# taste of home

## 2012 Healthy Cooking Annual Recipes

©2012 Reiman Media Group, LLC
5400 S. 60th St., Greendale WI 53129

International Standard Book Number (10):
1-61765-003-X

International Standard Book Number (13):
978-1-61765-003-1

International Standard Serial Number:
1944-7736

Printed in U.S.A.
13 5 7 9 10 8 6 4 2

Cover Photography:
Photographer: Dan Roberts
Food Stylist: Kathryn Conrad
Set Stylists: Melissa Haberman

Pictured on the Front Cover:
Turkey Meatballs & Sauce (p. 146);
Makeover Overnight French Toast (p. 87); Strawberry Spinach Salad (p. 38); and Makeover Pineapple Upside Cake (p. 238).

Pictured on the Back Cover:
Tuscan Chicken (p. 132); Artichoke Arugula Salad (p. 30); Ginger-Peach Milk Shakes (p. 8); and Quinoa Turkey Chili (p. 150).

Editor-in-Chief
Catherine Cassidy

Vice President, Executive Editor/Books
Heidi Reuter Lloyd

Creative Director
Howard Greenberg

Food Director
Diane Werner, RD

Senior Editor/Books
Mark Hagen

Associate Editor
Ellie Martin Cliffe

Associate Creative Director
Edwin Robles Jr.

Art Director
Gretchen Trautman

Content Production Manager
Julie Wagner

Layout Designer
Nancy Novak

Copy Chief
Deb Warlaumont Mulvey

Project Proofreader
Barbara Schuetz

Recipe Asset System Manager
Coleen Martin

Editor/Healthy Cooking
Stephen C. George

Art Director/Healthy Cooking
Nicholas Mork

Food Editor/Healthy Cooking
Peggy Woodward, RD

Recipe Testing and Editing
Taste of Home Test Kitchen

Food Photography
Taste of Home Photo Studio

Vice President, General Manager, RD Milwaukee
Lisa Karpinski

Vice President/Book Marketing
Dan Fink

Creative Director/Creative Marketing
James Palmen

THE READER'S DIGEST ASSOCIATION, INC.

President and Chief Executive Officer
Robert E. Guth

President, North America
Dan Lagani

# healthy cooking

## taste of home

### 2012 annual recipes

# Contents

From no-fuss nibbles to decadent desserts, you'll find everything you need in this edition of *Healthy Cooking Annual Recipes*. Consider these 17 chapters when you need a satisfying dish that contributes to a heart-smart lifestyle.

# Family Favorites

With *Healthy Cooking Annual Recipes*, it's a cinch to put satisfying all-time classics on the table...no matter how busy your day is. Best of all, no one will suspect they're eating lighter. Just ask Food Editor Peggy Woodward.

What do you think of when you hear the words "comfort food"? Satisfying stews and piping-hot casseroles? What about chocolate cakes? A few words you probably don't think of are "light" and "low-calorie." That's why I'm happy to bring you this edition of *Healthy Cooking Annual Recipes*!

Inside you'll find more than 400 family-favorite dishes that pare down calories, fat and sodium without sacrificing flavor. That means you'll feel good about serving stick-to-your-ribs meals because they won't pack on pounds. With all of these options, your family won't even notice that they're eating lighter!

Feel like Italian tonight? Check out Makeover Traditional Lasagna on page 122. It offers fewer calories than its full-fat counterpart, and it even contains 35% less sodium! Consider adding Artichoke Arugula Salad (p. 30) or Parmesan Herb Loaf (p. 202) to the lineup and a tasty yet health-minded dinner is ready.

In a rush? Enjoy a comforting bite without hitting the fast-food drive-thru. See the chapter "Ready in 30 Minutes" where you'll find quick dinner ideas that keep healthy eating goals in check. When the clock is ticking, consider Mom's Sloppy Tacos (p. 99), Pork 'n' Potato Skillet (p. 95) or Chicken Sausage Gyros (p. 106). These specialties are ready in half an hour, and they keep fat and calories at bay. You'll find more than 140 half-hour entrees sprinkled throughout the book!

If you crave sweets, you can still indulge with the fantastic treats found here. Consider Toffee Cheesecake Bars (p. 222) and Raspberry Baked Alaska Pie (p. 235). Not only will they satiate a sweet tooth, but each dessert provides a complete set of Nutrition Facts.

In fact, every item in *Healthy Cooking Annual Recipes* offers Nutrition Facts and many include Diabetic Exchanges. It's so easy to calculate points for various weight-loss programs, plan calorie-conscious menus and stick to low-sodium or low-carb meal plans with this information.

And because we know your time is valuable, we continue to include special-diet icons to help you find those dishes that may be of particular interest to you. Just see the key on the opposite page to understand what the four indicators stand for.

I know your gang will adore these trimmed-down takes on classic foods because most of them come from home cooks just like you and me! They know how to feed their families hearty meals without much fat yet keep flavor to a maximum—and they're happy to share those secrets.

We've tested all the recipes in the Healthy Cooking Test Kitchen, so you can rest assured that everything will turn out great whether it's the first time you make it or the fiftieth! And if your family is like mine, you'll be happily making these guilt-free comfort foods time and again!

*Peggy Woodward, RD*

Food Editor, *Healthy Cooking*

# Nutrition Facts Nuggets

## Nutritional Guidelines
All of the recipes in *Healthy Cooking Annual Recipes* cookbook fit the lifestyle of a health-conscious cook and his/her family. The recipes represent a variety of foods that will fit into any meal plan that is within the standards of the USDA's "MyPlate Plan" for moderately active adults (see box below).

## Facts
* Whenever a choice of ingredients is given in a recipe (such as 1/3 cup of sour cream or plain yogurt), the first ingredient listed is always the one calculated in the Nutrition Facts.
* When a range is given for an ingredient (such as 2 to 3 teaspoons), we calculate the first amount given.
* Only the amount of marinade absorbed during preparation is calculated.
* Garnishes listed in recipes are generally included in our calculations.

## Diabetic Exchanges
All recipes in *Healthy Cooking Annual Recipes* have been reviewed by a registered dietitian. Diabetic Exchanges are assigned to recipes in accordance with guidelines from the American Diabetic and American Dietetic associations.

The majority of recipes in this cookbook are suitable for diabetics, but please check the Diabetic Exchanges to make sure the recipe is in accordance with your doctor's instructions and fits your particular dietary guidelines.

## Special Diet Indicators
To help those on restricted diets easily find dishes to suit their needs, we clearly indicate recipes that are particularly low in fat, sodium or carbohydrates as well as those that contain no meat. You will find these colored special diet indicators directly after the recipe title where appropriate:

**F** One serving contains 3 grams or less of fat

**S** One serving contains 140 milligrams or less of sodium

**C** One serving contains 15 grams or less of carbohydrates

**M** Appetizers, salads, soups, side dishes and entrees that contain no meat

---

### A Word About Meat-Free Recipes

Enjoying meatless menus is a lifestyle choice that many people make. Others, however, prepare meat-free entrees only occasionally in order to cut back fat and calories or to simply mix-up their supper-time routines. Regardless of how often you prepare meatless recipes, you can easily find such dishes as identified with the meatless icon.

When flipping through this edition of *Healthy Cooking Annual Recipes*, please note that the icon highlights items that are meatless and not lacto-ovo vegetarian. As such, recipes containing eggs and cheese are marked as meat-free options.

Dishes that contain meat products such as marshmallows, marshmallow creme, gelatin and Worcestershire sauce are not labeled with a meatless icon.

Some dishes call for "reduced-sodium chicken broth or vegetable broth." While the Nutrition Facts for these recipes are published using the chicken broth as an ingredient, these dishes may offer the meatless icon since vegetarian broth is an option in the ingredient list.

So whether you depend on meatless meals for your family or simply want to try something new, look for the meatless icon to help you get the dinner bell ringing in no time!

---

## DAILY NUTRITION GUIDE

| | Women 25–50 | Women over 50 | Men 50–65 |
|---|---|---|---|
| **CALORIES** | 2,000 | 1,800 | 2,400 |
| **FAT** | 67 g or less | 60 g or less | 80 g or less |
| **SATURATED FAT** | 22 g or less | 20 g or less | 27 g or less |
| **CHOLESTEROL** | 300 mg or less | 300 mg or less | 300 mg or less |
| **SODIUM** | 2,300 mg or less | 1,500 mg or less | 1,500 mg or less |
| **CARBOHYDRATES** | 300 g | 270 g | 360 g |
| **FIBER** | 20-30 g | 20-30 g | 30-40 g |
| **PROTEIN** | 50 g | 45 g | 60 g |

This chart is only a guide. Requirements vary, depending on age, weight, height and amount of activity.
Children's dietary needs vary as they grow.

GLUTEN-FREE CHOCOLATE SNACK MIX

ORANGE & COFFEE MARTINI

TZATZIKI SHRIMP
CUCUMBER ROUNDS

Let's party! After all, watching what you eat doesn't mean avoiding favorite party fare. You can enjoy dips, snack mixes and all sorts of appetizers when you turn to this chapter's selection of munchies and beverages.

## Orange & Coffee Martini  F S C

**PREP/TOTAL TIME:** 5 min. **YIELD:** 1 serving

### HEALTHY COOKING TEST KITCHEN

*With its pretty jeweled appearance and complementary orange-coffee flavor, this impressive martini lends an elegant, upscale feel to any get-together.*

Ice cubes
- 2 oz. strong brewed coffee, cooled
- 1 oz. vodka
- 1/2 oz. orange liqueur
- 1/2 oz. hazelnut liqueur

**1.** Fill a mixing glass or tumbler three-fourths full with ice cubes. Add remaining ingredients; stir until condensation forms on outside of glass. Strain into a chilled cocktail glass. Serve immediately.

**Nutrition Facts:** 1/2 cup equals 172 calories, trace fat (trace saturated fat), 0 cholesterol, 2 mg sodium, 13 g carbohydrate, 0 fiber, trace protein.

## Lo-Cal Cheese Dip  F C

**PREP:** 5 min. + chilling **YIELD:** 1-3/4 cups

### JOYCE MONTAGUE • WICHITA, KANSAS

*Working in a local deli and retail outlet that sells herbs and spices gives me a chance to create many recipes. Cottage cheese is a heart-smart main ingredient in this savory dip that's terrific with crackers or veggies.*

- 2 cups (16 oz.) 2% cottage cheese
- 1 Tbsp. reduced-sodium beef bouillon granules
- 1 Tbsp. dried minced onion
- 2 tsp. lemon juice
Raw vegetables *or* crackers

**1.** In a blender, combine cottage cheese, bouillon, onion and lemon juice; cover and process until smooth. Cover and chill for at least 1 hour. Serve with vegetables or crackers.

**Nutrition Facts:** One serving (1/4 cup dip) equals 68 calories, 2 g fat (1 g saturated fat), 6 mg cholesterol, 291 mg sodium, 3 g carbohydrate, trace fiber, 9 g protein. **Diabetic Exchange:** 1 lean meat.

## Tzatziki Shrimp Cucumber Rounds  F S C

**PREP:** 25 min. **COOK:** 10 min./batch
**YIELD:** 24 appetizers

### SHANNON ROSE FLAHERTY • HAMPTON BAYS, NEW YORK

*I created this appetizer with what I had on hand one night, and now it's one of my husband's favorites! The bacon-wrapped shrimp, garlicky sauce and burst of cool cuke flavor make this a surefire crowd-pleaser.*

- 1/4 cup reduced-fat plain yogurt
- 2 Tbsp. finely chopped peeled cucumber
- 1/8 tsp. garlic salt
- 1/8 tsp. dill weed
- 6 bacon strips
- 24 peeled and deveined cooked medium shrimp, tails removed
- 2 medium cucumbers, cut into 1/4-in. slices

**1.** In a small bowl, combine the yogurt, chopped cucumber, garlic salt and dill; set aside.

**2.** Cut each bacon strip in half widthwise and then lengthwise. Wrap a piece of bacon around each shrimp. Secure with toothpicks.

**3.** In a large nonstick skillet coated with cooking spray, cook shrimp in batches over medium heat for 3-4 minutes on each side or until bacon is crisp.

**4.** Spoon a rounded 1/2 tsp. yogurt sauce onto each cucumber slice; top with shrimp.

**Nutrition Facts:** 1 appetizer equals 27 calories, 1 g fat (trace saturated fat), 18 mg cholesterol, 63 mg sodium, 1 g carbohydrate, trace fiber, 3 g protein.

Here's is a great way to keep **cucumbers fresh** longer. Purchase a plastic lettuce keeper and place up to six cucumbers in it. They don't get soft spots and stay fresh and crisp for almost 2 weeks. This should work with just about any veggie.

## Italian-Style Snack Mix F C M

**PREP/TOTAL TIME:** 15 min. **YIELD:** 1-1/2 qt.

**KATIE GOLWITZER • WILMINGTON, ILLINOIS**

*A touch of heat comes through in this tasty, toasty blend of cereals, pretzels and bagel chips. Parmesan, garlic and Italian seasonings boost the flavor of this fun energy mix.*

1-1/2 cups Corn Chex
1-1/2 cups Rice Chex
1-1/2 cups Wheat Chex
  1/2 cup garlic bagel chips
  1/2 cup miniature pretzels
    3 Tbsp. butter, melted
  1/2 tsp. garlic salt
  1/2 tsp. dried basil
  1/2 tsp. dried oregano
  1/2 tsp. crushed red pepper flakes
  1/4 tsp. onion powder
    2 Tbsp. grated Parmesan cheese

**1.** In a large microwave-safe bowl, combine the first five ingredients. In a small bowl, combine the butter, garlic salt, basil, oregano, pepper flakes and onion powder; pour over cereal mixture and toss to coat.

**2.** Microwave, uncovered, on high for 2 minutes, stirring once. Stir in cheese. Cook 4 minutes longer, stirring twice. Spread onto waxed paper to cool. Store in an airtight container.

**Editor's Note:** This recipe was tested in a 1,100-watt microwave.

**Nutrition Facts:** 1/2 cup equals 80 calories, 3 g fat (2 g saturated fat), 8 mg cholesterol, 235 mg sodium, 11 g carbohydrate, 1 g fiber, 2 g protein. **Diabetic Exchanges:** 1 starch, 1/2 fat.

## Ginger-Peach Milk Shakes F S

**PREP/TOTAL TIME:** 5 min. **YIELD:** 3 servings

**HEALTHY COOKING TEST KITCHEN**

*Is our milk shake better than yours? Give this treat from our Test Kitchen a try and see for yourself!*

  1 cup fat-free milk
  1 cup reduced-fat vanilla ice cream
  1 cup frozen unsweetened sliced peaches
1/4 tsp. ground ginger
Unsweetened chopped peaches

**1.** In a blender, combine all ingredients; cover and process until smooth. Pour into chilled glasses; garnish with chopped peaches. Serve immediately.

**Nutrition Facts:** 3/4 cup (calculated without garnish) equals 121 calories, 2 g fat (1 g saturated fat), 14 mg cholesterol, 67 mg sodium, 20 g carbohydrate, 1 g fiber, 5 g protein. **Diabetic Exchanges:** 1 starch, 1/2 fat.

## Blooming Onions F C M

**PREP:** 20 min. **BAKE:** 40 min. **YIELD:** 8 servings

**KENDRA DOSS • KANSAS CITY, MISSOURI**

*Instead of being battered and deep-fried, this onion is brushed with melted butter and mustard, sprinkled with bread crumbs and seasonings, and baked. It's an impressive-looking appetizer, and the dip can be used for veggies and crackers, too.*

  2 large sweet onions
  1 Tbsp. butter, melted
  2 tsp. Dijon mustard
  3 Tbsp. dry bread crumbs
1/4 tsp. salt
1/4 tsp. pepper
SAUCE:
1/4 cup fat-free sour cream

ITALIAN-STYLE SNACK MIX

GINGER-PEACH MILK SHAKES

1/4   cup fat-free mayonnaise
1-1/2 tsp. dried minced onion
1/4   tsp. garlic powder
1/4   tsp. dill weed

**1.** With a sharp knife, slice 1/2 in. off the top of the onions; peel onions. Cut each into 16 wedges to within 1/2 in. of root end.

**2.** Place each onion on a double thickness of heavy-duty foil (about 12 in. square). Fold foil around onions and seal tightly. Place in an ungreased 11-in. x 7-in. baking dish. Bake, uncovered, at 425° for 20 minutes.

**3.** In a small bowl, combine butter and mustard. Open foil; fold foil around onions. Brush butter mixture over onions; sprinkle with bread crumbs, salt and pepper.

**4.** Bake 18-22 minutes longer or until crisp-tender. Meanwhile, in a small bowl, combine sauce ingredients. Serve with onions.

**Nutrition Facts:** 1/4 onion with 1 Tbsp. sauce equals 65 calories, 2 g fat (1 g saturated fat), 6 mg cholesterol, 205 mg sodium, 11 g carbohydrate, 1 g fiber, 2 g protein. **Diabetic Exchanges:** 1 vegetable, 1/2 starch.

# Chunky Salsa  F S C M

**PREP:** 45 min. **PROCESS:** 15 min. **YIELD:** 7 pints

**DANA HAYES • CANTON, OHIO**

*My fresh-tasting salsa is wonderfully chunky. If you like it hotter, add more habanero peppers; if you prefer a mild salsa, simply add fewer.*

5   lbs. tomatoes
4   large green peppers, chopped
3   large onions, chopped
2   large sweet red peppers, chopped
2   habanero peppers, seeded and finely chopped
1   cup white vinegar
1   can (6 oz.) tomato paste
3   tsp. salt

**1.** Fill a Dutch oven two-thirds with water; bring to a boil. Score an "X" on the bottom of each tomato. Using a slotted spoon, place tomatoes, one at a time, in boiling water for 30-60 seconds. Remove tomatoes and immediately plunge in ice water. Discard peel; chop tomatoes.

**2.** In a stockpot, combine the remaining ingredients. Stir in tomatoes. Bring to a boil over medium-high heat. Reduce heat; simmer, uncovered, for 15-20 minutes or until desired thickness.

**3.** Carefully ladle hot mixture into seven hot 1-pint jars, leaving 1/2-in. headspace. Remove air bubbles; wipe rims and adjust lids. Process for 15 minutes in a boiling-water canner.

**Editor's Note:** We recommend wearing disposable gloves when cutting hot peppers. Avoid touching your face. The processing time listed is for altitudes of 1,000 feet or less. For altitudes up to 3,000 feet, add 5 minutes; 6,000 feet, add 10 minutes; 8,000 feet, add 15 minutes; 10,000 feet, add 20 minutes.

**Nutrition Facts:** 1/4 cup equals 18 calories, trace fat (trace saturated fat), 0 cholesterol, 131 mg sodium, 4 g carbohydrate, 1 g fiber, 1 g protein. **Diabetic Exchange:** Free food.

SPICED CHIPS AND
ROASTED TOMATILLO SALSA

# Spiced Chips and
# Roasted Tomatillo Salsa

**PREP:** 25 min. **BAKE:** 15 min. + cooling
**YIELD:** 10 servings

**MARY RELYEA • CANASTOTA, NEW YORK**

*My food processor does most of the work for me where this
green salsa is concerned. Studded with mango and splashed
with lime, it's yummy with no-fuss homemade chips.*

  10  flour tortillas (6 in.)
Cooking spray
  3  tsp. chili powder
  1  tsp. ground cumin
  1/2  tsp. salt
SALSA:
  3/4  lb. tomatillos, husks removed, quartered
  1  small onion, cut into wedges
  1  jalapeno pepper, halved and seeded
  2  garlic cloves
  3  Tbsp. fresh cilantro leaves
  1-1/2  tsp. lime juice
  1/2  tsp. salt
  1  medium mango, peeled and diced

**1.** Cut each tortilla into six wedges; place on
ungreased baking sheets. Spritz with cooking spray.
Combine the chili powder, cumin and salt; sprinkle
over wedges. Bake at 425° for 5-8 minutes or just
until edges begin to brown.

**2.** For salsa, place the tomatillos, onion, jalapeno and
garlic in a single layer in a 15-in. x 10-in. x 1-in.
baking pan coated with cooking spray. Broil 4-6 in.
from the heat for 14-17 minutes or until tender and
lightly browned, stirring once. Cool to room
temperature.

**3.** Transfer to a food processor; add the cilantro,
lime juice and salt. Cover and process until coarsely
chopped. Stir in mango. Refrigerate until serving.
Serve with chips.

**Editor's Note:** Wear disposable gloves when cutting hot
peppers; the oils can burn skin. Avoid touching your face.

**Nutrition Facts:** 6 chips with 1/4 cup salsa equals 127 calories,
4 g fat (trace saturated fat), 0 cholesterol, 470 mg sodium,
20 g carbohydrate, 2 g fiber, 4 g protein.

# Spiced Coffee F S C

**PREP/TOTAL TIME:** 20 min. **YIELD:** 2 servings

**JILL GARN • CHARLOTTE, MICHIGAN**

*Here's a quick and easy coffee made with instant granules. What's not to love about this autumnal beverage?*

- 2 cups water
- 5 tsp. instant coffee granules
- 1/2 cinnamon stick (3 in.)
- 4 whole cloves
- 5 tsp. sugar

Whipped topping, optional

**1.** In a small saucepan, combine the water, coffee granules, cinnamon stick and cloves. Bring to a boil. Remove from the heat; cover and let stand for 5-8 minutes. Strain and discard spices. Stir in sugar until dissolved. Ladle into mugs. Serve with whipped topping if desired.

**Nutrition Facts:** 1 cup (calculated without whipped topping) equals 46 calories, trace fat (trace saturated fat), 0 cholesterol, 1 mg sodium, 11 g carbohydrate, 0 fiber, trace protein. **Diabetic Exchange:** 1/2 starch.

# Greek Sandwich Bites C M

**PREP/TOTAL TIME:** 25 min. **YIELD:** 16 appetizers

**LYNN SCULLY • RANCHO SANTA FE, CALIFORNIA**

*My appetizer tastes just like traditional spanakopita, but it's much less work to prepare.*

- 1 medium onion, finely chopped
- 1 Tbsp. olive oil
- 2 garlic cloves, minced
- 1 lb. fresh baby spinach
- 1 cup (4 oz.) crumbled feta cheese
- 1/4 cup pine nuts, toasted
- 1/4 tsp. salt
- 1/4 tsp. pepper
- 1/8 tsp. ground nutmeg
- 8 slices Italian bread (1/2 in. thick)
- 4 tsp. butter, softened

**1.** In a large nonstick skillet, saute onion in oil until tender. Add garlic; cook 1 minute longer. Stir in the spinach; cook and stir until wilted. Drain. Stir in the feta, pine nuts, salt, pepper and nutmeg.

**2.** Spread over four bread slices; top with remaining bread. Spread outsides of sandwiches with butter. Grill, uncovered, over medium heat for 3-4 minutes or until bread is browned and cheese is melted, turning once. Cut each sandwich into quarters.

**Nutrition Facts:** 1 appetizer equals 87 calories, 5 g fat (2 g saturated fat), 6 mg cholesterol, 200 mg sodium, 8 g carbohydrate, 1 g fiber, 4 g protein. **Diabetic Exchanges:** 1 fat, 1/2 starch.

Greek Sandwich Bites make for a hearty appetizer so be sure to serve them with plates and napkins nearby. You may also wish to **dress them up** with frilly toothpicks or skewer each appetizer with a cherry tomato or olive garnish that sits nicely on top of each sandwich quarter.

GREEK SANDWICH BITES

SPICED COFFEE

# Iced Melon Moroccan Mint Tea F S

PREP/TOTAL TIME: 20 min.  YIELD: 5 servings

**SARAH BATT THRONE • EL CERRITO, CALIFORNIA**

*I grow mint on my balcony, and this refreshing beverage is a wonderful way to use it. It combines two of my favorite drinks—Moroccan Mint Tea and Honeydew Agua Fresca. For extra flair, add some ginger ale.*

2 cups water
12 fresh mint leaves
4 individual green tea bags
1/3 cup sugar
2-1/2 cups diced honeydew
1-1/2 cups ice cubes
Additional ice cubes

**1.** In a large saucepan, bring water to a boil. Remove from the heat; add mint leaves and tea bags. Cover and steep for 3-5 minutes. Discard the mint and tea bags. Stir in the sugar.

**2.** In a blender, process honeydew until blended. Add 1-1/2 cups ice and tea; process until blended. Serve over additional ice.

**Nutrition Facts:** 1 cup equals 81 calories, trace fat (trace saturated fat), 0 cholesterol, 9 mg sodium, 21 g carbohydrate, 1 g fiber, trace protein. **Diabetic Exchange:** 1 starch.

# Baked Veggie Chips C M

PREP/TOTAL TIME: 30 min.  YIELD: 7 servings

**CHRISTINE SCHENHER • SAN CLEMENTE, CALIFORNIA**

*Colorful roasted root vegetables are a fun, festive snack or casual side dish. These perfectly seasoned chips are so tasty they don't even need dip!*

1/2 lb. fresh beets (about 2 medium)
1 medium potato
1 medium sweet potato
1 medium parsnip
2 Tbsp. canola oil
2 Tbsp. grated Parmesan cheese
1/2 tsp. salt
1/2 tsp. garlic powder
1/2 tsp. dried oregano
Dash pepper

**1.** Peel vegetables and cut into 1/8-in. slices. Place in a large bowl. Drizzle with oil. Combine the remaining ingredients; sprinkle over vegetables and toss to coat.

**2.** Arrange in a single layer on racks in two ungreased 15-in. x 10-in. x 1-in. baking pans. Bake at 375° for 15-20 minutes or until golden brown, turning once.

**Nutrition Facts:** 1/2 cup equals 108 calories, 5 g fat (1 g saturated fat), 1 mg cholesterol, 220 mg sodium, 15 g carbohydrate, 2 g fiber, 2 g protein.

# Make-Ahead Crab Dip F C

PREP/TOTAL TIME: 10 min.  YIELD: 2 cups

**MARY DIAMOND • NEW PORT RICHEY, FLORIDA**

*Busy hostesses love the make-ahead convenience of this elegant dip with a lick of lemon and horseradish. Serve it with crackers or fresh veggies.*

3/4 cup fat-free mayonnaise
1/4 cup chili sauce
1 Tbsp. lemon juice
1 tsp. horseradish
1/2 tsp. garlic powder
1/4 tsp. pepper
2 cans (6 oz. *each*) lump crabmeat, drained
Assorted crackers or fresh vegetables

ICED MELON MOROCCAN MINT TEA

MAKE-AHEAD CRAB DIP

CHIPOTLE PEA SPREAD

**1.** In a small bowl, combine the first six ingredients; fold in crab. Chill until serving. Serve with crackers.

**Nutrition Facts:** 3 Tbsp. (calculated without crackers or vegetables) equals 54 calories, 1 g fat (trace saturated fat), 32 mg cholesterol, 349 mg sodium, 4 g carbohydrate, trace fiber, 7 g protein. **Diabetic Exchange:** 1 lean meat.

# Chipotle Pea Spread **C**

**PREP/TOTAL TIME:** 20 min. **YIELD:** 1-1/2 cups

**FRANCES "KAY" BOUMA • TRAIL, BRITISH COLUMBIA**

*I love hummus and bacon, but I needed to make something green for a Healthy Cooking contest. It took a few tries to come up with a recipe everyone loves. Hope you do, too!*

  2   cups frozen peas
1/3   cup grated Parmesan cheese
  3   cooked bacon strips, chopped
1/4   cup reduced-fat sour cream

  2   Tbsp. olive oil
  1   Tbsp. lime juice
  2   garlic cloves
  1   to 2 tsp. minced chipotle pepper in adobo sauce
1/4   tsp. pepper
Assorted fresh vegetables *or* crackers

**1.** In a small saucepan, bring 4 cups water to a boil. Add peas; cover and cook for 1 minute. Drain and immediately place peas in ice water. Drain and pat dry.

**2.** Place peas in a food processor; add the cheese, bacon, sour cream, oil, lime juice, garlic, chipotle pepper and pepper. Cover and process until smooth. Serve with vegetables or crackers.

**Nutrition Facts:** 1/4 cup (calculated without vegetables) equals 129 calories, 8 g fat (2 g saturated fat), 11 mg cholesterol, 207 mg sodium, 8 g carbohydrate, 2 g fiber, 6 g protein. **Diabetic Exchanges:** 1-1/2 fat, 1/2 starch.

# Curried Chicken And Rice Tartlets F S C

PREP: 30 min. BAKE: 10 min. YIELD: 24 appetizers

**HEALTHY COOKING TEST KITCHEN**

*These simple starters feature a yummy curried chicken filling that guests will love. A cute little phyllo dough cup makes the appetizers seem extra special.*

| | |
|---|---|
| 1/2 | cup reduced-sodium chicken broth |
| 1/4 | cup uncooked long grain rice |
| 3/4 | cup cubed cooked chicken breast |
| 1/2 | cup frozen peas and carrots, thawed and drained |
| 3 | Tbsp. reduced-fat mayonnaise |
| 1 | green onion, chopped |
| 1/2 | tsp. salt |
| 1/4 | tsp. pepper |
| 1/4 | tsp. curry powder |
| 1/8 | tsp. garlic powder |
| 1/8 | tsp. ground turmeric |
| 1/8 | tsp. ground coriander |

| | |
|---|---|
| 8 | sheets phyllo dough (14 in. x 9 in.) |

Butter-flavored cooking spray

Minced chives, optional

**1.** In a small saucepan, bring broth and rice to a boil. Reduce heat; cover and simmer for 15-18 minutes or until liquid is absorbed and rice is tender. In a large bowl. combine the rice, chicken, peas and carrots, mayonnaise, green onion and seasonings.

**2.** Place one sheet of phyllo dough on a work surface; spritz with butter-flavored spray. Top with another sheet of phyllo; spritz with spray. (Keep remaining phyllo covered with plastic wrap and a damp towel to prevent it from drying out.) Cut into 12 squares. Repeat three times, making 48 squares.

**3.** Stack two squares of layered phyllo in each of 24 muffin cups coated with cooking spray, rotating squares so corners do not overlap. Spoon 1 tablespoon rice mixture into each cup. Bake at 375° for 8-10 minutes or until golden brown. Garnish with chives if desired. Serve warm.

**Nutrition Facts:** 1 tartlet equals 35 calories, 1 g fat (trace saturated fat), 4 mg cholesterol, 96 mg sodium, 4 g carbohydrate, trace fiber, 2 g protein.

# Family-Favorite Taco Dip C

PREP/TOTAL TIME: 10 min. YIELD: 3 cups

**LAURIE ELLSWORTH • TULLY, NEW YORK**

*I've tasted many different dips, but this is my favorite. Not only does it feature a cream cheese base, but the tomato, olives and jalapeno pepper add a fun burst of color and flavor. Best of all, it comes together in just a few minutes!*

- 2 pkg. (8 oz. *each*) fat-free cream cheese
- 2 Tbsp. reduced-sodium taco seasoning
- 1 Tbsp. fat-free milk
- 1 cup (4 oz.) shredded cheddar cheese
- 1 medium tomato, diced
- 1/4 cup sliced ripe olives, drained
- 1/4 cup pickled jalapeno pepper

Baked tortilla chips

**1.** In a small bowl, beat the cream cheese, taco seasoning and milk until blended. Spread mixture into a 9-in. pie plate. Sprinkle with cheese, tomato, olives and jalapenos. Serve with chips.

**Nutrition Facts:** 1/4 cup (calculated without chips) equals 81 calories, 4 g fat (2 g saturated fat), 13 mg cholesterol, 393 mg sodium, 5 g carbohydrate, trace fiber, 8 g protein.

# Pineapple Salsa F S C

PREP/TOTAL TIME: 20 min. YIELD: 3-1/2 cups

**SUZI LAPAR • WAHIAWA, HAWAII**

*This mouthwatering salsa features fresh pineapple and a handful of seasonings. Serve it with tortilla chips or grilled chicken or fish for a jazzed-up meal.*

- 2 cups diced fresh pineapple
- 2 medium tomatoes, seeded and chopped
- 3/4 cup chopped sweet onion
- 1/4 cup minced fresh cilantro
- 1 jalapeno pepper, seeded and chopped
- 1 Tbsp. olive oil
- 1 tsp. ground coriander
- 3/4 tsp. ground cumin
- 1/2 tsp. salt
- 1/2 tsp. minced garlic

Tortilla chips

**1.** In a large bowl, combine the first 10 ingredients. Cover and refrigerate until serving. Serve with chips.

**Editor's Note:** Wear disposable gloves when cutting hot peppers; the oils can burn skin. Avoid touching your face.

**Nutrition Facts:** 1/4 cup (calculated without chips) equals 29 calories, 1 g fat (trace saturated fat), 0 cholesterol, 87 mg sodium, 5 g carbohydrate, 1 g fiber, trace protein. **Diabetic Exchange:** Free food.

To remove the seeds from a **tomato**, cut it in half horizontally and remove the stem. Holding a tomato half over a bowl or sink, scrape out seeds with a small spoon or squeeze the tomato to force out the seeds. Then slice or dice as directed in the recipe.

PINEAPPLE SALSA

FAMILY-FAVORITE TACO DIP

# Basil Citrus Cocktail F S C

PREP/TOTAL TIME: 10 min. YIELD: 1 serving

### HEALTHY COOKING TEST KITCHEN

*Fruity, fantastic and lighter in calories, this refreshing beverage is perfect for adult parties.*

      6   fresh basil leaves
1-1/2 to 2 cups ice cubes
      2   oz. white grapefruit juice
      2   oz. mandarin orange juice
    3/4   oz. gin
    1/2   oz. Domaine de Canton ginger liqueur

**1.** In a shaker, muddle the basil leaves.

**2.** Fill shaker three-fourths full with ice. Add the juices, gin and ginger liqueur; cover and shake for 10-15 seconds or until condensation forms on outside of shaker. Strain into a chilled cocktail glass.

**Nutrition Facts:** 1 serving equals 136 calories, trace fat (trace saturated fat), 0 cholesterol, trace sodium, 14 g carbohydrate, trace fiber, 1 g protein.

# Mulled Merlot F S C

PREP: 10 min. COOK: 1 hour YIELD: 9 servings

### HEALTHY COOKING TEST KITCHEN

*Here's a traditional beverage that's sure to warm you up!*

      4   cinnamon sticks (3 in.)
      4   whole cloves
      2   bottles (750 milliliters *each*) merlot
    1/2   cup sugar
    1/2   cup orange juice
    1/2   cup brandy
      1   medium orange, thinly sliced

**1.** Place cinnamon sticks and cloves on a double thickness of cheesecloth; bring up corners of cloth and tie with string to form a bag.

**2.** In a 3-qt. slow cooker, combine the wine, sugar, orange juice, brandy and orange slices. Add spice bag. Cover and cook on high for 1 hour or until heated through. Discard the spice bag and the orange slices. Serve warm.

**Nutrition Facts:** 1 serving (3/4 cup) equals 143 calories, trace fat (trace saturated fat), 0 cholesterol, 4 mg sodium, 15 g carbohydrate, trace fiber, trace protein.

# Parmesan Sesame Crackers F S C M

PREP: 25 min. BAKE: 15 min. + cooling YIELD: 4 dozen

### ELENA IORGA • HELENA, MONTANA

*I love these snacks! The rustic-looking crackers are crispy, crunchy and topped with cheese and plenty of seeds. Perfect for parties, they are only missing the preservatives and additives of store-bought alternatives.*

      2   cups all-purpose flour
    1/3   cup sesame seeds
    1/3   cup shredded Parmesan cheese
      2   Tbsp. poppy seeds
      1   tsp. baking powder
    1/2   tsp. salt
    2/3   cup plus 2 Tbsp. warm water, *divided*
    1/3   cup canola oil
      1   egg white

TOPPING:
      2   Tbsp. shredded Parmesan cheese
      1   Tbsp. sesame seeds
      1   Tbsp. poppy seeds

**1.** In a small bowl, combine the first six ingredients. Gradually add 2/3 cup water and oil, tossing with a fork until dough forms a ball. Turn onto a lightly floured surface; knead 8-10 times.

**2.** Divide dough in half. Roll each ball directly on a baking sheet coated with cooking spray into a 12-in. x 9-in. rectangle. Pierce dough with a fork.

BASIL CITRUS COCKTAIL

MULLED MERLOT

PARMESAN SESAME CRACKERS
NUTTY BLUE CHEESE SPREAD

**3.** Whisk together egg white and remaining water; brush over dough. Combine topping ingredients; sprinkle over tops.

**4.** Score dough in each pan into 24 pieces. Bake at 400° for 15-18 minutes or until golden brown. Immediately cut along the scored lines; cool in pans on wire racks. Store in an airtight container.

**Nutrition Facts:** 1 cracker equals 44 calories, 3 g fat (trace saturated fat), 1 mg cholesterol, 47 mg sodium, 4 g carbohydrate, trace fiber, 1 g protein.

# Nutty Blue Cheese Spread C

**PREP:** 15 min. + chilling  **YIELD:** 1-1/2 cups

**SHERRY HULSMAN • ELKTON, FLORIDA**

*With great blue cheese flavor and nice texture from the pecans, this super simple spread has a company-special feel. It's just perfect for formal and casual parties alike.*

> 1 pkg. (8 oz.) reduced-fat cream cheese
> 1-1/4 tsp. sugar
> 1/8 tsp. salt
> 1/4 cup crumbled blue cheese
> 3 Tbsp. finely chopped pecans, toasted
> Assorted crackers

**1.** In a large bowl, beat the cream cheese, sugar and salt until blended. Stir in blue cheese. Refrigerate for at least 1 hour. Just before serving, stir in pecans. Serve with crackers.

**Nutrition Facts:** 2 Tbsp. (calculated without crackers) equals 71 calories, 6 g fat (3 g saturated fat), 15 mg cholesterol, 144 mg sodium, 1 g carbohydrate, trace fiber, 3 g protein.

CHUTNEY CHEESE BALL

## Chutney Cheese Ball C M

PREP/TOTAL TIME: 15 min. YIELD: 2-1/2 cups

**PATRICIA SCHNEIDER • ROLLINSFORD, NEW HAMPSHIRE**

*This party starter goes great with crackers, bread cubes or fruit. Best of all, no one suspects it's light!*

- 1 pkg. (8 oz.) reduced-fat cream cheese
- 1 pkg. (8 oz.) fat-free cream cheese
- 1 cup (4 oz.) shredded reduced-fat Colby-Monterey Jack cheese
- 1/2 cup mango chutney
- 2 green onions, finely chopped
- 1 garlic clove, minced
- 1/4 tsp. salt
- 1/4 tsp. pepper
- 1/2 cup finely chopped walnuts
- 2 Tbsp. minced fresh parsley

Crackers, bread cubes and apples slices

**1.** In a small bowl, combine the first eight ingredients. Shape into a ball and roll in walnuts. Press parsley into ball; cover and chill until serving. Serve with crackers, bread cubes and apple slices.

**Nutrition Facts:** 2 Tbsp. (calculated without crackers) equals 99 calories, 5 g fat (3 g saturated fat), 12 mg cholesterol, 254 mg sodium, 7 g carbohydrate, trace fiber, 5 g protein. **Diabetic Exchanges:** 1 fat, 1/2 starch.

## Citrusy Fruit Kabobs F S

PREP/TOTAL TIME: 20 min. YIELD: 8 kabobs

**MARY RELYEA • CANASTOTA, NEW YORK**

*Fresh, fruity—and lower in sodium and fat—these grilled kabobs are great picks for health-minded hostesses.*

- 1/3 cup orange juice
- 2 Tbsp. lemon juice
- 4-1/2 tsp. honey
- 2 tsp. cornstarch

| 1-1/2 | tsp. grated lemon peel |
| 1/4 | tsp. ground allspice |
| 24 | fresh strawberries |
| 16 | cubes fresh pineapple |
| 2 | small bananas, cut into 1-in. pieces |
| 2 | tsp. minced fresh mint |

**1.** In a small saucepan, combine the first six ingredients. Bring to a boil; cook and stir for 2 minutes or until thickened. Remove from the heat; cool to room temperature.

**2.** Alternately thread an eighth of the fruit onto one metal or soaked wooden skewer. Repeat seven times. Brush with half of glaze. Moisten a paper towel with cooking oil; using long-handled tongs, lightly coat the grill rack.

**3.** Grill, covered, over medium heat for 5-7 minutes or until lightly browned, turning occasionally and basting frequently with remaining glaze. Just before serving, sprinkle with mint. Serve warm.

**Nutrition Facts:** 1 kabob equals 83 calories, trace fat (trace saturated fat), 0 cholesterol, 2 mg sodium, 21 g carbohydrate, 2 g fiber, 1 g protein. **Diabetic Exchange:** 1 fruit.

# Champagne Punch F S C

**PREP:** 5 min. + chilling **YIELD:** 16 servings

AMY SHORT • BARBOURSVILLE, WEST VIRGINIA

*A blend of four fruit juices pairs well with bubbly champagne in my party-pleasing punch. I like to add a strawberry garnish for a festive touch.*

| 4 | cups orange juice |
| 1 | cup ruby red grapefruit juice |
| 1/2 | cup lemon juice |
| 1/2 | cup lime juice |
| 2 | bottles (750 milliliters *each*) Champagne, chilled |

**1.** In a 3-qt. pitcher, combine the juices. Refrigerate until chilled. Just before serving, stir in Champagne. Serve in Champagne glasses.

**Nutrition Facts:** 3/4 cup equals 101 calories, trace fat (0 saturated fat), 0 cholesterol, trace sodium, 11 g carbohydrate, trace fiber, trace protein.

# Raspberry Merry F S C

**PREP/TOTAL TIME:** 5 min. **YIELD:** 1 serving

**HEALTHY COOKING TEST KITCHEN**

*Here's a lighter cocktail with a festive, merry flavor and plenty of holiday flair!*

| 5 | fresh raspberries |
| 1/4 | cup crushed ice |
| 1 | navel orange wedge |
| 1 | oz. pomegranate-flavored vodka |
| 1-1/2 | oz. Prosecco |

GARNISH:
Pomegranate seeds

**1.** In a shaker, muddle raspberries. Add ice. Squeeze the juice from the orange wedge into the shaker; add orange wedge and vodka. Cover and shake for 10-15 seconds or until condensation forms on outside of the shaker.

**2.** Strain into a chilled cocktail glass. Stir in Prosecco. Garnish with pomegranate seeds.

**Nutrition Facts:** 1 serving equals 112 calories, trace fat (trace saturated fat), 0 cholesterol, trace sodium, 5 g carbohydrate, 1 g fiber, trace protein.

CHAMPAGNE PUNCH

RASPBERRY MERRY

# BBQ Chicken Pizza Roll-Up F C

**PREP:** 15 min. **BAKE:** 15 min. + cooling
**YIELD:** 24 servings

**TRACEY BIRCH • QUEEN CREEK, ARIZONA**

*Warm slices of my hearty appetizer make a fab, filling snack with loads of sweet and tangy flavor.*

|       |                                                      |
|-------|------------------------------------------------------|
| 1     | tube (13.8 oz.) refrigerated pizza crust             |
| 1/4   | cup honey barbecue sauce                             |
| 1-1/2 | cups (6 oz.) shredded part-skim mozzarella cheese    |
| 1-1/2 | cups shredded cooked chicken breast                  |
| 1     | small red onion, finely chopped                      |
| 1/4   | cup minced fresh cilantro                            |
| 1     | tsp. Italian seasoning, optional                     |
| 1     | egg white                                            |
| 1     | Tbsp. water                                          |
| 1/4   | tsp. garlic powder                                   |

**1.** On a lightly floured surface, roll crust into a 12-in. x 9-in. rectangle; brush with barbecue sauce. Layer with cheese, chicken, onion, cilantro and Italian seasoning if desired.

**2.** Roll up jelly-roll style, starting with a long side; pinch seams to seal. Place seam side down on a baking sheet coated with cooking spray.

**3.** Beat the egg white and water; brush over top. Sprinkle with garlic powder. Bake at 400° for 15-20 minutes or until lightly browned. Cool for 10 minutes before slicing.

**Nutrition Facts:** 1 slice equals 81 calories, 2 g fat (1 g saturated fat), 11 mg cholesterol, 177 mg sodium, 9 g carbohydrate, trace fiber, 6 g protein. **Diabetic Exchanges:** 1 lean meat, 1/2 starch.

# Spicy Tomato Juice F

**PREP:** 45 min. + chilling **COOK:** 20 min.
**YIELD:** 15 servings

**MARTHA PHILBECK • LA FONTAINE, INDIANA**

*This zesty juice is good hot or cold. People love the spicy taste all year-round.*

|      |                                       |
|------|---------------------------------------|
| 12   | lbs. tomatoes                         |
| 9    | dried ancho chilies                   |
| 3    | medium onions, chopped                |
| 1    | celery rib, chopped                   |
| 1/4  | cup chopped seeded jalapeno pepper    |
| 1/2  | cup sugar                             |
| 1    | Tbsp. Worcestershire sauce            |
| 2    | tsp. salt                             |
| 1/4  | tsp. pepper                           |

**1.** Fill a Dutch oven two-thirds with water; bring to a boil. Score an "X" on the bottom of each tomato. Using a slotted spoon, place tomatoes, one at a time, in boiling water for 30-60 seconds. Remove tomatoes and immediately plunge in ice water. Discard peel; chop and place in a stockpot.

**2.** Add the chilies, onions, celery and jalapenos. Bring to a boil. Reduce heat; simmer, uncovered, for 20-25 minutes or until vegetables are tender. Cool slightly. In a food processor, process juice in batches until blended. Strain and discard seeds and pulp. Return puree to a large saucepan.

**3.** Stir in the remaining ingredients; heat through. Cool. To serve, refrigerate until chilled or transfer to storage containers. May be refrigerated for up to 3 days or frozen for up to 3 months.

**Editor's Note:** Wear disposable gloves when cutting hot peppers; the oils can burn skin. Avoid touching your face.

**Nutrition Facts:** 1 cup equals 134 calories, 2 g fat (trace saturated fat), 0 cholesterol, 351 mg sodium, 29 g carbohydrate, 7 g fiber, 5 g protein. **Diabetic Exchange:** 2 starch.

BBQ CHICKEN PIZZA ROLL-UP

SPICY TOMATO JUICE

# Triple Berry Salsa  F S C

**PREP/TOTAL TIME:** 20 min.  **YIELD:** 22 servings

**RAYMONDE BOURGEOIS • SWASTIKA, ONTARIO**

*Blueberries are so nutritious, low in calories and packed with vitamin C, fiber and disease-fighting antioxidants. My chunky salsa is a fresh, flavorful blend of berries and veggies that would be great over grilled chicken, too.*

1-1/2 cups fresh blueberries
3/4 cup chopped fresh strawberries
3/4 cup fresh raspberries
1 medium tomato, seeded and chopped
1 small sweet yellow pepper, chopped
1/4 cup finely chopped red onion
1/4 cup minced fresh cilantro
1 jalapeno pepper, seeded and minced
2 green onions, chopped

1 Tbsp. cider vinegar
1 Tbsp. olive oil
2 tsp. lime juice
2 tsp. orange juice
1 tsp. honey
1/4 tsp. salt
Baked tortilla chip scoops

**1.** In a large bowl, combine the first nine ingredients. In a small bowl, whisk the remaining ingredients. Drizzle over salsa; toss to coat. Chill until serving. Serve with chips.

**Editor's Note:** Wear disposable gloves when cutting hot peppers; the oils can burn skin. Avoid touching your face.

**Nutrition Facts:** 1/4 cup (calculated without chips) equals 20 calories, 1 g fat (trace saturated fat), 0 cholesterol, 28 mg sodium, 3 g carbohydrate, 1 g fiber, trace protein. **Diabetic Exchange:** Free food.

# Couscous Caps  F S C

PREP: 30 min. BAKE: 10 min. YIELD: 20 appetizers

**KENDRA DOSS • KANSAS CITY, MISSOURI**

*Couscous makes a pleasant change from bread crumbs in these savory appetizers—and provides nice texture as well.*

|       |                                                 |
|-------|-------------------------------------------------|
| 20    | large fresh mushrooms                           |
| 4     | green onions, chopped                           |
| 1     | cup reduced-sodium chicken broth, *divided*     |
| 1/3   | cup uncooked whole wheat couscous               |
| 1/4   | cup grated Parmesan cheese, *divided*           |
| 4     | tsp. reduced-fat mayonnaise                     |
| 1     | tsp. dried basil                                |
| 1/2   | tsp. dried tarragon                             |
| 1/2   | tsp. paprika                                    |

**1.** Remove stems from mushrooms and finely chop stems; set caps aside. In a large nonstick skillet coated with cooking spray, saute onions and chopped mushrooms until crisp-tender. Add 1/2 cup broth; cook and stir until liquid is evaporated and vegetables are tender, about 10 minutes.

**2.** Meanwhile, in a small saucepan, bring remaining broth to a boil. Stir in couscous. Remove from the heat; cover and let stand for 5-10 minutes or until broth is absorbed. Fluff with a fork. Add to onion mixture. Stir in 2 Tbsp. cheese, mayonnaise, basil and tarragon. Stuff into mushroom caps.

**3.** Place on a foil-lined baking sheet. Sprinkle with remaining cheese. Bake at 375° for 10-15 minutes or until mushrooms are tender. Just before serving, sprinkle with paprika.

**Nutrition Facts:** 1 stuffed mushroom equals 26 calories, 1 g fat (trace saturated fat), 1 mg cholesterol, 49 mg sodium, 4 g carbohydrate, 1 g fiber, 2 g protein.

# Granola-To-Go Bars **S**

PREP: 30 min. BAKE: 15 min. + cooling YIELD: 3 dozen

SALLY HAEN • MENOMONEE FALLS, WISCONSIN

*This grab-and-go goodie makes a portable breakfast or a hearty snack for a long day out. Chewy and sweet, these fruity oat bars really satisfy!*

3-1/2 cups quick-cooking oats
   1 cup chopped almonds
   1 egg, lightly beaten
2/3 cup butter, melted
1/2 cup honey
   1 tsp. vanilla extract
1/2 cup sunflower kernels
1/2 cup flaked coconut
1/2 cup chopped dried apples
1/2 cup dried cranberries
1/2 cup packed brown sugar
1/2 tsp. ground cinnamon

**1.** Combine the oats and the almonds in a 15-in. x 10-in. x 1-in. baking pan that has been coated with cooking spray. Bake at 350° for 15 minutes or until toasted, stirring occasionally.

**2.** In a large bowl, combine the egg, butter, honey and vanilla. Stir in the sunflower kernels, coconut, apples, cranberries, brown sugar and cinnamon. Stir in oat mixture.

**3.** Press into a 15-in. x 10-in. x 1-in. baking pan coated with cooking spray. Bake at 350° for 13-18 minutes or until set and edges are lightly browned. Cool on a wire rack. Carefully cut into bars. Store in an airtight container.

**Nutrition Facts:** 1 bar equals 130 calories, 7 g fat (3 g saturated fat), 15 mg cholesterol, 40 mg sodium, 16 g carbohydrate, 2 g fiber, 2 g protein.

# Peanut Caramel Corn

PREP: 20 min. BAKE: 45 min. YIELD: 2 qt.

LOIS WARD • PUSLIN, ONTARIO

*I found this lower-fat recipe a few years ago and always give it away in small packages at Christmas.*

   8 cups air-popped popcorn
1/2 cup salted peanuts
1/2 cup packed brown sugar
   3 Tbsp. light corn syrup
4-1/2 tsp. molasses
   1 Tbsp. butter
1/4 tsp. salt
1/2 tsp. vanilla extract
1/8 tsp. baking soda

**1.** Place popcorn and peanuts in a large bowl coated with cooking spray; set aside.

**2.** In a large heavy saucepan, combine the brown sugar, corn syrup, molasses, butter and salt. Bring to a boil over medium heat, stirring constantly. Boil for 2-3 minutes without stirring.

**3.** Remove from the heat; stir in vanilla and baking soda (mixture will foam). Quickly pour over popcorn and mix well.

**4.** Transfer to a 15-in. x 10-in. x 1-in. baking pan coated with cooking spray. Bake at 250° for 45 minutes, stirring every 15 minutes. Remove from pan and place on waxed paper to cool. Store in an airtight container.

**Nutrition Facts:** 1 cup equals 181 calories, 6 g fat (2 g saturated fat), 4 mg cholesterol, 155 mg sodium, 30 g carbohydrate, 2 g fiber, 3 g protein. **Diabetic Exchanges:** 2 starch, 1 fat.

PEANUT CARAMEL CORN

GRANOLA-TO-GO BARS

# California Wassail F S

**PREP/TOTAL TIME:** 30 min.  **YIELD:** 16 servings

**PATRICIA NIEH • PORTOLA VALLY, CALIFORNIA**

*Here's a healthy and delicious family-friendly punch that's a cozy way to welcome family and friends in from the cold or just celebrate the holiday season. Serve it in small cups, as it tastes best when piping hot!*

| | |
|---|---|
| 24 | whole cloves |
| 1 | large navel orange, cut into six wedges |
| 4 | cups orange juice |
| 4 | cups unsweetened apple juice |
| 4 | cups cranberry juice |
| 16 | maraschino cherries |
| 4 | cinnamon sticks (3 in.) |

**1.** Insert four cloves into each orange wedge. In a Dutch oven, combine the orange juice, apple juice and cranberry juice. Add orange wedges, cherries and cinnamon sticks.

**2.** Bring to a boil. Reduce heat; simmer, uncovered, for 15-20 minutes or until flavors are blended. Discard cinnamon sticks. Serve warm.

**Nutrition Facts:** 3/4 cup equals 101 calories, trace fat (trace saturated fat), 0 cholesterol, 3 mg sodium, 26 g carbohydrate, trace fiber, 1 g protein. **Diabetic Exchange:** 1-1/2 fruit.

When buying oranges, select those that are heavy for their size and feel firm. Avoid any with mold or spongy spots. Buying a **big bag of oranges** may be a bargain, but keep in mind that you can't see all areas on each orange. One pound equals about 3 medium oranges.

CALIFORNIA WASSAIL

# Gluten-Free Chocolate Snack Mix

**PREP/TOTAL TIME:** 25 min.  **YIELD:** 3 qt.

**ANGELA BUCHANAN • LONGMONT, COLORADO**

*Being gluten-intolerant, I experiment with a lot of recipes. This sweet snack is fun for kids and adults alike!*

| | |
|---|---|
| 5 | cups Chocolate Chex |
| 4 | cups Cinnamon Chex |
| 1 | cup salted cashews |
| 1 | cup dried banana chips |
| 6 | Tbsp. butter, cubed |
| 1 | cup flaked coconut |
| 1/4 | cup honey |
| 2 | Tbsp. baking cocoa |
| 1 | tsp. coconut extract |
| 1/2 | tsp. ground cinnamon |

**1.** In a large microwave-safe bowl, combine the cereals, cashews and banana chips. In a small microwave-safe bowl, melt butter. Add the coconut, honey, cocoa, extract and cinnamon; stir until blended. Pour over cereal mixture and toss to coat.

**2.** Microwave, uncovered, on high for 4 minutes, stirring every minute. Spread onto waxed paper to cool. Store in an airtight container.

**Editor's Note:** Read all ingredient labels for possible gluten content prior to use. Ingredient formulas can change, and production facilities vary among brands. If you're concerned that your brand may contain gluten, contact the company. This recipe was tested in a 1,100-watt microwave.

**Nutrition Facts:** 1/2 cup equals 182 calories, 10 g fat (5 g saturated fat), 8 mg cholesterol, 185 mg sodium, 23 g carbohydrate, 1 g fiber, 2 g protein.

# Tuscan Bean And Olive Spread C

**PREP/TOTAL TIME:** 20 min.  **YIELD:** 1-1/2 cups

**DIANE NEMITZ • LUDINGTON, MICHIGAN**

*Wonderful flavors of garlic, rosemary and basil blend in this hearty spread. Lucky enough to have leftovers? Serve it as a sandwich topper.*

| | |
|---|---|
| 6 | sun-dried tomato halves (not packed in oil), finely chopped |
| 1/2 | cup boiling water |
| 1 | can (15 oz.) white kidney or cannellini beans, rinsed and drained |
| 2 | Tbsp. water |
| 1 | Tbsp. olive oil |
| 1-1/2 | tsp. dried basil |
| 1 | garlic clove, halved |
| 1/2 | tsp. dried rosemary, crushed |
| 1/4 | tsp. pepper |
| 1/8 | tsp. crushed red pepper flakes |
| 1/4 | cup Greek olives, chopped |

Bagel chips

**1.** In a small bowl, combine tomatoes and boiling water. Let stand for 5 minutes; drain and set aside.

SPARKLING PARTY PUNCH

TUSCAN BEAN AND OLIVE SPREAD

GARLIC-HERB MINI QUICHES

**2.** Place the beans, water, oil, basil, garlic, rosemary, pepper and pepper flakes in a food processor; cover and process until blended. Stir in tomatoes. Transfer to a serving bowl; sprinkle with olives. Serve with bagel chips.

**Nutrition Facts:** 1/4 cup (calculated without chips) equals 99 calories, 4 g fat (1 g saturated fat), 0 cholesterol, 231 mg sodium, 12 g carbohydrate, 3 g fiber, 3 g protein.

# Sparkling Party Punch F S

**PREP/TOTAL TIME:** 5 min.  **YIELD:** 17 servings

### JAN WITTEVEEN • NORBORNE, MISSOURI

*This has been my "signature" punch for years. When, after several years of using it for the family Christmas party, the punch was changed to a festive red punch recipe, everyone wondered what happened to Jan's punch...needless to say, it has been the Sparkling (yellow) Party Punch ever since!*

  1  can (46 oz.) unsweetened pineapple juice, chilled
  3  cups apricot nectar *or* juice, chilled
  1  liter diet lemon-lime soda, chilled
Pineapple sherbet, optional

**1.** In a punch bowl, combine the pineapple juice, apricot nectar and soda. Top with scoops of sherbet if desired. Serve immediately.

**Nutrition Facts:** 3/4 cup (calculated without sherbet) equals 66 calories, trace fat (trace saturated fat), 0 cholesterol, 9 mg sodium, 16 g carbohydrate, trace fiber, trace protein. **Diabetic Exchange:** 1 fruit.

# Garlic-Herb Mini Quiches F S C M

**PREP/TOTAL TIME:** 25 min.  **YIELD:** 45 appetizers

### JOSEPHINE PIRO • EASTON, PENNSYLVANIA

*Looking for a wonderful way to ring in the New Year or celebrate an extra-special occasion? You've got it—and you need only five ingredients to make these tasty apps!*

  1  carton (6-1/2 oz.) reduced-fat spreadable garlic and herb cream cheese
  1/4  cup fat-free milk
  2  eggs
  3  pkg. (1.9 oz. *each*) frozen miniature phyllo tart shells
  2  Tbsp. minced fresh parsley
Minced chives, optional

**1.** In a small bowl, beat the cream cheese, milk and eggs. Place tart shells on an ungreased baking sheet; fill each with 2 tsp. mixture. Sprinkle with parsley.

**2.** Bake at 350° for 10-12 minutes or until filling is set and shells are lightly browned. Sprinkle with chives if desired. Serve warm.

**Nutrition Facts:** 1 mini quiche equals 31 calories, 2 g fat (trace saturated fat), 12 mg cholesterol, 32 mg sodium, 2 g carbohydrate, trace fiber, 1 g protein.

MAKEOVER CREAMY COLESLAW

PEAR COTTAGE CHEESE SALAD

OLIVE ORANGE SALAD

# Salads

Whether you prefer crispy greens, creamy pasta or refreshing fruit salads, this chapter's assortment of healthy specialties will keep you happy! Turn here for great meal starters, side salads or even meatless main dishes!

## Pear Cottage Cheese Salad C

PREP/TOTAL TIME: 10 min. YIELD: 6 servings

**JEANNIE THOMAS • DRY RIDGE, KENTUCKY**

*Perfect any time, this quick-to-fix snack makes a great pack-along lunch, too!*

    2  cups (16 oz.) 2% cottage cheese
    2  medium pears, chopped
    2  celery ribs, chopped
  1/3  cup chopped pecans
  1/2  tsp. ground ginger

**1.** In a large bowl, combine all ingredients. Chill until serving.

**Nutrition Facts:** 2/3 cup equals 135 calories, 6 g fat (1 g saturated fat), 9 mg cholesterol, 255 mg sodium, 14 g carbohydrate, 3 g fiber, 8 g protein. **Diabetic Exchanges:** 1 lean meat, 1 fat, 1/2 fruit.

## Makeover Creamy Coleslaw F

PREP: 10 min. + chilling YIELD: 8 servings

**RENEE ENDRESS • GALVA, ILLINOIS**

*Here's a lightened-up take on my family's favorite coleslaw recipe. The flavor is very much the same as our full-fat version, but for the sake of making it healthier, I'd say the slight change is definitely worth it!*

    2  pkg. (14 oz. *each*) coleslaw mix
  3/4  cup fat-free mayonnaise
  1/3  cup reduced-fat sour cream
  1/4  cup sugar
  3/4  tsp. seasoned salt
  1/2  tsp. ground mustard
  1/4  tsp. celery seed

**1.** Place coleslaw mix in a large bowl. In a small bowl, combine the remaining ingredients. Pour over coleslaw mix and toss to coat. Refrigerate for at least 2 hours before serving.

**Nutrition Facts:** 3/4 cup equals 85 calories, 2 g fat (1 g saturated fat), 6 mg cholesterol, 358 mg sodium, 16 g carbohydrate, 3 g fiber, 2 g protein. **Diabetic Exchange:** 1 starch.

## Olive Orange Salad

PREP/TOTAL TIME: 20 min. YIELD: 6 servings

**CAROL GAUS • ELK GROVE VILLAGE, ILLINOIS**

*This easy side salad is fancy enough to serve to dinner guests, but quick enough to make during the week. It pairs well with spicy meals, such as blackened fish or pasta with zesty sausage.*

    6  medium navel oranges
    6  lettuce leaves
    6  thin slices red onion, separated into rings
    6  Tbsp. sliced ripe olives
    6  Tbsp. Italian salad dressing

**1.** Peel and cut each orange widthwise into three slices. Place lettuce leaves on individual salad plates. Top with orange slices and onion. Sprinkle with olives; drizzle with dressing.

**Nutrition Facts:** 1 serving equals 138 calories, 7 g fat (1 g saturated fat), 0 cholesterol, 330 mg sodium, 20 g carbohydrate, 4 g fiber, 2 g protein. **Diabetic Exchanges:** 1 fruit, 1 fat.

## Honey Fruit Salad F S

PREP/TOTAL TIME: 10 min. YIELD: 4 servings

**DOROTHY DINNEAN • HARRISON, ARKANSAS**

*What's not to love about this refreshing assortment of berries and fruit? The delightful medley is even treated to a no-fuss dressing of honey, lemon juice and poppy seeds!*

    1  medium banana, chopped
    1  cup fresh blueberries
    1  cup fresh raspberries
    1  cup sliced fresh strawberries
    2  Tbsp. honey
  1/2  tsp. lemon juice
  1/4  tsp. poppy seeds

**1.** In a small bowl, combine banana and berries. In another small bowl, combine the honey, lemon juice and poppy seeds. Pour over fruit; toss to coat.

**Nutrition Facts:** 3/4 cup equals 109 calories, 1 g fat (trace saturated fat), 0 cholesterol, 2 mg sodium, 28 g carbohydrate, 5 g fiber, 1 g protein. **Diabetic Exchanges:** 1 fruit, 1/2 starch.

## Portobello Spinach Salad  S C M

**PREP:** 15 min. + marinating  **GRILL:** 10 min.
**YIELD:** 6 servings

**THOMAS MC CLEARY • KANSAS CITY, KANSAS**

*Grilled portobellos add a healthy heartiness to this meatless main-dish salad.*

- 1 cup orange juice
- 1/4 cup olive oil
- 4 tsp. grated orange peel
- 1 tsp. fennel seed
- 1/2 tsp. pepper
- 1/4 tsp. salt
- 1/2 lb. sliced baby portobello mushrooms
- 1 pkg. (6 oz.) fresh baby spinach
- 1 can (11 oz.) mandarin oranges, drained
- 1/2 medium red onion, thinly sliced
- 1/4 cup slivered almonds

**1.** In a small bowl, combine the first six ingredients. Pour 1/2 cup marinade into a large resealable plastic bag. Add the mushrooms; seal bag and turn to coat. Refrigerate for 15 minutes. Cover and refrigerate remaining marinade.

**2.** Drain mushrooms and discard marinade. Transfer mushrooms to a grill wok or basket. Grill, uncovered, over medium heat for 8-12 minutes or until tender, stirring frequently. Cool slightly.

**3.** Meanwhile, in a large bowl, combine the spinach, oranges, onion, almonds and grilled mushrooms.

**4.** Drizzle with reserved marinade; toss to coat. Serve immediately.

**Editor's Note:** If you do not have a grill wok or basket, use a disposable foil pan. Poke holes in the bottom of the pan with a meat fork to allow liquid to drain.

**Nutrition Facts:** 1 cup equals 129 calories, 8 g fat (1 g saturated fat), 0 cholesterol, 90 mg sodium, 12 g carbohydrate, 2 g fiber, 3 g protein. **Diabetic Exchanges:** 1-1/2 fat, 1 vegetable, 1/2 starch.

## Hawaiian Spinach Salad  F

**PREP/TOTAL TIME:** 25 min.  **YIELD:** 4 servings

**ANITA ASHE • SHERBROOKE, NOVA SCOTIA**

*Toss together fresh spinach, veggies, pineapple and ham for this light, lovely entree salad.*

- 4 cups fresh baby spinach
- 2 cups grape tomatoes
- 2/3 cup seeded chopped cucumber
- 1/2 cup sliced fresh mushrooms
- 8 slices red onion, halved
- 1 can (20 oz.) unsweetened pineapple chunks, drained
- 8 oz. sliced deli ham, julienned
- 1/3 cup fat-free poppy seed salad dressing

PORTOBELLO SPINACH SALAD

HAWAIIAN SPINACH SALAD

**1.** Divide spinach among four plates. Top with tomatoes, cucumber, mushrooms and onion. Arrange pineapple and ham over mushrooms. Drizzle with dressing.

**Nutrition Facts:** 2 cups equals 184 calories, 2 g fat (trace saturated fat), 29 mg cholesterol, 615 mg sodium, 31 g carbohydrate, 3 g fiber, 13 g protein. **Diabetic Exchanges:** 2 lean meat, 2 vegetable, 1/2 starch, 1/2 fruit.

# Taco Salad with a Twist ⓜ

**PREP/TOTAL TIME:** 25 min.  **YIELD:** 4 servings

**HEATHER CARROLL • COLORADO SPRINGS, COLORADO**

*You won't even miss the meat in this satisfying salad chock-full of beans, veggies and mouthwatering Southwest flavor.*

- 1 pkg. (5 oz.) spring mix salad greens
- 1 large tomato, seeded and chopped
- 1 large red onion, chopped
- 1 medium ripe avocado, peeled and chopped
- 1 cup canned black beans, rinsed and drained
- 4 green onions, chopped
- 1/2 cup shredded reduced-fat cheddar cheese
- 1/2 cup minced fresh cilantro

DRESSING:
- 1/2 cup green chili salsa
- 1/2 cup fat-free plain Greek yogurt
- 2 Tbsp. minced fresh cilantro
- 1 Tbsp. thinly sliced green onion
- 1 Tbsp. lemon juice
- 1 Tbsp. white wine vinegar
- 1 Tbsp. olive oil
- 1-1/2 tsp. honey
- 1/8 tsp. pepper

**1.** In a large bowl, combine the first eight ingredients. In a small bowl, whisk the remaining ingredients. Pour over salad mixture; toss to coat.

**Nutrition Facts:** 2 cups equals 277 calories, 14 g fat (3 g saturated fat), 10 mg cholesterol, 439 mg sodium, 29 g carbohydrate, 10 g fiber, 14 g protein. **Diabetic Exchanges:** 2 lean meat, 2 vegetable, 1-1/2 fat, 1 starch.

## Artichoke Arugula Salad

**PREP/TOTAL TIME:** 25 min. **YIELD:** 10 servings

**BARBARA BEGLEY • FAIRFIELD, OHIO**

*Packed with artichokes, dried cranberries and lots of fresh flavors, this salad is sure to be a favorite.*

    8   cups fresh arugula *or* baby spinach
    1   can (14 oz.) water-packed artichoke hearts,
        rinsed, drained and chopped
    1   cup dried cranberries
  3/4   cup chopped pecans, toasted
    4   green onions, chopped
  1/2   cup reduced-fat raspberry vinaigrette
  3/4   cup crumbled feta cheese

**1.** In a large bowl, combine the arugula, artichokes, cranberries, pecans and green onions. Drizzle with vinaigrette; toss to coat. Sprinkle with cheese.

**Nutrition Facts:** 1 cup equals 158 calories, 9 g fat (2 g saturated fat), 5 mg cholesterol, 314 mg sodium, 16 g carbohydrate, 2 g fiber, 4 g protein. **Diabetic Exchanges:** 1-1/2 fat, 1 starch.

## Beet Spinach Salad M

**PREP:** 10 min. **COOK:** 30 min. + cooling
**YIELD:** 4 servings

**DARLENE BRENDEN • SALEM, OREGON**

*Here's a colorful combination—beets, spinach, orange and apples. Tossing everything with a vinaigrette keeps it healthy.*

    6   small fresh beets (about 1-1/2 lb.)
    4   cups fresh baby spinach
    2   medium tart apples, peeled and sliced
    1   medium orange, sectioned
    3   Tbsp. raspberry hazelnut vinaigrette
    2   Tbsp. chopped hazelnuts, toasted

**1.** Scrub beets and trim tops to 1 in. Place in a Dutch oven and cover with water. Bring to a boil. Reduce heat; cover and simmer for 30-60 minutes or until the beets are tender. Remove beets from the water; cool. Peel beets and cut into 1-in. wedges.

**2.** Divide spinach among four plates. Top with apples, orange and beets. Drizzle with vinaigrette; sprinkle with hazelnuts.

**Nutrition Facts:** 1 serving equals 175 calories, 5 g fat (1 g saturated fat), 0 cholesterol, 252 mg sodium, 32 g carbohydrate, 5 g fiber, 4 g protein. **Diabetic Exchanges:** 2 starch, 1 fat.

# Feta Romaine Salad C M

**PREP/TOTAL TIME:** 15 min. **YIELD:** 6 servings

**MICHAEL VOLPATT • SAN FRANCISCO, CALIFORNIA**

*Feta cheese and Greek olives add a taste of the Mediterranean to this quick and easy dish.*

    1   bunch romaine, chopped
    3   plum tomatoes, seeded and chopped
    1   cup (4 oz.) crumbled feta cheese
    1   cup chopped seeded cucumber
  1/2   cup Greek olives, chopped
    2   Tbsp. minced fresh parsley
    2   Tbsp. minced fresh cilantro
    3   Tbsp. lemon juice
    2   Tbsp. olive oil
  1/4   tsp. pepper

**1.** In a large bowl, combine the first seven ingredients. In a small bowl, whisk the remaining ingredients. Drizzle over salad; toss to coat. Serve immediately.

**Nutrition Facts:** 1-1/3 cups equals 139 calories, 11 g fat (3 g saturated fat), 10 mg cholesterol, 375 mg sodium, 6 g carbohydrate, 3 g fiber, 5 g protein. **Diabetic Exchanges:** 2 fat, 1 vegetable.

# Light Green Goddess Salad Dressing C

**PREP/TOTAL TIME:** 10 min. **YIELD:** 2 cups

**PAGE ALEXANDER • BALDWIN CITY, KANSAS**

*Try my do-it-yourself version of a popular salad dressing that's lower in calories and fat but keeps all the flavor.*

    1   cup reduced-fat mayonnaise
  1/2   cup reduced-fat sour cream
  1/4   cup chopped green pepper
  1/4   cup packed fresh parsley sprigs
    3   anchovy fillets
    2   Tbsp. lemon juice
    2   green onion tops, coarsely chopped
    1   garlic clove, peeled
  1/4   tsp. pepper
  1/8   tsp. Worcestershire sauce

**1.** Place all ingredients in a blender; cover and process until smooth. Transfer to a bowl or jar; cover and store in the refrigerator.

**Nutrition Facts:** 2 Tbsp. equals 64 calories, 6 g fat (1 g saturated fat), 8 mg cholesterol, 153 mg sodium, 2 g carbohydrate, trace fiber, 1 g protein. **Diabetic Exchange:** 1 fat.

FETA ROMAINE SALAD

LIGHT GREEN GODDESS SALAD DRESSING

## Broccoli Tomato Salad F C M

**PREP:** 10 min. + chilling **YIELD:** 6 servings

**HELEN MEADOWS • TROUT CREEK, MONTANA**

*I found this recipe over 25 years ago. I made a few changes to it, and our family has enjoyed it ever since. The colorful combo is simply perfect for the holidays, but it's equally delightful at summer picnics.*

| | |
|---|---|
| 5 | cups broccoli florets |
| 1 | Tbsp. water |
| 1 | pint cherry tomatoes, cut in half |
| 2 | Tbsp. chopped green onion |
| 1/4 | cup fat-free mayonnaise |
| 1/4 | cup reduced-fat sour cream |
| 1 | Tbsp. lemon juice |
| 1/2 | tsp. salt |
| 1/4 | tsp. pepper |

**It takes longer to cook food when the microwave's power (wattage) is lower. We suggest that you start with a cook time that is one-third longer than what is called for in the recipe.**

BROCCOLI TOMATO SALAD

**1.** Place broccoli and water in a 2-qt. microwave-safe bowl. Cover and microwave on high for 1-1/2 to 2-1/2 minutes or until crisp-tender, stirring once; drain. Cool completely.

**2.** Place broccoli in a serving bowl; gently stir in tomatoes and onion. In a small bowl, combine the mayonnaise, sour cream, lemon juice, salt and pepper; pour over vegetables and stir gently. Cover and refrigerate for 1 hour.

**Editor's Note:** This recipe was tested in a 1,100-watt microwave.

**Nutrition Facts:** 3/4 cup equals 49 calories, 1 g fat (1 g saturated fat), 4 mg cholesterol, 304 mg sodium, 8 g carbohydrate, 3 g fiber, 3 g protein. **Diabetic Exchange:** 1 vegetable.

## Pepperoncini Arugula Salad F C M

**PREP/TOTAL TIME:** 5 min. **YIELD:** 4 servings

**TABITHA FREEMAN • MERIDEN, CONNECTICUT**

*This fantastic salad is short on time but not on taste. In about 5 minutes you can have a salad that goes well with just about any beef or pork dish.*

| | |
|---|---|
| 2 | cups fresh arugula *or* baby spinach |
| 2 | cups torn romaine |
| 1/4 | cup chopped red onion |
| 2 | pepperoncini, sliced |
| 1 | medium tomato, sliced |
| 1/4 | cup balsamic vinaigrette |

**1.** In a large salad bowl, combine the arugula, romaine, onion and tomato. Drizzle with vinaigrette; gently toss to coat.

**Editor's Note:** Look for pepperoncinis (pickled peppers) in the pickle and olive section of your grocery store.

**Nutrition Facts:** 1-1/4 cups equals 50 calories, 3 g fat (trace saturated fat), 0 cholesterol, 197 mg sodium, 6 g carbohydrate, 1 g fiber, 1 g protein. **Diabetic Exchanges:** 1 vegetable, 1/2 fat.

## Citrus-Marmalade Vinaigrette S C

**PREP/TOTAL TIME:** 10 min. **YIELD:** 3/4 cup

**SARAH VASQUES • MILFORD, NEW HAMPSHIRE**

*Add this fresh-tasting splash of citrus to a wide variety of salad mixings.*

| | |
|---|---|
| 1/3 | cup olive oil |
| 3 | Tbsp. lemon juice |
| 2 | Tbsp. orange marmalade |
| 4 | tsp. minced fresh thyme |
| 1 | Tbsp. Dijon mustard |
| 2 | tsp. grated lemon peel |
| 1/8 | tsp. salt |

**1.** In a small bowl whisk all ingredients. Chill until serving.

**Nutrition Facts:** 2 Tbsp. equals 128 calories, 12 g fat (2 g saturated fat), 0 cholesterol, 113 mg sodium, 6 g carbohydrate, trace fiber, trace protein. **Diabetic Exchanges:** 2 fat, 1/2 starch.

# Makeover Italian Pasta Salad C M

**PREP:** 25 min. + chilling **YIELD:** 8 servings

**HEALTHY COOKING TEST KITCHEN**

*Here's the perfect side dish for summer picnics or fall potlucks—and no one would ever guess that it's been slimmed down.*

1 cup uncooked whole wheat spiral pasta
1-1/2 cups halved cherry tomatoes
1 cup sliced fresh mushrooms
1/2 cup fat-free Italian salad dressing
1/4 cup chopped sweet red pepper
1/4 cup chopped green pepper
3 Tbsp. thinly sliced green onions
1/2 cup fat-free mayonnaise
1/3 cup grated Parmesan cheese
1/3 cup cubed provolone cheese
1 can (2-1/4 oz.) sliced ripe olives, drained

**1.** Cook pasta according to package directions; rinse with cold water and drain. Place in a large bowl; add the tomatoes, mushrooms, salad dressing, peppers and onions. Cover and refrigerate for at least 4 hours or overnight.

**2.** In a small bowl, combine mayonnaise and Parmesan cheese; stir in provolone cheese and olives. Gently fold into the pasta mixture. Chill until serving.

**Nutrition Facts:** 3/4 cup equals 101 calories, 4 g fat (2 g saturated fat), 9 mg cholesterol, 507 mg sodium, 12 g carbohydrate, 2 g fiber, 5 g protein. **Diabetic Exchanges:** 1 starch, 1/2 fat.

SPICY FRUIT SALAD

## Spicy Fruit Salad F S

**PREP/TOTAL TIME:** 15 min. **YIELD:** 10 servings

**REBECCA STURROCK • LONGVIEW, TEXAS**

*Definitely not your mother's fruit salad, this one balances cool fruit and hot spices to perfection.*

- 2 medium apples, halved and sliced
- 2 medium pears, halved and sliced
- 2 medium mangoes, peeled, halved and sliced
- 1 lb. fresh strawberries, sliced

VINAIGRETTE:
- 1/4 cup lime juice
- 1/4 cup orange juice
- 1/4 cup minced fresh cilantro
- 2 Tbsp. champagne vinegar
- 1-1/2 tsp. grated lime peel
- 1/4 tsp. sriracha Asian hot chili sauce *or* 1/8 tsp. hot pepper sauce

**1.** In a large bowl, combine the apples, pears, mangoes and strawberries. In a small bowl, whisk the juices, cilantro, vinegar, lime peel and hot chili sauce. Drizzle over fruit mixture; toss to coat.

**Nutrition Facts:** 3/4 cup equals 81 calories, trace fat (trace saturated fat), 0 cholesterol, 6 mg sodium, 21 g carbohydrate, 3 g fiber, 1 g protein. **Diabetic Exchange:** 1-1/2 fruit.

## Tangy Four-Bean Salad M

**PREP:** 20 min. + chilling **YIELD:** 12 servings

**SHARON CAIN • REVELSTOKE, BRITISH COLUMBIA**

*This colorful salad is easy to fix, and a no-fuss dressing lends sweet-sour flair. Green pepper and mushrooms help it stand out from other bean medleys.*

- 1 can (16 oz.) kidney beans, rinsed and drained
- 1 can (15 oz.) garbanzo beans or chickpeas, rinsed and drained
- 1 can (14-1/2 oz.) cut green beans, drained
- 1 can (14-1/2 oz.) cut wax beans, drained
- 1 cup sliced fresh mushrooms
- 1 cup chopped green pepper
- 1 cup chopped onion

DRESSING:
- 1/2 cup cider vinegar
- 1/3 cup sugar
- 1/4 cup canola oil

1 tsp. celery seed
1/2 tsp. pepper
1/4 tsp. salt
1/8 tsp. dried basil
1/8 tsp. dried oregano

**1.** In a large bowl, combine the beans, mushrooms, green pepper and onion. In a small bowl, whisk the dressing ingredients.

**2.** Pour dressing over bean mixture and stir to coat. Cover and refrigerate for at least 4 hours. Serve with a slotted spoon.

**Nutrition Facts:** 3/4 cup equals 162 calories, 6 g fat (trace saturated fat), 0 cholesterol, 366 mg sodium, 24 g carbohydrate, 5 g fiber, 5 g protein. **Diabetic Exchanges:** 1 starch, 1 vegetable, 1 fat.

# Mediterranean Tabbouleh

**PREP:** 25 min. + standing **BAKE:** 15 min.
**YIELD:** 8 servings

**KEITH DREITLEIN • CRANSTON, RHODE ISLAND**

*Fresh, filling and packed with flavor, this is a great make-ahead idea for a snack or mini-meal you can enjoy all weekend!*

| | |
|---|---|
| 1 | cup bulgur |
| 2 | cups boiling water |
| 5 | garlic cloves, unpeeled |
| 5 | Tbsp. olive oil, *divided* |
| 1/2 | lb. peeled and deveined cooked medium shrimp, chopped |
| 3 | medium tomatoes, seeded and chopped |
| 1 | medium cucumber, chopped |
| 1 | cup chopped sweet onion |
| 2 | green onions, thinly sliced |
| 1/2 | cup minced fresh parsley |
| 2 | Tbsp. minced fresh cilantro |
| 3 | Tbsp. lemon juice |

1/2 tsp. salt
1/4 tsp. pepper

**1.** Place bulgur in a large bowl. Stir in boiling water. Cover and let stand for 30 minutes or until most of the liquid is absorbed.

**2.** Meanwhile, place garlic on a double thickness of heavy-duty foil. Drizzle with 1/2 tsp. oil. Wrap foil around garlic. Bake at 425° for 15-20 minutes. Cool for 10-15 minutes.

**3.** Drain bulgur well; transfer to a large serving bowl. Stir in the shrimp, tomatoes, cucumber, onion, green onions, parsley and cilantro. Squeeze softened garlic into a small bowl and mash. Whisk in the lemon juice, salt, pepper and remaining oil; drizzle over salad. Toss to coat. Chill until serving.

**Nutrition Facts:** 3/4 cup equals 195 calories, 9 g fat (1 g saturated fat), 43 mg cholesterol, 199 mg sodium, 20 g carbohydrate, 5 g fiber, 9 g protein. **Diabetic Exchanges:** 1-1/2 fat, 1 starch, 1 lean meat, 1 vegetable.

To keep fresh parsley in the refrigerator for several weeks, wash the entire **bunch of parsley** in warm water, shake off all excess moisture, wrap in paper towel and seal in a plastic bag. If you need a longer storage time, remove paper towel and place the sealed bag in the freezer.

MEDITERRANEAN TABBOULEH

TANGY FOUR-BEAN SALAD

## Gingered Green Bean Salad  S C M

PREP/TOTAL TIME: 30 min.  YIELD: 8 servings

**TRISHA KRUSE • EAGLE, IDAHO**

*This crisp, summer salad keeps well in the refrigerator—if it lasts that long. The tangy sweetness and toasty flavor in the sesame dressing are almost addictive!*

- 2 lb. fresh green beans, trimmed
- 1 cup thinly sliced red onion, separated into rings
- 1 cup canned bean sprouts, rinsed and drained

VINAIGRETTE:
- 1/4 cup rice vinegar
- 2 Tbsp. sesame oil
- 1 Tbsp. minced fresh gingerroot
- 1 Tbsp. reduced-sodium soy sauce
- 2 tsp. sesame seeds, toasted
- 1 tsp. honey
- 1/2 tsp. minced garlic

**1.** Place green beans in a large saucepan and cover with water. Bring to a boil. Cook, uncovered, for 4-7 minutes or until crisp-tender. Drain and immediately place in ice water; drain and pat dry.

**2.** In a large salad bowl, combine the beans, onion and bean sprouts. In a small bowl, whisk the vinaigrette ingredients. Pour over bean mixture and toss to coat.

**Nutrition Facts:** 1 cup equals 88 calories, 4 g fat (1 g saturated fat), 0 cholesterol, 93 mg sodium, 12 g carbohydrate, 4 g fiber, 3 g protein. **Diabetic Exchanges:** 2 vegetable, 1 fat.

## Tortellini Chicken Salad

PREP: 25 min.  COOK: 15 min. + chilling
YIELD: 6 servings

**EDIE DESPAIN • LOGAN, UTAH**

*If you love pesto, you'll love it even more mixed with fresh veggies and chicken in this good-for-you summer salad.*

- 1 pkg. (9 oz.) refrigerated cheese tortellini
- 1 cup frozen peas
- 5 cups torn romaine
- 1-1/2 cups shredded carrots
- 2 cups cubed cooked chicken breast
- 1/2 cup julienned sweet red pepper
- 1/2 cup fat-free mayonnaise
- 1 jar (3 oz.) prepared pesto
- 1/4 cup buttermilk
- 2 Tbsp. minced fresh parsley

**1.** Cook tortellini according to package directions, adding the peas during the last 4-5 minutes of cooking. Drain and rinse in cold water.

**2.** In a large salad bowl, layer the romaine, carrots, chicken, tortellini and peas, and red pepper. In a small bowl, combine the mayonnaise, pesto and buttermilk. Spread over top. Sprinkle with parsley. Refrigerate until chilled.

**Nutrition Facts:** 1-1/2 cups equals 337 calories, 13 g fat (4 g saturated fat), 62 mg cholesterol, 525 mg sodium, 32 g carbohydrate, 5 g fiber, 25 g protein. **Diabetic Exchanges:** 3 lean meat, 2 starch, 1 fat.

GINGERED GREEN BEAN SALAD

TORTELLINI CHICKEN SALAD

ROASTED BEET-ORANGE SALAD

# Roasted Beet-Orange Salad F S C M

**PREP:** 20 min. + chilling  **BAKE:** 40 min.
**YIELD:** 6 servings

**KATHY RAIRIGH • MILFORD, INDIANA**

*Tender beets and tangy vinaigrette are the stars of this fresh, colorful salad.*

| | |
|---|---|
| 5 | whole fresh beets |
| 4 | green onions, thinly sliced |
| 1/4 | cup cider vinegar |
| 2 | Tbsp. olive oil |
| 1 | Tbsp. canola oil |
| 2 | Tbsp. sugar |
| 1/2 | tsp. salt |
| 1/2 | tsp. curry powder |
| 1/4 | tsp. white pepper |
| 6 | lettuce leaves |
| 2 | medium oranges, peeled and sectioned |

**1.** Place beets in an 11-in. x 7-in. baking dish; add 1 in. of water. Cover and bake at 400° for 40-45 minutes or until tender. Cool; peel, slice and quarter beets. In a large bowl, combine beets and green onions. In a small bowl, whisk the vinegar, oils, sugar, salt, curry and white pepper. Pour over beets; toss to coat. Cover and refrigerate for 2 hours.

**2.** Divide lettuce among six plates. Using a slotted spoon, top with beet mixture. Arrange orange sections over salad.

**Nutrition Facts:** 1 serving equals 59 calories, 2 g fat (trace saturated fat), 0 cholesterol, 96 mg sodium, 9 g carbohydrate, 1 g fiber, 1 g protein. **Diabetic Exchange:** 1/2 starch.

Olive oil can be stored tightly capped at room temperature or in the refrigerator for up to 1 year. When chilled, the oil turns cloudy and thick. Chilled **olive oil** will return to its original consistency when left at room temperature for a short period of time.

## Strawberry Spinach Salad [C]

**PREP:** 25 min.  **COOK:** 10 min.  **YIELD:** 8 servings

**MARY BUFORD SHAW • MT. PLEASANT, SOUTH CAROLINA**

*Here's a colorful salad packed full of flavor. Toasted walnuts add texture and crunch.*

- 3 bacon strips, chopped
- 3 Tbsp. rice vinegar
- 2 Tbsp. honey
- 5 tsp. olive oil
- 1 tsp. Dijon mustard
- 1/2 tsp. pepper
- 1/4 tsp. salt
- 1 pkg. (6 oz.) fresh baby spinach
- 2 medium navel oranges, peeled and chopped
- 12 fresh strawberries, quartered
- 1 cup thinly sliced cucumber
- 1/2 cup thinly sliced red onion
- 1 medium carrot, shredded
- 1/2 cup chopped walnuts, toasted

**1.** In a small skillet, cook bacon over medium heat until crisp. Remove to paper towels with a slotted spoon; drain.

**2.** In a small bowl, whisk the vinegar, honey, oil, mustard, pepper and salt. In a large bowl, combine the spinach, oranges, strawberries, cucumber, onion and carrot. Pour dressing over salad; toss to coat. Sprinkle with walnuts and bacon. Serve immediately.

**Nutrition Facts:** 1 cup equals 142 calories, 9 g fat (1 g saturated fat), 3 mg cholesterol, 168 mg sodium, 15 g carbohydrate, 3 g fiber, 3 g protein. **Diabetic Exchanges:** 1-1/2 fat, 1 starch.

## Chicken Curry Fruit Salad

**PREP:** 20 min. + chilling  **YIELD:** 6 servings

**PJ ANDERSON • SALT LAKE CITY, UTAH**

*Perfect for a special spring luncheon, this refreshing combo blends chicken, apple, celery and grapes with a splash of lime and the crunch of nuts and chow mein noodles. Yum!*

- 4 cups cubed cooked chicken breasts
- 2 celery ribs, diced
- 1 cup seedless red grapes, halved

1 medium apple, peeled and diced
1 small red onion, diced
1 cup fat-free mayonnaise
1 Tbsp. orange marmalade
2 tsp. lime juice
1 tsp. curry powder
1/2 cup lightly salted cashews
1/2 cup chow mein noodles

**1.** In a large bowl, combine the first five ingredients. In a small bowl, combine the mayonnaise, marmalade, lime juice and curry. Pour over chicken mixture and toss to coat. Cover and refrigerate for at least 1 hour.

**2.** Just before serving, sprinkle with cashews and chow mein noodles.

**Nutrition Facts:** 1-1/3 cups equals 305 calories, 11 g fat (2 g saturated fat), 76 mg cholesterol, 431 mg sodium, 22 g carbohydrate, 3 g fiber, 30 g protein. **Diabetic Exchanges:** 4 lean meat, 1 starch, 1 fat, 1/2 fruit.

# Makeover Loaded Baked Potato Salad

**PREP:** 20 min. **BAKE:** 30 min. + cooling
**YIELD:** 12 servings (3/4 cup each)

## HEALTHY COOKING TEST KITCHEN

*Crispy bacon, crunchy pickle, cheddar cheese and a creamy dressing are guaranteed to make this salad a family favorite.*

2-1/2 lb. small unpeeled red potatoes, cubed
1/2 tsp. salt
1/4 tsp. pepper
2 hard-cooked eggs, chopped
4 bacon strips, cooked and crumbled
1/2 cup shredded reduced-fat cheddar cheese
1 cup chopped sweet onion
1 dill pickle, chopped
1/2 cup reduced-fat sour cream
1/2 cup fat-free mayonnaise
1 tsp. prepared mustard

**1.** Place potatoes in a 15-in. x 10-in. x 1-in. baking pan coated with cooking spray; sprinkle with salt and pepper. Bake, uncovered, at 425° for 30-35 minutes or until tender. Cool on a wire rack.

**2.** In a large bowl, combine the potatoes, eggs, bacon, cheese, onion and pickle. In a small bowl, combine the sour cream, mayonnaise and mustard; pour over the potato mixture and toss to coat.

**Nutrition Facts:** 3/4 cup equals 133 calories, 4 g fat (2 g saturated fat), 45 mg cholesterol, 340 mg sodium, 19 g carbohydrate, 2 g fiber, 6 g protein. **Diabetic Exchanges:** 1 starch, 1 medium-fat meat.

Reduced-fat cheese products refer to products that contain at least **25% less fat** than the original version. These products can be used in most recipes that are heated or melted. Fat-free cheese must contain less than 0.5 g fat per serving.

MAKEOVER LOADED BAKED POTATO SALAD

CHICKEN CURRY FRUIT SALAD

# Cannellini Bean Salad

**PREP/TOTAL TIME:** 30 min. **YIELD:** 5 servings

**ALDEN THORNTON • WARRENTON, OREGON**

*I've had this recipe quite a long time, although I have changed it somewhat from the original. It has always been popular, particularly when served at picnics and potlucks.*

- 1 large sweet red pepper
- 2 cans (15 oz. *each*) white kidney or cannellini beans, rinsed and drained
- 1 medium red onion, sliced and separated into rings
- 1/4 cup minced fresh basil
- 3 Tbsp. red wine vinegar
- 2 Tbsp. olive oil
- 1/4 tsp. salt
- 1/4 tsp. pepper

**1.** Cut red pepper in half; remove seeds. Broil pepper cut side down 4 in. from the heat until skin is blistered and charred, about 8 minutes. Immediately place pepper in a small bowl; cover and let stand for 15-20 minutes.

**2.** Peel off and discard charred skin. Cut pepper into strips; place in a large bowl. Add the beans, onion and basil. In a jar with a tight-fitting lid, combine the vinegar, oil, salt and pepper; shake well. Pour over bean mixture; toss to coat.

**Nutrition Facts:** 3/4 cup equals 190 calories, 6 g fat (1 g saturated fat), 0 cholesterol, 472 mg sodium, 26 g carbohydrate, 7 g fiber, 7 g protein. **Diabetic Exchanges:** 1-1/2 starch, 1 lean meat, 1 fat.

# Makeover Fluffy Lime Salad  S

**PREP:** 15 min. + chilling **YIELD:** 8 servings

**HEALTHY COOKING TEST KITCHEN**

*Loaded with crunchy walnuts, tangy pineapple and lip-smacking lime flavor, this refreshing salad could even double as dessert!*

- 1 can (8 oz.) unsweetened crushed pineapple, undrained
- 1 pkg. (.3 oz.) sugar-free lime gelatin
- 3 Tbsp. water
- 6 oz. reduced-fat cream cheese
- 1 cup miniature marshmallows
- 1/2 cup chopped walnuts
- 1 carton (8 oz.) frozen reduced-fat whipped topping, thawed

**1.** Drain pineapple, reserving juice; set pineapple aside. In a small saucepan, combine the gelatin, water and reserved juice. Cook and stir over low heat until gelatin is dissolved. Refrigerate until syrupy, about 30 minutes.

**2.** In a small bowl, beat cream cheese until fluffy. Stir in gelatin mixture, marshmallows, walnuts and pineapple. Fold in whipped topping.

**3.** Transfer to a serving bowl. Cover and refrigerate for 2 hours or until set.

**Nutrition Facts:** 3/4 cup equals 206 calories, 12 g fat (7 g saturated fat), 15 mg cholesterol, 125 mg sodium, 21 g carbohydrate, 1 g fiber, 4 g protein.

# Frosted Fruit Salad  F S

**PREP/TOTAL TIME:** 10 min. **YIELD:** 6 servings

**ANN FOX • AUSTIN, TEXAS**

*I came up with this breakfast recipe that's easy, light, delicious and uses up the bananas and apples I always have on hand.*

MAKEOVER FLUFFY LIME SALAD

CANNELLINI BEAN SALAD

STRAWBERRY SALAD WITH MOJITO VINAIGRETTE

2 large apples, cut into 3/4-in. cubes
2 medium firm bananas, sliced
2 tsp. lemon juice
1 carton (6 oz.) fat-free sugar-free raspberry yogurt
1/4 cup raisins
1 Tbsp. sunflower kernels

**1.** In a large bowl, combine apples and bananas. Sprinkle with lemon juice; toss to coat. Stir in the yogurt, raisins and sunflower kernels.

**Nutrition Facts:** 3/4 cup equals 124 calories, 1 g fat (trace saturated fat), 1 mg cholesterol, 31 mg sodium, 28 g carbohydrate, 3 g fiber, 3 g protein. **Diabetic Exchange:** 2 fruit.

# Strawberry Salad With Mojito Vinaigrette

**PREP/TOTAL TIME:** 20 min. **YIELD:** 5 servings

**DONNA MARIE RYAN • TOPSFIELD, MASSACHUSETTS**

*Mojitos are a fun summery drink and the inspiration behind this refreshing side salad. No rum was used in my recipe, but it certainly could be added to the vinaigrette.*

1/4 cup white wine vinegar
4 fresh strawberries, hulled

2 Tbsp. water
2 Tbsp. lime juice
2 Tbsp. coarsely chopped fresh mint
2 Tbsp. honey
1/4 tsp. salt
Dash pepper
2 Tbsp. olive oil

SALAD:
1 pkg. (5 oz.) spring mix salad greens
2 cups fresh strawberries, hulled and sliced
1 small red onion, thinly sliced
3 oz. fresh goat cheese, crumbled
1/4 cup chopped walnuts

**1.** In a blender, combine the first eight ingredients. While processing, gradually add oil in a steady stream. Set aside.

**2.** Divide salad greens among five salad plates; top with strawberries, onion, cheese and walnuts. Drizzle with vinaigrette.

**Nutrition Facts:** 1-1/2 cups salad with 2 Tbsp. vinaigrette equals 178 calories, 11 g fat (3 g saturated fat), 11 mg cholesterol, 195 mg sodium, 17 g carbohydrate, 3 g fiber, 4 g protein. **Diabetic Exchanges:** 2 fat, 1 vegetable, 1/2 starch, 1/2 fruit.

CUBAN-STYLE PORK SANDWICHES

BLACK BEAN-PUMPKIN SOUP

OPEN-FACED HAM AND APPLE MELT

# Soups & Sandwiches

Whether you need a hearty lunch or a casual weeknight dinner, you can skip the fast-food drive-thru thanks to these tasty options. Enjoy the recipes alone or paired with a green salad for a healthy meal in no time.

## Open-Faced Ham and Apple Melts F

PREP/TOTAL TIME: 15 min.  YIELD: 4 servings

SALLY MALONEY • DALLAS, GEORGIA

*As a homework snack or light lunch, these yummy melts combine the crunch of sweet apple with the tangy flavor of ham and Dijon mustard!*

    2   whole wheat English muffins, split
    2   tsp. Dijon mustard
    4   slices deli ham
  1/2   medium apple, thinly sliced
    2   slices reduced-fat Swiss cheese, halved

**1.** Place English muffin halves cut side up on a baking sheet. Broil 4-6 in. from the heat for 2-3 minutes or until golden brown.

**2.** Spread with mustard. Top with ham, apple slices and cheese. Broil 3-4 minutes longer or until cheese is melted.

**Nutrition Facts:** 1 muffin half equals 130 calories, 3 g fat (1 g saturated fat), 14 mg cholesterol, 429 mg sodium, 17 g carbohydrate, 3 g fiber, 10 g protein.

## Turkey Avocado Sandwiches

PREP/TOTAL TIME: 10 min.  YIELD: 2 servings

DAVE BREMSON • PLANTATION, FLORIDA

*Hearty and delicious, these satisfying sandwiches have just the right amount of heat!*

    3   oz. fat-free cream cheese
    2   tsp. taco sauce
    4   drops hot pepper sauce
    4   slices whole wheat bread
    4   oz. sliced cooked turkey
  1/2   medium ripe avocado, peeled and sliced
    1   medium tomato, sliced
    2   to 4 Tbsp. minced fresh cilantro
    2   lettuce leaves

**1.** In a large bowl, beat cream cheese until smooth. Beat in taco sauce and pepper sauce; spread over bread.

**2.** Layer the turkey, avocado and tomato on two bread slices; sprinkle with cilantro. Top with lettuce and remaining bread.

**Nutrition Facts:** 1 sandwich equals 399 calories, 11 g fat (2 g saturated fat), 52 mg cholesterol, 617 mg sodium, 40 g carbohydrate, 7 g fiber, 33 g protein. **Diabetic Exchanges:** 3 lean meat, 2 starch, 1 vegetable, 1 fat.

## Black Bean-Pumpkin Soup M

PREP: 30 min.  COOK: 30 min.  YIELD: 8 servings (2 qt.)

JENNIFER FISHER • AUSTIN, TEXAS

*This is such a healthy recipe, packed with protein from the beans and vitamins from the pumpkin.*

    2   cans (15 oz. *each*) black beans, rinsed and drained
    1   can (14-1/2 oz.) diced tomatoes, drained
    2   medium onions, finely chopped
    1   tsp. olive oil
    3   garlic cloves, minced
    1   tsp. ground cumin
    3   cups vegetable broth
    1   can (15 oz.) solid-pack pumpkin
    2   Tbsp. cider vinegar
  1/2   tsp. pepper
    2   Tbsp. bourbon, optional
  1/2   cup reduced-fat sour cream
  1/2   cup thinly sliced green onions
  1/2   cup roasted salted pumpkin seeds

**1.** Place beans and tomatoes in a food processor; cover and process until blended. Set aside.

**2.** In a Dutch oven, saute onions in oil until tender. Add garlic and cumin; saute 1 minute longer. Stir in the broth, pumpkin, vinegar, pepper and bean mixture. Bring to a boil. Reduce heat; cover and simmer for 20 minutes.

**3.** Stir in bourbon if desired. Garnish each serving with sour cream, green onions and pumpkin seeds.

**Nutrition Facts:** 1 cup (calculated without bourbon) equals 238 calories, 8 g fat (2 g saturated fat), 5 mg cholesterol, 716 mg sodium, 30 g carbohydrate, 9 g fiber, 13 g protein. **Diabetic Exchanges:** 1-1/2 starch, 1-1/2 fat, 1 lean meat, 1 vegetable.

## Makeover Beef & Potato Soup

**PREP:** 30 min.  **COOK:** 6-1/2 hours
**YIELD:** 10 servings (3 qt.)

**SHEILA HOLDERMAN • BERTHOLD, NORTH DAKOTA**

*Slow cooker ease makes this healthy version of our favorite soups a Christmas Eve tradition after church services.*

- 1-1/2 lbs. lean ground beef (90% lean)
- 3/4 cup chopped onion
- 1/2 cup all-purpose flour
- 2 cans (14-1/2 oz. *each*) reduced-sodium chicken broth, *divided*
- 5 medium potatoes, peeled and cubed
- 5 medium carrots, chopped
- 3 celery ribs, chopped
- 3 tsp. dried basil
- 2 tsp. dried parsley flakes
- 1 tsp. garlic powder
- 1/2 tsp. pepper
- 12 oz. reduced-fat process cheese (Velveeta), cubed
- 1-1/2 cups 2% milk
- 1/2 cup reduced-fat sour cream

**1.** In a large skillet, cook beef and onion over medium heat until meat is no longer pink; drain. Combine flour and 1 can broth until smooth. Add to beef mixture. Bring to a boil; cook and stir for 2 minutes or until thickened.

**2.** Transfer to a 5-qt. slow cooker. Stir in the potatoes, carrots, celery, seasonings and remaining broth. Cover and cook on low for 6-7 hours or until vegetables are tender.

**3.** Stir in cheese and milk. Cover and cook 30 minutes longer or until cheese is melted. Just before serving, stir in sour cream.

**Nutrition Facts:** 1-1/4 cups equals 327 calories, 11 g fat (5 g saturated fat), 61 mg cholesterol, 832 mg sodium, 32 g carbohydrate, 3 g fiber, 25 g protein.

## Seafood Salad Pitas F

**PREP:** 20 min. + chilling  **YIELD:** 8 servings

**LINDA EVANCOE-COBLE • LEOLA, PENNSYLVANIA**

*You can make this lovely, interesting sandwich as a refreshing light lunch...or pair it with a hearty soup for a change-of-pace supper.*

- 2 cups chopped imitation crabmeat (about 10 oz.)
- 1/2 lb. cooked medium shrimp, peeled, deveined and chopped (about 1 cup)
- 2 celery ribs, chopped
- 1/2 cup thinly sliced green onions
- 3/4 cup fat-free mayonnaise
- 3/4 tsp. seafood seasoning
- 1/4 tsp. salt
- 1/8 tsp. pepper
- 8 whole wheat pita pocket halves

**1.** In a large bowl, combine the crab, shrimp, celery and onions. In a small bowl, combine the mayonnaise, seafood seasoning, salt and pepper. Pour over crab mixture; toss to coat. Cover and refrigerate for at least 2 hours. Spoon into pita halves.

**Nutrition Facts:** 1 filled pita half equals 162 calories, 2 g fat (trace saturated fat), 27 mg cholesterol, 755 mg sodium, 28 g carbohydrate, 3 g fiber, 10 g protein. **Diabetic Exchanges:** 2 starch, 1 lean meat.

MAKEOVER BEEF & POTATO SOUP

SEAFOOD SALAD PITAS

# Roasted Garlic Butternut Soup

**PREP:** 35 min. **COOK:** 20 min.
**YIELD:** 9 servings (2-1/4 qt.)

**ROBIN HAAS • CRANSTON, RHODE ISLAND**

*This lower-fat soup is creamy, really intense in flavor and offers 545 mg of potassium.*

- 1 whole garlic bulb
- 1 tsp. olive oil
- 1 medium butternut squash (3 lb.), peeled and cubed
- 1 medium sweet potato, peeled and cubed
- 1 large onion, chopped
- 2 Tbsp. butter
- 3-1/4 cups water
- 1 can (14-1/2 oz.) reduced-sodium chicken broth
- 1 tsp. paprika
- 1/2 tsp. pepper
- 1/4 tsp. salt
- 9 Tbsp. crumbled blue cheese

**1.** Remove papery outer skin from garlic (do not peel or separate cloves). Cut top off of garlic bulb. Brush with oil; wrap in heavy-duty foil. Bake at 425° for 30-35 minutes or until softened. Cool for 10-15 minutes.

**2.** Meanwhile, in a Dutch oven, saute the squash, sweet potato and onion in butter until crisp-tender. Add the water, broth, paprika, pepper and salt; squeeze softened garlic into pan. Bring to a boil. Reduce heat; cover and simmer for 20-25 minutes or until vegetables are tender. Cool slightly.

**3.** In a food processor, process soup in batches until smooth. Return all to pan and heat through. Ladle into bowls; top with blue cheese.

**Nutrition Facts:** 1 cup soup with 1 Tbsp. blue cheese equals 144 calories, 6 g fat (3 g saturated fat), 13 mg cholesterol, 340 mg sodium, 21 g carbohydrate, 5 g fiber, 4 g protein.
**Diabetic Exchanges:** 1 starch, 1 fat.

# Easy Minestrone

**PREP:** 25 min. **COOK:** 40 min.
**YIELD:** 11 servings (2-3/4 qt.)

**LAUREN BRENNAN • HOOD RIVER, OREGON**

*This recipe is special to me because it's one of the few dinners my entire family loves. And I can feel good about serving it because it's nutritious and low in fat.*

|     |     |
| --- | --- |
| 2   | large carrots, diced |
| 2   | celery ribs, chopped |
| 1   | medium onion, chopped |
| 1   | Tbsp. olive oil |
| 1   | Tbsp. butter |
| 2   | garlic cloves, minced |
| 2   | cans (14-1/2 oz. *each*) reduced-sodium chicken broth |
| 2   | cans (8 oz. *each*) no-salt-added tomato sauce |
| 1   | can (16 oz.) kidney beans, rinsed and drained |
| 1   | can (15 oz.) garbanzo beans *or* chickpeas, rinsed and drained |
| 1   | can (14-1/2 oz.) diced tomatoes, undrained |

|       |     |
| ---   | --- |
| 1-1/2 | cups shredded cabbage |
| 1     | Tbsp. dried basil |
| 1-1/2 | tsp. dried parsley flakes |
| 1     | tsp. dried oregano |
| 1/2   | tsp. pepper |
| 1     | cup uncooked whole wheat elbow macaroni |
| 11    | tsp. grated Parmesan cheese |

**1.** In a large saucepan, saute the carrots, celery and onion in oil and butter until tender. Add garlic; cook 1 minute longer.

**2.** Stir in the broth, tomato sauce, beans, tomatoes, cabbage, basil, parsley, oregano and pepper. Bring to a boil. Reduce heat; cover and simmer for 20 minutes. Meanwhile, cook pasta according to package directions; drain.

**3.** Return soup to a boil. Stir in pasta; heat through. Ladle into bowls. Sprinkle with cheese.

**Nutrition Facts:** 1 cup equals 180 calories, 4 g fat (1 g saturated fat), 4 mg cholesterol, 443 mg sodium, 29 g carbohydrate, 7 g fiber, 8 g protein. **Diabetic Exchanges:** 2 starch, 1 lean meat.

# Saucy Portobello Pitas

**PREP:** 25 min. **COOK:** 10 min. **YIELD:** 4 servings

**LISA HUNDLEY • ABERDEEN, NORTH CAROLINA**

*Portobello mushrooms replace spicy lamb in this healthier version of a gyro. The sandwich is served with the refreshing cucumber-mint yogurt sauce of the Greek classic.*

## CUCUMBER SAUCE:

- 1 cup (8 oz.) reduced-fat plain yogurt
- 1/2 cup chopped peeled cucumber
- 1/4 to 1/3 cup minced fresh mint
- 1 Tbsp. grated lemon peel
- 1 Tbsp. lemon juice
- 1 tsp. garlic powder

## PITAS:

- 4 large portobello mushrooms, stems removed
- 1/2 tsp. pepper
- 1/4 tsp. onion powder
- 1/4 tsp. garlic powder
- 1/4 tsp. Greek seasoning
- 2 Tbsp. canola oil
- 8 pita pocket halves, warmed
- 8 thin slices red onion, separated into rings
- 8 slices tomato

**1.** In a small bowl, combine the cucumber sauce ingredients. Cover and refrigerate until serving.

**2.** Sprinkle mushrooms with pepper, onion powder, garlic powder and Greek seasoning. In a large skillet, cook mushrooms in oil for 3-5 minutes on each side or until tender.

**3.** Cut pita breads in half; line each with a slice of onion and tomato. Cut mushrooms in half; place in pitas. Serve with cucumber sauce.

**Nutrition Facts:** 2 filled pita halves with 1/3 cup sauce equals 303 calories, 9 g fat (1 g saturated fat), 3 mg cholesterol, 411 mg sodium, 45 g carbohydrate, 4 g fiber, 11 g protein. **Diabetic Exchanges:** 3 starch, 1 fat.

# So Easy Gazpacho  C M

**PREP:** 10 min. + chilling **YIELD:** 5 servings

**LORNA SIRTOLI • CORTLAND, NEW YORK**

*My daughter got this lovely salad recipe from a college friend and shared it with me. Now I serve it often as an appetizer. It certainly is the talk of the party.*

- 2 cups tomato juice
- 4 medium tomatoes, peeled and finely chopped
- 1/2 cup chopped seeded peeled cucumber
- 1/3 cup finely chopped onion
- 1/4 cup olive oil
- 1/4 cup cider vinegar
- 1 tsp. sugar
- 1 garlic clove, minced
- 1/4 tsp. salt
- 1/4 tsp. pepper

**1.** In a large bowl, combine all ingredients. Cover and refrigerate for at least 4 hours or until chilled.

**Nutrition Facts:** 1 cup equals 146 calories, 11 g fat (2 g saturated fat), 0 cholesterol, 387 mg sodium, 11 g carbohydrate, 2 g fiber, 2 g protein.

SO EASY GAZPACHO

SAUCY PORTOBELLO PITAS

## Shrimp 'n' Mushroom Lettuce Wraps  [C]

**PREP:** 40 min. **COOK:** 10 min. **YIELD:** 4 servings

MARY BETH VULTEE • OCEAN BEACH, NORTH CAROLINA

*Here's a nutritious but special option for a luncheon. To add some hands-on fun, serve the filling on a platter with the lettuce leaves on the side, and let your guests wrap their own.*

- 1 Tbsp. water
- 1 Tbsp. lime juice
- 1 Tbsp. cider vinegar
- 1 Tbsp. reduced-sodium soy sauce
- 1/4 cup reduced-fat creamy peanut butter
- 1 Tbsp. chopped jalapeno pepper
- 3/4 tsp. minced fresh gingerroot
- 1 garlic clove, peeled
- 3/4 tsp. sesame oil
- 3/4 tsp. honey
- 1 lb. uncooked medium shrimp, peeled, deveined and coarsely chopped
- 1/4 tsp. salt
- 1/4 tsp. pepper
- 2 tsp. canola oil, *divided*
- 1 pkg. (6 oz.) portobello mushrooms, coarsely chopped
- 1/2 cup chopped red onion
- 1 cup canned bean sprouts
- 1/4 cup minced fresh cilantro
- 2 Tbsp. minced fresh basil
- 4 green onions, sliced
- 2 Tbsp. chopped salted peanuts
- 8 Bibb *or* Boston lettuce leaves

**1.** For sauce, in a blender, combine the first 10 ingredients; cover and process until smooth. Set aside.

**2.** Sprinkle shrimp with salt and pepper. In a large nonstick skillet, saute shrimp in 1 tsp. canola oil for 4-6 minutes or until shrimp turn pink; remove and keep warm.

**3.** In the same skillet, saute mushrooms and red onion in remaining oil for 5-8 minutes or until tender. Return shrimp to the pan. Add bean sprouts, cilantro and basil; cook and stir for 1 minute or until heated through.

**4.** Remove from the heat; stir in green onions and peanuts. Divide among lettuce leaves; drizzle each with 1 Tbsp. sauce. Fold lettuce over filling.

**Editor's Note:** Wear disposable gloves when cutting hot peppers; the oils can burn skin. Avoid touching your face.

**Nutrition Facts:** 2 wraps with 2 Tbsp. sauce equals 268 calories, 12 g fat (2 g saturated fat), 168 mg cholesterol, 619 mg sodium, 15 g carbohydrate, 4 g fiber, 26 g protein. **Diabetic Exchanges:** 3 lean meat, 2 fat, 1 vegetable, 1/2 starch.

## Mediterranean Chicken Sandwiches

**PREP:** 20 min. + chilling **YIELD:** 6 servings

MARCIA FULLER • SHERIDAN, MONTANA

*Here's a refreshing lunch flavored with oregano and mint.*

- 1-1/4 lbs. boneless skinless chicken breasts, cut into 1-in. strips
- 2 medium tomatoes, seeded and chopped
- 1/2 cup sliced, quartered seeded cucumber
- 1/2 cup sliced sweet onion
- 2 Tbsp. cider vinegar
- 1 Tbsp. olive oil
- 1 Tbsp. minced fresh oregano *or* 1 tsp. dried oregano
- 1 to 2 tsp. minced fresh mint *or* 1/2 tsp. dried mint
- 1/4 tsp. salt
- 6 whole wheat pita pocket halves, warmed
- 6 lettuce leaves

**1.** In a large nonstick skillet coated with cooking spray, cook chicken for 5 minutes or until no longer pink. Remove from the skillet; cool slightly.

**2.** In a large bowl, combine the chicken, tomatoes, cucumber and onion. In a small bowl, whisk the vinegar, oil, oregano, mint and salt. Pour over chicken mixture; toss gently.

**3.** Cover and refrigerate for at least 1 hour. Line pita halves with lettuce; fill with chicken mixture, using a slotted spoon.

**Nutrition Facts:** 1 sandwich equals 227 calories, 4 g fat (1 g saturated fat), 55 mg cholesterol, 335 mg sodium, 22 g carbohydrate, 3 g fiber, 26 g protein. **Diabetic Exchanges:** 3 lean meat, 1 starch, 1 vegetable.

SHRIMP 'N' MUSHROOM LETTUCE WRAPS

TURKEY–SWEET POTATO SOUP

## Turkey-Sweet Potato Soup ⬛F

**PREP:** 20 min. **COOK:** 30 min. **YIELD:** 4 servings

**RADINE KELLOGG • FAIRVIEW, ILLINOIS**
*This yummy soup brings the flavors and aroma of Thanksgiving to my table all year long.*

|       |                                          |
|-------|------------------------------------------|
| 2     | cups water                               |
| 2     | tsp. sodium-free chicken bouillon granules |
| 2     | medium sweet potatoes, cubed             |
| 1     | can (14-3/4 oz.) cream-style corn        |
| 1     | Tbsp. minced fresh sage                  |
| 1/4   | tsp. pepper                              |
| 1     | Tbsp. cornstarch                         |
| 1     | cup 2% milk                              |
| 2     | cups cubed cooked turkey breast          |

**1.** In a large saucepan, bring water and bouillon to a boil. Add sweet potatoes. Reduce heat; cover and cook for 10-15 minutes or until potatoes are tender. Stir in the corn, sage and pepper; heat through. Combine cornstarch and milk until smooth. Stir into pan. Bring to a boil; cook and stir for 2 minutes or until thickened. Stir in turkey; heat through.

**Nutrition Facts:** 1-1/2 cups equals 275 calories, 3 g fat (1 g saturated fat), 65 mg cholesterol, 374 mg sodium, 39 g carbohydrate, 3 g fiber, 26 g protein. **Diabetic Exchanges:** 3 lean meat, 2-1/2 starch.

## Greek Sloppy Joes

**PREP/TOTAL TIME:** 25 min. **YIELD:** 6 servings

**SONYA LABBE • LOS ANGELES, CALIFORNIA**
*Here's a tasty take on an all-time family classic. For a great meal, add a green salad dotted with olives and feta cheese.*

|       |                                      |
|-------|--------------------------------------|
| 1     | lb. lean ground beef (90% lean)      |
| 1     | small red onion, chopped             |
| 1     | can (15 oz.) tomato sauce            |
| 1     | tsp. dried oregano                   |
| 2     | cups chopped romaine                 |
| 6     | kaiser rolls, split and toasted      |
| 1/2   | cup crumbled feta cheese             |

**1.** In a large skillet, cook beef and onion over medium heat until meat is no longer pink; drain. Stir in tomato sauce and oregano. Bring to a boil. Reduce heat; simmer, uncovered, for 8-10 minutes or until sauce thickens slightly, stirring occasionally.

**2.** Place romaine on roll bottoms. Top each with 1/2 cup meat mixture and sprinkle with feta. Replace roll tops.

**Nutrition Facts:** 1 sandwich equals 335 calories, 10 g fat (4 g saturated fat), 52 mg cholesterol, 767 mg sodium, 36 g carbohydrate, 3 g fiber, 23 g protein. **Diabetic Exchanges:** 3 lean meat, 2 starch, 1 vegetable.

CUBAN-STYLE PORK SANDWICHES

## Cuban-Style Pork Sandwiches

**PREP:** 20 min.  **COOK:** 6 hours + standing
**YIELD:** 10 servings

**ROBIN HAAS • CRANSTON, RHODE ISLAND**

*Loaded with tangy flavor, this is a slow-cooked version of a favorite restaurant-style sandwich. If you don't have a panini maker, tuck the sandwiches under the broiler until the bread is browned and the cheese is melted.*

|   |   |
|---|---|
| 1 | large onion, cut into wedges |
| 3/4 | cup reduced-sodium chicken broth |
| 1 | cup minced fresh parsley |
| 7 | garlic cloves, minced, *divided* |
| 2 | Tbsp. cider vinegar |
| 1 | Tbsp. plus 1-1/2 tsp. lemon juice, *divided* |
| 2 | tsp. ground cumin |
| 1 | tsp. ground mustard |

|   |   |
|---|---|
| 1 | tsp. dried oregano |
| 1/2 | tsp. salt |
| 1/2 | tsp. pepper |
| 1 | boneless pork shoulder butt roast (3 to 4 lb.) |
| 1-1/4 | cups fat-free mayonnaise |
| 2 | Tbsp. Dijon mustard |
| 10 | whole wheat hamburger buns, split |
| 1-1/4 | cups (5 oz.) shredded reduced-fat Swiss cheese |
| 1 | medium onion, thinly sliced and separated into rings |
| 2 | whole dill pickles, sliced |

**1.** Place onion wedges and broth in a 5-qt. slow cooker. In a small bowl, combine the parsley, 5 garlic cloves, vinegar, 1 Tbsp. lemon juice, cumin, mustard, oregano, salt and pepper; rub over pork. Add to slow cooker. Cover and cook on low for 6-8 hours or until meat is tender.

**2.** Remove meat; let stand for 10 minutes before slicing. In another small bowl, combine the mayonnaise, mustard and remaining garlic and lemon juice; spread over buns. Layer bun bottoms with pork, cheese, sliced onion and pickles; replace tops.

**3.** Cook on a panini maker or indoor grill for 2-3 minutes or until buns are browned and cheese is melted.

**Nutrition Facts:** 1 sandwich equals 415 calories, 18 g fat (6 g saturated fat), 90 mg cholesterol, 943 mg sodium, 32 g carbohydrate, 5 g fiber, 33 g protein.

# Italian Sausage Bean Soup

**PREP:** 20 min.  **COOK:** 1-1/2 hours
**YIELD:** 8 servings (3 qt.)

**GLENNA REIMER • GIG HARBOR, WASHINGTON**

*In the cold months, I like to put on a big pot of this comforting soup. It cooks away while I do other things, such as baking bread, crafting or even cleaning the house.*

- 1 lb. bulk Italian sausage
- 1 medium onion, finely chopped
- 3 garlic cloves, sliced
- 4 cans (14-1/2 oz. *each*) reduced-sodium chicken broth
- 2 cans (15 oz. *each*) pinto beans, rinsed and drained
- 1 can (14-1/2 oz.) diced tomatoes, undrained
- 1 cup medium pearl barley
- 1 large carrot, sliced
- 1 celery rib, sliced
- 1 tsp. minced fresh sage
- 1/2 tsp. minced fresh rosemary *or* 1/8 tsp. dried rosemary, crushed
- 6 cups chopped fresh kale

**1.** In a Dutch oven, cook sausage and onion over medium heat until meat is no longer pink. Add garlic; cook 1 minute longer. Drain.

**2.** Stir in the broth, beans, tomatoes, barley, carrot, celery, sage and rosemary. Bring to a boil. Reduce heat; cover and simmer for 45 minutes.

**3.** Stir in kale; return to a boil. Reduce heat; cover and simmer for 25-30 minutes or until vegetables are tender and kale is wilted.

**Nutrition Facts:** 1-1/2 cups equals 339 calories, 9 g fat (3 g saturated fat), 23 mg cholesterol, 1,100 mg sodium, 48 g carbohydrate, 11 g fiber, 19 g protein.

# Creamy Turnip Soup

**PREP:** 20 min.  **COOK:** 20 min.
**YIELD:** 9 servings (2-1/4 qt.)

**LIZ WHEELER • WILMINGTON, VERMONT**

*Nearby Wardsboro, Vermont, hosts a fall festival where one of the entrees is this delicious soup. It reheats wonderfully in a slow cooker.*

- 1 medium onion, chopped
- 2 Tbsp. butter
- 3 garlic cloves, minced

- 1/2 cup white wine *or* reduced-sodium chicken broth
- 3 lb. turnips, peeled and cut into 1-in. cubes
- 1 carton (32 oz.) reduced-sodium chicken broth
- 1 medium potato, peeled and cubed
- 1 cup half-and-half cream
- 1/2 tsp. salt
- 1/2 tsp. ground nutmeg
- 3 cups fresh baby spinach
- 1/2 tsp. olive oil

**1.** In a Dutch oven, saute onion in butter until tender. Add garlic; cook 1 minute longer. Stir in wine. Bring to a boil; cook until liquid is reduced by half.

**2.** Add the turnips, broth and potato. Bring to a boil. Reduce heat; simmer, uncovered, for 20-25 minutes or until vegetables are tender. Cool slightly.

**3.** In a food processor, process soup in batches until smooth. Return all to pan. Stir in the cream, salt and nutmeg; heat through. Meanwhile, in a large nonstick skillet, saute spinach in oil until tender. Garnish soup with spinach.

**Nutrition Facts:** 1 cup equals 138 calories, 6 g fat (3 g saturated fat), 20 mg cholesterol, 526 mg sodium, 17 g carbohydrate, 4 g fiber, 4 g protein. **Diabetic Exchanges:** 1 starch, 1 fat.

Found in grocery stores in bulk or in cellophane bags, baby spinach can be eaten cooked or uncooked. It is a tender variety of spinach that has a **small, flat leaf.** The bagged variety is usually pre-washed.

CREAMY TURNIP SOUP

# Easy Tortellini Soup

**PREP/TOTAL TIME:** 30 min.  **YIELD:** 6 servings

**GAYE THOMPSON • ST. CHARLES, MISSOURI**

*Quick, simple and colorful, this soup makes a cozy cup or even a light lunch on blustery days. Veggies add nutrition, and cheese tortellini makes it hearty and delicious.*

- 1 medium onion, chopped
- 1 tsp. olive oil
- 1 garlic clove, minced
- 2 cans (14-1/2 oz. *each*) reduced-sodium chicken broth
- 1 can (14-1/2 oz.) diced tomatoes, undrained
- 1 pkg. (9 oz.) refrigerated cheese tortellini *or* tortellini of your choice
- 3 cups chopped fresh spinach
- 1 Tbsp. balsamic vinegar
- 1/4 tsp. pepper
- Shredded Parmesan cheese, optional

**1.** In a Dutch oven, saute onion in oil until tender. Add garlic; cook 1 minute longer. Stir in broth and tomatoes. Bring to a boil. Reduce heat; simmer, uncovered, for 10 minutes, stirring occasionally.

**2.** Add tortellini; cook for 7-9 minutes or until tender. Stir in the spinach, vinegar and pepper. Cook and stir until heated through and spinach is wilted. Sprinkle with cheese.

**Nutrition Facts:** 1 cup (calculated without cheese) equals 178 calories, 4 g fat (2 g saturated fat), 18 mg cholesterol, 652 mg sodium, 27 g carbohydrate, 3 g fiber, 9 g protein. **Diabetic Exchanges:** 1 starch, 1 lean meat, 1 vegetable.

# Veggie Chicken Pitas

**PREP/TOTAL TIME:** 30 min.  **YIELD:** 5 servings

**BILL PARKIS • WILMINGTON, NORTH CAROLINA**

*These delicious pita pockets are literally stuffed with veggies, chicken and cheese. They make for great on-the-go dinners. (But bring a napkin!)*

- 1 medium red onion, sliced
- 1 cup julienned carrots
- 1 cup chopped fresh broccoli
- 1 cup fresh snow peas
- 2 Tbsp. olive oil
- 1/2 tsp. minced garlic
- 1 cup cubed cooked chicken
- 1 jar (7 oz.) roasted sweet red peppers, drained and chopped
- 1/4 cup white wine *or* chicken broth
- 1/2 tsp. dried oregano
- 1/2 tsp. cayenne pepper
- 10 pita pocket halves
- 1/3 cup shredded part-skim mozzarella cheese
- 1/3 cup shredded cheddar cheese

**1.** In a large skillet, saute the onion, carrots, broccoli and peas in oil for 4-5 minutes or until tender. Add garlic; cook 1 minute longer.

**2.** Stir in the chicken, red peppers, wine, oregano and cayenne. Bring to a boil. Reduce heat; simmer, uncovered, for 5-6 minutes or until heated through. Spoon mixture into pita breads; sprinkle with cheeses.

**Nutrition Facts:** 2 stuffed pita halves equals 373 calories, 12 g fat (4 g saturated fat), 37 mg cholesterol, 595 mg sodium, 43 g carbohydrate, 4 g fiber, 19 g protein. **Diabetic Exchanges:** 2 starch, 2 lean meat, 2 vegetable, 1 fat.

EASY TORTELLINI SOUP

VEGGIE CHICKEN PITAS

CALYPSO BURRITOS

# Calypso Burritos M

**PREP/TOTAL TIME:** 30 min. **YIELD:** 8 servings

**DARLENE DEEG • VERNON, BRITISH COLUMBIA**

*Because these burritos are packed with a bounty of beans, veggies, cheese and salsa, my husband doesn't notice he's not getting meat. Set out toppings such as sour cream, chopped tomatoes and avocado.*

|       |                                          |
|-------|------------------------------------------|
| 2     | small zucchini, shredded                 |
| 2     | medium carrots, shredded                 |
| 1     | medium onion, finely chopped             |
| 1     | Tbsp. canola oil                         |
| 1     | can (16 oz.) kidney beans, rinsed and drained |
| 1     | can (15 oz.) black beans, rinsed and drained |
| 1-1/2 | cups frozen corn, thawed                 |
| 3/4   | cup salsa                                |
| 2     | Tbsp. reduced-sodium taco seasoning      |
| 2     | tsp. ground cumin                        |
| 1     | cup (4 oz.) shredded part-skim mozzarella cheese |
| 1/4   | cup minced fresh cilantro                |
| 8     | flour tortillas (8 in.), warmed          |

**1.** In a large skillet over medium heat, cook and stir the zucchini, carrots and onion in oil for 3-5 minutes or until tender. Stir in the beans, corn, salsa, taco seasoning and cumin. Cook and stir for 5-7 minutes or until vegetables are tender.

**2.** Remove from the heat. Stir in cheese and cilantro. Spoon about 2/3 cupful filling off center on each tortilla. Fold sides and ends over filling and roll up.

**Nutrition Facts:** 1 burrito equals 349 calories, 7 g fat (2 g saturated fat), 8 mg cholesterol, 744 mg sodium, 55 g carbohydrate, 8 g fiber, 16 g protein.

## Zesty Dill Tuna Sandwiches

**PREP/TOTAL TIME:** 15 min.  **YIELD:** 2 servings

**JENNY DUBINSKY • INWOOD, WEST VIRGINIA**

*I absolutely love tuna salad. With this recipe, I brought together all of my favorite things to make the best tuna salad sandwich ever!*

| | |
|---|---|
| 1 | can (5 oz.) light water-packed tuna, drained |
| 1/4 | cup reduced-fat mayonnaise |
| 1 | Tbsp. grated Parmesan cheese |
| 1 | Tbsp. sweet pickle relish |
| 1 | Tbsp. minced fresh parsley |
| 1 | tsp. spicy brown mustard |
| 1/4 | tsp. dill weed |
| 1/8 | tsp. onion powder |
| 1/8 | tsp. curry powder |
| 1/8 | tsp. garlic powder |
| 4 | slices whole wheat bread |

**1.** In a small bowl, combine the first 10 ingredients. Spread over two slices of bread. Top with the remaining bread.

**Nutrition Facts:** 1 sandwich equals 346 calories, 13 g fat (3 g saturated fat), 34 mg cholesterol, 877 mg sodium, 29 g carbohydrate, 4 g fiber, 27 g protein. **Diabetic Exchanges:** 3 lean meat, 2 starch, 1-1/2 fat.

## Italian Pulled Pork Sandwiches

**PREP:** 20 min.  **COOK:** 8 hours  **YIELD:** 12 servings

**LIA DELLARIO • MIDDLEPORT, NEW YORK**

*Enjoy all the flavors of Italian sausage sandwiches with this healthier alternative.*

| | |
|---|---|
| 1 | Tbsp. fennel seed, crushed |
| 1 | Tbsp. steak seasoning |
| 1 | tsp. cayenne pepper, optional |
| 1 | boneless pork shoulder butt roast (3 lbs.) |
| 1 | Tbsp. olive oil |

- 2 medium green *or* sweet red peppers, thinly sliced
- 2 medium onions, thinly sliced
- 1 can (14-1/2 oz.) diced tomatoes, undrained
- 12 whole wheat hamburger buns, split

**1.** In a small bowl, combine the fennel seed, steak seasoning and cayenne if desired. Rub over pork. In a large skillet, brown roast in oil on all sides. Place in a 4- or 5-qt. slow cooker. Add the peppers, onions and tomatoes; cover and cook on low for 8-10 hours or until meat is tender.

**2.** Remove roast; cool slightly. Skim fat from cooking juices. Shred pork with two forks and return to slow cooker; heat through. Using a slotted spoon, place 1/2 cup meat mixture on each bun.

**Editor's Note:** This recipe was tested with McCormick's Montreal Steak Seasoning. Look for it in the spice aisle.

**Nutrition Facts:** 1 sandwich equals 288 calories, 8 g fat (2 g saturated fat), 56 mg cholesterol, 454 mg sodium, 27 g carbohydrate, 5 g fiber, 26 g protein. **Diabetic Exchanges:** 3 lean meat, 2 starch.

# Hearty Split Pea Soup

**PREP:** 30 min. **COOK:** 7 hours
**YIELD:** 6 servings (2-1/4 qt.)

### DEBRA KEIL • OWASSO, OKLAHOMA

*We started a 39-day Soup Challenge to eat healthier after the holidays, figuring if "Survivor" contestants could last 39 days on little food, surely we could survive on soup! This was a family favorite—chunky, hearty and smooth.*

- 1 large onion, chopped
- 1 cup chopped celery
- 1 cup chopped fresh carrots
- 1 tsp. dried thyme
- 2 Tbsp. olive oil
- 1 pkg. (16 oz.) dried green split peas, rinsed
- 4 cups vegetable broth
- 2 cups water
- 6 oz. Canadian bacon, chopped
- 1/4 tsp. pepper

**1.** In a large skillet, saute the onion, celery, carrots and thyme in oil until tender.

**2.** Transfer to a 5-qt. slow cooker. Add the peas, broth and water. Cover and cook on low for 7-8 hours or until peas are tender.

**3.** Cool slightly. In a blender, process half of the soup until smooth. Return all to the slow cooker. Add bacon and pepper; heat through.

**Nutrition Facts:** 1-1/2 cups equals 363 calories, 7 g fat (1 g saturated fat), 10 mg cholesterol, 945 mg sodium, 53 g carbohydrate, 21 g fiber, 24 g protein.

# Southwest Chicken Soup  F

**PREP:** 15 min. **COOK:** 25 min. **YIELD:** 5 servings

### WILL SMITH • BEEBE, ARKANSAS

*Simmer up a big pot of this hearty soup on Sunday. Then, reheat and ladle it up for lunches during the week! Serve the change-of-pace dish with corn bread and baked tortilla chips.*

- 1/2 lb. boneless skinless chicken breast, cut into 3/4-in. pieces
- 2 tsp. canola oil
- 1 small sweet red pepper, finely chopped
- 1 medium onion, chopped
- 1 garlic clove, minced
- 2 cans (14-1/2 oz. *each*) reduced-sodium chicken broth
- 1 can (15 oz.) black beans, rinsed and drained
- 1 cup frozen corn
- 1 medium lime, peeled, seeded and finely chopped
- 1 jalapeno pepper, seeded and chopped
- 1/4 tsp. pepper
- 1/8 to 1/4 tsp. cayenne pepper
- 1 small tomato, peeled, seeded and chopped
- 2 green onions, sliced

**1.** In a large nonstick saucepan, saute chicken in oil until no longer pink. Remove and keep warm.

**2.** In the same pan, saute red pepper and onion until tender. Add the garlic; cook 1 minute longer. Add the broth, beans, corn, lime, jalapeno, black pepper and cayenne; bring to a boil. Reduce heat; cover and simmer for 10 minutes.

**3.** Stir in the tomato, green onions and chicken; heat through.

**Editor's Note:** Wear disposable gloves when cutting hot peppers; the oils can burn skin. Avoid touching your face.

**Nutrition Facts:** 1-1/2 cups equals 199 calories, 3 g fat (trace saturated fat), 25 mg cholesterol, 621 mg sodium, 26 g carbohydrate, 6 g fiber, 17 g protein. **Diabetic Exchanges:** 2 lean meat, 1-1/2 starch, 1 vegetable.

SOUTHWEST CHICKEN SOUP

# Butternut Turkey Soup **F**

**PREP:** 30 min. **COOK:** 35 min. **YIELD:** 6 servings (2 qt.)

**DENISE LAROCHE • HUDSON, NEW HAMPSHIRE**

*Although hearty with lots of nutritious vegetables and turkey, this soup is also light and luscious.*

|     |     |
| --- | --- |
| 3 | shallots, thinly sliced |
| 1 | tsp. olive oil |
| 3 | cups reduced-sodium chicken broth |
| 3 | cups cubed peeled butternut squash (3/4-in. cubes) |
| 2 | medium red potatoes, cut into 1/2-in. cubes |
| 1-1/2 | cups water |
| 2 | tsp. minced fresh thyme |
| 1/2 | tsp. pepper |
| 2 | whole cloves |
| 3 | cups cubed cooked turkey breast |

**1.** In a large saucepan coated with cooking spray, cook shallots in oil over medium heat until tender. Stir in the broth, squash, potatoes, water, thyme and pepper.

**2.** Place cloves on a double thickness of cheesecloth; bring up corners of cloth and tie with string to form a bag. Stir into soup. Bring to a boil. Reduce heat; cover and simmer for 10-15 minutes or until vegetables are tender. Stir in turkey; heat through. Discard spice bag.

**Nutrition Facts:** 1-1/3 cups equals 192 calories, 2 g fat (trace saturated fat), 60 mg cholesterol, 332 mg sodium, 20 g carbohydrate, 3 g fiber, 25 g protein. **Diabetic Exchanges:** 3 lean meat, 1 starch.

# Veggie Tortellini Soup **M**

**PREP:** 15 min. **COOK:** 20 min. **YIELD:** 7 servings

**PRISCILLA GILBERT • INDIAN HARBOUR BEACH, FLORIDA**

*Italian cuisine has more to offer than spaghetti and pizza. Just check out this healthy, mouthwatering soup. I've served it to company with rave reviews along with requests for the recipe.*

|     |     |
| --- | --- |
| 3 | medium carrots, chopped |
| 1 | large onion, chopped |
| 1 | Tbsp. olive oil |
| 4 | garlic cloves, minced |
| 2 | cans (14-1/2 oz. *each*) vegetable broth |
| 2 | medium zucchini, chopped |
| 4 | plum tomatoes, chopped |
| 2 | cups refrigerated cheese tortellini |
| 1/3 | cup chopped fresh spinach |
| 1 | tsp. minced fresh rosemary *or* 1/4 tsp. dried rosemary, crushed |
| 1/4 | tsp. pepper |
| 1 | Tbsp. red wine vinegar |

**1.** In a Dutch oven, saute the carrots and onion in oil until the onion is tender. Add the garlic; cook 1 minute longer.

**2.** Stir in the broth, zucchini, tomatoes, tortellini, spinach, rosemary and pepper. Bring to a boil. Reduce heat; cover and simmer for 8-10 minutes or until the tortellini are tender. Just before serving, stir in the vinegar.

**Nutrition Facts:** 1 cup equals 155 calories, 5 g fat (2 g saturated fat), 13 mg cholesterol, 693 mg sodium, 24 g carbohydrate, 3 g fiber, 6 g protein. **Diabetic Exchanges:** 1 starch, 1 vegetable, 1/2 fat.

BUTTERNUT TURKEY SOUP

VEGGIE TORTELLINI SOUP

PEANUTTY ASIAN LETTUCE WRAPS

## Peanutty Asian Lettuce Wraps

**PREP/TOTAL TIME:** 30 min.  **YIELD:** 6 servings

**MANDY RIVERS • LEXINGTON, SOUTH CAROLINA**

*This recipe packs so much flavor into a beautiful, healthy presentation. I love to serve it as an hors d'oeuvre or as the main dish when I have folks over. It's always a hit! I usually offer it with a little extra hoisin on the side.*

| | |
|---|---|
| 1-1/2 | lbs. lean ground turkey |
| 1/2 | cup shredded carrot |
| 2 | Tbsp. minced fresh gingerroot |
| 4 | garlic cloves, minced |
| 1 | can (8 oz.) whole water chestnuts, drained and chopped |
| 4 | green onions, chopped |
| 1/2 | cup chopped fresh snow peas |
| 1/3 | cup reduced-sodium teriyaki sauce |
| 1/4 | cup hoisin sauce |
| 3 | Tbsp. creamy peanut butter |
| 1 | Tbsp. rice vinegar |
| 1 | Tbsp. sesame oil |
| 12 | Bibb lettuce leaves |

Additional hoisin sauce, optional

**1.** In a large skillet, cook turkey and carrot over medium heat until meat is no longer pink and carrot is tender; drain. Add ginger and garlic; cook 1 minute longer.

**2.** Stir in the chestnuts, onions, snow peas, teriyaki sauce, hoisin sauce, peanut butter, vinegar and oil; heat through. Divide among lettuce leaves; drizzle with additional hoisin sauce if desired. Fold lettuce over filling.

**Nutrition Facts:** 2 lettuce wraps (calculated without additional hoisin sauce) equals 313 calories, 16 g fat (4 g saturated fat), 90 mg cholesterol, 613 mg sodium, 18 g carbohydrate, 3 g fiber, 24 g protein. **Diabetic Exchanges:** 3 lean meat, 2 vegetable, 2 fat, 1/2 starch.

HEARTY LEEK AND POTATO SOUP

# Hearty Leek and
# Potato Soup M

**PREP:** 20 min. **COOK:** 30 min. **YIELD:** 8 servings (2 qt.)

**RACHEL TAYLOR • SPRINGFIELD, TENNESSEE**

*This thick, flavorful soup is a winner in our home and makes a
nice starter dish. The leeks and green pepper offer a fantastic
addition to traditional potato soup.*

| | |
|---|---|
| 3 | celery ribs, chopped |
| 2 | medium onions, chopped |
| 3 | medium leeks (white portion only), chopped |
| 1 | medium green pepper, chopped |

| | |
|---|---|
| 2 | jalapeno peppers, seeded and chopped |
| 6 | garlic cloves, minced |
| 2 | Tbsp. olive oil |
| 4 | medium potatoes, peeled and cubed |
| 2 | cans (14-1/2 oz. *each*) vegetable broth |
| 1 | cup water |
| 1/2 | tsp. pepper |
| 1/4 | tsp. salt |
| 3 | Tbsp. all-purpose flour |
| 1/4 | cup fat-free milk |
| 1/2 | cup reduced-fat sour cream |
| 2 | green onions, chopped |

**1.** In a nonstick Dutch oven, saute the celery, onions, leeks, green pepper, jalapenos and garlic in oil until tender. Add the potatoes, broth, water, pepper and salt. Bring to a boil. Reduce heat; cover and simmer for 10-15 minutes or until potatoes are tender, stirring occasionally.

**2.** Combine flour and milk until smooth; stir into soup. Cook and stir for 2 minutes or until thickened and bubbly. Reduce heat to low. Stir in sour cream and green onions until blended; heat through (do not boil).

**Editor's Note:** Wear disposable gloves when cutting hot peppers; the oils can burn skin. Avoid touching your face.

**Nutrition Facts:** 1 cup equals 180 calories, 5 g fat (1 g saturated fat), 5 mg cholesterol, 598 mg sodium, 30 g carbohydrate, 3 g fiber, 4 g protein. **Diabetic Exchanges:** 1-1/2 starch, 1 vegetable, 1 fat.

# Cashew Turkey Salad Sandwiches

PREP/TOTAL TIME: 15 min.  YIELD: 4 servings

**MARY WILHELM • SPARTA, WISCONSIN**

*One bite and you're sure to be hooked on this sweet and savory sandwich. It's protein-packed, so you can feel good about it while you munch.*

1-1/2 cups cubed cooked turkey breast
1/4 cup thinly sliced celery
2 Tbsp. chopped dried apricots
2 Tbsp. chopped unsalted cashews
1 green onion, chopped
1/4 cup reduced-fat mayonnaise
2 Tbsp. reduced-fat plain yogurt
1/4 tsp. salt
1/4 tsp. pepper
4 lettuce leaves
8 slices pumpernickel bread

**1.** In a small bowl, combine the turkey, celery, apricots, cashews and onion. In another bowl, combine the mayonnaise, yogurt, salt and pepper; add to turkey mixture and stir to coat.

**2.** Place a lettuce leaf on half of the bread slices; top each with 1/2 cup turkey salad and remaining bread.

**Nutrition Facts:** 1 sandwich equals 298 calories, 9 g fat (2 g saturated fat), 51 mg cholesterol, 664 mg sodium, 32 g carbohydrate, 4 g fiber, 22 g protein. **Diabetic Exchanges:** 2 starch, 2 lean meat, 1-1/2 fat.

# Mexican Lettuce Wraps

PREP/TOTAL TIME: 20 min.  YIELD: 6 servings

**JUNE BARRUS • SPRINGVILLE, UTAH**

*This recipe proved to be a winner, not only when wrapped in lettuce, but also when served as a dip with tortilla chips. It is so easy to make ahead, chill and take for a picnic or potluck.*

3 cups cubed cooked chicken breast
1 can (15 oz.) black beans, rinsed and drained
1 medium tomato, seeded and finely chopped
1 can (4 oz.) chopped green chilies

1/2 cup salsa
1/4 cup finely chopped onion
1/4 cup finely chopped sweet red pepper
1 Tbsp. lime juice
1/2 tsp. ground cumin
1/2 tsp. seasoned salt
1/4 tsp. garlic powder
1 medium ripe avocado, peeled and finely chopped
12 Bibb or Boston lettuce leaves
1/2 cup reduced-fat sour cream

**1.** In a large bowl, combine the first 11 ingredients. Refrigerate until serving.

**2.** Just before serving, stir in avocado. Place 1/2 cup chicken mixture on each lettuce leaf; top each with 2 tsp. sour cream. Fold lettuce over filling.

**Nutrition Facts:** 2 wraps equals 259 calories, 8 g fat (2 g saturated fat), 61 mg cholesterol, 478 mg sodium, 19 g carbohydrate, 6 g fiber, 26 g protein. **Diabetic Exchanges:** 3 lean meat, 1 starch, 1 vegetable, 1 fat.

To keep lettuce crisp and fresh, wash it in cold water and drain very well. Use a salad spinner or pat dry with paper towels. Store **washed lettuce** in a resealable plastic bag or an airtight container with a dry paper towel in the bottom to absorb leftover moisture.

MEXICAN LETTUCE WRAPS

## Skinny Turkey-Vegetable Soup F

PREP: 30 min.  COOK: 35 min.
YIELD: 6 servings (2-1/4 qt.)

**CHARLOTTE WELCH • UTICA, NEW YORK**

*The blend of flavors and colors in this hearty soup will bring everyone at the table back for more.*

- 2 medium onions, chopped
- 2 medium carrots, halved and thinly sliced
- 2 celery ribs, chopped
- 1/2 cup chopped sweet red pepper
- 1 Tbsp. olive oil
- 3 garlic cloves, minced
- 4 cups water
- 1 can (10 oz.) diced tomatoes and green chilies, undrained
- 1/2 cup frozen peas
- 1 bay leaf
- 4 tsp. sodium-free chicken bouillon granules
- 1/2 tsp. dried basil
- 1/2 tsp. dried thyme
- 1/4 tsp. ground cumin
- 1/4 tsp. pepper
- 1/4 to 1/2 tsp. hot pepper sauce, optional
- 1/2 cup uncooked whole wheat orzo pasta
- 2 cups cubed cooked turkey breast
- 1 Tbsp. minced fresh cilantro

**1.** In a large saucepan, saute the onions, carrots, celery and red pepper in oil until tender. Add garlic; cook 2 minutes longer. Stir in the water, tomatoes, peas, bay leaf, bouillon, basil, thyme, cumin, pepper and pepper sauce if desired. Bring to a boil. Reduce heat; simmer, uncovered, for 15 minutes.

**2.** Meanwhile, cook orzo according to package directions; drain. Stir orzo and turkey into soup; heat through. Discard bay leaf. Sprinkle with cilantro.

**Nutrition Facts:** 1-1/2 cups equals 191 calories, 3 g fat (1 g saturated fat), 40 mg cholesterol, 257 mg sodium, 22 g carbohydrate, 5 g fiber, 18 g protein. **Diabetic Exchanges:** 2 lean meat, 1 starch, 1 vegetable, 1/2 fat.

> Because of orzo's similar shape and mild flavor, this pasta can be substituted for rice in many recipes. Nutritionally speaking, the two are alike as well. Ounce for ounce, **rice and orzo** contain a similar amount of fat, sugar, carbohydrates and even sodium.

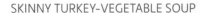

SKINNY TURKEY-VEGETABLE SOUP

## Bistro Tuna Sandwiches

PREP: 25 min.  GRILL: 10 min.  YIELD: 4 servings

**SONYA LABBE • LOS ANGELES, CALIFORNIA**

*Your family and friends will love this fun French take on a grilled tuna sandwich. Tucked into a crusty baguette, it's fast, easy and packed with veggies and fresh flavor.*

- 2 Tbsp. Greek olives
- 1 Tbsp. capers, drained
- 1 Tbsp. lemon juice
- 1 tsp. grated lemon peel
- 1 garlic clove, peeled
- 1 Tbsp. plus 2 tsp. olive oil, *divided*
- 2 tuna steaks (6 oz. *each*)
- 1/4 tsp. pepper
- 1 French bread baguette (10-1/2 oz.)
- 1/3 cup reduced-fat mayonnaise
- 2 Tbsp. Dijon mustard
- 1/4 cup roasted sweet red peppers, drained and cut into strips
- 4 slices red onion
- 4 Boston lettuce leaves

**1.** Place the olives, capers, lemon juice, peel, garlic and 1 Tbsp. oil in a food processor; cover and process until finely chopped. Set aside.

**2.** Brush tuna with remaining oil; sprinkle with pepper. Using long-handled tongs, moisten a paper towel with cooking oil and lightly coat the grill rack. For medium-rare, grill tuna, covered, over high heat or broil 3-4 in. from the heat for 3-4 minutes on each side or until slightly pink in the center.

**3.** Cut baguette in half horizontally. Grill bread cut side down, uncovered, for 1-2 minutes or until toasted. Slice tuna into 1/2-in. thick slices. Combine mayonnaise and mustard until smooth; spread over baguette bottoms. Layer with peppers, onion, tuna, olive mixture and lettuce; replace tops. Cut into slices.

SPICY BLACK BEAN SOUP

**Nutrition Facts:** 1 sandwich equals 456 calories, 16 g fat (2 g saturated fat), 45 mg cholesterol, 1,044 mg sodium, 48 g carbohydrate, 2 g fiber, 29 g protein.

# Spicy Black Bean Soup  F M

**PREP:** 25 min.  **COOK:** 40 min.  **YIELD:** 12 servings

**TIA MUSSER • HUDSON, INDIANA**

*A splash of sherry enhances this filling, easy-to-make soup. For a milder flavor, remove the ribs and seeds from the jalapeno before dicing.*

- 1 large red onion, chopped
- 1 medium sweet red pepper, chopped
- 1 jalapeno pepper, seeded and minced
- 2 Tbsp. olive oil
- 3 garlic cloves, minced
- 3 cans (15 oz. *each*) black beans, rinsed and drained
- 3-1/2 cups vegetable broth
- 1 can (14-1/2 oz.) diced tomatoes with mild green chilies, undrained
- 1 can (4 oz.) chopped green chilies
- 1/3 cup sherry or additional vegetable broth
- 2 Tbsp. minced fresh cilantro
- 1/2 cup fat-free sour cream
- 1/4 cup shredded cheddar cheese

**1.** In a Dutch oven, saute onion and peppers in oil until tender. Add garlic; cook 1 minute longer.

**2.** Stir in the beans, broth, tomatoes and chopped green chilies. Bring to a boil. Reduce heat; simmer, uncovered, for 25 minutes. Add sherry and cilantro; cook 5 minutes longer.

**3.** Remove from the heat; cool slightly. Place half of soup in a blender; cover and process until pureed. Return to the pan and heat through. Top each serving with 2 tsp. sour cream and 1 tsp. cheese.

**Editor's Note:** Wear disposable gloves when cutting hot peppers; the oils can burn skin. Avoid touching your face.

**Nutrition Facts:** 3/4 cup equals 150 calories, 3 g fat (1 g saturated fat), 4 mg cholesterol, 667 mg sodium, 23 g carbohydrate, 5 g fiber, 7 g protein.

SPICY PEPPER SLAW

PEAR APPLESAUCE

LEMON COUSCOUS WITH BROCCOLI

# Side Dishes

Need a great veggie to complement your beef roast? How about a no-fuss pasta salad to serve alongside a turkey sub? The simple side dishes offered here are great ways to complete menus and keep calories and fat at bay!

## Lemon Couscous With Broccoli F

**PREP/TOTAL TIME:** 25 min. **YIELD:** 6 servings

**BETH DAUENHAUER • PUEBLO, COLORADO**

*A splash of lemon brightens this versatile side dish. It combines whole wheat couscous with fresh broccoli and a sprinkling of almonds on top.*

> 4 cups fresh broccoli florets, cut into small pieces
> 1 Tbsp. olive oil
> 1 cup uncooked whole wheat couscous
> 2 garlic cloves, minced
> 1-1/4 cups reduced-sodium chicken broth
> 1 tsp. grated lemon peel
> 1 tsp. lemon juice
> 1/2 tsp. salt
> 1/2 tsp. dried basil
> 1/4 tsp. coarsely ground pepper
> 1 Tbsp. slivered almonds, toasted

**1.** In a large skillet, saute broccoli in oil until crisp-tender. Add couscous and garlic; saute 1-2 minutes longer.

**2.** Stir in the broth, lemon peel, lemon juice, salt, basil and pepper. Bring to a boil. Remove from the heat; cover and let stand for 5-10 minutes or until broth is absorbed. Fluff with a fork. Sprinkle with toasted almonds.

**Nutrition Facts:** 2/3 cup equals 115 calories, 3 g fat (trace saturated fat), 0 cholesterol, 328 mg sodium, 18 g carbohydrate, 4 g fiber, 5 g protein. **Diabetic Exchanges:** 1 starch, 1/2 fat.

## Corn and Bean Medley M

**PREP/TOTAL TIME:** 25 min. **YIELD:** 6 servings

**WENDY CAMPBELL • NEW WILMINGTON, PENNSYLVANIA**

*Frozen corn and edamame make this side dish a breeze to toss together. The black beans and green pepper add a nice touch, and the garlic salt and cayenne really pump up the flavor.*

> 1 small green pepper, chopped
> 1/3 cup chopped onion
> 1-1/2 tsp. butter
> 1-1/2 tsp. olive oil
> 1-3/4 cups frozen corn, thawed
> 1-1/2 cups frozen shelled edamame, thawed
> 3/4 cup black beans, rinsed and drained
> 1/4 tsp. garlic salt
> 1/8 tsp. cayenne pepper

**1.** In a large nonstick skillet, saute green pepper and onion in butter and oil until tender. Add the remaining ingredients. Cook and stir over medium heat for 4-5 minutes or until heated through.

**Nutrition Facts:** 2/3 cup equals 137 calories, 4 g fat (1 g saturated fat), 3 mg cholesterol, 148 mg sodium, 19 g carbohydrate, 4 g fiber, 7 g protein. **Diabetic Exchanges:** 1-1/2 starch, 1/2 fat.

## Pear Applesauce F S

**PREP/TOTAL TIME:** 30 min. **YIELD:** about 2 cups

**JENNY COHEN • BALTIMORE, MARYLAND**

*Here's a great way to satisfy your sweet tooth. Best of all, it's fat-free and only 120 calories!*

> 3 medium apples, peeled and coarsely chopped
> 2 medium pears, peeled and coarsely chopped
> 3/4 cup water
> 2 Tbsp. sugar
> 1/4 tsp. ground cinnamon
> 1/8 tsp. ground nutmeg

**1.** In a large saucepan, combine all ingredients. Bring to a boil. Reduce heat; cover and simmer for 15-20 minutes or until tender, stirring occasionally. Mash until sauce is desired consistency. Serve warm or cold.

**Nutrition Facts:** 1/2 cup equals 120 calories, trace fat (trace saturated fat), 0 cholesterol, 1 mg sodium, 31 g carbohydrate, 4 g fiber, trace protein. **Diabetic Exchanges:** 2 fruit, 1/2 starch.

# Sunny Snow Peas F C M

**PREP/TOTAL TIME:** 25 min.  **YIELD:** 6 servings

**KATHLEEN BAILEY • CHESTER SPRINGS, PENNSYLVANIA**

*Turn crispy snow peas into something special by tossing them with this lovely honey-orange sauce. I enjoy serving fresh vegetables, especially when I can prepare a sauce that seems to add the bright warmth of the sun.*

- 1/2 cup orange juice
- 2 Tbsp. honey
- 1 Tbsp. butter
- 1 to 2 tsp. grated orange peel
- 1/2 tsp. salt
- 1/8 tsp. ground cardamom
- 1 lb. fresh snow peas or sugar snap peas

**1.** In a small saucepan, combine the orange juice, honey, butter, orange peel, salt and cardamom; bring to a boil. Reduce heat; simmer, uncovered, until mixture is reduced by half, about 15 minutes.

**2.** Meanwhile, in another saucepan, bring 1 in. of water to a boil. Add peas. Reduce heat; cover and simmer for 3-4 minutes or until crisp-tender. Drain and transfer to a serving bowl. Add orange juice mixture and toss to coat.

**Nutrition Facts:** 2/3 cup equals 80 calories, 2 g fat (1 g saturated fat), 5 mg cholesterol, 213 mg sodium, 14 g carbohydrate, 2 g fiber, 2 g protein. **Diabetic Exchanges:** 1 vegetable, 1/2 starch.

# Cheese Smashed Potatoes M

**PREP:** 10 min.  **COOK:** 25 min.  **YIELD:** 4 servings

**JANET HOMES • SURPRISE, ARIZONA**

*Try this delicious, versatile side dish with a variety of entrees. It's perfect for a summer barbecue or a winter feast!*

- 1 lb. small red potatoes, quartered
- 1 cup fresh cauliflowerets
- 2/3 cup shredded reduced-fat cheddar cheese
- 1/4 cup reduced-fat sour cream
- 1/4 tsp. salt

**1.** Place potatoes in a large saucepan and cover with water. Bring to a boil. Reduce heat; cover and cook for 10 minutes. Add cauliflower; cook 10 minutes longer or until vegetables are tender.

**2.** Drain; mash with cheese, sour cream and salt.

**Nutrition Facts:** 3/4 cup equals 161 calories, 5 g fat (3 g saturated fat), 18 mg cholesterol, 292 mg sodium, 21 g carbohydrate, 3 g fiber, 8 g protein. **Diabetic Exchanges:** 1 starch, 1 medium-fat meat.

# Herbed Twice-Baked Potatoes M

**PREP:** 1-1/4 hours  **BAKE:** 15 min.  **YIELD:** 4 servings

**RUTH ANDREWSON • LEAVENWORTH, WASHINGTON**

*Light cream cheese, garlic powder and butter make these classic potatoes irresistible. You can replace the basil with parsley.*

- 2 medium baking potatoes
- 1-1/2 oz. reduced-fat cream cheese, cubed
- 1 Tbsp. minced chives
- 1/4 tsp. salt
- 1/4 tsp. dried basil
- Dash cayenne pepper
- 3 Tbsp. fat-free milk
- 3 tsp. butter, melted, *divided*
- Dash garlic powder
- Dash paprika

HERBED TWICE-BAKED POTATOES

SUNNY SNOW PEAS

RIGATONI CHARD TOSS

**1.** Scrub and pierce potatoes. Bake at 375° for 1 hour or until tender. Cool for 10 minutes. Cut potatoes in half lengthwise. Scoop out pulp, leaving thin shells.

**2.** In a large bowl, mash pulp with cream cheese, chives, salt, basil and cayenne. Add milk and 1-1/2 tsp. butter; mash. Spoon into potato shells. Drizzle with remaining butter; sprinkle with garlic powder and paprika.

**3.** Place on an ungreased baking sheet. Bake for 15-20 minutes or until heated through.

**Nutrition Facts:** 1/2 stuffed potato equals 150 calories, 5 g fat (3 g saturated fat), 15 mg cholesterol, 234 mg sodium, 23 g carbohydrate, 2 g fiber, 4 g protein. **Diabetic Exchanges:** 1-1/2 starch, 1 fat.

# Rigatoni Chard Toss

**PREP:** 25 min.   **COOK:** 20 min.   **YIELD:** 11 servings

**CAROLYN KUMPE • EL DORADO, CALIFORNIA**

*Fresh chard and tomatoes add fiber and vitamins to this hearty, colorful side dish.*

- 8  oz. uncooked rigatoni or large tube pasta
- 1  bunch Swiss chard, coarsely chopped
- 1  small onion, thinly sliced
- 2  Tbsp. olive oil
- 2  garlic cloves, minced
- 3  medium tomatoes, chopped
- 1  can (15 oz.) white kidney or cannellini beans, rinsed and drained
- 1/2  tsp. salt
- 1/8  tsp. crushed red pepper flakes
- 1/8  tsp. fennel seed, crushed
- 1/8  tsp. pepper
- 1/4  cup minced fresh basil
- 1/2  cup grated Parmesan cheese

**1.** Cook rigatoni according to package directions.

**2.** Meanwhile, in a large skillet, saute chard and onion in oil for 4 minutes. Add garlic; cook 2 minutes longer. Stir in the tomatoes, beans, salt, pepper flakes, fennel and pepper; cook 3-4 minutes longer or until chard is tender.

**3.** Drain pasta, reserving 1/4 cup cooking liquid. Stir basil, rigatoni and reserved liquid into skillet; heat through. Transfer to a serving bowl; sprinkle with Parmesan cheese.

**Nutrition Facts:** 3/4 cup equals 159 calories, 4 g fat (1 g saturated fat), 3 mg cholesterol, 291 mg sodium, 24 g carbohydrate, 3 g fiber, 7 g protein. **Diabetic Exchanges:** 1-1/2 starch, 1/2 fat.

> Drain pasta thoroughly in a colander without rinsing when it is to be served with a sauce or combined in a baked dish. Rinsing pasta can wash away starch that may help to slightly thicken the pasta sauce. Pasta can be rinsed in a colander when it is to be served cold.

## Sweet Onion Spoon Bread Ⓜ

PREP: 15 min.  BAKE: 25 min.  YIELD: 9 servings

**HEATHER THOMAS • FREDERICKSBURG, VIRGINIA**

*This unique recipe has been a family secret for years. The layers of tangy cheese, sour cream and sweet onions in this moist corn bread taste so great together! Chopped green chilies could add some fun zip.*

1-1/3  cups chopped sweet onions
   1  Tbsp. butter
   1  can (8-1/4 oz.) cream-style corn
   1  pkg. (8-1/2 oz.) corn bread/muffin mix
   2  egg whites, lightly beaten
   2  Tbsp. fat-free milk
 1/2  cup reduced-fat sour cream
 1/3  cup shredded sharp cheddar cheese

**1.** In a small nonstick skillet coated with cooking spray, saute onions in butter until tender; set aside.

**2.** Meanwhile, in a large bowl, combine the corn, muffin mix, egg whites and milk. Pour into a 9-in. square baking dish coated with cooking spray. Combine sour cream and onions; spread over batter. Sprinkle with cheese.

**3.** Bake, uncovered, at 350° for 25-30 minutes or until a toothpick inserted near the center comes out clean.

**Nutrition Facts:** 1 piece equals 191 calories, 6 g fat (3 g saturated fat), 18 mg cholesterol, 361 mg sodium, 29 g carbohydrate, 1 g fiber, 6 g protein. **Diabetic Exchanges:** 2 starch, 1/2 fat.

# Lemon Risotto With Broccoli F

**PREP:** 25 min. **COOK:** 30 min. **YIELD:** 8 servings

**JUDY GREBETZ • RACINE, WISCONSIN**

*Here's a creamy, rich party-special alternative to potatoes. It seems time-consuming, but it's really quite easy, and the results are sure to impress. Try it with a chicken entree, or add a handful of mushrooms and enjoy it as a light main course. A sprinkling of chopped green onion makes an easy garnish.*

|     |     |
|-----|-----|
| 3 | cans (14-1/2 oz. *each*) reduced-sodium chicken broth |
| 1 | small onion, finely chopped |
| 1 | Tbsp. olive oil |
| 1-1/2 | cups uncooked arborio rice |
| 2 | tsp. grated lemon peel |
| 1/2 | cup dry white wine *or* additional reduced-sodium chicken broth |
| 3 | cups chopped fresh broccoli |
| 1/3 | cup grated Parmesan cheese |
| 1 | Tbsp. lemon juice |
| 2 | tsp. minced fresh thyme |

**1.** In a large saucepan, heat broth and keep warm. In a large nonstick skillet coated with cooking spray, saute onion in oil until tender. Add rice and lemon peel; cook and stir for 2-3 minutes.

**2.** Reduce heat; stir in wine. Cook and stir until all of the liquid is absorbed. Carefully stir in 1 cup warm broth; cook and stir until all of the liquid is absorbed. Stir in broccoli.

**3.** Add remaining broth, 1/2 cup at a time, stirring constantly. Allow liquid to absorb between additions. Cook until risotto is creamy and rice is almost tender. (Cooking time is about 20 minutes.)

**4.** Remove from the heat; stir in cheese and lemon juice. Sprinkle with thyme. Serve immediately.

**Nutrition Facts:** 2/3 cup equals 198 calories, 3 g fat (1 g saturated fat), 3 mg cholesterol, 447 mg sodium, 34 g carbohydrate, 1 g fiber, 7 g protein. **Diabetic Exchanges:** 2 starch, 1/2 fat.

# Roasted Pepper Salad F C M

**PREP:** 15 min. **BAKE:** 25 min. **YIELD:** 6 servings

**TRISHA KRUSE • EAGLE, IDAHO**

*Here's a pretty, quick-prep side that will go with a summer full of grilled entrees.*

|     |     |
|-----|-----|
| 2 | cups cherry tomatoes, halved |
| 1/2 | cup minced fresh basil |
| 8 | garlic cloves, minced |
| 1 | Tbsp. balsamic vinegar |
| 1/2 | tsp. salt |
| 1/2 | tsp. pepper |
| 3 | large sweet yellow peppers, halved and seeded |
| 2 | Tbsp. shredded Parmesan cheese |

**1.** In a small bowl, combine the tomatoes, basil, garlic, vinegar, salt and pepper. Spoon 1/3 cup into each pepper half.

**2.** Transfer to a 13-in. x 9-in. baking dish coated with cooking spray. Cover and bake at 400° for 20 minutes. Uncover; sprinkle with cheese. Bake 5-10 minutes longer or until cheese is melted.

**Nutrition Facts:** 1 stuffed pepper half equals 51 calories, 1 g fat (trace saturated fat), 1 mg cholesterol, 233 mg sodium, 10 g carbohydrate, 2 g fiber, 2 g protein. **Diabetic Exchange:** 2 vegetable.

# Lemon Roasted Potatoes F

**PREP:** 10 min. **BAKE:** 35 min. **YIELD:** 6 servings

**MITZI SENTIFF • ANNAPOLIS, MARYLAND**

*Delicious with almost any meat or fish dinner, these crispy potatoes are really something special. Tangy lemon permeates the potatoes and adds marvelous flavor.*

|     |     |
|-----|-----|
| 2 | lbs. small red potatoes, quartered |
| 1 | medium lemon, halved and sliced |
| 1 | Tbsp. olive oil |
| 2 | tsp. minced fresh rosemary |
| 1/2 | tsp. salt |
| 1/8 | tsp. coarsely ground pepper |

**1.** In a large bowl, combine all ingredients; toss to coat. Arrange in a single layer in a 15-in. x 10-in. x 1-in. baking pan coated with cooking spray. Bake at 425° for 35-40 minutes or until potatoes are golden and tender.

**Nutrition Facts:** 3/4 cup equals 132 calories, 2 g fat (trace saturated fat), 0 cholesterol, 207 mg sodium, 25 g carbohydrate, 3 g fiber, 3 g protein. **Diabetic Exchanges:** 1-1/2 starch, 1/2 fat.

LEMON ROASTED POTATOES

# Hot and Zesty Quinoa M

**PREP/TOTAL TIME:** 25 min. **YIELD:** 4 servings

**SANDRA LETIZIA • PROVIDENCE, RHODE ISLAND**

*I created this healthy whole grain side to serve my family instead of potatoes or rice. It's so easy and has a little kick. Quinoa's a nurturing grain and a complete protein.*

- 1 cup water
- 1/2 cup quinoa, rinsed
- 1 small onion, finely chopped
- 1 tsp. olive oil
- 2 garlic cloves, minced
- 1 can (10 oz.) diced tomatoes and green chilies
- 2 Tbsp. chopped marinated quartered artichoke hearts
- 2 Tbsp. grated Parmesan cheese

**1.** In a small saucepan, bring water to a boil. Add quinoa. Reduce heat; cover and simmer for 12-15 minutes or until liquid is absorbed. Remove from the heat; fluff with a fork.

**2.** In a large skillet, saute onion in oil until tender. Add garlic; cook 1 minute longer. Add tomatoes and green chilies. Bring to a boil over medium heat. Reduce heat; simmer, uncovered, for 10 minutes. Stir in quinoa and artichoke; heat through. Sprinkle with the cheese.

**Editor's Note:** Look for quinoa in the cereal, rice or organic food aisle.

**Nutrition Facts:** 1/2 cup equals 135 calories, 5 g fat (1 g saturated fat), 2 mg cholesterol, 361 mg sodium, 20 g carbohydrate, 2 g fiber, 5 g protein. **Diabetic Exchanges:** 1 starch, 1 vegetable, 1 fat.

# Spicy Pepper Slaw C M

**PREP:** 20 min. + chilling **YIELD:** 8 servings

**CHERYL MC CLEARY • KANSAS CITY, KANSAS**

*I love coleslaw but wanted to jazz it up and make it just a little healthier. This recipe not only makes a good side dish, but it's also great as a relish on a chicken sandwich or burger. Jalapenos give it just the right kick.*

- 3 cups shredded cabbage
- 2 celery ribs, chopped
- 1 medium green pepper, julienned
- 1 cup cut fresh green beans (1-in. pieces)
- 1 cup cut fresh asparagus (1-in. pieces)
- 1 bunch green onions, chopped
- 1 banana pepper, seeded and chopped
- 2 jalapeno peppers, seeded and chopped
- 2 serrano peppers, seeded and chopped
- 1/2 cup cider vinegar
- 3 Tbsp. olive oil
- 1 Tbsp. lime juice
- 1 Tbsp. minced fresh thyme
- 1 Tbsp. snipped fresh dill
- 1 Tbsp. minced fresh cilantro
- 1 tsp. salt
- 1 tsp. pepper

**1.** In a large bowl, combine the first nine ingredients. In a small bowl, whisk the remaining ingredients; pour over salad and toss to coat. Refrigerate for at least 1 hour before serving.

**Editor's Note:** Wear disposable gloves when cutting hot peppers; the oils can burn skin. Avoid touching your face.

**Nutrition Facts:** 1 cup equals 76 calories, 5 g fat (1 g saturated fat), 0 cholesterol, 314 mg sodium, 6 g carbohydrate, 3 g fiber, 2 g protein. **Diabetic Exchanges:** 1 vegetable, 1 fat.

HOT AND ZESTY QUINOA

SPICY PEPPER SLAW

# Spinach and Rice F

PREP: 20 min. COOK: 40 min. YIELD: 8 servings

LAURA NURSE • LILBURN, GEORGIA

*Dill and oregano do a nice job of dressing up this dish. It makes a pleasing side with savory lamb or pork chops.*

| | |
|---|---|
| 6 | green onions, chopped |
| 1 | Tbsp. olive oil |
| 1 | cup uncooked brown rice |
| 2-3/4 | cups water |
| 1/3 | cup snipped fresh dill |
| 2 | Tbsp. minced fresh oregano |
| 3/4 | tsp. salt |
| 1/4 | tsp. pepper |
| 1 | pkg. (6 oz.) fresh baby spinach |

**1.** In a large saucepan, saute onions in oil until tender. Add rice; cook and stir for 3-4 minutes or until rice is lightly browned.

**2.** Stir in the water, dill, oregano, salt and pepper. Bring to a boil. Reduce heat; cover and simmer for 35-40 minutes or until rice is tender. Add spinach; heat through.

**Nutrition Facts:** 3/4 cup equals 110 calories, 3 g fat (trace saturated fat), 0 cholesterol, 242 mg sodium, 20 g carbohydrate, 2 g fiber, 3 g protein. **Diabetic Exchanges:** 1 starch, 1 vegetable.

# Roasted Dijon Broccoli C M

PREP/TOTAL TIME: 20 min. YIELD: 4 servings

AMY WINGENTER • TUSCALOOSA, ALABAMA

*A hint of red wine vinegar and Dijon mustard wonderfully flavor this quick, easy and very versatile side dish. If you'd like, feel free to add a little more garlic or even a dash of red pepper flakes for extra flair!*

| | |
|---|---|
| 1 | bunch broccoli, cut into florets |
| 2 | Tbsp. olive oil |
| 1 | Tbsp. red wine vinegar |
| 1 | tsp. Dijon mustard |
| 1 | garlic clove, minced |
| 1/4 | tsp. salt |
| 1/4 | tsp. pepper |

**1.** Place broccoli on a baking sheet. In a small bowl, whisk the remaining ingredients. Drizzle over broccoli; toss to coat.

**2.** Bake, uncovered, at 425° for 10-15 minutes or until tender.

**Nutrition Facts:** 1 cup equals 106 calories, 7 g fat (1 g saturated fat), 0 cholesterol, 219 mg sodium, 9 g carbohydrate, 5 g fiber, 5 g protein. **Diabetic Exchanges:** 2 vegetable, 1 fat.

SAVORY GREEN BEANS

## Savory Green Beans F C M

PREP/TOTAL TIME: 30 min.  YIELD: 6 servings

**CAROL ANN HAYDEN • EVERSON, WASHINGTON**

*This was my mother's favorite way to fix green beans. She always grew savory in her garden, which is the key ingredient to this recipe's fresh flavor. Not only is this dish low in fat, but it goes well with just about any main course.*

- 3/4 cup chopped sweet red pepper
- 1 Tbsp. canola oil
- 1 garlic clove, minced
- 1-1/2 lbs. fresh green beans, trimmed and cut into 2-in. pieces
- 1/2 cup water
- 2 Tbsp. minced fresh savory or 2 tsp. dried savory
- 1 Tbsp. minced chives
- 1/2 tsp. salt

**1.** In a large skillet, saute red pepper in oil for 2-3 minutes or until tender. Add garlic; cook 1 minute longer. Stir in the green beans, water, savory, chives and salt. Bring to a boil. Reduce heat; cover and simmer for 8-10 minutes or until beans are crisp-tender.

**Nutrition Facts:** 3/4 cup equals 59 calories, 3 g fat (trace saturated fat), 0 cholesterol, 203 mg sodium, 9 g carbohydrate, 4 g fiber, 2 g protein. **Diabetic Exchanges:** 2 vegetable, 1/2 fat.

## Spanish Rice with Bacon

PREP: 5 min.  COOK: 40 min.  YIELD: 6 servings

**DAVID BIAS • SILOAM SPRINGS, ARKANSAS**

*I add bacon to this zippy rice dish for a flavorful change of pace. Being big fans of Mexican food, my family loves this simple recipe.*

- 6 bacon strips, diced
- 1 Tbsp. canola oil
- 1 medium onion, chopped
- 1 cup uncooked long grain rice
- 1-3/4 cups water
- 2 large tomatoes, chopped

1 medium green pepper, chopped
2 jalapeno peppers, seeded and chopped
1 to 1-1/2 tsp. chili powder
1/2 tsp. salt

**1.** In a large skillet, cook bacon over medium heat until crisp. Remove to paper towels. Add oil to the drippings; saute onion for 3 minutes. Add rice; stir until golden brown, about 5 minutes. Stir in the remaining ingredients. Bring to a boil.

**2.** Reduce heat; cover and simmer for 30 minutes or until rice is tender. Sprinkle with bacon.

**Editor's Note:** Wear disposable gloves when cutting hot peppers; the oils can burn skin. Avoid touching your face.

**Nutrition Facts:** 3/4 cup equals 287 calories, 12 g fat (4 g saturated fat), 16 mg cholesterol, 514 mg sodium, 34 g carbohydrate, 2 g fiber, 10 g protein. **Diabetic Exchanges:** 2 starch, 2 fat, 1 vegetable.

# Creamy Grilled Potato Salad  M

PREP: 15 min.  GRILL: 25 min.  YIELD: 6 servings

**GAYLE ROBINSON • CARROLLTON, GEORGIA**

*I grill just about everything in the summer to avoid turning on my oven—including this salad. Friends dubbed this "The Best Potato Salad You'll Ever Put in Your Mouth!"*

8 medium red potatoes (about 2 lbs.), cut into 1-in. slices
2 Tbsp. olive oil
1/2 tsp. garlic salt
1/4 tsp. paprika
1/4 tsp. pepper
1 cup fat-free mayonnaise
2 hard-cooked eggs, chopped
1 dill pickle spear, chopped
3 Tbsp. dill pickle juice
1 Tbsp. spicy brown mustard

**1.** Place the first five ingredients in a large bowl; toss to coat. Moisten a paper towel with cooking oil; using long-handled tongs, lightly coat the grill rack. Grill potatoes, covered, over medium heat for 25-30 minutes or until tender, turning once. Cool. Cut into quarters and place in a large bowl.

**2.** In a small bowl, combine remaining ingredients. Pour over potatoes; toss to coat. Serve immediately. Refrigerate leftovers.

**Nutrition Facts:** 3/4 cup equals 209 calories, 8 g fat (1 g saturated fat), 75 mg cholesterol, 651 mg sodium, 30 g carbohydrate, 4 g fiber, 5 g protein. **Diabetic Exchanges:** 2 starch, 1 fat.

# Makeover Spinach and Artichoke Casserole  M

PREP: 35 min.  BAKE: 30 min.  YIELD: 12 servings

**JUDY ARMSTRONG • PRAIRIEVILLE, LOUISIANA**

*Spinach never tasted better than in this creamy, colorful dish that's now even healthier and more delicious!*

5 celery ribs, finely chopped
2 medium sweet red peppers, chopped

2 medium onions, finely chopped
2 Tbsp. butter
1 Tbsp. canola oil
6 garlic cloves, minced
3 Tbsp. all-purpose flour
1 cup half-and-half cream
1 cup fat-free milk
3 cups (12 oz.) shredded reduced-fat Mexican cheese blend
4 pkg. (10 oz. *each*) frozen chopped spinach, thawed and squeezed dry
2 cans (14 oz. *each*) water-packed artichoke hearts, rinsed, drained and quartered
1 tsp. salt
1 tsp. cayenne pepper
1 tsp. pepper
1/2 tsp. crushed red pepper flakes
1 cup grated Parmesan cheese

**1.** In a Dutch oven, saute the celery, red peppers and onions in butter and oil until tender. Add garlic; cook 1 minute longer. Stir in flour until blended; gradually add cream and milk. Bring to a boil; cook and stir for 2 minutes or until thickened. Stir in shredded cheese until melted.

**2.** Add the spinach, artichokes, salt, cayenne, pepper and pepper flakes. Transfer to a 13-in. x 9-in. baking dish coated with cooking spray. Sprinkle with Parmesan cheese.

**3.** Bake, uncovered, at 350° for 30-35 minutes or until bubbly.

**Nutrition Facts:** 1 cup equals 245 calories, 13 g fat (7 g saturated fat), 41 mg cholesterol, 781 mg sodium, 17 g carbohydrate, 4 g fiber, 17 g protein.

MAKEOVER SPINACH AND ARTICHOKE CASSEROLE

## Slow-Roasted Tomatoes C M

PREP: 20 min. BAKE: 3 hours + cooling
YIELD: 4 cups

**JULIE TILNEY • DOWNEY, CALIFORNIA**

*I love tomatoes, and these are so versatile. You can also use them in sandwiches, omelets and to top broiled chicken.*

| | |
|---|---|
| 20 | plum tomatoes (about 5 lbs.) |
| 1/4 | cup olive oil |
| 5 | tsp. Italian seasoning |
| 2-1/2 | tsp. salt |

**1.** Cut tomatoes into 1/2-in. slices. Brush with oil; sprinkle with Italian seasoning and salt.

**2.** Place on racks coated with cooking spray in foil-lined 15-in. x 10-in. x 1-in. baking pans. Bake, uncovered, at 325° for 3 to 3-1/2 hours or until tomatoes are deep brown around the edges and shriveled. Cool for 10-15 minutes. Serve warm or at room temperature.

**3.** Store in an airtight container in the refrigerator for up to 1 week or freeze for up to 3 months. Bring tomatoes to room temperature before using.

**Nutrition Facts:** 1/4 cup equals 45 calories, 4 g fat (trace saturated fat), 0 cholesterol, 373 mg sodium, 3 g carbohydrate, 1 g fiber, 1 g protein.

## Snow Pea & Carrot Saute F M

PREP/TOTAL TIME: 20 min. YIELD: 5 servings

**HEALTHY COOKING TEST KITCHEN**

*With bright carrot strips and green snow peas, this makes a colorful dish with any entree. Short on time? You can also buy matchstick carrots at the grocery store.*

| | |
|---|---|
| 1 | lb. fresh snow peas |
| 1 | Tbsp. butter |
| 2 | medium carrots, julienned |
| 1 | garlic clove, minced |
| 3 | Tbsp. honey |
| 1/4 | tsp. salt |
| 1/8 | tsp. pepper |

**1.** In a large skillet, saute snow peas in butter for 3 minutes. Add carrots and garlic; saute 1-2 minutes longer or until vegetables are crisp-tender. Add remaining ingredients; heat through.

**Nutrition Facts:** 3/4 cup equals 108 calories, 3 g fat (1 g saturated fat), 6 mg cholesterol, 155 mg sodium, 20 g carbohydrate, 3 g fiber, 3 g protein. **Diabetic Exchanges:** 2 vegetable, 1/2 starch.

## Grilled Summer Squash C M

PREP/TOTAL TIME: 25 min. YIELD: 4 servings

**LISA FINNEGAN • FORKED RIVER, NEW JERSEY**

*Grilling food in foil packets creates steam, so it cooks in its own juices, which makes this summer squash flavorful and keeps it light. Best of all, there's no cleanup! Just remember to keep the packet small enough to easily take off the grill.*

| | |
|---|---|
| 2 | medium yellow summer squash, sliced |
| 2 | medium sweet red peppers, sliced |
| 1 | large sweet onion, halved and sliced |
| 2 | Tbsp. olive oil |
| 2 | garlic cloves, minced |
| 1 | tsp. sugar |
| 1/4 | tsp. salt |
| 1/4 | tsp. pepper |

SNOW PEA & CARROT SAUTE

GRILLED SUMMER SQUASH

**1.** In a large bowl, combine all ingredients. Divide between two double thicknesses of heavy-duty foil (about 18 in. x 12 in.). Fold foil around vegetable mixture and seal tightly.

**2.** Grill, covered, over medium heat for 10-15 minutes or until vegetables are tender. Open foil carefully to allow steam to escape.

**Nutrition Facts:** 3/4 cup equals 124 calories, 7 g fat (1 g saturated fat), 0 cholesterol, 159 mg sodium, 15 g carbohydrate, 3 g fiber, 3 g protein. **Diabetic Exchanges:** 2 vegetable, 1-1/2 fat.

# Makeover Pecan Corn Pudding Ⓜ

**PREP:** 20 min. **BAKE:** 45 min. **YIELD:** 12 servings

**SHARON BESHOAR • MONTROSE, COLORADO**

*Every bit as rich and creamy as my original recipe, this magical makeover has crunchy pecans, loads of cheese and a touch of jalapeno. It's destined to become a favorite!*

|   |   |
|---|---|
| 1 | cup yellow cornmeal |
| 3/4 | tsp. baking soda |
| 3 | eggs |
| 1-1/4 | cups buttermilk |
| 3/4 | cup reduced-fat butter, melted |
| 2 | cans (one 14-3/4 oz., one 8-1/4 oz.) cream-style corn |
| 2 | cups frozen corn |
| 2 | medium onions, chopped |

|   |   |
|---|---|
| 1-1/2 | cups (6 oz.) shredded sharp reduced-fat cheddar cheese |
| 4 | jalapeno peppers, seeded and chopped |
| 1/2 | cup chopped pecans, toasted |

**1.** In a large bowl, combine cornmeal and baking soda. In a small bowl, whisk the eggs, buttermilk and butter. Add cream-style corn, corn and onions. Stir into dry ingredients just until moistened.

**2.** Pour half the mixture into a 13-in. x 9-in. baking dish coated with cooking spray. Sprinkle with cheese and jalapenos. Top with remaining batter; sprinkle with pecans.

**3.** Bake, uncovered, at 350° for 45-50 minutes or until a thermometer reads 160°. Serve warm.

**Editor's Note:** This recipe was tested with Land O'Lakes light stick butter. We recommend wearing disposable gloves when cutting hot peppers. Avoid touching your face.

**Nutrition Facts:** 3/4 cup equals 269 calories, 15 g fat (6 g saturated fat), 79 mg cholesterol, 465 mg sodium, 31 g carbohydrate, 3 g fiber, 10 g protein.

> White cornmeal is more popular in the South and yellow cornmeal is preferred in the North. Blue cornmeal can be found in specialty stores. All three types can be used interchangeably in recipes.

# Heirloom Tomato Tart Ⓜ

PREP: 20 min. BAKE: 10 min. + cooling
YIELD: 6 servings

**KATHRYN CONRAD • MILWAUKEE, WISCONSIN**

*What a great way to showcase a summer harvest of tomatoes! Refrigerated pie pastry makes this pretty side dish easy, while goat cheese and fresh basil lend Mediterranean flair.*

- 2 tsp. cornmeal, *divided*
- 1 refrigerated pie pastry
- Cooking spray
- 3 Tbsp. shredded Asiago cheese
- 3 large heirloom tomatoes, cut into 1/4-in. slices
- 3 small heirloom tomatoes, cut into 1/4-in. slices
- 1 Tbsp. extra-virgin olive oil
- 1/2 tsp. coarsely ground pepper
- 1/4 tsp. salt
- 1/4 cup crumbled goat *or* feta cheese
- Fresh basil leaves, optional

**1.** Sprinkle a large baking sheet with 1 tsp. cornmeal.

**2.** On a lightly floured surface, roll pastry into a 12-in. circle; transfer to prepared pan. Spritz dough with cooking spray. Sprinkle with remaining cornmeal, pressing cornmeal gently into dough. Prick thoroughly with a fork. Sprinkle with Asiago cheese.

**3.** Bake at 450° for 10 minutes or until lightly browned. Cool on a wire rack.

**4.** Layer with tomatoes. Drizzle with olive oil; sprinkle with pepper and salt. Top with goat cheese; garnish with basil if desired. Serve immediately.

**Nutrition Facts:** 1 slice equals 236 calories, 14 g fat (6 g saturated fat), 16 mg cholesterol, 270 mg sodium, 24 g carbohydrate, 2 g fiber, 4 g protein.

# Grilled Cherry Tomatoes S C M

**PREP/TOTAL TIME:** 20 min. **YIELD:** 6 servings

**LUCY MEYRING • WALDEN, COLORADO**

*This tasty side dish is seasoned with herbs and butter. Just tuck the foil packet beside any meat you happen to be grilling and you'll have dinner in a flash. Just be sure to cut the foil large enough to fold the edges over twice to seal.*

> 2 pints cherry tomatoes, halved
> 2 garlic cloves, minced
> 1/2 tsp. dried oregano
> 3 Tbsp. butter

**1.** Place tomatoes on a double thickness of heavy-duty foil (about 24 in. x 12 in.). In a small skillet, saute garlic and oregano in butter for 2 minutes. Pour over tomatoes. Fold foil around tomatoes and seal tightly.

**2.** Grill, covered, over medium heat for 4-5 minutes on each side or until tomatoes are heated through. Open foil carefully to allow steam to escape.

**Nutrition Facts:** 1/2 cup equals 73 calories, 6 g fat (4 g saturated fat), 15 mg cholesterol, 67 mg sodium, 5 g carbohydrate, 1 g fiber, 1 g protein. **Diabetic Exchanges:** 1 vegetable, 1 fat.

# Italian Vegetable Medley C M

**PREP/TOTAL TIME:** 15 min. **YIELD:** 4 servings

**MARGARET WILSON • SUN CITY, CALIFORNIA**

*Round out a variety of menus with this veggie side that lends a delicious pop of color. If you can, use leftover vegetables. People are always surprised at how easy this dish is because the flavors are so bold and the colors are so bright! Feel free to experiment with different vegetable blends if you'd like.*

> 1 pkg. (16 oz.) frozen broccoli stir-fry vegetable blend
> 2 Tbsp. grated Parmesan cheese
> 1 Tbsp. seasoned bread crumbs
> 1/8 tsp. garlic powder
> 1/8 tsp. seasoned salt
> 1/8 tsp. pepper
> 1 Tbsp. butter

**1.** Microwave vegetables according to package directions. Meanwhile, in a small bowl, combine the cheese, bread crumbs, garlic powder, seasoned salt and pepper.

**2.** Drain vegetables; stir in butter. Sprinkle with cheese mixture.

**Nutrition Facts:** 3/4 cup equals 79 calories, 4 g fat (2 g saturated fat), 10 mg cholesterol, 174 mg sodium, 7 g carbohydrate, 2 g fiber, 2 g protein. **Diabetic Exchanges:** 1 vegetable, 1/2 fat.

# Grilled Potatoes F M

**PREP:** 10 min. **GRILL:** 30 min. **YIELD:** 4 servings

**JENA COFFEY • ROCK HILL, MISSOURI**

*Need a simple sidekick to serve with steaks or chops? Try these bursting-with-flavor potatoes. I make the recipe for picnics and potlucks. The potatoes turn out tender and well-seasoned. Plus, there's one less pot to wash.*

> 1 Tbsp. olive oil
> 2 garlic cloves, minced
> 1/2 tsp. dried basil
> 1/4 tsp. salt
> 1/8 tsp. pepper
> 3 medium baking potatoes, peeled and cut into 1-in. cubes

**1.** In a large bowl, combine the first five ingredients. Add potatoes; toss to coat. Spoon onto a greased double thickness of heavy-duty foil (about 18 in. square).

**2.** Fold foil around potato mixture and seal tightly. Grill, covered, over medium heat for 30-35 minutes or until potatoes are tender, turning once. Open foil carefully to allow steam to escape.

**Nutrition Facts:** 3/4 cup equals 126 calories, 3 g fat (trace saturated fat), 0 cholesterol, 151 mg sodium, 22 g carbohydrate, 2 g fiber, 2 g protein. **Diabetic Exchanges:** 1-1/2 starch, 1/2 fat.

> To make **seasoned bread crumbs**, simply break slices of dried bread into pieces and process in a blender or food processor until you have fine crumbs. Then season the crumbs to accommodate your family's tastes.

GRILLED POTATOES

## Agave Roasted Parsnips 🆂 🅼

PREP: 20 min. BAKE: 20 min. YIELD: 6 servings

**KATHLEEN THORSON • MENOMONEE FALLS, WISCONSIN**

*Deliciously sweet and aromatic, this dinner addition nicely spices up any traditional meal.*

- 6 medium parsnips, peeled and sliced
- 2 medium carrots, sliced
- 1 medium leek (white portion only), sliced
- 3 garlic cloves, sliced
- 2 Tbsp. butter, melted
- 2 Tbsp. agave nectar or honey
- 1/8 tsp. ground cinnamon
- 1/8 tsp. ground nutmeg

**1.** Divide the parsnips, carrots, leek and garlic between two 15-in. x 10-in. x 1-in. baking pans coated with cooking spray. Combine the remaining ingredients; drizzle over vegetables and toss to coat.

**2.** Bake, uncovered, at 425° for 20-25 minutes or until tender, stirring occasionally.

**Nutrition Facts:** 3/4 cup equals 187 calories, 4 g fat (3 g saturated fat), 10 mg cholesterol, 60 mg sodium, 37 g carbohydrate, 7 g fiber, 3 g protein.

## Makeover Streusel-Topped Sweet Potatoes 🆂 🅼

PREP: 25 min. BAKE: 20 min. YIELD: 12 servings

**TAMRA DUNCAN • LINCOLN, ARKANSAS**

*People really do eat with their eyes, and no one ever misses the fat and calories in this dish when they see how yummy and attractive this lightened-up version is.*

- 6 medium sweet potatoes
- 1/2 cup reduced-fat butter, melted
- 3 eggs, lightly beaten
- 1/4 cup unsweetened apple juice
- 1-1/2 tsp. vanilla extract

TOPPING:
- 3/4 cup packed brown sugar
- 1/2 cup flaked coconut
- 1/2 cup chopped pecans
- 1/4 cup reduced-fat butter, melted

**1.** Scrub and pierce sweet potatoes; place on a microwave-safe plate. Microwave, uncovered, on high for 15-18 minutes or until tender, turning once.

**2.** When cool enough to handle, cut each potato in half lengthwise. Scoop out the pulp, leaving thin shells. In a large bowl, mash the pulp with butter and eggs. Stir in juice and vanilla. Carefully spoon into potato shells.

**3.** Divide between two 13-in. x 9-in. baking dishes coated with cooking spray. Combine the topping ingredients; spoon over potatoes. Bake at 375° for 20-25 minutes or until a thermometer reads 160°.

**Editor's Note:** This recipe was tested with Land O'Lakes light stick butter in a 1,100-watt microwave.

**Nutrition Facts:** 1 stuffed potato half equals 260 calories, 12 g fat (5 g saturated fat), 68 mg cholesterol, 136 mg sodium, 37 g carbohydrate, 3 g fiber, 4 g protein.

AGAVE ROASTED PARSNIPS

MAKEOVER STREUSEL-TOPPED SWEET POTATOES

MAKEOVER SAUSAGE PECAN STUFFING

## Lemon-Garlic Green Beans F S C M

PREP/TOTAL TIME: 20 min.  YIELD: 4 servings

**GAIL ORSILLO • LYNNWOOD, WASHINGTON**

*My brother made this light stovetop dish as his contribution to Christmas dinner one year. We liked it so much that it became a mainstay in our house.*

- 1 lb. fresh green beans, trimmed and cut into 2-in. pieces
- 2 tsp. olive oil
- 2 garlic cloves, minced
- 1 Tbsp. lemon juice
- 1/4 tsp. coarsely ground pepper
- 1/8 tsp. salt

**1.** In a large nonstick skillet coated with cooking spray, cook and stir beans in oil over medium heat for 10-13 minutes or until crisp-tender.

**2.** Add garlic; cook 1 minute longer. Stir in the lemon juice, pepper and salt.

**Nutrition Facts:** 3/4 cup equals 54 calories, 2 g fat (trace saturated fat), 0 cholesterol, 80 mg sodium, 8 g carbohydrate, 3 g fiber, 2 g protein. **Diabetic Exchanges:** 1 vegetable, 1/2 fat.

## Makeover Sausage Pecan Stuffing

PREP: 30 min.  BAKE: 30 min.  YIELD: 12 servings

**HEALTHY COOKING TEST KITCHEN**

*Nothing about this moist, pecan-topped stuffing says "light." The fabulous flavors are sure to captivate friends and family.*

- 1 lb. lean ground turkey
- 2 cups sliced fresh mushrooms
- 2 celery ribs, chopped
- 1 medium onion, chopped
- 1 tsp. fennel seed
- 1/4 tsp. cayenne pepper
- 1/8 tsp. ground nutmeg
- 3 garlic cloves, minced
- 1 loaf (16 oz.) day-old white bread, cubed
- 1 large tart apple, chopped
- 2 tsp. rubbed sage
- 1-1/2 tsp. salt
- 1-1/2 tsp. poultry seasoning
- 1/2 tsp. pepper
- 2 eggs
- 1 cup reduced-sodium chicken broth
- 1/2 cup chopped pecans

**1.** In a Dutch oven, cook the turkey, mushrooms, celery, onion, fennel seed, cayenne and nutmeg over medium heat until turkey is no longer pink. Add garlic; cook 1 minute longer. Drain.

**2.** Transfer to a large bowl. Add the bread, apple, sage, salt, poultry seasoning and pepper. Whisk eggs and broth; pour over bread mixture and toss to coat. Transfer to a 13-in. x 9-in. baking dish coated with cooking spray; sprinkle with pecans.

**3.** Bake, uncovered, at 350° for 30-35 minutes or until top is lightly browned and a thermometer reads 160°.

**Nutrition Facts:** 3/4 cup equals 226 calories, 9 g fat (2 g saturated fat), 65 mg cholesterol, 654 mg sodium, 25 g carbohydrate, 2 g fiber, 12 g protein. **Diabetic Exchanges:** 1-1/2 starch, 1 lean meat, 1 fat.

DUCHESS POTATOES

# Duchess Potatoes

PREP: 35 min.  BAKE: 20 min.  YIELD: 6 servings

**HEALTHY COOKING TEST KITCHEN**

*Potatoes always make for cozy, comfort-food flavor. Here, they're also presented in an attractive package!*

|       |                                        |
|-------|----------------------------------------|
| 2     | lbs. russet potatoes, peeled and quartered |
| 3     | egg yolks                              |
| 3     | Tbsp. fat-free milk                    |
| 2     | Tbsp. butter                           |
| 1     | tsp. salt                              |
| 1/4   | tsp. pepper                            |
| 1/8   | tsp. ground nutmeg                     |
| 1     | egg, lightly beaten                    |

**1.** Place potatoes in a large saucepan and cover with water. Bring to a boil. Reduce heat; cover and simmer for 15-20 minutes or until tender. Drain.

**2.** Over very low heat, stir potatoes for 1-2 minutes or until steam has evaporated. Press through a potato ricer or strainer into a large bowl. Stir in the egg yolks, milk, butter, salt, pepper and nutmeg.

**3.** Using a pastry bag or heavy-duty resealable plastic bag and a large star tip, pipe potatoes into six mounds on a parchment paper-lined baking sheet. Brush with beaten egg. Bake at 400° for 20-25 minutes or until golden brown.

**Nutrition Facts:** 1 serving equals 158 calories, 7 g fat (3 g saturated fat), 134 mg cholesterol, 437 mg sodium, 21 g carbohydrate, 1 g fiber, 4 g protein.

# Easy Baked Mushrooms  S C M

PREP/TOTAL TIME: 30 min.  YIELD: 4 servings

**DENISE DIPACE • MEDFORD, NEW JERSEY**

*This savory side couldn't be much easier or more delicious. The mushrooms are wonderful alongside steaks and other beefy dishes as well as pork entrees.*

1 lb. medium fresh mushrooms, halved
2 Tbsp. olive oil
1/4 cup seasoned bread crumbs
1/4 tsp. garlic powder
1/4 tsp. pepper
Fresh parsley, optional

**1.** Place mushrooms on a baking sheet. Drizzle with oil; toss to coat. In a bowl, combine the bread crumbs, garlic powder and pepper; sprinkle over mushrooms.

**2.** Bake, uncovered, at 425° for 18-20 minutes or until lightly browned. Garnish with parsley if desired.

**Nutrition Facts:** 3/4 cup equals 116 calories, 8 g fat (1 g saturated fat), 0 cholesterol, 112 mg sodium, 10 g carbohydrate, 2 g fiber, 4 g protein.

# Rice with Chilies 'n' Veggies F M

**PREP:** 15 min. **COOK:** 30 min. **YIELD:** 8 servings

**KATE SELNER • LINO LAKES, MINNESOTA**

*I turned to a particular dish when I wanted to use peppers I grew in my garden. I promptly rewrote the recipe to include several other fresh veggies, and this was the result. It's a perfect complement for just about anything.*

1/3 cup fat-free milk
1/2 cup frozen corn, thawed
1 cup uncooked long grain rice
2 tsp. canola oil
1 large onion, chopped
1 medium zucchini, chopped
1 medium sweet red pepper, chopped
1/2 cup chopped carrot
1 can (4 oz.) chopped green chilies
1 garlic clove, minced
2 cups vegetable broth
1 bay leaf

**1.** Place milk and corn in a food processor. Cover and process until smooth; set aside. In a large skillet, saute rice in oil for 5-6 minutes or until lightly browned. Stir in the onion, zucchini, red pepper, carrot, chilies, garlic and corn mixture; cook for 1 minute.

**2.** Stir in broth and bay leaf; bring to a boil. Reduce heat; cover and simmer for 20 minutes or until rice is tender and liquid is absorbed. Discard bay leaf.

**Nutrition Facts:** 3/4 cup equals 134 calories, 2 g fat (trace saturated fat), trace cholesterol, 318 mg sodium, 27 g carbohydrate, 2 g fiber, 4 g protein. **Diabetic Exchanges:** 1 starch, 1 vegetable, 1/2 fat.

# Garlic and Artichoke Roasted Potatoes M

**PREP:** 15 min. **BAKE:** 35 min. **YIELD:** 10 servings

**MARIE RIZZIO • INTERLOCHEN, MICHIGAN**

*I like to put this simple dish into the oven to roast with the main course. The artichokes give it a gourmet appeal.*

2-1/2 lbs. medium red potatoes, cut into 1-1/2-in. cubes
2 pkg. (8 oz. *each*) frozen artichoke hearts
8 garlic cloves, halved
3 Tbsp. olive oil
3/4 tsp. salt
1/4 tsp. pepper
1/4 cup lemon juice
2 Tbsp. minced fresh parsley
1 tsp. grated lemon peel

**1.** Place the potatoes, artichokes and garlic in a 15-in. x 10-in. x 1-in. baking pan coated with cooking spray. Combine the oil, salt and pepper; drizzle over vegetables and toss to coat.

**2.** Bake, uncovered, at 425° for 35-40 minutes or until tender, stirring occasionally. Transfer to a large bowl. Add lemon juice, parsley and lemon peel; toss to coat. Serve warm.

**Nutrition Facts:** 3/4 cup equals 143 calories, 4 g fat (1 g saturated fat), 0 cholesterol, 209 mg sodium, 24 g carbohydrate, 4 g fiber, 4 g protein. **Diabetic Exchanges:** 1 starch, 1 vegetable, 1 fat.

**Need grated lemon peel? Citrus peel** can be grated into fine shreds with a Microplane grater. For slightly thicker shreds, use the zester; for long, continuous strips, use a stripper. Remove only the colored portion of the peel.

GARLIC AND ARTICHOKE ROASTED POTATOES

## Sweet Corn and Potato Gratin Ⓜ

PREP: 30 min.  BAKE: 45 min. + standing
YIELD: 8 servings

**JENNIFER OLSON • PLEASANTON, CALIFORNIA**

*This tasty side combines the distinctive flavors of garlic and onion, and kids love the crispy topping, too!*

- 1 medium onion, thinly sliced
- 2 Tbsp. butter
- 2 Tbsp. all-purpose flour
- 2 garlic cloves, minced
- 1 tsp. salt
- 1/2 tsp. pepper
- 1 cup whole milk
- 2 lbs. medium Yukon Gold potatoes, peeled and cut into 1/8-in. slices
- 2 cups fresh *or* frozen corn
- 1 can (8-1/4 oz.) cream-style corn
- 3/4 cup panko (Japanese) bread crumbs
- 1 Tbsp. butter, melted

**1.** In a large saucepan, saute onion in butter until tender. Stir in the flour, garlic, salt and pepper until blended; gradually add milk. Stir in potatoes. Bring to a boil. Reduce heat; cook and stir for 8-10 minutes or until potatoes are crisp-tender.

**2.** Stir in corn and cream-style corn. Transfer to an 8-in. square baking dish coated with cooking spray.

**3.** In a small bowl, combine bread crumbs and butter; sprinkle over potatoes. Bake at 350° for 45-50 minutes or until golden brown and potatoes are tender. Let stand for 10 minutes before serving.

**Nutrition Facts:** 3/4 cup equals 213 calories, 6 g fat (3 g saturated fat), 14 mg cholesterol, 452 mg sodium, 37 g carbohydrate, 3 g fiber, 5 g protein. **Diabetic Exchanges:** 2 starch, 1 fat.

## Mustard Brussels Sprouts Ⓜ

PREP/TOTAL TIME: 25 min.  YIELD: 5 servings

**LEAH-ANNE SCHNAPP • GROVE CITY, OHIO**

*Mustard boosts the green flavor of the sprouts in this versatile favorite. It's lovely served with chicken or pork chops.*

- 1-1/2 lb. fresh brussels sprouts
- 1/3 cup chopped shallots
- 1 Tbsp. butter
- 1/3 cup half-and-half cream
- 4-1/2 tsp. Dijon mustard
- 1/4 tsp. salt
- 1/4 tsp. dried tarragon
- 1/8 tsp. pepper
- 2 Tbsp. grated Parmesan cheese

**1.** Cut an "X" in the core of each brussels sprout. In a Dutch oven, bring 1/2 in. of water to a boil. Add brussels sprouts; cover and cook for 8-12 minutes or until tender.

**2.** Meanwhile, in a small saucepan, saute shallots in butter until tender. Add the cream, mustard, salt, tarragon and pepper. Cook and stir over medium heat until thickened. Drain sprouts; add cream mixture and heat through. Sprinkle with cheese.

SWEET CORN AND POTATO GRATIN

MUSTARD BRUSSELS SPROUTS

ASIAN BROCCOLI AND MUSHROOMS

**Nutrition Facts:** 1 cup equals 121 calories, 5 g fat (3 g saturated fat), 16 mg cholesterol, 316 mg sodium, 16 g carbohydrate, 5 g fiber, 6 g protein. **Diabetic Exchanges:** 2 vegetable, 1 fat.

# Garlic-Chive Baked Fries M

**PREP:** 15 min. **BAKE:** 20 min. **YIELD:** 4 servings

### HEALTHY COOKING TEST KITCHEN

*Yes, you do want fries with that—especially these crispy, golden-brown fries, full of garlic flavor and just a little bit of heat from pepper.*

    4   medium russet potatoes
    1   Tbsp. olive oil
    4   tsp. dried minced chives
  1/2   tsp. salt
  1/2   tsp. garlic powder
  1/4   tsp. pepper

**1.** Cut potatoes into 1/4-in. julienned strips. Rinse well and pat dry. Drizzle with oil and sprinkle with chives, salt, garlic powder and pepper; toss to coat. Arrange in a single layer on two 15-in. x 10-in. x 1-in. baking pans coated with cooking spray.

**2.** Bake at 450° for 20-25 minutes or until lightly browned, turning once.

**Nutrition Facts:** 1 serving equals 200 calories, 4 g fat (1 g saturated fat), 0 cholesterol, 308 mg sodium, 39 g carbohydrate, 4 g fiber, 5 g protein.

# Asian Broccoli And Mushrooms C M

**PREP/TOTAL TIME:** 20 min. **YIELD:** 4 servings

### CARLA PEELE • MULLINS, SOUTH CAROLINA

*What a great way to round out a meal! These vegetables are easily dressed up with sesame oil and ground chipotle pepper.*

    3   cups fresh broccoli florets
    4   oz. sliced baby portobello mushrooms
    1   Tbsp. olive oil
    1   tsp. sesame oil
    1   tsp. butter
    3   garlic cloves, minced
  1/2   tsp. seasoning blend
  1/4   tsp. ground chipotle pepper

**1.** In a large nonstick skillet coated with cooking spray, saute broccoli and mushrooms in olive oil, sesame oil and butter until tender. Add the garlic, seasoning blend and ground chipotle pepper; cook 1 minute longer.

**Editor's Note:** This recipe was tested with Nature's Seasons seasoning blend by Morton. It can be found in the spice aisle of your grocery store.

**Nutrition Facts:** 3/4 cup equals 74 calories, 6 g fat (1 g saturated fat), 3 mg cholesterol, 214 mg sodium, 5 g carbohydrate, 2 g fiber, 3 g protein. **Diabetic Exchanges:** 1 vegetable, 1 fat.

HEARTY PEPPER STRATA

FLUFFY PUMPKIN PANCAKES

MAKEOVER HASH BROWN CASSEROLE

# Good Mornings

You're sure to spring out of bed each morning when you start the day with any of these light and lively breakfast dishes. Whether you need an on-the-go sipper or a brunch contribution, this chapter has you covered.

## Makeover Hash Brown Casserole

**PREP:** 15 min.  **BAKE:** 40 min.  **YIELD:** 8 servings

**KELLY KIRBY • WESTVILLE, NOVA SCOTIA**

*This new, revised and lightened-up recipe is just as tasty as the original full-fat version!*

- 1 pkg. (30 oz.) frozen shredded hash brown potatoes, thawed
- 1 can (10-3/4 oz.) reduced-fat reduced-sodium condensed cream of chicken soup, undiluted
- 1 cup (4 oz.) shredded reduced-fat sharp cheddar cheese
- 2/3 cup reduced-fat sour cream
- 1 small onion, chopped
- 1/2 tsp. salt
- 1/2 tsp. pepper
- 1/4 cup crushed cornflakes
- 1 Tbsp. butter, melted

**1.** In a large bowl, combine the first seven ingredients. Transfer to a 13-in. x 9-in. baking dish coated with cooking spray. Combine cornflakes and butter; sprinkle over top. Bake at 350° for 40-45 minutes or until golden brown.

**Nutrition Facts:** 1-1/4 cups equals 203 calories, 7 g fat (4 g saturated fat), 24 mg cholesterol, 443 mg sodium, 27 g carbohydrate, 2 g fiber, 9 g protein. **Diabetic Exchanges:** 2 starch, 1 medium-fat meat.

## Honey Cinnamon Milk  **F** **S**

**PREP/TOTAL TIME:** 10 min.  **YIELD:** 1 serving

**LEONY SANTOSO • WINTER, VIRGINIA**

*I know you'll enjoy this warm, soothing beverage on a bleak wintry day. It's a nice alternative to hot cocoa or tea.*

- 1 cup fat-free milk
- 1 cinnamon stick (3 in.)
- Dash ground nutmeg
- Dash ground allspice
- 1-1/2 tsp. honey

**1.** In a small saucepan, combine the milk, cinnamon stick, nutmeg and allspice. Cook and stir over medium heat until heated through; whisk in honey. Serve warm in a mug; garnish with cinnamon stick.

**Nutrition Facts:** 1 cup equals 117 calories, trace fat (trace saturated fat), 5 mg cholesterol, 103 mg sodium, 21 g carbohydrate, trace fiber, 8 g protein. **Diabetic Exchanges:** 1 fat-free milk, 1/2 starch.

## Hearty Pepper Strata  **M**

**PREP:** 15 min. + chilling  **BAKE:** 50 min. + standing  **YIELD:** 8 servings

**HEALTHY COOKING TEST KITCHEN**

*Here's a hearty make-ahead strata that's as satisfying and delicious for dinner as it is for breakfast. You'll want to give this eye-opening recipe a try!*

- 9 slices whole wheat bread, cubed
- 1 pkg. (14 oz.) frozen pepper strips
- 1 cup sliced fresh mushrooms
- 1 medium onion, chopped
- 1 Tbsp. canola oil
- 8 eggs
- 8 egg whites
- 2-1/2 cups fat-free milk
- 1 cup (4 oz.) shredded cheddar cheese
- 1/2 tsp. salt
- 1/2 tsp. pepper

**1.** Place bread cubes in a 13-in. x 9-in. baking dish coated with cooking spray; set aside.

**2.** In a large skillet, saute the peppers, mushrooms and onion in oil until tender. In a large bowl, combine the eggs, egg whites, milk, cheese, salt, pepper and vegetable mixture; pour over the top. Cover and refrigerate overnight.

**3.** Remove from the refrigerator 30 minutes before baking. Bake, uncovered, at 350° for 50-60 minutes or until a knife inserted near the center comes out clean. Let stand for 10 minutes before cutting.

**Nutrition Facts:** 1 piece equals 283 calories, 12 g fat (5 g saturated fat), 228 mg cholesterol, 546 mg sodium, 22 g carbohydrate, 3 g fiber, 21 g protein. **Diabetic Exchanges:** 2 medium-fat meat, 1 starch, 1 vegetable, 1/2 fat.

# Zucchini Frittata C M

PREP: 20 min. BAKE: 20 min. YIELD: 4 servings

**MICHELLE SANDOVAL • ESCALON, CALIFORNIA**

*Surprisingly hearty, with a fresh veggie flavor as big as its serving size, this cheesy frittata also qualifies as a nice lunch option or late-night supper.*

- 1 large onion, chopped
- 2 medium zucchini, halved and thinly sliced
- 1 cup thinly sliced fresh mushrooms
- 4-1/2 tsp. butter
- 3 eggs
- 1/3 cup fat-free milk
- 1 tsp. Dijon mustard
- 1/2 tsp. ground mustard
- 1/4 tsp. salt
- 1/4 tsp. pepper
- 1 cup (4 oz.) shredded reduced-fat Swiss cheese
- 2 Tbsp. dry bread crumbs

**1.** In a large skillet, saute the onion, zucchini and mushrooms in butter until tender; drain. Transfer to an 8-in. square baking dish coated with cooking spray.

**2.** In a large bowl, whisk the eggs, milk, mustards, salt and pepper; pour over vegetable mixture. Sprinkle with cheese and bread crumbs. Bake, uncovered, at 375° for 18-22 minutes or until set. Let stand for 5 minutes.

**Nutrition Facts:** 1 piece equals 209 calories, 10 g fat (5 g saturated fat), 182 mg cholesterol, 391 mg sodium, 13 g carbohydrate, 2 g fiber, 17 g protein. **Diabetic Exchanges:** 2 medium-fat meat, 1 vegetable, 1 fat.

ZUCCHINI FRITTATA

# Makeover Noodle Kugel M

PREP: 15 min. BAKE: 45 min. + standing
YIELD: 15 servings

**CATHY TANG • REDMOND, WASHINGTON**

*I can finally feel good serving this fabulous brunch dish, particularly now that it's lower in saturated fat and cholesterol than my original recipe.*

- 1 pkg. (12 oz.) yolk-free noodles
- 2 Tbsp. butter, melted
- 2 cups (16 oz.) 1% cottage cheese
- 1-1/2 cups sugar
- 4 eggs
- 1 cup egg substitute
- 1 cup (8 oz.) reduced-fat sour cream
- 1 cup reduced-fat ricotta cheese

TOPPING:
- 1/2 cup cinnamon graham cracker crumbs (about 3 whole crackers)
- 1 Tbsp. butter, melted

**1.** Cook noodles according to package directions; drain. Toss with butter; set aside.

**2.** In a large bowl, beat the cottage cheese, sugar, eggs, egg substitute, sour cream and ricotta cheese until well blended. Stir in noodles.

**3.** Transfer to a 13-in. x 9-in. baking dish coated with cooking spray. Combine cracker crumbs and butter; sprinkle over top.

**4.** Bake, uncovered, at 350° for 45-50 minutes or until a thermometer reads 160°. Let stand for 10 minutes before cutting.

**Nutrition Facts:** 1 piece equals 271 calories, 6 g fat (3 g saturated fat), 73 mg cholesterol, 235 mg sodium, 41 g carbohydrate, 1 g fiber, 13 g protein. **Diabetic Exchanges:** 2-1/2 starch, 1 lean meat, 1/2 fat.

# Mustard Ham Strata C

PREP: 15 min. + chilling BAKE: 45 min.
YIELD: 12 servings

**DOLORES ZORNOW • POYNETTE, WISCONSIN**

*I had this at a bed-and-breakfast years ago. They were kind enough to share the recipe, and I've made it many times since.*

- 12 slices day-old bread, crusts removed and cubed
- 1-1/2 cups cubed fully cooked ham
- 1 cup chopped green pepper
- 3/4 cup shredded cheddar cheese
- 3/4 cup shredded Monterey Jack cheese
- 1/3 cup chopped onion
- 7 eggs
- 3 cups whole milk
- 3 tsp. ground mustard
- 1 tsp. salt

**1.** In a 13-in. x 9-in. baking dish coated with cooking spray, layer the bread cubes, ham, green pepper, cheeses and onion. In a large bowl, combine the eggs, milk, mustard and salt. Pour over top. Cover and refrigerate overnight.

GOOD MORNING FRITTATA

**2.** Remove from the refrigerator 30 minutes before baking. Bake, uncovered, at 325° for 45-50 minutes or until a knife inserted near the center comes out clean. Let stand for 5 minutes before cutting.

**Nutrition Facts:** 1 piece equals 198 calories, 11 g fat (5 g saturated fat), 153 mg cholesterol, 648 mg sodium, 11 g carbohydrate, 1 g fiber, 13 g protein. **Diabetic Exchanges:** 2 medium-fat meat, 1 starch.

# Good Morning Frittata C

**PREP/TOTAL TIME:** 20 min. **YIELD:** 2 servings

**MARY RELYEA • CANASTOTA, NEW YORK**

*Start the day bright with this light, fluffy, fast-fixing dish. Orange peppers add sunshiny sweetness.*

  1   cup egg substitute
1/4  cup fat-free milk
1/8  tsp. pepper
Dash salt

1/4  cup chopped sweet orange pepper
  2   green onions, thinly sliced
1/2  tsp. canola oil
1/3  cup cubed fully cooked ham
1/4  cup shredded reduced-fat cheddar cheese

**1.** In a small bowl, whisk the egg substitute, milk, pepper and salt; set aside. In an 8-in. ovenproof skillet, saute orange pepper and onions in oil until tender. Add ham; heat through. Reduce heat; top with egg mixture. Cover and cook for 4-6 minutes or until nearly set.

**2.** Uncover skillet; sprinkle with cheese. Broil 3-4 in. from the heat for 2-3 minutes or until eggs are completely set. Let stand for 5 minutes. Cut into wedges.

**Nutrition Facts:** 1 slice equals 169 calories, 6 g fat (3 g saturated fat), 23 mg cholesterol, 727 mg sodium, 7 g carbohydrate, 1 g fiber, 21 g protein. **Diabetic Exchanges:** 3 lean meat, 1/2 starch.

## Fluffy Pumpkin Pancakes

PREP: 15 min.  COOK: 10 min./batch  YIELD: 4 pancakes

**MINDY BAUKNECHT • TWO RIVERS, WISCONSIN**

*These pancakes are also delicious served with butter or whipped topping and a sprinkle of pumpkin pie spice. Freeze any extras in a single layer on a cookie sheet, then store in a freezer bag. They're great fresh out of the toaster!*

  1/3  cup all-purpose flour
  1/3  cup whole wheat flour
    2  Tbsp. sugar
  1/2  tsp. baking powder
  1/2  tsp. baking soda
  1/4  tsp. pumpkin pie spice
  1/8  tsp. ground cinnamon
Dash salt
  1/2  cup fat-free milk
  1/3  cup vanilla yogurt
  1/3  cup canned pumpkin
    1  egg, lightly beaten
    1  Tbsp. canola oil
  1/8  tsp. vanilla extract
Maple syrup

**1.** In a large bowl, combine the first eight ingredients. In another bowl, whisk the milk, yogurt, pumpkin, egg, oil and vanilla; stir into dry ingredients just until moistened.

**2.** Pour batter by 1/2 cupfuls onto a hot griddle coated with cooking spray; turn when bubbles form on top. Cook until the second side is golden brown. Serve with syrup.

**Nutrition Facts:** 2 pancakes (calculated without syrup) equals 360 calories, 11 g fat (2 g saturated fat), 109 mg cholesterol, 579 mg sodium, 55 g carbohydrate, 5 g fiber, 13 g protein.

# Baked Blueberry & Peach Oatmeal M

**PREP:** 20 min. **BAKE:** 35 min. **YIELD:** 9 servings

**ROSEMARIE WELESKI • NATRONA HEIGHTS, PENNSYLVANIA**

*This oatmeal bake is a staple in our home. It's very easy to prepare the night before; just keep the dry and wet ingredients separate until ready to bake. I've tried a variety of fruits, but the blueberry and peach is the most requested combo.*

- 3 cups old-fashioned oats
- 1/2 cup packed brown sugar
- 2 tsp. baking powder
- 1/2 tsp. salt
- 2 egg whites
- 1 egg
- 1-1/4 cups fat-free milk
- 1/4 cup canola oil
- 1 tsp. vanilla extract
- 1 can (15 oz.) sliced peaches in juice, drained and chopped
- 1 cup fresh *or* frozen blueberries
- 1/3 cup chopped walnuts
- Additional fat-free milk, optional

**1.** In a large bowl, combine the oats, brown sugar, baking powder and salt. Whisk the egg whites, egg, milk, oil and vanilla; add to dry ingredients and stir until blended. Let stand for 5 minutes. Stir in peaches and blueberries.

**2.** Transfer to an 11-in. x 7-in. baking dish coated with cooking spray. Sprinkle with walnuts. Bake, uncovered, at 350° for 35-40 minutes or until top is lightly browned and a thermometer reads 160°. Serve with additional milk if desired.

**Nutrition Facts:** 1 serving (calculated without additional milk) equals 277 calories, 11 g fat (1 g saturated fat), 24 mg cholesterol, 263 mg sodium, 38 g carbohydrate, 3 g fiber, 8 g protein. **Diabetic Exchanges:** 2 starch, 2 fat, 1/2 fruit.

# Waffle Sandwich

**PREP/TOTAL TIME:** 20 min. **YIELD:** 1 serving

**MICHELE MCHENRY • BELLINGHAM, WASHINGTON**

*Keep 'em going right through to lunchtime with this quick and hefty breakfast sandwich idea!*

- 1 slice Canadian bacon
- 1 egg
- 1 green onion, chopped
- 2 frozen low-fat multigrain waffles
- 1 Tbsp. shredded reduced-fat cheddar cheese

**1.** In a small nonstick skillet coated with cooking spray, cook bacon for 1-2 minutes on each side or until lightly browned. Remove and keep warm.

**2.** Whisk egg and green onion. In the same skillet, add egg mixture. Cook and stir until completely set.

**3.** Meanwhile, prepare waffles according to package directions. Place one waffle on a plate. Layer with bacon, egg mixture, cheese and remaining waffle.

**Nutrition Facts:** 1 sandwich equals 261 calories, 10 g fat (3 g saturated fat), 223 mg cholesterol, 733 mg sodium, 30 g carbohydrate, 3 g fiber, 16 g protein. **Diabetic Exchanges:** 2 starch, 2 medium-fat meat.

# Makeover Overnight French Toast M

**PREP:** 15 min. + chilling **BAKE:** 25 min. **YIELD:** 8 servings

**SONYA LABBE • LOS ANGELES, CALIFORNIA**

*We tried this lighter version recently, and the whole family really loved it! You can bet this dish is going to become a brand-new family favorite.*

- 4 eggs
- 1 cup egg substitute
- 3 cups fat-free milk
- 1/4 cup sugar
- 2 tsp. vanilla extract
- 1/4 tsp. salt
- 16 slices French bread (1 in. thick)

BERRY SAUCE:
- 2 pkg. (12 oz. *each*) frozen unsweetened mixed berries, thawed
- 1/4 cup sugar

**1.** In a large bowl, combine the eggs, egg substitute, milk, sugar, vanilla and salt. Place bread slices in two ungreased 13-in. x 9-in. baking dishes; pour egg mixture over top. Cover and refrigerate overnight.

**2.** Coat two 15-in. x 10-in. x 1-in. baking pans with butter-flavored cooking spray. Carefully transfer bread to prepared pans. Bake, uncovered, at 400° for 15 minutes. Carefully turn slices over. Bake 10-15 minutes longer or until golden and slightly puffed.

**3.** Meanwhile, combine berries and sugar. Serve with French toast.

**Nutrition Facts:** 2 slices French toast with 1/3 cup sauce equals 294 calories, 4 g fat (1 g saturated fat), 108 mg cholesterol, 486 mg sodium, 50 g carbohydrate, 3 g fiber, 13 g protein.

MAKEOVER OVERNIGHT FRENCH TOAST

# Makeover Farm Girl Breakfast Casserole C M

PREP: 15 min. BAKE: 35 min. YIELD: 8 servings

**NANCY ZIMMERMAN • CAPE MAY COURT HOUSE, NEW JERSEY**

*I served this lightened-up makeover casserole to my husband, Ken. He said it was fluffy and very good!*

- 4 eggs
- 1-1/2 cups egg substitute
- 1/2 cup all-purpose flour
- 1 tsp. baking powder
- 2 cups (16 oz.) 1% cottage cheese
- 2 cups (8 oz.) shredded reduced-fat Monterey Jack cheese *or* reduced-fat Mexican cheese blend, *divided*
- 1 can (4 oz.) chopped green chilies

**1.** In a large bowl, beat eggs and egg substitute on medium-high speed for 3 minutes or until light and lemon-colored. Combine flour and baking powder; gradually add to egg mixture and mix well. Stir in the cottage cheese, 1-1/2 cups shredded cheese and chilies.

**2.** Pour into a 13-in. x 9-in. baking dish coated with cooking spray. Bake, uncovered, at 350° for 35-40 minutes or until a knife inserted near the center comes out clean. Sprinkle with remaining cheese. Let stand for 5 minutes before serving.

**Nutrition Facts:** 1 piece equals 210 calories, 9 g fat (4 g saturated fat), 128 mg cholesterol, 665 mg sodium, 10 g carbohydrate, trace fiber, 24 g protein.

MAKEOVER FARM GIRL BREAKFAST CASSEROLE

# Southwestern Eggs Benedict

PREP: 35 min. COOK: 10 min. YIELD: 4 servings

**CATHY HALL • PHOENIX, ARIZONA**

*This colorful dish makes a beautiful, hearty, rise-and-shine breakfast. The potatoes and pepper are tender; the poached eggs are perfect; and the flavor combination is wonderful.*

- 4 medium red potatoes, cubed
- 3 Tbsp. water
- 1 small sweet red pepper, sliced
- 1/2 cup sliced sweet onion
- 2 tsp. olive oil
- 4 turkey bacon strips, chopped and cooked
- 1/4 tsp. salt
- 1/4 tsp. pepper

SAUCE:
- 1-1/2 tsp. butter
- 1 Tbsp. all-purpose flour
- 1/8 tsp. salt
- 1/8 tsp. pepper
- 3/4 cup fat-free milk
- 1/4 cup shredded reduced-fat Colby-Monterey Jack cheese
- 1 Tbsp. chopped green chilies

EGGS:
- 1 Tbsp. white vinegar
- 4 eggs
  Chopped plum tomatoes and minced fresh cilantro, optional

**1.** Place potatoes and water in a microwave-safe dish. Cover and microwave on high for 4-5 minutes or until tender; drain. In a large skillet, saute pepper and onion in oil until onion is tender. Add the potatoes, bacon, salt and pepper; saute 8-10 minutes longer or until potatoes are lightly browned.

**2.** In a small saucepan, melt butter. Stir in the flour, salt and pepper until smooth. Gradually add milk. Bring to a boil; cook and stir for 1 minute or until thickened. Stir in cheese and chilies; cook and stir until cheese is melted.

**3.** Meanwhile, place 2-3 in. of water in a large skillet with high sides; add vinegar. Bring to a boil; reduce heat and simmer gently. Break cold eggs, one at a time, into a custard cup or saucer; holding the cup close to the surface of the water, slip each egg into water.

**4.** Cook, uncovered, until whites are completely set and yolks are still soft, about 4 minutes. Divide potato mixture among four plates. Using a slotted spoon, lift eggs out of water and place on potato mixture. Top with sauce; sprinkle with tomatoes and cilantro if desired.

**Nutrition Facts:** 1 cup potato mixture with 1 poached egg and 2 Tbsp. sauce (calculated without optional ingredients) equals 277 calories, 13 g fat (5 g saturated fat), 235 mg cholesterol, 585 mg sodium, 26 g carbohydrate, 3 g fiber, 14 g protein. **Diabetic Exchanges:** 2 medium-fat meat, 1 starch, 1 fat.

# Yogurt Pancakes M

**PREP:** 15 min.  **COOK:** 5 min./batch  **YIELD:** 12 pancakes

**CHERYLL BABER • HOMEDALE, IDAHO**

*Get your day off to a great start. Short on time? Make a batch on the weekend.*

- 2 cups all-purpose flour
- 2 Tbsp. sugar
- 2 tsp. baking powder
- 1 tsp. baking soda
- 2 eggs
- 2 cups (16 oz.) plain yogurt
- 1/4 cup water

Semisweet chocolate chips, dried cranberries, sliced ripe bananas and coarsely chopped pecans, optional

**1.** In a small bowl, combine the flour, sugar, baking powder and baking soda. In another bowl, whisk the eggs, yogurt and water. Stir into dry ingredients just until moistened.

**2.** Pour batter by 1/4 cupfuls onto a hot griddle coated with cooking spray. Sprinkle with optional ingredients if desired. Turn when bubbles form on top; cook until the second side is golden brown.

**3.** To freeze, arrange cooled pancakes in a single layer on sheet pans. Freeze overnight or until frozen. Transfer to a resealable plastic freezer bag. May be frozen for up to 2 months.

**To use frozen pancakes:** Place pancake on a microwave-safe plate; microwave on high for 40-50 seconds or until heated through.

**Nutrition Facts:** 2 pancakes (calculated without optional ingredients) equals 242 calories, 5 g fat (2 g saturated fat), 81 mg cholesterol, 403 mg sodium, 40 g carbohydrate, 1 g fiber, 9 g protein. **Diabetic Exchange:** 3 starch.

DELIGHTFUL APPLE-PINEAPPLE DRINK

# Delightful Apple-Pineapple Drink  F  S

PREP: 5 min.  COOK: 30 min.  YIELD: 8 servings

**NANCY JOHNSON • LAVERNE, OKLAHOMA**

*Chase winter doldrums and chills with this warm and tangy fruit drink that will appeal to both kids and adults. Not overly sweet, it has a nice touch of nutmeg and cinnamon.*

|       |                                    |
|-------|------------------------------------|
| 4     | cups unsweetened apple juice       |
| 4     | cups unsweetened pineapple juice   |
| 2     | Tbsp. lemon juice                  |
| 2     | Tbsp. honey                        |
| 4     | cinnamon sticks (3 in.)            |
| 1/8   | tsp. ground nutmeg                 |

Additional cinnamon sticks (3 in.), optional

**1.** In a large saucepan, combine the juices, honey, cinnamon sticks and nutmeg. Bring to a boil. Reduce heat; simmer, uncovered, for 25-30 minutes or until flavors are blended. Discard cinnamon. Serve warm in mugs with additional cinnamon sticks if desired.

**Nutrition Facts:** 1 cup equals 142 calories, trace fat (trace saturated fat), 0 cholesterol, 6 mg sodium, 35 g carbohydrate, trace fiber, 1 g protein.

# Prosciutto Egg Panini

PREP/TOTAL TIME: 30 min.  YIELD: 8 servings

**ERIN RENOUF MYLROIE • SANTA CLARA, UTAH**

*Try a yummy new twist on the usual bacon and egg sandwich. It's a breakfast worth waking up for!*

|       |                                    |
|-------|------------------------------------|
| 3     | eggs                               |
| 2     | egg whites                         |
| 6     | Tbsp. fat-free milk                |
| 1     | green onion, thinly sliced         |
| 1     | Tbsp. Dijon mustard                |
| 1     | Tbsp. maple syrup                  |
| 8     | slices sourdough bread             |
| 8     | thin slices prosciutto *or* deli ham |
| 1/2   | cup shredded sharp cheddar cheese  |
| 8     | tsp. butter                        |

**1.** In a small bowl, whisk the eggs, egg whites, milk and onion. Coat a large skillet with cooking spray and place over medium heat. Add egg mixture; cook and stir over medium heat until completely set.

**2.** Combine mustard and syrup; spread over four bread slices. Layer with scrambled eggs, prosciutto and cheese; top with remaining bread. Butter outsides of sandwiches.

**3.** Cook on a panini maker or indoor grill for 3-4 minutes or until bread is browned and cheese is melted. Cut each panini in half to serve.

**Nutrition Facts:** 1/2 sandwich equals 228 calories, 10 g fat (5 g saturated fat), 111 mg cholesterol, 640 mg sodium, 21 g carbohydrate, 1 g fiber, 13 g protein. **Diabetic Exchanges:** 1-1/2 starch, 1-1/2 fat, 1 lean meat.

# Mini Ham 'n' Cheese Frittatas  C

PREP: 15 min.  BAKE: 25 min.  YIELD: 8 servings

**SUSAN WATT • BASKING RIDGE, NEW JERSEY**

*Portion control is easy with these healthful mini frittatas—and so is breakfast!*

|       |                                           |
|-------|-------------------------------------------|
| 1/4   | lb. cubed fully cooked ham                |
| 1     | cup (4 oz.) shredded fat-free cheddar cheese |
| 6     | eggs                                      |
| 4     | egg whites                                |
| 3     | Tbsp. minced chives                       |
| 2     | Tbsp. fat-free milk                       |
| 1/4   | tsp. salt                                 |
| 1/4   | tsp. pepper                               |

**1.** Divide ham among eight muffin cups coated with cooking spray; top with cheese. In a large bowl, beat eggs and whites. Beat in the chives, milk, salt and pepper. Pour over cheese, filling each muffin cup three-fourths full.

**2.** Bake at 375° for 22-25 minutes or until a knife inserted near the center comes out clean. Carefully run a knife around edges to loosen; remove from pan. Serve warm.

**Nutrition Facts:** 1 frittata equals 106 calories, 4 g fat (1 g saturated fat), 167 mg cholesterol, 428 mg sodium, 2 g carbohydrate, trace fiber, 14 g protein. **Diabetic Exchange:** 2 medium-fat meat.

PROSCIUTTO EGG PANINI

MINI HAM 'N' CHEESE FRITTATAS

# Gluten-Free Banana Pancakes

**PREP:** 15 min. **COOK:** 5 min./batch **YIELD:** 12 pancakes

**SHAREN GUSTAFSON • SOUTH LYON, MICHIGAN**

*When one of my sons and I had to change to a gluten-free diet, I searched for recipes that tasted great. These pancakes are low-cal as well. I cook extras and freeze them. Then, when I'm short on time, I toss a couple in the toaster. You'll love the chocolate flavor and fluffy texture.*

| | |
|---|---|
| 1 | cup gluten-free all-purpose baking flour |
| 3 | tsp. baking powder |
| 1/2 | tsp. salt |
| 2/3 | cup gluten-free rice milk |
| 1/4 | cup unsweetened applesauce |
| 2 | Tbsp. olive oil |
| 3 | tsp. vanilla extract |
| 1-1/3 | cups mashed ripe bananas (3 medium) |
| 1/2 | cup semisweet chocolate chips, optional |

Maple syrup

**1.** In a large bowl, combine the flour, baking powder and salt. In another bowl, whisk the rice milk, applesauce, oil and vanilla; stir into dry ingredients just until moistened. Stir in bananas and chocolate chips if desired.

**2.** Pour batter by 1/4 cupfuls onto a hot griddle coated with cooking spray; turn when bubbles form on top. Cook until the second side is golden brown. Serve with syrup.

GLUTEN-FREE BANANA PANCAKES

**Editor's Note:** Read all ingredient labels for possible gluten content prior to use. Ingredient formulas can change, and production facilities vary among brands. If you're concerned that your brand may contain gluten, contact the company.

**Nutrition Facts:** 2 pancakes (calculated without chocolate chips and syrup) equals 173 calories, 6 g fat (1 g saturated fat), 0 cholesterol, 407 mg sodium, 30 g carbohydrate, 3 g fiber, 3 g protein. **Diabetic Exchanges:** 2 starch, 1 fat.

# Good Mornin' Pancake Mix

**PREP:** 15 min. **COOK:** 5 min./batch
**YIELD:** 10 pancakes per batch

**SHARON SUTTON • LINDSEY, OHIO**

*I love these moist, fluffy pancakes on a wintry day. They make a perfect gift for family and friends. Just put the mix in two plastic bags tied with ribbons, and don't forget to include the easy prep directions.*

| | |
|---|---|
| 2 | cups all-purpose flour |
| 1-1/4 | cups whole wheat flour |
| 1 | cup buttermilk blend powder |
| 1 | cup old-fashioned oats |
| 1/3 | cup sugar |
| 3 | Tbsp. baking powder |
| 3 | tsp. baking soda |
| 1 | tsp. dried orange peel |
| 1/2 | tsp. ground cinnamon |
| 1 | cup golden raisins |
| 1 | cup sliced almonds, toasted |

ADDITIONAL INGREDIENTS (FOR EACH BATCH):

| | |
|---|---|
| 1 | egg |
| 3/4 | cup water |
| 2 | Tbsp. canola oil |

**1.** Place the first nine ingredients in a food processor; cover and process until oats are ground. Place 1 cup in each of four resealable plastic bags. In each of four separate resealable plastic bags, place 1/4 cup raisins and 1/4 cup almonds. Store for up to 6 months. **Yield:** 4 batches (6 cups mix).

**2.** To prepare pancakes, in a large bowl, combine the contents of one pancake mix bag and one fruit-nut bag. In a small bowl, whisk the egg, water and oil. Stir into dry ingredients just until moistened.

**3.** Pour batter by 1/4 cupfuls onto a hot griddle coated with cooking spray. Turn when bubbles form on top; cook until second side is golden brown.

**Nutrition Facts:** 2 pancakes equals 236 calories, 10 g fat (1 g saturated fat), 46 mg cholesterol, 416 mg sodium, 31 g carbohydrate, 3 g fiber, 8 g protein. **Diabetic Exchanges:** 2 starch, 1 fat.

# Delectable Granola

**PREP:** 20 min. **BAKE:** 30 min. + cooling **YIELD:** 11 cups

**LORI STEVENS • RIVERTON, UTAH**

*A great make-ahead recipe! Be sure to remove from the cookie sheets within 20 minutes after baking to prevent sticking.*

| | |
|---|---|
| 8 | cups old-fashioned oats |
| 1 | cup finely chopped almonds |
| 1 | cup finely chopped pecans |

1/2 cup flaked coconut
1/2 cup packed brown sugar
1/2 cup canola oil
1/2 cup honey
1/4 cup maple syrup
2 tsp. ground cinnamon
1-1/2 tsp. salt
2 tsp. vanilla extract
Plain yogurt, optional

**1.** In a large bowl, combine the oats, almonds, pecans and coconut. In a small saucepan, combine the brown sugar, oil, honey, maple syrup, cinnamon and salt. Heat for 3-4 minutes over medium heat until sugar is dissolved. Remove from the heat; stir in vanilla. Pour over the oat mixture; stir to coat.

**2.** Transfer to two 15-in. x 10-in. x 1-in. baking pans coated with cooking spray. Bake at 350° for 30-35 minutes or until crisp, stirring every 10 minutes.

Cool completely on wire racks. Store in an airtight container. Serve with yogurt if desired.

**Nutrition Facts:** 1/2 cup (calculated without yogurt) equals 288 calories, 15 g fat (2 g saturated fat), 0 cholesterol, 170 mg sodium, 36 g carbohydrate, 4 g fiber, 6 g protein. **Diabetic Exchanges:** 2-1/2 starch, 2 fat.

To soften brown sugar, place a slice of bread or an apple wedge with it in a covered container for a few days. If you're in a hurry, microwave the **brown sugar** on high for 20-30 seconds. Repeat if necessary, watching it carefully, because the sugar will begin to melt. Always store brown sugar in an airtight container.

MOM'S SLOPPY TACOS

PORK 'N' POTATO SKILLET

MEXICAN BEANS AND RICE

One of the hardest parts about maintaining a healthy diet is cooking light on busy nights. The next time the kitchen clock is ticking, turn to this chapter of quick family favorites instead. Each dish is ready in 30 minutes!

## Pork 'n' Potato Skillet

**PREP/TOTAL TIME:** 20 min. **YIELD:** 4 servings

**MARY TALLMAN • ARBOR VITAE, WISCONSIN**

*This scrumptious skillet dinner makes the ideal hurry-up entree for a hungry family. Round out the meal with steamed vegetables or a rustic green salad.*

| | |
|---|---|
| 4 | boneless pork loin chops (1 in. thick and 4 oz. *each*) |
| 1/4 | tsp. pepper |
| 1 | Tbsp. olive oil |
| 4 | medium red potatoes, thinly sliced |
| 1 | medium onion, sliced |
| 1 | tsp. dried oregano |
| 1 | cup chicken broth |
| 1/2 | cup diced roasted sweet red peppers |

**1.** Sprinkle pork chops with pepper. In a large skillet, cook chops in oil over medium heat for 2-3 minutes on each side or until chops are lightly browned; drain. Remove and keep warm.

**2.** In the same skillet, saute the potatoes, onion and oregano for 6-8 minutes or until potatoes are almost tender. Stir in broth and red peppers; bring to a boil.

**3.** Top with pork chops. Reduce heat; cover and simmer for 4-6 minutes or until a thermometer reads 145°, stirring occasionally. Let stand 5 minutes before serving.

**Nutrition Facts:** 1 serving (prepared with reduced-sodium broth) equals 292 calories, 10 g fat (3 g saturated fat), 55 mg cholesterol, 297 mg sodium, 24 g carbohydrate, 3 g fiber, 26 g protein. **Diabetic Exchanges:** 3 lean meat, 1 starch, 1 vegetable.

## Sweet Mustard Salmon C

**PREP/TOTAL TIME:** 25 min. **YIELD:** 4 servings

**CORTNEY CLAESON • SPOKANE, WASHINGTON**

*Lemon juice, mustard and brown sugar add something special to this salmon dish.*

| | |
|---|---|
| 4 | salmon fillets (6 oz. *each*) |
| 2 | Tbsp. lemon juice |
| 3 | Tbsp. yellow mustard |
| 1/4 | cup packed brown sugar |

**1.** Place salmon on a 15-in. x 10-in. x 1-in. baking pan coated with cooking spray. Drizzle with lemon juice; brush with mustard. Sprinkle with brown sugar.

**2.** Bake, uncovered, at 375° for 12-15 minutes or until fish flakes easily with a fork.

**Nutrition Facts:** 1 fillet equals 326 calories, 16 g fat (3 g saturated fat), 85 mg cholesterol, 218 mg sodium, 15 g carbohydrate, trace fiber, 29 g protein. **Diabetic Exchanges:** 4 lean meat, 1-1/2 fat, 1 starch.

## Mexican Beans and Rice M

**PREP/TOTAL TIME:** 30 min. **YIELD:** 4 servings

**LORRAINE CALAND • THUNDER BAY, ONTARIO**

*This skillet supper is terrific for a cold or rainy day. It's easy, comforting and really fills the tummy. Sometimes I switch up pinto beans for kidney beans or white rice for brown.*

| | |
|---|---|
| 2 | celery ribs, chopped |
| 1 | medium green pepper, chopped |
| 1 | medium onion, chopped |
| 1 | Tbsp. canola oil |
| 1 | can (28 oz.) diced tomatoes, undrained |
| 1 | can (16 oz.) kidney beans, rinsed and drained |
| 2 | cups cooked brown rice |
| 2 | tsp. Worcestershire sauce |
| 1-1/2 | tsp. chili powder |
| 1/4 | tsp. pepper |
| 1/4 | cup shredded cheddar cheese |
| 1/4 | cup reduced-fat sour cream |
| 2 | green onions, chopped |

**1.** In a large nonstick skillet, saute the celery, green pepper and onion in oil until tender.

**2.** Stir in the tomatoes, beans, rice, Worcestershire sauce, chili powder and pepper. Bring to a boil. Reduce heat; cover and simmer for 7-9 minutes or until heated through. Top with cheese, sour cream and green onions.

**Nutrition Facts:** 1-1/2 cups equals 354 calories, 8 g fat (3 g saturated fat), 13 mg cholesterol, 549 mg sodium, 58 g carbohydrate, 12 g fiber, 15 g protein.

# Chicken Stir-Fry with Noodles

PREP/TOTAL TIME: 30 min. YIELD: 4 servings

**BEVERLY NORRIS • EVANSTON, WYOMING**

*This nutritious meal is fast-fixing, filling and full of flavor and vitamins. Feel free to garnish individual servings with a sprinkling of chopped pecans or green onions. For extra crunch, try adding a handful of chow mein noodles right before serving.*

|     |     |
|-----|-----|
| 8 | oz. uncooked whole wheat spaghetti |
| 1 | head bok choy (16 oz.) |
| 1 | lb. boneless skinless chicken breasts, cubed |
| 2 | Tbsp. canola oil, *divided* |
| 1 | celery rib, sliced |
| 1/2 | cup chopped green pepper |
| 1/2 | cup chopped sweet red pepper |
| 1/3 | cup chopped onion |
| 6 | Tbsp. reduced-sodium teriyaki sauce |

**1.** Cook the spaghetti according to package. directions; drain.

**2.** Meanwhile, cut off and discard root end of bok choy. Cut leaves from stalks; coarsely chop and set aside. Cut stalks into 1-in. pieces.

**3.** In a large skillet or wok, stir-fry chicken in 1 Tbsp. oil until no longer pink. Remove and keep warm.

**4.** Stir-fry the bok choy stalks, celery, peppers and onion in remaining oil for 4 minutes. Add bok choy

leaves; stir-fry 2-4 minutes longer or until vegetables are crisp-tender. Stir in teriyaki sauce. Add chicken and spaghetti; heat through.

**Nutrition Facts:** 1-1/2 cups equals 434 calories, 11 g fat (1 g saturated fat), 63 mg cholesterol, 623 mg sodium, 53 g carbohydrate, 9 g fiber, 35 g protein.

# Honey Chicken Stir-Fry

PREP/TOTAL TIME: 30 min. YIELD: 4 servings

**CAROLINE SPERRY • ALLENTOWN, MICHIGAN**

*I'm a new mom, and my schedule is very dependent upon our young son. So I like meals that can be ready in as little time as possible. This all-in-one stir-fry with a hint of sweetness from honey is a big time-saver.*

|     |     |
|-----|-----|
| 1 | lb. boneless skinless chicken breasts, cut into 1-in. pieces |
| 1 | garlic clove, minced |
| 3 | tsp. olive oil, *divided* |
| 3 | Tbsp. honey |
| 2 | Tbsp. reduced-sodium soy sauce |
| 1/8 | tsp. salt |
| 1/8 | tsp. pepper |
| 1 | pkg. (16 oz.) frozen broccoli stir-fry vegetable blend |
| 2 | tsp. cornstarch |
| 1 | Tbsp. cold water |

Hot cooked rice

**1.** In a large nonstick skillet, stir-fry chicken and garlic in 2 tsp. oil for 1 minute. Add the honey, soy sauce, salt and pepper. Cook and stir until chicken is lightly browned and no longer pink. Remove the chicken and keep warm.

**2.** In the same pan, stir-fry the vegetables in remaining oil for 4-5 minutes or until tender. Return chicken to the pan; stir to coat. Combine cornstarch and cold water until smooth; gradually stir into chicken mixture. Bring to a boil; cook and stir for 1 minute or until thickened. Serve with rice.

**Nutrition Facts:** 1 cup stir-fry mixture (calculated without rice) equals 243 calories, 5 g fat (1 g saturated fat), 66 mg cholesterol, 470 mg sodium, 19 g carbohydrate, 3 g fiber, 28 g protein. **Diabetic Exchanges:** 3 lean meat, 3 vegetable.

# Shrimp Orzo with Feta

PREP/TOTAL TIME: 25 min. YIELD: 4 servings

**SARAH HUMMEL • MOON TOWNSHIP, PENNSYLVANIA**

*Simple yet special, this refreshing pasta dish is one of my favorites. You can serve it as a main course or as a side.*

|     |     |
|-----|-----|
| 1-1/4 | cups uncooked whole wheat orzo pasta |
| 2 | garlic cloves, minced |
| 2 | Tbsp. olive oil |
| 2 | medium tomatoes, chopped |
| 2 | Tbsp. lemon juice |
| 1-1/4 | lbs. uncooked large shrimp, peeled and deveined |
| 2 | Tbsp. minced fresh cilantro |
| 1/4 | tsp. pepper |
| 1/2 | cup crumbled feta cheese |

CHICKEN STIR-FRY WITH NOODLES

**1.** Cook orzo according to package directions.
Meanwhile, in a large skillet, saute garlic in oil for
 minute. Add tomatoes and lemon juice. Bring to a
 oil. Reduce heat; stir in shrimp. Simmer, uncovered,
 or 4-5 minutes or until shrimp turn pink.

**2.** Drain orzo. Add the orzo, cilantro and pepper to
 he shrimp mixture; heat through. Sprinkle with the
 eta cheese.

**Nutrition Facts:** 1 cup equals 406 calories, 12 g fat (3 g
 aturated fat), 180 mg cholesterol, 307 mg sodium, 40 g
 arbohydrate, 9 g fiber, 33 g protein. **Diabetic Exchanges:**
 lean meat, 2 starch, 1 fat.

# Simple Chicken Soup  F

**PREP/TOTAL TIME:** 20 min.  **YIELD:** 6 servings

UE WEST • ALVORD, TEXAS

*revised a recipe that my family loved so it would be lighter
nd easier to make. It's a hearty and healthy meal served with
 green salad and fresh bread.*

2 cans (14-1/2 oz. *each*) reduced-sodium
  chicken broth
1 Tbsp. dried minced onion
1 pkg. (16 oz.) frozen mixed vegetables
2 cups cubed cooked chicken breast
2 cans (10-3/4 oz. *each*) reduced-fat
  reduced-sodium condensed cream of chicken
  soup, undiluted

**1.** In a large saucepan, bring broth and onion to a
boil. Reduce heat. Add the vegetables; cover and cook
for 6-8 minutes or until crisp-tender. Stir in chicken
and soup; heat through.

**Nutrition Facts:** 1-1/3 cups equals 195 calories, 3 g fat (1 g
saturated fat), 44 mg cholesterol, 820 mg sodium, 21 g
carbohydrate, 3 g fiber, 19 g protein.

When chicken pieces are on sale, try to buy several
packages and bake all of it at once. Bake the chicken skin
side up on foil-lined pans. When cooled, remove the skin
and bones, cube the meat and freeze **the chicken** in
measured portions to use in quick suppers.

CHICKEN CHOW MEIN

# Chicken Chow Mein

PREP/TOTAL TIME: 30 min.  YIELD: 2 servings

BETH DAUENHAUER • PUEBLO, COLORADO

*When we go out for Chinese food, my husband always orders chicken chow mein. I created this recipe using richer-flavored tamari sauce rather than soy.*

- 1 Tbsp. cornstarch
- 2/3 cup reduced-sodium chicken broth
- 1 tsp. reduced-sodium soy sauce
- 1/2 tsp. salt
- 1/4 tsp. ground ginger
- 1/4 lb. sliced fresh mushrooms
- 2/3 cup thinly sliced celery
- 1/4 cup sliced onion
- 1/4 cup thinly sliced green pepper
- 2 Tbsp. julienned carrot
- 1 tsp. canola oil
- 1 garlic clove, minced
- 1 cup cubed cooked chicken breast
- 1 cup cooked brown rice
- 2 Tbsp. chow mein noodles

**1.** In a small bowl, combine the cornstarch, broth, soy sauce, salt and ginger until smooth; set aside.

**2.** In a large skillet or wok, stir-fry the mushrooms, celery, onion, pepper and carrot in oil for 5 minutes. Add garlic; stir-fry 1-2 minutes longer or until vegetables are crisp-tender.

**3.** Stir cornstarch mixture and add to the pan. Bring to a boil; cook and stir for 2 minutes or until thickened. Add chicken; heat through. Serve with rice; sprinkle with chow mein noodles.

**Nutrition Facts:** 1 cup chow mein with 1/2 cup cooked brown rice and 1 Tbsp. chow mein noodles equals 307 calories, 7 g fat (1 g saturated fat), 54 mg cholesterol, 984 mg sodium, 35 g carbohydrate, 4 g fiber, 27 g protein. **Diabetic Exchanges:** 3 lean meat, 2 starch, 1 vegetable, 1/2 fat.

# Vegetable Pizza ⓜ

PREP/TOTAL TIME: 30 min.  YIELD: 8 slices

BEVERLY LITTLE • MARIETTA, GEORGIA

*An assortment of fresh veggies tops this delicious meatless pizza. Feel free to use any vegetables you like. I often add a few sliced black olives.*

- 1 tube (13.8 oz.) refrigerated pizza crust
- 1/2 cup sliced fresh mushrooms
- 1/2 cup chopped onion
- 1/2 cup chopped fresh broccoli
- 1/2 cup chopped green pepper
- 1/2 cup chopped fresh baby spinach
- 1 cup meatless spaghetti sauce
- 2 plum tomatoes, thinly sliced
- 2 cups (8 oz.) shredded part-skim mozzarella cheese

**1.** Unroll pizza crust into a 15-in. x 10-in. x 1-in. baking pan coated with cooking spray; flatten dough and build up edges slightly. Bake at 400° for 8 minutes.

**2.** Meanwhile, in a nonstick skillet coated with cooking spray, saute the mushrooms, onion, broccoli, green pepper and spinach until crisp-tender.

**3.** Spread spaghetti sauce over crust. Top with sauteed vegetables, tomatoes and cheese. Bake for 15-20 minutes or until crust is golden brown and cheese is melted. Let pizza stand for 10 minutes before serving.

**Nutrition Facts:** 1 serving equals 263 calories, 10 g fat (6 g saturated fat), 33 mg cholesterol, 644 mg sodium, 24 g carbohydrate, 2 g fiber, 18 g protein. **Diabetic Exchanges:** 1-1/2 starch, 1 medium-fat meat.

# Mom's Sloppy Tacos

PREP/TOTAL TIME: 30 min.  YIELD: 6 servings

KAMI JONES • AVONDALE, ARIZONA

*No matter how hectic the weeknight, there's always time to serve your family a healthy meal with recipes this easy and good!*

- 1-1/2 lbs. extra-lean ground beef (95% lean)
- 1 can (15 oz.) tomato sauce
- 3/4 tsp. garlic powder
- 1/2 tsp. salt
- 1/4 tsp. pepper
- 1/4 tsp. cayenne pepper
- 12 taco shells, warmed

Optional toppings: shredded lettuce and cheese, chopped tomatoes, avocado and olives

**1.** In a large skillet, cook beef over medium heat until no longer pink. Stir in the tomato sauce, garlic powder, salt, pepper and cayenne. Bring to a boil. Reduce heat; simmer, uncovered, for 10 minutes.

**2.** Fill each taco shell with 1/4 cup beef mixture and toppings of your choice.

**Nutrition Facts:** 2 tacos (calculated without optional toppings) equals 264 calories, 10 g fat (4 g saturated fat), 65 mg cholesterol, 669 mg sodium, 17 g carbohydrate, 1 g fiber, 25 g protein. **Diabetic Exchanges:** 3 lean meat, 1 starch, 1 fat.

MOM'S SLOPPY TACOS

# Honey-Mustard Chicken Sandwiches

PREP/TOTAL TIME: 20 min. YIELD: 4 servings

**CHRISTINA LEVRANT • HENDERSON, NEVADA**

*These hearty, mouthwatering sandwiches are homemade "fast food" more delicious than the kind you go out for.*

| | |
|---|---|
| 1/4 | cup Dijon mustard |
| 2 | Tbsp. honey |
| 1 | tsp. dried oregano |
| 1 | tsp. water |
| 1/4 | tsp. garlic powder |
| 1/8 to 1/4 | tsp. cayenne pepper |
| 4 | boneless skinless chicken breast halves (4 oz. *each*) |
| 4 | sandwich buns, split |
| 1 | cup shredded lettuce |
| 8 | thin tomato slices |

**1.** In a small bowl, combine the first six ingredients. Broil chicken 4 in. from the heat for 4-7 minutes on each side or until a thermometer reads 170°, brushing occasionally with mustard mixture. Serve on buns with lettuce and tomato.

**Nutrition Facts:** 1 sandwich equals 391 calories, 7 g fat (2 g saturated fat), 63 mg cholesterol, 813 mg sodium, 49 g carbohydrate, 2 g fiber, 32 g protein. **Diabetic Exchanges:** 3 starch, 3 lean meat.

# Favorite Layered Salad

PREP/TOTAL TIME: 20 min. YIELD: 8 servings

**JODI ANDERSON • OVERBROOK, KANSAS**

*Perfect for potlucks, this salad offers the best that summer produce has to offer, and it looks so beautiful layered in a glass bowl. It's almost too pretty to dig into—almost!*

| | |
|---|---|
| 2 | cups torn romaine |
| 2 | cups fresh baby spinach |
| 1 | cup sliced fresh mushrooms |
| 1 | cup grape tomatoes |
| 1/2 | cup shredded carrot |
| 1 | medium red onion, halved and sliced |
| 1 | medium sweet red pepper, chopped |
| 1 | medium cucumber, sliced |
| 1 | cup frozen peas, thawed |
| 1/2 | cup Miracle Whip Light |
| 3 | Tbsp. sugar |
| 1/2 | cup shredded cheddar cheese |
| 3 | Tbsp. crumbled cooked bacon |

**1.** In a 3-qt. trifle bowl or glass bowl, combine romaine and spinach. Layer with mushrooms, tomatoes, carrot, onion, pepper, cucumber and peas.

**2.** Combine the Miracle Whip and sugar; spread over the peas. Sprinkle with the cheese and bacon. Chill until serving.

**Nutrition Facts:** 1-1/2 cups equals 131 calories, 6 g fat (2 g saturated fat), 14 mg cholesterol, 293 mg sodium, 16 g carbohydrate, 3 g fiber, 5 g protein. **Diabetic Exchanges:** 1 vegetable, 1 fat, 1/2 starch.

FAVORITE LAYERED SALAD

HONEY-MUSTARD CHICKEN SANDWICHES

# Asian Chicken with Pasta

**PREP/TOTAL TIME:** 25 min. **YIELD:** 6 servings

**REBECCA SAMS • OAK HARBOR, OHIO**

*Mild flavors make this a dish even picky eaters will like. The coleslaw mix brings a pleasing crunch to the veggie-filled recipe.*

1/2 lb. uncooked angel hair pasta
1 lb. chicken tenderloins, cut into 1-in. cubes
1/3 cup prepared balsamic vinaigrette
1/3 cup prepared Italian salad dressing
1 pkg. (12 oz.) broccoli coleslaw mix
1/2 lb. sliced fresh mushrooms
3/4 cup julienned sweet red pepper
1/2 cup sliced onion
1/2 tsp. garlic powder
1/2 tsp. ground ginger
1/4 tsp. salt
1/8 tsp. pepper

**1.** Cook pasta according to package directions. Meanwhile, in a large skillet, saute chicken in vinaigrette and salad dressing until no longer pink. Remove and keep warm.

**2.** In the same skillet, saute the coleslaw mix, mushrooms, red pepper and onion until tender. Add the seasonings. Stir in the chicken; heat through. Drain pasta. Add to chicken mixture; toss to coat.

**Nutrition Facts:** 1-1/2 cups equals 320 calories, 8 g fat (1 g saturated fat), 44 mg cholesterol, 474 mg sodium, 38 g carbohydrate, 4 g fiber, 25 g protein. **Diabetic Exchanges:** 3 lean meat, 2 starch, 1 vegetable, 1 fat.

# Garden Vegetable Wraps

**PREP/TOTAL TIME:** 25 min. **YIELD:** 4 servings

**BARBARA BLAKE • WEST BRATTLEBORO, VERMONT**

*My husband and I love these light, tasty wraps for lunch. I found the recipe years ago, and it was an instant hit.*

1/2 cup reduced-fat garlic-herb cheese spread
4 flour tortillas (10 in.)
1-1/4 cups chopped seeded tomatoes
1-1/4 cups julienned fresh spinach
3/4 cup chopped sweet red pepper
2 bacon strips, cooked and crumbled
1/4 tsp. coarsely ground pepper

**1.** Spread 2 Tbsp. cheese spread over each tortilla. Top with tomatoes, spinach, red pepper, bacon and pepper. Roll up tightly.

**Nutrition Facts:** 1 wrap equals 314 calories, 10 g fat (5 g saturated fat), 21 mg cholesterol, 614 mg sodium, 37 g carbohydrate, 8 g fiber, 12 g protein. **Diabetic Exchanges:** 2-1/2 starch, 2 fat, 1 vegetable.

SWEET & SPICY SALMON FILLETS

## Sweet & Spicy Salmon Fillets C

PREP/TOTAL TIME: 25 min.  YIELD: 4 servings

**SUSAN BORDERS • GALENA, OHIO**

*Tender and moist, this baked salmon has a hit of heat, and a mango salsa lends sweetness. Stir any leftover salsa into chili.*

|   |   |
|---|---|
| 4 | salmon fillets (6 oz. *each*) |
| 1/2 | tsp. garlic powder |
| 1/2 | tsp. cayenne pepper |
| 3/4 | cup mango salsa |

**1.** Place salmon on a 15-in. x 10-in. baking pan coated with cooking spray. Sprinkle with garlic powder and cayenne. Spoon salsa over top.

**2.** Bake at 375° for 12-15 minutes or until fish flakes easily with a fork.

**Nutrition Facts:** 1 fillet equals 281 calories, 16 g fat (3 g saturated fat), 85 mg cholesterol, 355 mg sodium, 2 g carbohydrate, trace fiber, 29 g protein. **Diabetic Exchanges:** 4 lean meat, 2 fat.

## Better Than Fried Shrimp F S C

PREP/TOTAL TIME: 30 min.  YIELD: 2-1/2 dozen

**CHER SCHWARTZ • ELLISVILLE, MISSOURI**

*Coating with panko bread crumbs, spraying with cooking spray and then baking give this shrimp a wonderful crunch without all the saturated fat and calories of deep-frying.*

|   |   |
|---|---|
| 1-1/2 | cups panko (Japanese) bread crumbs |
| 2 | egg whites |
| 1 | Tbsp. fat-free milk |
| 3 | Tbsp. all-purpose flour |
| 3 | tsp. seafood seasoning |
| 1/4 | tsp. salt |
| 1/4 | tsp. pepper |
| 30 | uncooked large shrimp, peeled and deveined |

Olive oil-flavored cooking spray

**1.** Place bread crumbs in a shallow bowl. In another shallow bowl, combine egg whites and milk. In a third shallow bowl, combine flour, seafood seasoning, salt and pepper. Dip shrimp in the flour mixture, egg mixture, then bread crumbs.

**2.** Place shrimp on a baking sheet coated with cooking spray; spritz shrimp with cooking spray.

**3.** Bake at 400° for 8-12 minutes or until shrimp turn pink and coating is golden brown, turning once.

**Nutrition Facts:** 1 shrimp equals 28 calories, 1 g fat (trace saturated fat), 20 mg cholesterol, 86 mg sodium, 2 g carbohydrate, trace fiber, 3 g protein.

## Pear Chutney Chicken

PREP/TOTAL TIME: 30 min.  YIELD: 4 servings

**SHEILA O'CONNELL BERG • LUCAS VALLEY, CALIFORNIA**

*With the unique combination of flavors in this recipe, dinner is sure to satisfy. My freezer is rarely without servings of this dish that my grandson calls "Pear Chix." We love it!*

|   |   |
|---|---|
| 1 | can (15-1/4 oz.) sliced pears |
| 4 | boneless skinless chicken breast halves (4 oz. *each*) |
| 2 | Tbsp. all-purpose flour |
| 1/4 | tsp. pepper |
| 2 | Tbsp. olive oil |
| 1/2 | cup chopped onion |
| 1/2 | cup mango chutney |
| 1 | to 2 Tbsp. lemon juice |
| 3/4 | to 1 tsp. curry powder |

**1.** Drain pears, reserving 1/4 cup juice; set pears and juice aside.

**2.** Flatten chicken to 1/4-in. thickness.

**3.** In a large resealable bag, combine flour and pepper. Add chicken in batches and shake to coat.

**4.** In a large skillet, cook chicken in oil over medium heat for 5-6 minutes on each side or until no longer pink. Remove and keep warm.

**5.** In the same skillet, combine the onion, chutney, lemon juice, curry powder and reserved pear juice. Bring to a boil.

**6.** Add chicken and pears. Reduce heat; simmer, uncovered, for 3-5 minutes or until heated through. Serve immediately.

**Nutrition Facts:** 1 serving equals 395 calories, 9 g fat (2 g saturated fat), 63 mg cholesterol, 404 mg sodium, 51 g carbohydrate, 1 g fiber, 24 g protein.

PEAR CHUTNEY CHICKEN

# Feta Shrimp Tacos

**PREP/TOTAL TIME:** 30 min.  **YIELD:** 4 servings

**ATHENA RUSSELL • FLORENCE, SOUTH CAROLINA**

*Taco seasoning and feta cheese work remarkably well together in these refreshing tacos. It's a good thing you get two per serving, because you won't want to stop at one!*

|   |   |
|---|---|
| 2 | cups shredded red cabbage |
| 1/4 | cup finely chopped sweet onion |
| 1 | banana pepper, finely chopped |
| 1/4 | cup Miracle Whip Light |
| 1 | Tbsp. cider vinegar |
| 1 | Tbsp. stone-ground mustard |
| 1/4 | tsp. pepper |
| 1 | lb. uncooked medium shrimp, peeled and deveined |
| 1 | Tbsp. reduced-sodium taco seasoning |
| 1 | Tbsp. olive oil |
| 8 | whole wheat tortillas (8 in.) |
| 3/4 | cup crumbled feta cheese |

Sliced avocado, optional

**1.** In a small bowl, combine the cabbage, onion and banana pepper. In another small bowl, whisk the Miracle Whip, vinegar, mustard and pepper. Pour over cabbage mixture and toss to coat. Chill mixture until serving.

**2.** Sprinkle shrimp with taco seasoning. In a large nonstick skillet, saute shrimp in oil for 3-4 minutes or until shrimp turn pink. Place shrimp on tortillas; top with cheese, coleslaw and avocado if desired.

**Nutrition Facts:** 2 tacos (calculated without avocado) equals 527 calories, 18 g fat (4 g saturated fat), 153 mg cholesterol, 1,021 mg sodium, 55 g carbohydrate, 6 g fiber, 31 g protein.

FETA SHRIMP TACOS

# Strawberry Puff Pancake

**PREP/TOTAL TIME:** 30 min.  **YIELD:** 4 servings

**BRENDA MORTON • HALE CENTER, TEXAS**

*I've cut this recipe to 2 eggs and 1/2 cup milk for my husband and me, and it works just fine. It's yummy with strawberry or blueberry topping. You could even garnish it with whipped topping for a light dessert.*

|   |   |
|---|---|
| 2 | Tbsp. butter |
| 3 | eggs |
| 3/4 | cup fat-free milk |
| 1 | tsp. vanilla extract |
| 3/4 | cup all-purpose flour |
| 1/8 | tsp. salt |
| 1/8 | tsp. ground cinnamon |
| 1/4 | cup sugar |
| 1 | Tbsp. cornstarch |
| 1/2 | cup water |
| 1 | cup sliced fresh strawberries |

Confectioners' sugar

**1.** Place butter in a 9-in. pie plate; place in a 400° oven for 4-5 minutes or until melted. Meanwhile, in a small bowl, whisk the eggs, milk and vanilla. In another small bowl, combine the flour, salt and cinnamon; whisk into egg mixture until blended.

**2.** Pour into prepared pie plate. Bake for 15-20 minutes or until sides are crisp and golden brown.

**3.** In a small saucepan, combine sugar and cornstarch. Stir in water until smooth; add strawberries. Cook and stir over medium heat until thickened. Coarsely mash strawberries. Serve with pancake. Dust with confectioners' sugar.

**Nutrition Facts:** 1 slice with 1/3 cup sauce (calculated without confectioners' sugar) equals 277 calories, 10 g fat (5 g saturated fat), 175 mg cholesterol, 187 mg sodium, 38 g carbohydrate, 2 g fiber, 9 g protein. **Diabetic Exchanges:** 2-1/2 starch, 1 medium-fat meat, 1 fat.

# Spinach Tomato Linguine Ⓜ

**PREP/TOTAL TIME:** 25 min.  **YIELD:** 4 servings

**ROSEMARY AVERKAMP • GENOA, WISCONSIN**

*Chock-full of garden freshness, this colorful toss makes an excellent meatless entree or even a side dish. Sometime I substitute penne pasta and add cooked chicken for a heartier main meal. Using garlic-flavored feta cheese is a great touch.*

|   |   |
|---|---|
| 8 | oz. uncooked linguine |
| 3 | cups chopped seeded plum tomatoes |
| 1 | pkg. (10 oz.) frozen chopped spinach, thawed and squeezed dry |
| 1/2 | cup chopped green onions |
| 1 | tsp. olive oil |
| 1/4 | tsp. salt |
| 1/4 | tsp. garlic salt |
| 4 | oz. crumbled feta cheese |

**1.** Cook linguine according to package directions. Meanwhile, in a large nonstick skillet, saute the tomatoes, spinach and onions in oil until tomatoes

TANGERINE CASHEW SNAPPER

are softened. Sprinkle with salt and garlic salt. Reduce heat. Stir in the cheese; until heated through.

**2.** Drain linguine; transfer to a serving bowl. Add tomato mixture; toss to coat.

**Nutrition Facts:** 1 cup equals 357 calories, 11 g fat (5 g saturated fat), 25 mg cholesterol, 646 mg sodium, 52 g carbohydrate, 6 g fiber, 15 g protein. **Diabetic Exchanges:** 2-1/2 starch, 2 vegetable, 1 lean meat, 1 fat.

## Tangerine Cashew Snapper

**PREP/TOTAL TIME:** 30 min. **YIELD:** 4 servings

**CRYSTAL BRUNS • ILIFF, COLORADO**

*Loads of delicious toppings make this fast-to-fix supper option stunning to both the palate and the eye!*

      4  tangerines
      2  Tbsp. lime juice
      2  Tbsp. reduced-sodium soy sauce
      1  Tbsp. brown sugar
      2  tsp. minced fresh gingerroot
      1  tsp. sesame oil
    1/8  tsp. crushed red pepper flakes
      4  red snapper fillets (4 oz. *each*)
    1/3  cup chopped unsalted cashews
      2  green onions, thinly sliced

**1.** Peel, slice and remove seeds from 2 tangerines; chop the fruit and place in a small bowl. Squeeze juice from remaining tangerines; add to bowl. Stir in the lime juice, soy sauce, brown sugar, ginger, sesame oil and pepper flakes.

**2.** Place fillets in a 13-in. x 9-in. baking dish coated with cooking spray. Pour tangerine mixture over fillets; sprinkle with cashews and green onions. Bake, uncovered, at 425° for 15-20 minutes or until fish flakes easily with a fork.

**Nutrition Facts:** 1 fillet with about 2 Tbsp. sauce equals 260 calories, 8 g fat (2 g saturated fat), 40 mg cholesterol, 358 mg sodium, 22 g carbohydrate, 2 g fiber, 26 g protein. **Diabetic Exchanges:** 3 lean meat, 1 fruit, 1 fat.

CHICKEN SAUSAGE GYROS

## Chicken Sausage Gyros

**PREP/TOTAL TIME:** 20 min. **YIELD:** 4 servings

**KERRI GEORGE • BERNE, INDIANA**

*Surprise your family after a day at the beach with this fast, filling meal in minutes. Casual and hearty, the whole wheat pitas are packed with veggies—and flavor.*

- 1 pkg. (12 oz.) fully cooked spinach and feta chicken sausage links *or* flavor of your choice, cut into 1/4-in. slices
- 1 cup (8 oz.) reduced-fat sour cream
- 1/4 cup finely chopped cucumber
- 1-1/2 tsp. red wine vinegar
- 1-1/2 tsp. olive oil
- 1/2 tsp. garlic powder
- 4 whole wheat pita breads (6 in.)
- 1 plum tomato, sliced
- 1/2 small onion, thinly sliced

**1.** In a large skillet coated with cooking spray, cook sausage over medium heat until heated through.

**2.** Meanwhile, in a small bowl, combine the sour cream, cucumber, vinegar, oil and garlic powder. Serve chicken sausage on pita breads with tomato, onion and cucumber sauce.

**Nutrition Facts:** 1 gyro with 1/4 cup sauce equals 418 calories, 15 g fat (6 g saturated fat), 75 mg cholesterol, 873 mg sodium, 42 g carbohydrate, 5 g fiber, 27 g protein. **Diabetic Exchanges:** 3 starch, 3 lean meat, 1-1/2 fat.

# Cheese Ravioli with Pumpkin Alfredo Sauce

PREP/TOTAL TIME: 30 min. YIELD: 6 servings

CHERI NEUSTIFTER • STURTEVANT, WISCONSIN

*When I first made this recipe everyone thought: Pumpkin on pasta? Ewww! But once they tasted it, they couldn't believe how much they liked it! A warm, comforting and delicious blend of flavors.*

- 1 pkg. (25 oz.) frozen cheese ravioli
- 3 Tbsp. all-purpose flour
- 2 cups fat-free milk
- 1 can (14-1/2 oz.) reduced-sodium chicken broth
- 3 garlic cloves, minced
- 2 Tbsp. butter
- 1/2 cup shredded Parmesan cheese
- 1/2 cup canned pumpkin
- 1/4 cup minced fresh parsley
- 1-1/2 tsp. minced fresh sage
- Dash ground nutmeg
- 1/4 cup pine nuts, toasted
- 1/4 cup chopped walnuts, toasted

**1.** Cook ravioli according to package directions. Meanwhile, in a large bowl, whisk the flour, milk and broth.

**2.** In a large skillet, saute garlic in butter until tender. Stir in the milk mixture, cheese, pumpkin, parsley, sage and nutmeg. Cook, uncovered, over medium heat for 10-15 minutes or until thickened, stirring occasionally.

**3.** Drain ravioli and gently stir into sauce. Sprinkle with nuts.

**Nutrition Facts:** 1 cup equals 420 calories, 16 g fat (6 g saturated fat), 29 mg cholesterol, 662 mg sodium, 50 g carbohydrate, 4 g fiber, 19 g protein.

# Scrambled Egg Muffins C

PREP/TOTAL TIME: 30 min. YIELD: 1 dozen

CATHY LARKINS • MARSHFIELD, MISSOURI

*After enjoying scrambled egg muffins at a local restaurant, I came up with this savory version that my husband likes even better. Freeze the extras to reheat on busy mornings.*

- 1/2 lb. bulk pork sausage
- 12 eggs
- 1/2 cup chopped onion
- 1/4 cup chopped green pepper
- 1/2 tsp. salt
- 1/4 tsp. garlic powder
- 1/4 tsp. pepper
- 1/2 cup shredded cheddar cheese

**1.** In a large skillet, cook sausage over medium heat until no longer pink; drain.

**2.** In a large bowl, beat eggs. Add the onion, green pepper, salt, garlic powder and pepper. Stir in sausage and cheese.

**3.** Spoon by 1/3 cupfuls into muffin cups coated with cooking spray. Bake at 350° for 20-25 minutes or until a knife inserted near the center comes out clean.

**Nutrition Facts:** 1 muffin equals 133 calories, 10 g fat (4 g saturated fat), 224 mg cholesterol, 268 mg sodium, 2 g carbohydrate, trace fiber, 9 g protein.

CHEESE RAVIOLI WITH PUMPKIN ALFREDO SAUCE

SCRAMBLED EGG MUFFINS

MUSHROOM POT ROAST

SKILLET BEEF STROGANOFF

MAKEOVER PHILLY STEAK
AND CHEESE STROMBOLI

# Beef Entrees

Have a meat-and-potato lover in your family? Consider the lip-smacking specialties in this chapter! You'll find more than two dozen beefy main courses so satisfying, no one will guess they're eating healthy!

## Mushroom Pot Roast [C]

PREP: 25 min. COOK: 6 hours YIELD: 10 servings

**ANGIE STEWART • TOPEKA, KANSAS**

*Wow! The wine-warmed flavors in this recipe are amazing! Packed with wholesome veggies and tender beef, this is one company-special dish all ages will like. Serve with mashed potatoes to enjoy every last drop of the rich, beefy gravy.*

| | |
|---|---|
| 1 | boneless beef chuck roast (3 to 4 lbs.) |
| 1/2 | tsp. salt |
| 1/4 | tsp. pepper |
| 1 | Tbsp. canola oil |
| 1-1/2 | lb. sliced fresh shiitake mushrooms |
| 2-1/2 | cups thinly sliced onions |
| 1-1/2 | cups reduced-sodium beef broth |
| 1-1/2 | cups dry red wine or additional reduced-sodium beef broth |
| 1 | can (8 oz.) tomato sauce |
| 3/4 | cup chopped peeled parsnips |
| 3/4 | cup chopped celery |
| 3/4 | cup chopped carrots |
| 8 | garlic cloves, minced |
| 2 | bay leaves |
| 1-1/2 | tsp. dried thyme |
| 1 | tsp. chili powder |
| 1/4 | cup cornstarch |
| 1/4 | cup water |

Mashed potatoes

**1.** Sprinkle roast with salt and pepper. In a Dutch oven, brown roast in oil on all sides. Transfer to a 6-qt. slow cooker. Add the mushrooms, onions, broth, wine, tomato sauce, parsnips, celery, carrots, garlic, bay leaves, thyme and chili powder. Cover and cook on low for 6-8 hours or until meat is tender.

**2.** Remove meat and vegetables to a serving platter; keep warm. Discard bay leaves. Skim fat from cooking juices; transfer juices to a small saucepan. Bring liquid to a boil. Combine cornstarch and water until smooth; gradually stir into the pan. Bring to a boil; cook and stir for 2 minutes or until thickened. Serve with mashed potatoes, meat and vegetables.

**Nutrition Facts:** 4 oz. cooked beef with 2/3 cup vegetables and 1/2 cup gravy (calculated without potatoes) equals

310 calories, 14 g fat (5 g saturated fat), 89 mg cholesterol, 363 mg sodium, 14 g carbohydrate, 3 g fiber, 30 g protein. **Diabetic Exchanges:** 4 lean meat, 2 vegetable, 1-1/2 fat.

## Makeover Philly Steak And Cheese Stromboli

PREP: 30 min. BAKE: 25 min. + standing YIELD: 8 servings

**BARBIE MILLER • OAKDALE, MINNESOTA**

*It's just not Christmas Eve at our house without this traditional stromboli—and now it's lower in fat and calories!*

| | |
|---|---|
| 2 | large green peppers, julienned |
| 1/2 | lb. sliced fresh mushrooms |
| 1 | large onion, halved and sliced |
| 2 | Tbsp. canola oil |
| 1/2 | tsp. garlic powder |
| 1/4 | tsp. pepper |
| 1 | loaf (1 lb.) frozen whole wheat bread dough, thawed |
| 12 | oz. reduced-fat process cheese (Velveeta), sliced |
| 1/2 | lb. shaved deli roast beef, chopped |
| 1 | egg white |
| 1 | tsp. water |
| 1/4 | cup shredded part-skim mozzarella cheese |

**1.** In a large nonstick skillet, saute the peppers, mushrooms and onion in oil until tender. Stir in garlic powder and pepper; set aside.

**2.** On a baking sheet coated with cooking spray, roll dough into a 15-in. x 10-in. rectangle. Layer half of the sliced cheese, all of roast beef and vegetable mixture lengthwise over half of dough to within 1/2 in. of edges. Top with remaining sliced cheese. Fold dough over filling; pinch the seams to seal and tuck ends under.

**3.** Combine egg white and water; brush over dough. Cut slits in top. Bake at 350° for 20-25 minutes or until golden brown. Sprinkle with mozzarella cheese. Bake 5 minutes longer or until cheese is melted. Let stand for 10 minutes before cutting.

**Nutrition Facts:** 1 slice equals 331 calories, 12 g fat (3 g saturated fat), 33 mg cholesterol, 1,055 mg sodium, 38 g carbohydrate, 5 g fiber, 23 g protein.

# Basil Burgers with Sun-Dried Tomato Mayonnaise

**PREP:** 25 min.  **GRILL:** 10 min.  **YIELD:** 6 servings

**VIRGINIA KOCHIS • SPRINGFIELD, VIRGINIA**

*I often end up with a bumper crop of basil, and here's a favorite way to use some of it. These burgers feature great Italian flavor. And who can resist their gooey, cheesy centers or the scrumptious topping?*

- 1/4 cup sun-dried tomatoes (not packed in oil)
- 1 cup boiling water
- 1 cup fat-free mayonnaise
- 2 tsp. Worcestershire sauce
- 1/4 cup fresh basil leaves, coarsely chopped
- 2 tsp. Italian seasoning
- 2 garlic cloves, minced
- 1/2 tsp. pepper
- 1/4 tsp. salt
- 1-1/2 lb. lean ground beef (90% lean)
- 3/4 cup shredded part-skim mozzarella cheese
- 6 whole wheat hamburger buns, split

Additional fresh basil leaves, optional

**1.** In a small bowl, combine tomatoes and water. Let stand for 5 minutes; drain. In a food processor, combine mayonnaise and tomatoes; cover and process until blended. Chill until serving.

**2.** In a large bowl, combine the Worcestershire sauce, basil, Italian seasoning, garlic, pepper and salt. Crumble beef over mixture and mix well. Shape into 12 thin patties. Place 2 Tbsp. cheese on six patties; top with the remaining patties and press edges firmly to seal.

**3.** Moisten a paper towel with cooking oil; using long-handled tongs, lightly coat the grill rack. Grill burgers, covered, over medium heat or broil 4 in. from the heat for 5-7 minutes on each side or until a thermometer reads 160° and juices run clear. Serve on buns with mayonnaise mixture and additional basil if desired.

**Nutrition Facts:** 1 burger equals 368 calories, 15 g fat (6 g saturated fat), 83 mg cholesterol, 816 mg sodium, 30 g carbohydrate, 5 g fiber, 30 g protein. **Diabetic Exchanges:** 4 lean meat, 2 starch, 1/2 fat.

BASIL BURGERS WITH SUN-DRIED TOMATO MAYONNAISE

# Mexican Meat Loaf

**PREP:** 25 min.  **BAKE:** 55 min. + standing
**YIELD:** 8 servings

**MARY RELYEA • CANASTOTA, NEW YORK**

*Welcome your family in from the cold with this moist and delicious meat loaf that offers wonderful taco flavor. This is down-home comfort food at its healthy best!*

- 1 large onion, chopped
- 1 large sweet red pepper, chopped
- 3 garlic cloves, minced
- 1 Tbsp. olive oil
- 1 cup dry bread crumbs
- 2 tsp. chili powder
- 1 tsp. salt
- 1 tsp. dried oregano
- 1/2 tsp. ground cumin
- 1/2 tsp. pepper
- 1 can (14-1/2 oz.) diced tomatoes with mild green chilies, *divided*
- 1/3 cup plain yogurt
- 1 egg, lightly beaten
- 2 lbs. lean ground beef (90% lean)

**1.** In a large nonstick skillet, saute the onion, red pepper and garlic in oil until tender. Transfer to a large bowl. Stir in the bread crumbs, chili powder, salt, oregano, cumin, pepper, 2/3 cup diced tomatoes with green chilies, yogurt and egg. Crumble beef over mixture and mix well.

**2.** Shape into a loaf and place in an 11-in. x 7-in. baking dish coated with cooking spray. Spoon the remaining diced tomatoes over top. Bake, uncovered, at 350° for 55-60 minutes or until no pink remains and a thermometer reads 160°. Drain if necessary; let stand for 15 minutes before slicing.

**Nutrition Facts:** 1 slice equals 296 calories, 13 g fat (5 g saturated fat), 98 mg cholesterol, 672 mg sodium, 18 g carbohydrate, 3 g fiber, 26 g protein. **Diabetic Exchanges:** 3 lean meat, 1 starch, 1/2 fat.

# Chili Mac Casserole

**PREP:** 20 min.  **BAKE:** 25 min.  **YIELD:** 6 servings

**JANET KANZLER • YAKIMA, WASHINGTON**

*With wagon wheel pasta and popular Tex-Mex ingredients, this beefy main dish is sure to be a hit with adults and kids. Simply add a mixed green salad with any light dressing you like for a complete dinner.*

CHILI MAC CASSEROLE

1   cup uncooked wagon wheel pasta
1   lb. lean ground beef (90% lean)
1/2 cup chopped onion
1/2 cup chopped green pepper
1   can (15 oz.) turkey chili with beans
1   can (14-1/2 oz.) stewed tomatoes, undrained
1   cup crushed baked tortilla chip scoops
1   cup (4 oz.) shredded reduced-fat cheddar
    cheese, *divided*
1/4 cup uncooked instant rice
1   tsp. chili powder
1/4 tsp. salt
1/8 tsp. pepper

**1.** Cook pasta according to package directions. Meanwhile, in a large nonstick skillet, cook the beef, onion and green pepper over medium heat until meat is no longer pink; drain. Stir in the chili, tomatoes, chips, 1/2 cup cheese, rice, chili powder, salt and pepper. Drain pasta; add to beef mixture.

**2.** Transfer to a 2-qt. baking dish coated with cooking spray. Sprinkle with remaining cheese. Bake, uncovered, at 350° for 25-30 minutes or until cheese is melted.

**Nutrition Facts:** 1 cup equals 358 calories, 11 g fat (5 g saturated fat), 60 mg cholesterol, 847 mg sodium, 36 g carbohydrate, 4 g fiber, 28 g protein. **Diabetic Exchange:** 3 lean meat, 2 starch, 1 vegetable.

To **chop an onion,** peel and cut in half from the root to the top. Leaving root attached, cut vertically through the onion, leaving the root end uncut. Then, simply cut across the onion, discarding the root end.

## Easy Burgundy Stew C

**PREP:** 20 min. **BAKE:** 3 hours **YIELD:** 7 servings

**COLEEN BALCH • CLAY, NEW YORK**

*Watching your salt intake? This satisfying stew has almost 2/3 less sodium than many off-the-shelf "beef stew cup" products. To lower the sodium even further, replace the diced tomatoes with no-salt-added diced tomatoes.*

| | |
|---|---|
| 1 | boneless beef chuck roast (2 lbs.), cut into 1-in. cubes |
| 1 | can (14-1/2 oz.) diced tomatoes, undrained |
| 1/2 | lb. sliced fresh mushrooms |
| 4 | medium carrots, sliced |
| 2 | medium onions, sliced |
| 2 | celery ribs, chopped |
| 1 | cup Burgundy wine *or* reduced-sodium beef broth |
| 1 | Tbsp. minced fresh thyme *or* 1 tsp. dried thyme |
| 1/2 | tsp. salt |
| 1/2 | tsp. ground mustard |
| 1/4 | tsp. pepper |
| 3 | Tbsp. all-purpose flour |
| 1 | cup water |

**1.** In an ovenproof Dutch oven, combine the first 11 ingredients. Combine flour and water until smooth. Gradually stir into stew. Cover and bake at 325° for 3 hours or until meat and vegetables are tender, stirring every 30 minutes.

**Nutrition Facts:** 1 cup equals 287 calories, 13 g fat (5 g saturated fat), 84 mg cholesterol, 332 mg sodium, 15 g carbohydrate, 4 g fiber, 28 g protein. **Diabetic Exchanges:** 3 lean meat, 2 vegetable, 1 fat.

## Veggie Steak Fajitas

**PREP/TOTAL TIME:** 25 min. **YIELD:** 4 servings

**BECKY TONEY • TARPON SPRINGS, FLORIDA**

*Since I used to live in Mexico, I love re-creating the flavors I enjoyed there. This is one of my favorite quick meals!*

| | |
|---|---|
| 1 | beef top sirloin steak (1 lb.), thinly sliced |
| 2 | tsp. ground cumin |
| 1/8 | tsp. salt |
| 3 | tsp. canola oil, *divided* |
| 1 | large onion, julienned |
| 1 | small sweet red pepper, julienned |
| 1 | small green pepper, julienned |

2 Tbsp. minced fresh cilantro

4 whole wheat tortillas (8 in.), warmed

Optional ingredients: Shredded lettuce, chopped
tomato and reduced-fat
sour cream

**1.** Sprinkle beef with cumin and salt. In a large
skillet, saute beef in 2 tsp. oil until no longer pink.
Remove and set aside.

**2.** In the same skillet, saute onion and peppers in
remaining oil until tender. Stir in cilantro. Return
beef to the pan; heat through.

**3.** Spoon onto tortillas; fold in sides. Serve with
lettuce, tomato and sour cream if desired.

**Nutrition Facts:** 1 fajita (calculated without optional
ingredients) equals 344 calories, 11 g fat (2 g saturated fat),
46 mg cholesterol, 299 mg sodium, 28 g carbohydrate, 4 g
fiber, 29 g protein. **Diabetic Exchanges:** 3 lean meat, 1-1/2
starch, 1 vegetable, 1 fat.

# Salisbury Steak with Gravy

**PREP:** 15 min. **BAKE:** 50 min. **YIELD:** 4 servings

**DANELLE WEIHER • VERNDALE, MINNESOTA**

*This recipe was shared at a WeightWatchers meeting I
attended, and my whole family really enjoys it. I like that it's
so tasty and quick to prepare.*

1/2 cup fat-free milk

14 fat-free saltines, crushed

2 Tbsp. dried minced onion

2 tsp. dried parsley flakes

1 lb. lean ground beef (90% lean)

1 jar (12 oz.) fat-free beef gravy

2 Tbsp. ketchup

2 tsp. Worcestershire sauce

1/4 tsp. pepper

**1.** In a large bowl, combine the milk, saltines, onion
and parsley. Crumble beef over mixture and mix well.
Shape into four patties. Place in an 8-in. square
baking dish coated with cooking spray.

**2.** In a small bowl, combine the gravy, ketchup,
Worcestershire and pepper; pour over patties. Bake,
uncovered, at 350° for 50-55 minutes or until a
thermometer reads 160°.

**Nutrition Facts:** 1 salisbury steak equals 266 calories, 9 g fat
(4 g saturated fat), 77 mg cholesterol, 727 mg sodium, 21 g
carbohydrate, 1 g fiber, 24 g protein. **Diabetic Exchanges:**
3 lean meat 1-1/2 starchs.

# Skillet Beef Stroganoff C

**PREP:** 25 min. **COOK:** 1-1/4 hours **YIELD:** 6 servings

**ALJENE WENDLING • SEATTLE, WASHINGTON**

*This has been a favorite of mine for 40 years. I like using
horseradish, which gives the dish an extra zing.*

5 cups sliced fresh mushrooms

1 large onion, sliced

1 Tbsp. reduced-fat butter

1/3 to 1/2 cup hot water

1 Tbsp. prepared horseradish

1/2 tsp. salt

1/8 tsp. pepper

1/4 cup all-purpose flour

1 beef flank steak (1-1/4 lb.), cut into 2-in. strips

1 cup (8 oz.) reduced-fat sour cream

Hot cooked noodles

**1.** In a large skillet, saute mushrooms and onion in
butter until tender. With a slotted spoon, transfer to
a large bowl; stir in the water, horseradish, salt and
pepper. Set aside.

**2.** Place flour in a large resealable plastic bag. Add
beef, a few pieces at a time. Seal bag; shake to coat.

**3.** In the same skillet, brown the beef in batches.
Return all of the beef to the pan; top with the
mushroom mixture.

**4.** Bring to a boil. Reduce heat; cover and simmer for
1-1/4 to 1-1/2 hours or until beef is tender, stirring
occasionally. Remove from the heat; stir in sour
cream. Serve with noodles.

**Editor's Note:** This recipe was tested with Land O'Lakes light
stick butter.

**Nutrition Facts:** 2/3 cup (calculated without noodles) equals
246 calories, 11 g fat (6 g saturated fat), 62 mg cholesterol,
302 mg sodium, 11 g carbohydrate, 1 g fiber, 24 g protein.
**Diabetic Exchanges:** 3 lean meat, 1 starch, 1 fat.

To perk up your own **beef stroganoff** recipe, add an
envelope of ranch salad dressing/dip mix to the sour
cream before stirring it into the rice or noodles. You can
also sprinkle in a few teaspoons of dill weed.

SKILLET BEEF STROGANOFF

# Gingered Beef Stir-Fry

**PREP/TOTAL TIME:** 20 min. **YIELD:** 4 servings

**DEBBIE WILLIAMS • ASHLAND, OHIO**

*Stir-fry is popular in our home because it's so quick to fix. My oldest son especially likes this version. With its pleasant ginger flavor, sweet red peppers and bright green snap peas, it's easy to see why!*

| | |
|---|---|
| 1-1/2 | tsp. sugar |
| 1 | tsp. cornstarch |
| 1/4 | cup cold water |
| 3 | Tbsp. reduced-sodium soy sauce |
| 2 | tsp. sesame oil, *divided* |
| 1 | beef flank steak (1 lb.), cut into thin strips |
| 1 | jar (8 oz.) whole baby corn, drained |
| 1/4 | cup julienned sweet red pepper |
| 2 | tsp. minced fresh gingerroot |
| 2 | tsp. minced garlic |
| 1/4 | lb. fresh sugar snap peas |
| 3 | cups hot cooked rice |

**1.** In a small bowl, combine sugar and cornstarch. Stir in the water, soy sauce and 1 tsp. oil until smooth; set aside. In a large nonstick skillet or wok, stir-fry beef in remaining oil for 4-5 minutes or until no longer pink.

**2.** Add the corn, red pepper, ginger and garlic; stir-fry for 2-3 minutes or until vegetables are crisp-tender. Add peas; stir-fry 30 seconds longer. Stir soy sauce mixture and add to the pan. Bring to a boil; cook and stir for 2 minutes or until thickened. Serve with rice.

**Nutrition Facts:** 1 cup beef mixture with 3/4 cup rice equals 377 calories, 12 g fat (4 g saturated fat), 48 mg cholesterol, 618 mg sodium, 41 g carbohydrate, 2 g fiber, 25 g protein. **Diabetic Exchanges:** 3 lean meat, 2 starch, 1 vegetable, 1/2 fat.

# Lasagna Corn Carne

**PREP:** 30 min. **BAKE:** 45 min. + standing
**YIELD:** 12 servings

**MARY LOU WILLS • LA PLATA, MARYLAND**

*Packed with lean ground beef and nutritious veggies, here's a dinner dish that's as good as it is good for you!*

| | |
|---|---|
| 1 | lb. lean ground beef (90% lean) |
| 1 | jar (16 oz.) salsa |
| 1 | can (16 oz.) kidney beans, rinsed and drained |
| 1 | can (14-3/4 oz.) cream-style corn |
| 1 | large onion, chopped |
| 1 | medium green pepper, chopped |
| 1 | celery rib, chopped |
| 3 | garlic cloves, minced |
| 1 | Tbsp. minced fresh basil *or* 1 tsp. dried basil |
| 1 | tsp. salt |
| 1 | tsp. chili powder |
| 12 | lasagna noodles, cooked, rinsed and drained |
| 2 | cups (8 oz.) shredded part-skim mozzarella cheese |
| 1/2 | cup grated Parmesan cheese |

**1.** In a large skillet, cook beef over medium heat until no longer pink; drain. Add the salsa, beans, vegetables, garlic and seasonings. Bring to a boil. Reduce heat; cover and simmer for 15 minutes.

**2.** Spread a fourth of the meat sauce in a 13-in. x 9-in. baking dish coated with cooking spray; top with four noodles. Repeat layers once. Top with half of the remaining sauce; sprinkle with half of the cheeses. Layer with remaining noodles, sauce and cheeses.

GINGERED BEEF STIR-FRY

LASAGNA CORN CARNE

**3.** Cover and bake at 350° for 30 minutes. Uncover; bake 15-20 minutes longer or until heated through. Let stand for 15 minutes before cutting.

**Nutrition Facts:** 1 piece equals 292 calories, 8 g fat (4 g saturated fat), 37 mg cholesterol, 674 mg sodium, 36 g carbohydrate, 4 g fiber, 20 g protein. **Diabetic Exchanges:** 2-1/2 starch, 2 lean meat.

## Fiesta Grilled Flank Steak ⒸC

**PREP:** 20 min. + marinating   **GRILL:** 15 min.
**YIELD:** 4 servings

**ROXANNE CHAN • ALBANY, CALIFORNIA**

*Whether you broil this tasty steak or slap it on the grill, the acid in the marinade's lime and pineapple juice will help tenderize it. Pair this with sweet potatoes for a colorful, hearty summer hit!*

| | |
|---|---|
| 1/2 | cup unsweetened pineapple juice |
| 1 | Tbsp. lime juice |
| 1/2 | tsp. garlic salt |
| 1/2 | tsp. ground cumin |
| 1 | beef flank steak (1 lb.) |
| 1 | cup cubed fresh pineapple |
| 1/2 | cup salsa verde |

| | |
|---|---|
| 1 | medium ripe avocado, peeled and cubed |
| 1 | green onion, finely chopped |
| 1 | Tbsp. minced fresh cilantro |

**1.** In a large resealable plastic bag, combine the pineapple juice, lime juice, garlic salt and cumin. Score the surface of the beef, making diamond shapes 1/4 in. deep; place in bag. Seal bag and turn to coat; refrigerate for 8 hours or overnight.

**2.** In a small bowl, combine the pineapple, salsa, avocado, green onion and cilantro. Cover and chill until serving.

**3.** Drain beef and discard marinade. Using long-handled tongs, moisten a paper towel with cooking oil and lightly coat the grill rack. Grill steak, covered, over medium heat or broil 4 in. from the heat for 6-8 minutes on each side or until meat reaches desired doneness (for medium-rare, a thermometer should read 145°; medium, 160°; well-done, 170°).

**4.** Let stand for 5 minutes; thinly slice across the grain. Serve with salsa.

**Nutrition Facts:** 3 oz. cooked beef with 1/2 cup salsa equals 274 calories, 15 g fat (4 g saturated fat), 54 mg cholesterol, 322 mg sodium, 12 g carbohydrate, 4 g fiber, 24 g protein. **Diabetic Exchanges:** 3 lean meat, 1 fat, 1/2 fruit.

## Beef & Blue Cheese Tart

**PREP:** 20 min. **BAKE:** 15 min. **YIELD:** 6 servings

**JUDY BATSON • TAMPA, FLORIDA**

*This elegant yet rustic recipe goes together in minutes and is so simple. It's just perfect for entertaining!*

| | |
|---|---|
| 1/2 | lb. lean ground beef (90% lean) |
| 1-3/4 | cups sliced fresh mushrooms |
| 1/2 | medium red onion, thinly sliced |
| 1/4 | tsp. salt |
| 1/4 | tsp. pepper |
| 1 | tube (13.8 oz.) refrigerated pizza crust |
| 1/2 | cup reduced-fat sour cream |
| 2 | tsp. Italian seasoning |
| 1/2 | tsp. garlic powder |
| 3/4 | cup crumbled blue cheese |

**1.** In a large skillet, cook the beef, mushrooms and onion over medium heat until meat is no longer pink; drain. Stir in salt and pepper; set aside.

**2.** On a lightly floured surface, roll crust into a 15-in. x 12-in. rectangle. Carefully transfer to a parchment paper-lined baking sheet.

**3.** In a small bowl, combine the sour cream, Italian seasoning and garlic powder; spread over crust to within 2 in. of edges. Spoon beef mixture over top. Fold up edges of crust over the filling, leaving the center uncovered.

**4.** Bake at 425° for 15-18 minutes or until crust is golden. Using the parchment paper, slide tart onto a wire rack. Sprinkle with blue cheese; let stand for 5 minutes before slicing.

**Nutrition Facts:** 1 slice equals 328 calories, 12 g fat (5 g saturated fat), 43 mg cholesterol, 803 mg sodium, 35 g carbohydrate, 1 g fiber, 19 g protein. **Diabetic Exchanges:** 2 starch, 2 lean meat, 2 fat.

## Chipotle Beef & Rice

**PREP/TOTAL TIME:** 30 min. **YIELD:** 4 servings

**AYSHA SCHURMAN • AMMON, IDAHO**

*Made completely in the skillet, this savory, moist mix of ground beef, lime, salsa, peppers and cheese offers creamy comfort. Chipotle pepper adds just the right amount of heat.*

| | |
|---|---|
| 1 | lb. extra-lean ground beef (95% lean) |
| 1/3 | cup chopped green onions |
| 1/3 | cup chopped green pepper |
| 2 | cups cooked brown rice |
| 1 | cup salsa |
| 1 | cup (8 oz.) fat-free sour cream |
| 2 | Tbsp. finely chopped pickled pepper rings |
| 1 | Tbsp. lime juice |
| 1 | tsp. ground chipotle pepper |
| 3/4 | cup shredded reduced-fat cheddar cheese, *divided* |

**1.** In a large skillet, cook the beef, onions and pepper over medium heat until beef is no longer pink; drain.

**2.** Stir in the rice, salsa, sour cream, pepper rings, lime juice, chipotle pepper and 1/2 cup cheese. Cook and stir until heated through. Sprinkle with remaining cheese. Cover and let stand for 5 minutes or until cheese is melted.

**Nutrition Facts:** 1-1/2 cups equals 403 calories, 11 g fat (6 g saturated fat), 90 mg cholesterol, 495 mg sodium, 39 g carbohydrate, 2 g fiber, 35 g protein. **Diabetic Exchanges:** 4 lean meat, 2-1/2 starch, 1/2 fat.

# One-For-All Marinated Beef C

**PREP:** 10 min. + marinating **GRILL:** 6 min. + standing **YIELD:** 6 servings

**SUE SAUER • DEER RIVER, MINNESOTA**

*I use this great marinade not just for beef but for everything I grill—from pork chops to chicken. The marinade's main ingredient, orange juice, is low in calories, and it makes for a good tenderizer.*

 3/4 cup orange juice
 1/4 cup reduced-sodium soy sauce
 2 Tbsp. brown sugar
 2 Tbsp. prepared mustard
 1 Tbsp. canola oil
 2 garlic cloves, minced
 1 beef flank steak (1-1/2 lbs.)

**1.** In a large resealable plastic bag, combine the first six ingredients; add steak. Seal bag and turn to coat; refrigerate for 4 hours or overnight.

**2.** Drain and discard marinade. Using long-handled tongs, moisten a paper towel with cooking oil and lightly coat the grill rack. Grill steak, covered, over medium heat or broil 4 in. from the heat for 6-8 minutes on each side or until meat reaches desired doneness (for medium-rare, a thermometer should read 145°; medium, 160°; well-done, 170°). Let stand for 10 minutes before slicing.

**Nutrition Facts:** 3 oz. cooked beef equals 206 calories, 10 g fat (4 g saturated fat), 56 mg cholesterol, 305 mg sodium, 4 g carbohydrate, 1 g fiber, 23 g protein. **Diabetic Exchanges:** 3 lean meat, 1 fat.

# Beefy Tomato Rice Skillet

**PREP/TOTAL TIME:** 25 min. **YIELD:** 6 servings

**ELLYN GRAEBERT • YUMA, ARIZONA**

*I put this together one day with what I had on hand. It's quick on busy nights or in the summer when we're camping.*

 1 lb. ground beef
 1 cup chopped celery
 2/3 cup chopped onion
 1/2 cup chopped green pepper
 1 can (11 oz.) whole kernel corn, drained
 1 can (10-3/4 oz.) condensed tomato soup, undiluted
 1 cup water
 1 tsp. Italian seasoning
 1 cup uncooked instant rice

**1.** In a large skillet over medium heat, cook the beef, celery, onion and pepper until meat is no longer pink and vegetables are tender; drain.

**2.** Add the corn, soup, water and Italian seasoning; bring to a boil. Stir in rice; cover and remove from the heat. Let stand for 10 minutes or until rice is tender.

**Nutrition Facts:** 1 cup equals 266 calories, 7 g fat (3 g saturated fat), 37 mg cholesterol, 506 mg sodium, 30 g carbohydrate, 2 g fiber, 17 g protein. **Diabetic Exchanges:** 2 lean meat, 2 vegetable, 1 starch, 1 fat.

ONE-FOR-ALL MARINATED BEEF

BEEFY TOMATO RICE SKILLET

# Beef Kabobs with Chutney Sauce

**PREP:** 15 min. + marinating **GRILL:** 5 min.
**YIELD:** 8 kabobs (about 1/2 cup sauce)

**JUDY THOMPSON • ANKENY, IOWA**

*I created this speedy grilled entree for our daughter, who's a fan of Indian food. The mango chutney and subtle curry give the beef a sweet yet spicy flavor.*

    1/4  cup mango chutney
      1  Tbsp. water
      1  Tbsp. cider vinegar
      1  tsp. curry powder
    1/4  tsp. cayenne pepper
      1  lb. beef top sirloin steak, cut into 1/4-in. strips

CHUTNEY SAUCE:
    1/2  cup plain yogurt
      3  Tbsp. mango chutney
      1  tsp. lemon juice
    1/2  tsp. curry powder
    1/4  tsp. ground cumin
    1/8  tsp. cayenne pepper

Add flavor to beef with **marinades.** Always marinate in the refrigerator in a glass container or plastic resealable storage bag. If a marinade is also used as a basting sauce, reserve some before adding it to the uncooked beef.

**1.** In a large resealable plastic bag, combine the first five ingredients; add the beef. Seal bag and turn to coat; refrigerate overnight.

**2.** In a small bowl, combine the sauce ingredients. Cover and refrigerate until serving.

**3.** Drain and discard marinade. Thread beef onto eight metal or soaked wooden skewers.

**4.** Moisten a paper towel with cooking oil; using long-handled tongs, lightly coat the grill rack. Grill kabobs, covered, over medium heat or broil 4 in. from the heat for 4-6 minutes or until meat reaches desired doneness, turning occasionally. Serve beef with sauce.

**Nutrition Facts:** 2 skewers with 2 Tbsp. sauce equals 258 calories, 6 g fat (2 g saturated fat), 50 mg cholesterol, 321 mg sodium, 23 g carbohydrate, trace fiber, 25 g protein. **Diabetic Exchanges:** 3 lean meat, 1-1/2 starch.

# Hungarian Goulash

**PREP:** 20 min. **COOK:** 7 hours **YIELD:** 12 servings

**MARCIA DOYLE • POMPANO BEACH, FLORIDA**

*Talk about your heirloom recipes! My grandmother made this for my mother when she was a child, and my mother made it for us to enjoy. Sour cream gives it a creamy richness.*

      3  medium onions, chopped
      2  medium carrots, chopped
      2  medium green peppers, chopped
      3  lb. beef stew meat, cut into 1-in. cubes
    1/2  tsp. plus 1/4 tsp. salt, *divided*
    1/2  tsp. plus 1/4 tsp. pepper, *divided*
      2  Tbsp. olive oil
  1-1/2  cups reduced-sodium beef broth
    1/4  cup all-purpose flour
      3  Tbsp. paprika
      2  Tbsp. tomato paste
      1  tsp. caraway seeds
      1  garlic clove, minced
Dash sugar
     12  cups uncooked whole wheat egg noodles
      1  cup (8 oz.) reduced-fat sour cream

**1.** Place the onions, carrots and green peppers in a 5-qt. slow cooker. Sprinkle meat with 1/2 tsp. salt and 1/2 tsp. pepper. In a large skillet, brown meat in oil in batches. Transfer to slow cooker.

**2.** Add broth to skillet, stirring to loosen browned bits from pan. Combine the flour, paprika, tomato paste, caraway seeds, garlic, sugar and remaining salt and pepper; stir into skillet. Bring to a boil; cook and stir for 2 minutes or until thickened. Pour over the meat. Cover and cook on low for 7-9 hours or until the meat is tender.

**3.** Meanwhile, cook noodles according to package directions. Stir sour cream into slow cooker. Drain noodles; serve with goulash.

**Nutrition Facts:** 2/3 cup goulash with 1 cup noodles equals 388 calories, 13 g fat (4 g saturated fat), 78 mg cholesterol, 285 mg sodium, 41 g carbohydrate, 7 g fiber, 31 g protein. **Diabetic Exchanges:** 3 lean meat, 2 starch, 1 vegetable, 1 fat.

BEEF KABOBS WITH CHUTNEY SAUCE

## Grilled Sirloin Teriyaki c

**PREP:** 10 min. + marinating **GRILL:** 10 min.
**YIELD:** 2 servings

**AGNES WARD • STRATFORD, ONTARIO**

*The marinade for this very tender Asian-style beef also works well with fish, chicken and pork. It's perfect for two!*

| | |
|---|---|
| 3 | Tbsp. reduced-sodium soy sauce |
| 4-1/2 | tsp. brown sugar |
| 1 | Tbsp. rice vinegar |
| 1-1/2 | tsp. minced fresh gingerroot |
| 1 | garlic clove, minced |
| 1/8 | tsp. crushed red pepper flakes |
| 1 | beef top sirloin steak (1 in. thick and 1/2 lb.) |

**1.** In a large resealable plastic bag, combine the first six ingredients. Add the steak; seal bag and turn to coat. Refrigerate for 8 hours or overnight.

**2.** Drain and discard marinade. Using long-handled tongs, moisten a paper towel with cooking oil and lightly coat the grill rack. Grill beef, covered, over medium heat or broil 4 in. from the heat for 4-5 minutes on each side or until meat reaches desired doneness (for medium-rare, a thermometer should read 145°; medium, 160°; well-done, 170°).

**Nutrition Facts:** 3 oz. cooked beef equals 163 calories, 5 g fat (2 g saturated fat), 46 mg cholesterol, 279 mg sodium, 4 g carbohydrate, trace fiber, 25 g protein. **Diabetic Exchange:** 3 lean meat.

TERIYAKI BEEF TENDERLOIN

# Teriyaki Beef Tenderloin [C]

**PREP:** 10 min. + marinating **BAKE:** 45 min. + standing
**YIELD:** 8 servings

**LILY JULOW • GAINESVILLE, FLORIDA**

*A beautiful glaze coats this fantastic tenderloin that's as easy as it is delicious. All you have to do is throw some ingredients together and let the marinade do all the work.*

- 1 cup sherry *or* reduced-sodium beef broth
- 1/2 cup reduced-sodium soy sauce
- 1 envelope onion soup mix
- 1/4 cup packed brown sugar
- 1 beef tenderloin roast (2 lbs.)
- 2 Tbsp. water

**1.** In a large bowl, combine the sherry, soy sauce, soup mix and brown sugar. Pour 1 cup into a large resealable plastic bag; add tenderloin. Seal bag and turn to coat; refrigerate for 5 hours or overnight. Cover and refrigerate remaining marinade.

**2.** Drain and discard marinade. Place tenderloin on a rack in a shallow roasting pan. Bake, uncovered, at 425° for 45-50 minutes or until meat reaches desired doneness (for medium-rare, a thermometer should read 145°; medium, 160°; well-done, 170°), basting often with 1/3 cup reserved marinade. Let stand for 10-15 minutes.

**3.** Meanwhile, in a small saucepan, bring water and remaining marinade to a rolling boil for 1 minute or until sauce is slightly reduced. Slice beef; serve with sauce.

**Nutrition Facts:** 3 oz. cooked beef with 1 Tbsp. sauce equals 242 calories, 11 g fat (4 g saturated fat), 72 mg cholesterol, 695 mg sodium, 7 g carbohydrate, trace fiber, 24 g protein. **Diabetic Exchanges:** 3 lean meat, 1/2 starch.

# Little Meat Loaves [C]

**PREP:** 15 min. **BAKE:** 45 min. **YIELD:** 8 servings

**PAUL SOPER • SIERRA VISTA, ARIZONA**

*I've wanted to reduce the fat in my meat loaf for many years, so I finally came up with this recipe. By starting with lean ground beef and not adding any egg yolks, I reduced the total fat considerably. Making individual loaves cuts the cooking time by almost half.*

- 3 egg whites
- 1/2 cup fat-free plain yogurt
- 1 can (6 oz.) tomato paste
- 1 Tbsp. Worcestershire sauce
- 1/2 cup quick-cooking oats
- 1 small onion, chopped
- 2 Tbsp. dried parsley flakes
- 1 tsp. salt
- 1 tsp. poultry seasoning
- 1/2 tsp. garlic powder
- 1/2 tsp. pepper
- 2 lbs. lean ground beef (90% lean)
- 1/2 cup ketchup

**1.** In a large bowl, combine the first 11 ingredients. Crumble beef over mixture and mix well. Shape into eight loaves.

**2.** Place on a rack coated with cooking spray in a shallow baking pan. Bake, uncovered, at 350° for 30 minutes. Spoon ketchup over the loaves. Bake 15 minutes longer or until a thermometer reads 160° and meat is no longer pink.

**Nutrition Facts:** 1 meat loaf equals 264 calories, 11 g fat (4 g saturated fat), 42 mg cholesterol, 633 mg sodium, 15 g carbohydrate, 2 g fiber, 27 g protein. **Diabetic Exchanges:** 3 lean meat, 1 starch, 1/2 fat.

# Black Bean and Beef Tostadas

**PREP/TOTAL TIME:** 30 min. **YIELD:** 4 servings

**SUSAN BROWN • KANSAS CITY, KANSAS**

*Just a handful of ingredients add up to one of our family's favorites. It's also easy to double for casual get-togethers!*

- 8 oz. lean ground beef (90% lean)
- 1 can (10 oz.) diced tomatoes and green chilies, undrained
- 1 can (15 oz.) black beans, rinsed and drained
- 1 can (16 oz.) refried beans
- 8 tostada shells

Optional toppings: shredded lettuce, shredded reduced-fat Mexican cheese blend, sour cream *and/or* salsa

**1.** In a large skillet, cook beef over medium heat until no longer pink; drain. Stir in tomatoes. Bring to a boil. Reduce heat; simmer, uncovered, for 6-8 minutes or until liquid is reduced to 2 Tbsp. Stir in black beans; heat through.

**2.** Spread refried beans over tostada shells. Top with beef mixture. Serve with toppings of your choice.

**Nutrition Facts:** 2 tostadas (calculated without toppings) equals 390 calories, 11 g fat (3 g saturated fat), 44 mg cholesterol, 944 mg sodium, 49 g carbohydrate, 12 g fiber, 24 g protein. **Diabetic Exchanges:** 3 starch, 3 lean meat.

BLACK BEAN AND BEEF TOSTADAS

## Savory Marinated Flank Steak  [C]

**PREP:** 10 min. + marinating **GRILL:** 15 min.
**YIELD:** 6 servings

### LISA RUEHLOW • BLAINE, MINNESOTA

*A handful of kitchen staples come together quickly in this flavorful marinade that really perks up flank steak!*

- 3 Tbsp. canola oil
- 2 Tbsp. lemon juice
- 2 Tbsp. Worcestershire sauce
- 1 Tbsp. dried minced garlic
- 1 Tbsp. Greek seasoning
- 1 Tbsp. brown sugar
- 1 tsp. onion powder
- 1 beef flank steak (1-1/2 lbs.)

**1.** In a large resealable plastic bag, combine the first seven ingredients; add the steak. Seal bag and turn to coat; refrigerate for 6 hours or overnight.

**2.** Drain and discard marinade. Moisten a paper towel with cooking oil; using long-handled tongs, lightly coat the grill rack. Grill steak, covered, over medium heat or broil 4 in. from heat for 6-8 minutes on each side or until steak reaches desired doneness (for medium-rare, a thermometer should read 145°; medium, 160°; well-done, 170°).

**3.** To serve, thinly slice across the grain.

**Nutrition Facts:** 3 oz. cooked beef equals 196 calories, 11 g fat (4 g saturated fat), 54 mg cholesterol, 269 mg sodium, 2 g carbohydrate, trace fiber, 22 g protein. **Diabetic Exchanges:** 3 lean meat, 1/2 fat.

## Hearty Beans and Rice

**PREP:** 10 min.  **COOK:** 25 min.  **YIELD:** 5 servings

### BARB MUSGROVE • FORT ATKINSON, WISCONSIN

*Filling, fast-fixing and fabulous flavor make this satisfying dish destined to become a family favorite.*

- 1 lb. lean ground beef (90% lean)
- 1 can (15 oz.) black beans, rinsed and drained
- 1 can (14-1/2 oz.) diced tomatoes with mild green chilies, undrained
- 1-1/3 cups frozen corn, thawed
- 1 cup water
- 1/4 tsp. salt
- 1-1/2 cups instant brown rice

**1.** In a large saucepan, cook beef over medium heat until no longer pink; drain. Stir in the beans, tomatoes, corn, water and salt. Bring to a boil. Stir in rice; return to a boil. Reduce heat; cover and simmer for 5 minutes. Remove from the heat; let stand, covered, for 5 minutes.

**Nutrition Facts:** 1-1/4 cups equals 376 calories, 9 g fat (3 g saturated fat), 56 mg cholesterol, 647 mg sodium, 47 g carbohydrate, 7 g fiber, 26 g protein. **Diabetic Exchanges:** 3 starch, 3 lean meat, 1 vegetable.

## Makeover Traditional Lasagna

**PREP:** 45 min.  **BAKE:** 70 min. + standing
**YIELD:** 12 servings

### MICHELLE BEHAN • LITTLETON, COLORADO

*Here's a special recipe that's so good, it's become our family's Christmas Eve tradition. This light version allows us to enjoy it without the guilt!*

- 1 lb. extra-lean ground beef (95% lean)
- 1 pkg. (14 oz.) breakfast turkey sausage links, casings removed and crumbled
- 3 cans (8 oz. *each*) no-salt-added tomato sauce
- 1 can (6 oz.) tomato paste

SAVORY MARINATED FLANK STEAK

HEARTY BEANS AND RICE

2 garlic cloves, minced

2 tsp. sugar

1-1/2 tsp. Italian seasoning

1/2 tsp. pepper

9 whole wheat lasagna noodles

3 eggs, lightly beaten

2 cups (16 oz.) 2% cottage cheese

1 carton (15 oz.) reduced-fat ricotta cheese

1/2 cup grated Parmesan cheese

3 Tbsp. minced fresh parsley

1-1/2 cups (6 oz.) shredded part-skim mozzarella cheese

6 slices provolone cheese

**1.** In a large skillet, cook beef and sausage over medium heat until meat is no longer pink; drain. Add the tomato sauce, tomato paste, garlic, sugar, Italian seasoning and pepper. Bring to a boil. Reduce heat; cover and simmer for 15 minutes. Meanwhile, cook noodles according to package directions; drain.

**2.** In a small bowl, combine the eggs, cottage cheese, ricotta cheese, Parmesan and parsley. Spread 1 cup meat sauce into a 13-in. x 9-in. baking dish coated with cooking spray. Layer with three noodles, half of the cheese mixture, 1-1/3 cups sauce and 1/2 cup mozzarella cheese. Repeat layers. Top with remaining noodles and sauce.

**3.** Cover and bake at 350° for 55-60 minutes or until bubbly. Top with provolone and remaining mozzarella cheese. Bake, uncovered, 15-20 minutes longer or until the cheese is melted. Let stand for 15 minutes before cutting.

**Nutrition Facts:** 1 piece equals 361 calories, 15 g fat (7 g saturated fat), 133 mg cholesterol, 634 mg sodium, 23 g carbohydrate, 3 g fiber, 32 g protein.

A half cup of creamed cottage cheese contains about 115 calories, while 1% cottage cheese has about 80 calories. A half cup of **ricotta cheese** made with whole milk contains about 215 calories, while ricotta made partly with skim milk has only 170 calories per half cup.

## Sirloin Steak with Rich Mushroom Gravy C

PREP/TOTAL TIME: 30 min. YIELD: 4 servings

**HEALTHY COOKING TEST KITCHEN**

*Toasting the flour to a light tan color gives this gravy a full flavor and thickness, without using much additional fat. The gravy can be thinned with broth to taste.*

|       |                                                      |
|-------|------------------------------------------------------|
| 1/4   | cup all-purpose flour                                |
| 1     | cup reduced-sodium beef broth                        |
| 1     | beef top sirloin steak (1-1/4 lbs.)                  |
| 1/2   | tsp. salt                                            |
| 1/4   | tsp. pepper                                          |
| 1     | Tbsp. canola oil                                     |
| 1/2   | lb. sliced fresh mushrooms                           |
| 1     | garlic clove, minced                                 |
| 1/2   | tsp. dried rosemary, crushed                         |
| 1/8   | tsp. salt                                            |
| 1/4   | cup sherry *or* additional reduced-sodium beef broth |
| 1     | Tbsp. butter                                         |

**1.** In a large skillet over medium-high heat, cook and stir flour for 4-5 minutes or until light tan in color. Immediately transfer to a small bowl; whisk in broth until smooth. Set aside.

**2.** Sprinkle beef with salt and pepper. In the same skillet, cook beef in oil over medium heat for 5-6 minutes on each side or until meat reaches desired doneness (for medium-rare, a thermometer should read 145°; medium, 160°; well-done, 170°). Remove and keep warm.

**3.** In the same skillet, saute mushrooms until tender. Add the garlic, rosemary and salt; saute 1 minute longer. Stir in the sherry. Stir flour mixture; add to the pan. Bring to a boil; cook and stir for 1 minute or until thickened. Stir in butter until melted. Serve with steak.

**Nutrition Facts:** 4 oz. cooked beef with 1/2 cup gravy equals 289 calories, 12 g fat (4 g saturated fat), 66 mg cholesterol, 565 mg sodium, 9 g carbohydrate, 1 g fiber, 33 g protein. **Diabetic Exchanges:** 4 lean meat, 1 vegetable, 1 fat.

## Mexican Beef & Pasta

PREP/TOTAL TIME: 30 min. YIELD: 8 servings

**CHRISTINE RICHARDSON • MAPLE GROVE, MINNESOTA**

*Your family will love the hearty flavors of this skillet supper. You'll love that it's fast home cooking done light and chock-full of healthier ingredients. Topped with crushed corn chips for extra crunch, it's a must-try recipe.*

|   |                                                          |
|---|----------------------------------------------------------|
| 3 | cups uncooked whole wheat spiral pasta                   |
| 1 | lb. lean ground beef (90% lean)                          |
| 1 | small onion, chopped                                     |
| 2 | cans (14-1/2 oz. *each*) no-salt-added diced tomatoes, undrained |
| 1 | can (15 oz.) black beans, rinsed and drained             |

1 cup frozen corn, thawed
1 cup chunky salsa
1 can (4 oz.) chopped green chilies
1 can (2-1/4 oz.) sliced ripe olives, drained
3 Tbsp. taco seasoning
1/2 cup reduced-fat sour cream
Crushed tortilla chips, optional

**1.** Cook pasta according to package directions; drain. Meanwhile, in a large skillet, cook beef and onion over medium heat until meat is no longer pink; drain.

**2.** Stir in the pasta, tomatoes, beans, corn, salsa, green chilies, olives and taco seasoning. Bring to a boil. Reduce heat; simmer, uncovered, for 8-10 minutes or until heated through. Top with sour cream and crushed chips if desired.

**Nutrition Facts:** 1-1/4 cups beef mixture with 1 Tbsp. reduced-fat sour cream (calculated without chips) equals 305 calories, 7 g fat (3 g saturated fat), 40 mg cholesterol, 737 mg sodium, 40 g carbohydrate, 7 g fiber, 20 g protein. **Diabetic Exchanges:** 2 starch, 2 lean meat, 2 vegetable.

## Makeover Beef & Sausage Lasagna

**PREP:** 45 min. **BAKE:** 45 min. + standing
**YIELD:** 12 servings

**JACOB KITZMAN • SEATTLE, WASHINGTON**

*Here's a healthier version of my popular meat-lover's lasagna. This recipe really trims the cholesterol and saturated fat, so I can enjoy it a bit more regularly...which is a good thing!*

3/4 lb. lean ground beef (90% lean)
3/4 lb. Italian turkey sausage links, casings removed
1 medium onion, chopped
1 medium green pepper, chopped
1 jar (26 oz.) spaghetti sauce
1 pkg. (8 oz.) reduced-fat cream cheese, cubed
1 cup (8 oz.) 1% cottage cheese
1 egg, lightly beaten

1 Tbsp. minced fresh parsley
6 whole wheat lasagna noodles, cooked and drained
1 cup (4 oz.) shredded reduced-fat Italian cheese blend
3 tsp. Italian seasoning, *divided*
1 cup (4 oz.) shredded part-skim mozzarella cheese

**1.** In a large skillet, cook the beef, sausage, onion and green pepper over medium heat until meat is no longer pink; drain. Set aside 1 cup spaghetti sauce; stir remaining sauce into meat mixture. Bring to a boil. Reduce heat; simmer, uncovered, for 8-10 minutes or until thickened.

**2.** In a small saucepan, melt cream cheese over medium heat. Remove from the heat. Stir in the cottage cheese, egg and parsley.

**3.** Spread meat sauce into a 13-in. x 9-in. baking dish coated with cooking spray. Top with three noodles, Italian cheese blend, 1-1/2 tsp. Italian seasoning and cream cheese mixture. Layer with remaining noodles and reserved spaghetti sauce; sprinkle with mozzarella and remaining Italian seasoning.

**4.** Cover and bake at 350° for 35 minutes. Bake, uncovered, for 10-15 minutes or until bubbly. Let stand for 15 minutes before cutting.

**Nutrition Facts:** 1 piece equals 298 calories, 15 g fat (7 g saturated fat), 78 mg cholesterol, 772 mg sodium, 17 g carbohydrate, 3 g fiber, 23 g protein. **Diabetic Exchanges:** 3 lean meat, 1-1/2 fat, 1 starch.

MEXICAN BEEF & PASTA

MAKEOVER BEEF & SAUSAGE LASAGNA

CHICKEN SAUSAGES WITH PEPPERS

MAKEOVER BACON CHICKEN ALFREDO

ITALIAN RESTAURANT CHICKEN

# Chicken Favorites

## Makeover Bacon Chicken Alfredo

**PREP:** 30 min. **COOK:** 15 min. **YIELD:** 8 servings

**IRENE SULLIVAN • LAKE MILLS, WISCONSIN**

*This healthier version of her bacon chicken Alfredo offers all the creamy comfort and rich homey flavor of the original, but slashes the calories, cholesterol and sodium.*

- 1 pkg. (16 oz.) whole wheat fettuccine
- 8 bacon strips, chopped
- 1 lb. boneless skinless chicken breasts, cubed
- 1/2 tsp. salt, *divided*
- 1/4 tsp. pepper
- 2 garlic cloves, minced
- 1 Tbsp. butter
- 3 Tbsp. cornstarch
- 3 cups 2% milk
- 1 cup half-and-half cream
- 1 pkg. (10 oz.) frozen chopped spinach, thawed and squeezed dry
- 1 cup grated Parmigiano-Reggiano cheese, *divided*
- 1/2 tsp. Italian seasoning

**1.** Cook fettuccine according to package directions. Meanwhile, in a large skillet, cook bacon over medium heat until crisp. Remove to paper towels to drain.

**2.** Sprinkle chicken with 1/4 tsp. salt and pepper. Cook chicken and garlic in butter over medium heat for 4-6 minutes or until meat is no longer pink; remove and keep warm.

**3.** Combine cornstarch and milk until smooth; stir into skillet. Add cream and remaining salt. Bring to a boil; cook and stir for 2 minutes or until thickened. Add the spinach, chicken, 3/4 cup cheese, Italian seasoning and half of the bacon; cook and stir until cheese is melted.

**4.** Drain fettuccine; add to chicken mixture. Cook and stir until heated through. Sprinkle with remaining cheese and bacon.

**Nutrition Facts:** 1 cup equals 465 calories, 14 g fat (7 g saturated fat), 72 mg cholesterol, 584 mg sodium, 51 g carbohydrate, 7 g fiber, 32 g protein.

## Italian Restaurant Chicken C

**PREP:** 25 min. **BAKE:** 50 min. **YIELD:** 6 servings

**PATRICIA NIEH • PORTOLA VALLEY, CALIFORNIA**

*Here's a nutritious dish that's a favorite with family and friends. While the chicken and sauce cook, I make pasta to serve with it. The moist, tender, richly seasoned chicken is something special!*

- 1 broiler/fryer chicken (3 lbs.), cut up and skin removed
- 1/2 tsp. salt
- 1/4 tsp. pepper
- 2 Tbsp. olive oil
- 1 small onion, finely chopped
- 1/4 cup finely chopped celery
- 1/4 cup finely chopped carrot
- 3 garlic cloves, minced
- 1/2 cup dry red wine *or* reduced-sodium chicken broth
- 1 can (28 oz.) crushed tomatoes
- 1 bay leaf
- 1 tsp. minced fresh rosemary *or* 1/4 tsp. dried rosemary, crushed
- 1/4 cup minced fresh basil

**1.** Sprinkle chicken with salt and pepper. In an ovenproof Dutch oven, brown chicken in oil in batches. Remove and keep warm.

**2.** In the same pan, saute the onion, celery, carrot and garlic in pan drippings until tender. Add wine, stirring to loosen browned bits from pan.

**3.** Stir in the tomatoes, bay leaf, rosemary and chicken; bring to a boil.

**4.** Cover and bake at 325° for 50-60 minutes or until chicken is tender. Discard bay leaf; sprinkle with basil.

**Nutrition Facts:** 3 oz. cooked chicken with 2/3 cup sauce equals 254 calories, 11 g fat (2 g saturated fat), 73 mg cholesterol, 442 mg sodium, 12 g carbohydrate, 3 g fiber, 27 g protein. **Diabetic Exchanges:** 3 lean meat, 2 vegetable, 1 fat.

# Chicken Fajita Pizza

PREP/TOTAL TIME: 30 min.  YIELD: 6 servings

**CARRIE SHAUB • MOUNT JOY, PENNSYLVANIA**

*This recipe has always been a hit! Even my kids like it—and it's such a great way to sneak in extra vegetables.*

| | |
|---|---|
| 1 | pkg. (13.8 oz.) refrigerated pizza crust |
| 8 | oz. boneless skinless chicken breasts, cut into thin strips |
| 1 | tsp. canola oil, *divided* |
| 1 | medium onion, sliced |
| 1 | medium sweet red pepper, sliced |
| 1 | medium green pepper, sliced |
| 1 | tsp. chili powder |
| 1/2 | tsp. ground cumin |
| 1 | garlic clove, minced |
| 1/4 | cup chunky salsa |
| 2 | cups (8 oz.) shredded reduced-fat Mexican cheese blend |
| 1 | Tbsp. minced fresh cilantro |

Sour cream and additional salsa, optional

**1.** Unroll dough into a 15-in. x 10-in. x 1-in. baking pan coated with cooking spray; flatten dough and build up edges slightly. Bake at 425° for 8-10 minutes or until edges are lightly browned.

**2.** Meanwhile, in a large nonstick skillet coated with cooking spray, cook chicken over medium heat in 1/2 tsp. oil for 4-6 minutes or until no longer pink; remove and keep warm.

**3.** In the same pan, saute the onion, peppers, chili powder and cumin in remaining oil until crisp-tender. Add the garlic; cook 1 minute longer. Stir in the salsa and chicken.

**4.** Sprinkle half of the cheese over prepared crust; top with chicken mixture and remaining cheese.

CHICKEN FAJITA PIZZA

Bake for 8-10 minutes or until crust is golden brown and cheese is melted. Sprinkle with cilantro. Serve with sour cream and additional salsa if desired.

**Nutrition Facts:** 1 piece (calculated without optional ingredients) equals 351 calories, 12 g fat (4 g saturated fat), 48 mg cholesterol, 767 mg sodium, 38 g carbohydrate, 2 g fiber, 25 g protein. **Diabetic Exchanges:** 3 lean meat, 2 starch, 1 vegetable, 1/2 fat.

# Lemon-Olive Chicken with Orzo

PREP/TOTAL TIME: 30 min.  YIELD: 4 servings

**NANCY BROWN • DAHINDA, ILLINOIS**

*This quick recipe is a healthy all-in-one meal. I just add a tossed salad for a menu the entire family loves!*

| | |
|---|---|
| 4 | boneless skinless chicken thighs (about 1 lb.) |
| 1 | Tbsp. olive oil |
| 1 | can (14-1/2 oz.) reduced-sodium chicken broth |
| 2/3 | cup uncooked whole wheat orzo pasta |
| 4 | lemon wedges |
| 1/2 | cup pitted Greek olives, sliced |
| 1 | Tbsp. lemon juice |
| 1 | tsp. dried oregano |
| 1/4 | tsp. salt |
| 1/4 | tsp. pepper |

**1.** In a large nonstick skillet, brown chicken in oil; drain and set aside. Add broth to skillet, stirring to loosen browned bits from pan.

**2.** Bring to a boil. Stir in the orzo, lemon wedges, olives, lemon juice, oregano, salt and pepper. Return to a boil. Reduce heat; simmer, uncovered, for 5 minutes, stirring occasionally.

**3.** Return chicken to the skillet. Cover and cook for 5-7 minutes or until chicken juices run clear and pasta is tender.

**Nutrition Facts:** 1 serving equals 346 calories, 17 g fat (3 g saturated fat), 76 mg cholesterol, 784 mg sodium, 22 g carbohydrate, 5 g fiber, 26 g protein. **Diabetic Exchanges:** 3 lean meat, 2 fat, 1 starch.

# Chicken Sausages With Peppers C

PREP/TOTAL TIME: 30 min.  YIELD: 4 servings

**DEBORAH SCHAEFER • DURAND, MICHIGAN**

*Ready in just half an hour, this is one savory main course you will turn to time and again!*

| | |
|---|---|
| 1 | small onion, halved and sliced |
| 1 | small sweet orange pepper, julienned |
| 1 | small sweet red pepper, julienned |
| 1 | Tbsp. olive oil |
| 1 | garlic clove, minced |
| 1 | pkg. (12 oz.) fully cooked apple chicken sausage links or flavor of your choice, cut into 1-in. pieces |

**1.** In a large nonstick skillet, saute onion and peppers in oil until crisp-tender. Add garlic; cook 1 minute longer. Stir in sausages; heat through.

FAVORITE JAMBALAYA

**Nutrition Facts:** 1 cup equals 208 calories, 11 g fat (2 g saturated fat), 60 mg cholesterol, 483 mg sodium, 14 g carbohydrate, 1 g fiber, 15 g protein. **Diabetic Exchanges:** 2 lean meat, 1 vegetable, 1/2 starch, 1/2 fat.

# Favorite Jambalaya

PREP: 20 min. COOK: 25 min. YIELD: 6 servings

### HEALTHY COOKING TEST KITCHEN

*This zesty jambalaya trumps most ready-made jambalaya mixes. Not only does our recipe include fresh vegetables, but we use our own seasonings to boost flavor.*

| | |
|---|---|
| 1/2 | lb. boneless skinless chicken breasts, cubed |
| 1/4 | lb. smoked turkey sausage, halved lengthwise and sliced |
| 1 | large onion, chopped |
| 1 | medium green pepper, chopped |
| 1 | celery rib, chopped |
| 1 | Tbsp. canola oil |
| 2 | garlic cloves, minced |
| 2 | cans (14-1/2 oz. *each*) no-salt-added diced tomatoes, undrained |
| 1 | bay leaf |
| 1 | tsp. Cajun seasoning |
| 1 | tsp. dried thyme |
| 1/4 | tsp. cayenne pepper |
| 1/4 | tsp. pepper |
| 1 | lb. uncooked medium shrimp, peeled and deveined |
| 3 | cups hot cooked brown rice |

**1.** In a nonstick Dutch oven, saute the chicken, sausage, onion, green pepper and celery in oil until chicken is no longer pink. Add garlic; cook 1 minute longer. Stir in the tomatoes, bay leaf, Cajun seasoning, thyme, cayenne and pepper.

**2.** Bring to a boil. Reduce heat; cover and simmer for 15 minutes. Add shrimp; cook 5-6 minutes longer or until shrimp turn pink. Discard bay leaf. Serve with the rice.

**Nutrition Facts:** 1 cup jambalaya with 1/2 cup rice equals 302 calories, 6 g fat (1 g saturated fat), 125 mg cholesterol, 450 mg sodium, 34 g carbohydrate, 5 g fiber, 27 g protein. **Diabetic Exchanges:** 3 lean meat, 2 vegetable, 1 starch.

## Lentil & Chicken Sausage Stew

PREP: 15 min.  COOK: 8 hours  YIELD: 6 servings

**JAN VALDEZ • CHICAGO, ILLINOIS**

*No matter how chilly the weather, this hearty and healthy soup will warm up your family right down to their toes! It's packed with veggies and the comforting flavors of autumn. Serve with cornbread or rolls to soak up every last drop.*

- 1 carton (32 oz.) reduced-sodium chicken broth
- 1 can (28 oz.) diced tomatoes, undrained
- 3 fully cooked spicy chicken sausage links (3 oz. *each*), cut into 1/2-in. slices
- 1 cup dried lentils, rinsed
- 1 medium onion, chopped
- 1 medium carrot, chopped
- 1 celery rib, chopped
- 2 garlic cloves, minced
- 1/2 tsp. dried thyme

**1.** In a 4- or 5-qt. slow cooker, combine all ingredients. Cover and cook on low for 8-10 hours or until lentils are tender.

**Nutrition Facts:** 1-1/2 cups equals 231 calories, 4 g fat (1 g saturated fat), 33 mg cholesterol, 803 mg sodium, 31 g carbohydrate, 13 g fiber, 19 g protein. **Diabetic Exchanges:** 2 lean meat, 2 vegetable, 1 starch.

# Mango Barbecued Jerk Chicken Thighs [C]

PREP: 20 min. + marinating  COOK: 20 min.
YIELD: 4 servings

**KAREN CAMBIOTTI • STROUDSBURG, PENNSYLVANIA**

*I like my food bursting with flavor, so I love to experiment with all different ethnic recipes. Sweet, tangy barbecue sauce goes well with the heat of the jerk-seasoned marinade in this recipe. Ease of prep plus an appealing presentation make it great for entertaining. And friends always come back for seconds!*

-  2  Tbsp. orange juice
- 1-1/2 tsp. lime juice
- 1-1/2 tsp. olive oil
-  1  Tbsp. Caribbean jerk seasoning
-  1  garlic clove, minced
-  4  boneless skinless chicken thighs (about 1 lb.)

BARBECUE SAUCE:
-  3  Tbsp. mango chutney
- 1-1/2 tsp. lime juice
- 1-1/2 tsp. honey
-  1  tsp. Dijon mustard
- 1/4 tsp. Chinese five-spice powder
- 1/4 tsp. minced fresh gingerroot
-  1  Tbsp. minced fresh cilantro
- 1-1/2 tsp. sesame seeds, toasted
-  1  tsp. grated orange peel

**1.** In a large resealable plastic bag, combine the first five ingredients; add the chicken. Seal bag and turn to coat; refrigerate for 8 hours or overnight.

**2.** For barbecue sauce, in a small bowl, combine the chutney, lime juice, honey, mustard, five-spice powder and ginger; set aside. In another small bowl, combine the cilantro, sesame seeds and orange peel; set aside.

**3.** Drain and discard marinade. Broil chicken 4-6 in. from the heat for 7 minutes. Turn and broil for 6 minutes. Baste with half of the barbecue sauce. Broil 3-5 minutes longer or until chicken juices run clear. Place on a serving dish. Sprinkle cilantro mixture over chicken. Serve with remaining sauce.

**Nutrition Facts:** 1 chicken thigh equals 232 calories, 9 g fat (2 g saturated fat), 76 mg cholesterol, 297 mg sodium, 14 g carbohydrate, trace fiber, 21 g protein. **Diabetic Exchanges:** 3 lean meat, 1 starch.

# Curried Chicken and Rice Ring

PREP: 30 min.  BAKE: 35 min.  YIELD: 6 servings

**HEALTHY COOKING TEST KITCHEN**

*Here's an impressive change-of-pace entree that's sure to liven up meals. Best of all, it's a meal-in-one specialty! Simply add a healthy green salad, and dinner is ready.*

-  1  cup reduced-sodium chicken broth
- 1/2 cup uncooked long grain rice
- 1-1/2 cups cubed cooked chicken breast
-  1  cup frozen peas and carrots, thawed and drained
-  6  Tbsp. reduced-fat mayonnaise
-  2  green onions, chopped
-  1  tsp. salt
- 1/2 tsp. pepper
- 1/2 tsp. curry powder
- 1/4 tsp. garlic powder
- 1/4 tsp. ground turmeric
- 1/4 tsp. ground coriander
- 12  sheets phyllo dough (14 in. x 9 in.)

Butter-flavored cooking spray

**1.** In a small saucepan, bring broth and rice to a boil. Reduce heat; cover and simmer for 15-18 minutes or until liquid is absorbed and rice is tender.

**2.** In a large bowl combine the rice, chicken, peas and carrots, mayonnaise, green onion and seasonings.

**3.** Coat a 10-in. fluted tube pan with cooking spray. Drape one sheet of phyllo over pan and push down over hole. Repeat twice, rotating sheets to cover sides of pan and letting edges of dough hang over sides. Spritz with butter-flavored spray; repeat.

**4.** Spoon filling into pan. Top with remaining phyllo in the same manner. Fold edges over into pan; spray with butter-flavored cooking spray. Bake at 375° for 30-35 minutes or until lightly browned. Let the ring stand for 10 minutes before removing from the pan to a serving platter.

**Nutrition Facts:** 1 piece equals 248 calories, 8 g fat (1 g saturated fat), 32 mg cholesterol, 740 mg sodium, 30 g carbohydrate, 2 g fiber, 15 g protein.

CURRIED CHICKEN AND RICE RING

# Tuscan Chicken C

PREP: 25 min. COOK: 15 min. YIELD: 4 servings

**CARLA WELLS • SOMERSET, KENTUCKY**

*I created this recipe one night when I was looking for a new way to prepare chicken. It's moist, tender, saucy and healthy, too. I recently lost 30-some pounds, and this is one dish I prepare often.*

|     |     |
| --- | --- |
| 4   | boneless skinless chicken breast halves (6 oz. *each*) |
| 1/4 | tsp. pepper |
| 2   | Tbsp. olive oil |
| 1   | *each* medium green, sweet red and yellow peppers, julienned |
| 2   | thin slices prosciutto *or* deli ham, chopped |
| 2   | garlic cloves, minced |
| 1   | can (14-1/2 oz.) diced tomatoes, undrained |
| 1/4 | cup reduced-sodium chicken broth |
| 2   | Tbsp. minced fresh basil *or* 2 tsp. dried basil |
| 1   | tsp. minced fresh oregano *or* 1/4 tsp. dried oregano |

**1.** Sprinkle chicken with pepper. In a large nonstick skillet, brown chicken in oil. Remove and keep warm. In the same skillet, saute peppers and prosciutto until peppers are tender. Add garlic; cook 1 minute longer.

**2.** Add the tomatoes, broth, basil, oregano and chicken. Bring to a boil. Reduce heat; cover and simmer for 12-15 minutes or until a thermometer reads 170°.

**Nutrition Facts:** 1 chicken breast half with 1 cup vegetable mixture equals 304 calories, 12 g fat (2 g saturated fat), 100 mg cholesterol, 389 mg sodium, 11 g carbohydrate, 3 g fiber, 38 g protein. **Diabetic Exchanges:** 5 lean meat, 2 vegetable, 1 fat.

TUSCAN CHICKEN

# Sassy Chicken & Peppers C

PREP/TOTAL TIME: 25 min. YIELD: 2 servings

**DORIS HEATH • FRANKLIN, NORTH CAROLINA**

*Sharing supper with a friend who's watching his or her weight? Taco seasoning, salsa and a squirt of lime add up to a nice summery flavor for chicken—but a slim 239 calories for you!*

|     |     |
| --- | --- |
| 2   | boneless skinless chicken breast halves (4 oz. *each*) |
| 2   | tsp. taco seasoning |
| 4   | tsp. canola oil, *divided* |
| 1   | small onion, halved and sliced |
| 1/2 | small green bell pepper, julienned |
| 1/2 | small sweet red pepper, julienned |
| 1/4 | cup salsa |
| 1   | Tbsp. lime juice |

**1.** Sprinkle the chicken with seasoning. In a small nonstick skillet, cook chicken in 2 tsp. oil over medium heat for 4-5 minutes on each side or until juices run clear. Remove and keep warm.

**2.** Saute onion and peppers in remaining oil until crisp-tender; stir in salsa and lime juice. Spoon mixture over chicken.

**Nutrition Facts:** 1 serving equals 239 calories, 12 g fat (1 g saturated fat), 63 mg cholesterol, 377 mg sodium, 8 g carbohydrate, 1 g fiber, 24 g protein. **Diabetic Exchanges:** 3 lean meat, 2 fat, 1 vegetable.

# Chicken with Berry Wine Sauce C

PREP: 35 min. GRILL: 10 min. YIELD: 4 servings

**ELIZABETH WRIGHT • RALEIGH, NORTH CAROLINA**

*An impressive ruby-red sauce makes this grilled entree a natural choice for summer entertaining.*

|     |     |
| --- | --- |
| 1   | cup fresh strawberries, halved |
| 1   | cup fresh raspberries |
| 1   | cup merlot *or* red grape juice |
| 2   | Tbsp. sugar |
| 4   | boneless skinless chicken breast halves (6 oz. *each*) |
| 1/2 | tsp. salt |
| 1/2 | tsp. pepper |

Thinly sliced fresh basil leaves

**1.** In a small saucepan, combine the strawberries, raspberries, merlot and sugar. Bring to a boil. Reduce heat; simmer, uncovered, for 25-30 minutes or until thickened, stirring occasionally.

**2.** Meanwhile, moisten a paper towel with cooking oil; using long-handled tongs, lightly coat the grill rack. Sprinkle the chicken with salt and pepper. Grill chicken, covered, over medium heat or broil 4 in. from the heat for 4-7 minutes on each side or until a thermometer reads 170°.

**3.** Serve with berry sauce; garnish with basil.

**Nutrition Facts:** 1 chicken breast half with 2 Tbsp. sauce equals 251 calories, 4 g fat (1 g saturated fat), 94 mg cholesterol, 378 mg sodium, 13 g carbohydrate, 3 g fiber, 35 g protein. **Diabetic Exchanges:** 5 lean meat, 1/2 starch, 1/2 fruit.

# Spicy Chicken and Rice

PREP: 20 min. COOK: 5-1/2 hours YIELD: 8 servings

**JESSICA COSTELLO • WESTMINSTER, MASSACHUSETTS**

*As a working mom with two kids, I have little time to prepare something hearty during the week. This recipe is easily tossed together in the morning and fabulous to come home to after a long day. Both my picky eaters love it!*

- 4 boneless skinless chicken breast halves (6 oz. *each*)
- 2 cans (14-1/2 oz. *each*) diced tomatoes with mild green chilies, undrained
- 2 medium green peppers, chopped
- 1 medium onion, chopped
- 1 garlic clove, minced
- 1 tsp. smoked paprika
- 3/4 tsp. salt
- 1/2 tsp. ground cumin
- 1/2 tsp. ground chipotle pepper
- 6 cups cooked brown rice
- 1 can (15 oz.) black beans, rinsed and drained
- 1/2 cup shredded cheddar cheese
- 1/2 cup reduced-fat sour cream

**1.** Place chicken in a 4- or 5-qt. slow cooker. In a large bowl, combine the tomatoes, green peppers, onion, garlic, paprika, salt, cumin and chipotle pepper; pour over chicken. Cover and cook on low for 5-6 hours or until chicken is tender.

**2.** Shred chicken with two forks and return to the slow cooker. Stir in rice and beans; heat through. Garnish with cheese and sour cream.

**Nutrition Facts:** 1-1/3 cups chicken mixture with 1 Tbsp. cheese and 1 Tbsp. sour cream equals 389 calories, 7 g fat (3 g saturated fat), 59 mg cholesterol, 817 mg sodium, 53 g carbohydrate, 7 g fiber, 27 g protein.

# Chicken Pasta Skillet

**PREP/TOTAL TIME:** 30 min. **YIELD:** 6 servings

**HEATHER MCCLINTOCK • COLUMBUS, OHIO**

*I was inspired to come up with a healthier mac and cheese dish—something with a little fiber and some veggies. My husband doesn't like health food, but he loved this!*

- 3 cups uncooked whole wheat spiral pasta
- 2 cups fresh broccoli florets
- 2 Tbsp. butter
- 2 Tbsp. plus 1 tsp. all-purpose flour
- 1-1/4 cups reduced-sodium chicken broth
- 1/2 cup fat-free half-and-half
- 4 oz. reduced-fat process cheese (Velveeta), cubed
- 1 tsp. garlic-herb seasoning blend
- 1/4 tsp. salt
- 2-1/2 cups cubed cooked chicken breast
- 1/2 cup shredded cheddar cheese

**1.** In a large saucepan, cook pasta according to package directions, adding the broccoli during the last 2 minutes of cooking; drain.

**2.** In a large skillet, melt butter. Combine flour and broth until smooth; stir into pan. Add half-and-half. Bring to a boil; cook and stir for 1 minute or until thickened. Add the process cheese, seasoning blend and salt; stir until smooth. Stir in pasta mixture and chicken; heat through.

**3.** Remove from the heat; sprinkle with cheddar cheese. Cover and let stand for 5-10 minutes or until cheese is melted.

**Nutrition Facts:** 1-1/4 cups equals 335 calories, 11 g fat (6 g saturated fat), 72 mg cholesterol, 671 mg sodium, 29 g carbohydrate, 4 g fiber, 29 g protein. **Diabetic Exchanges:** 3 lean meat, 2 starch, 1 fat.

# Garden Chicken Cacciatore C

**PREP:** 15 min. **COOK:** 8-1/2 hours **YIELD:** 12 servings

**MARTHA SCHIRMACHER • STERLING HEIGHTS, MICHIGAN**

*Here's the perfect Italian meal to serve company. While simmering, it frees you up to visit with your guests and always receives rave reviews. Mangia!*

- 12 boneless skinless chicken thighs (about 3 lbs.)
- 2 medium green peppers, chopped
- 1 can (14-1/2 oz.) diced tomatoes with basil, oregano and garlic, undrained
- 1 can (6 oz.) tomato paste
- 1 medium onion, sliced
- 1/2 cup reduced-sodium chicken broth
- 1/4 cup dry red wine *or* additional reduced-sodium chicken broth
- 3 garlic cloves, minced
- 3/4 tsp. salt
- 1/8 tsp. pepper
- 2 Tbsp. cornstarch
- 2 Tbsp. water

**1.** Place chicken in a 4-qt. slow cooker. In a small bowl, combine the green peppers, tomatoes, tomato paste, onion, broth, wine, garlic, salt and pepper. Cover and cook on low for 8-10 hours or until chicken is tender.

**2.** Combine the cornstarch and water until the mixture is smooth; gradually stir into slow cooker. Cover and cook on high 30 minutes longer or until the sauce is thickened.

**Nutrition Facts:** 1 chicken thigh with scant 1/2 cup sauce equals 207 calories, 9 g fat (2 g saturated fat), 76 mg cholesterol, 410 mg sodium, 8 g carbohydrate, 1 g fiber, 23 g protein. **Diabetic Exchanges:** 3 lean meat, 1 vegetable, 1/2 fat.

Garlic that's been finely chopped by hand and garlic that's been put through a press can be used **interchangeably** in recipes. Choose whichever is most convenient for you.

GARDEN CHICKEN CACCIATORE

## Spinach-Stuffed Chicken Rolls C

**PREP:** 30 min. **COOK:** 20 min. **YIELD:** 4 servings

**VIRGINIA ANTHONY • JACKSONVILLE, FLORIDA**

*I've been making this pretty, festive-looking dish for years and people often ask for the recipe. Convenient for company, it can be made ahead of time right up to the point of dusting with flour and browning.*

- 1/3 cup sun-dried tomatoes (not packed in oil)
- 1 cup boiling water
- 4 boneless skinless chicken breast halves (4 oz. *each*)
- 1-1/2 tsp. minced fresh rosemary *or* 1/2 tsp. dried rosemary, crushed
- 1/2 tsp. pepper
- 1/4 tsp. salt
- 1 pkg. (10 oz.) frozen chopped spinach, thawed and squeezed dry
- 1 Tbsp. golden raisins
- 1 Tbsp. reduced-fat cream cheese
- 2 tsp. pine nuts
- 2 Tbsp. all-purpose flour
- 2 tsp. olive oil
- 1 cup reduced-sodium chicken broth
- 1/2 cup minced fresh basil
- 3 garlic cloves, minced
- 1-1/2 tsp. cornstarch
- 1 Tbsp. cold water
- 2 medium tomatoes, chopped

**1.** Place dried tomatoes in a small bowl. Cover with boiling water; let stand for 5 minutes. Drain, reserving 1/2 cup water; chop tomatoes and set aside.

**2.** Flatten chicken to 1/4-in. thickness; sprinkle with rosemary, pepper and salt. In a small bowl, combine the spinach, raisins, cream cheese, pine nuts and sun-dried tomatoes. Spread 1/4 cup spinach mixture over each chicken breast. Roll up and secure with toothpicks. Place flour in a shallow bowl; coat chicken with flour.

**3.** In a large nonstick skillet coated with cooking spray over medium heat, brown chicken in oil. Add the broth, basil, garlic and reserved water. Bring to a boil. Reduce heat; cover and simmer for 10-12 minutes or until a thermometer reads 170°.

**4.** Combine cornstarch and cold water until smooth. Stir into pan. Bring to a boil; cook and stir for 1 minute or until thickened. Add tomatoes; heat through. Discard toothpicks.

**Nutrition Facts:** 1 stuffed chicken roll with 1/3 cup tomato mixture equals 226 calories, 7 g fat (2 g saturated fat), 65 mg cholesterol, 512 mg sodium, 14 g carbohydrate, 4 g fiber, 28 g protein. **Diabetic Exchanges:** 3 lean meat, 2 vegetable, 1 fat.

## Baked Caesar Chicken C

**PREP:** 10 min. **BAKE:** 30 min. **YIELD:** 4 servings

**KIRSTEN NORGAARD • ASTORIA, OREGON**

*Easy, fast to fix and delicious, this meal maker is a winner!*

- 4 boneless skinless chicken breast halves (6 oz. *each*)
- 1/2 cup fat-free creamy Caesar salad dressing
- 1 medium ripe avocado, peeled and cubed
- 1/4 cup shredded Parmesan cheese, *divided*

**1.** Place chicken in an 11-in. x 7-in. baking dish coated with cooking spray.

**2.** In a small bowl, combine the salad dressing, avocado and 2 Tbsp. cheese; spoon over chicken. Bake, uncovered, at 375° for 30-35 minutes or until a thermometer reads 170°. Sprinkle with the remaining cheese.

**Nutrition Facts:** 1 chicken breast half equals 320 calories, 12 g fat (3 g saturated fat), 98 mg cholesterol, 530 mg sodium, 15 g carbohydrate, 4 g fiber, 38 g protein. **Diabetic Exchanges:** 5 lean meat, 1 starch, 1 fat.

## Curried Chicken And Rice Bundles

**PREP:** 30 min. **BAKE:** 15 min. **YIELD:** 6 servings

**HEALTHY COOKING TEST KITCHEN**

*Looking to liven up a special menu? Consider these tasty bundles! Their cute presentation is sure to impress, but the savory filling is what will keep folks talking.*

- 1 cup reduced-sodium chicken broth
- 1/2 cup uncooked long grain rice
- 1-1/2 cups cubed cooked chicken breast

BAKED CAESAR CHICKEN

CURRIED CHICKEN AND RICE BUNDLES

1 cup frozen peas and carrots, thawed and drained

6 Tbsp. reduced-fat mayonnaise

2 green onions, chopped

1 tsp. salt

1/2 tsp. pepper

1/2 tsp. curry powder

1/4 tsp. garlic powder

1/4 tsp. ground turmeric

1/4 tsp. ground coriander

12 sheets phyllo dough (14 in. x 9 in.)

Butter-flavored cooking spray

6 whole chives

**1.** In a small saucepan, bring broth and rice to a boil. Reduce heat; cover and simmer for 15-18 minutes or until liquid is absorbed and rice is tender.

**2.** In a large bowl, combine the rice, chicken, peas and carrots, mayonnaise, green onions and seasonings.

**3.** Place one sheet of phyllo on a work surface; spritz with butter-flavored spray. Top with another sheet of phyllo; spritz with spray. Place 1/2 cup of the rice filling in the center. Bring the corners together and twist; tie bundle closed with a chive. Repeat with the remaining ingredients.

**4.** Place on a baking sheet coated with cooking spray. Bake at 375° for 12-15 minutes or until bundles are lightly browned.

**Nutrition Facts:** 1 bundle equals 248 calories, 8 g fat (1 g saturated fat), 32 mg cholesterol, 740 mg sodium, 30 g carbohydrate, 2 g fiber, 15 g protein.

# Chicken with Celery Root Puree

**PREP:** 30 min. **COOK:** 15 min. **YIELD:** 4 servings

**TASTE OF HOME TEST KITCHEN**

*Celeriac, or celery root, is a root veggie than combines well with other seasonal ingredients and adds nice texture and flavor to this puree.*

- 4 boneless skinless chicken breast halves (6 oz. *each*)
- 1/2 tsp. pepper
- 1 Tbsp. canola oil, *divided*
- 1 large celery root, peeled and chopped
- 2 cups chopped peeled butternut squash
- 1 small onion, chopped
- 2 garlic cloves, minced
- 1 can (5-1/2 oz.) unsweetened apple juice
- 1/4 tsp. salt

**1.** Sprinkle chicken with pepper. In a large nonstick skillet coated with cooking spray, brown chicken in 2 tsp. oil. Remove and keep warm. In the same skillet, saute the celery root, squash and onion in remaining oil until squash is crisp-tender. Add garlic; cook 1 minute longer.

**2.** Add the apple juice, salt and chicken. Bring to a boil. Reduce heat; cover and simmer for 12-15 minutes or until a thermometer reads 170°.

**3.** Remove chicken and keep warm. Transfer vegetable mixture to a food processor. Cover and process until smooth. Return to the pan; heat through. Serve with chicken.

**Nutrition Facts:** 1 chicken breast half with 2/3 cup puree equals 328 calories, 8 g fat (1 g saturated fat), 94 mg cholesterol, 348 mg sodium, 28 g carbohydrate, 5 g fiber, 37 g protein. **Diabetic Exchanges:** 5 lean meat, 2 starch, 1/2 fat.

# Provolone Chicken Pizza

**PREP/TOTAL TIME:** 25 min. **YIELD:** 6 servings

**SHELLY BEVINGTON-FISHER • HERMISTON, OREGON**

*Just pick up a ready-made pizza crust and rotisserie chicken on the way home, and enjoy a fresh, cheesy pizza in less time than it takes to order one that's not even half as good!*

- 1 prebaked 12-in. thin whole wheat pizza crust
- 1/2 cup reduced-fat ranch salad dressing
- 6 slices reduced-fat provolone cheese
- 2 cups shredded cooked chicken breast
- 1 medium tomato, thinly sliced
- 2 green onions, thinly sliced
- 1 Tbsp. grated Parmesan cheese

**1.** Place crust on an ungreased 12-in. pizza pan or baking sheet; spread with salad dressing. Top with provolone cheese, chicken, tomato and onions. Sprinkle with Parmesan cheese. Bake at 450° for 10-12 minutes or until cheese is melted and edges are lightly browned.

**Nutrition Facts:** 1 slice equals 306 calories, 12 g fat (4 g saturated fat), 52 mg cholesterol, 636 mg sodium, 26 g carbohydrate, 4 g fiber, 25 g protein. **Diabetic Exchanges:** 3 lean meat, 1-1/2 starch, 1 fat.

# Asian Chicken Pasta Salad

**PREP/TOTAL TIME:** 30 min. **YIELD:** 6 servings

**NICOLE FILIZETTI • JACKSONVILLE, FLORIDA**

*Packed with veggies, chicken, whole wheat pasta and just the right amount of heat, this main-dish salad is definitely special.*

- 3 cups uncooked whole wheat spiral pasta
- 2 cups cubed cooked chicken breast
- 2 cups fresh broccoli florets
- 1-1/2 cups fresh sugar snap peas, trimmed and halved
- 1 can (8 oz.) bamboo shoots
- 1 small sweet red pepper, chopped
- 3 Tbsp. rice vinegar
- 3 Tbsp. peanut oil
- 3 Tbsp. reduced-sodium soy sauce
- 2 Tbsp. sesame oil
- 3 garlic cloves, minced
- 2 tsp. minced fresh gingerroot
- 1/2 tsp. crushed red pepper flakes
- 1/2 tsp. pepper

**1.** Cook pasta according to package directions. Meanwhile, in a large bowl, combine the chicken, broccoli, peas, bamboo shoots and red pepper.

**2.** In a small bowl, whisk the remaining ingredients. Pour over chicken mixture; toss to coat. Drain pasta and rinse in cold water; add to salad.

**Nutrition Facts:** 1-2/3 cups equals 321 calories, 14 g fat (2 g saturated fat), 36 mg cholesterol, 344 mg sodium, 29 g carbohydrate, 6 g fiber, 21 g protein. **Diabetic Exchanges:** 2 lean meat, 2 fat, 1-1/2 starch, 1 vegetable.

ASIAN CHICKEN PASTA SALAD

# Thai Chicken Pasta Salad

PREP/TOTAL TIME: 30 min. YIELD: 8 servings

BETH DAUENHAUER • PUEBLO, COLORADO

*This healthier twist on traditional Pad Thai has only 1/3 the sodium of similar name-brand products—and it's ready to serve in just 30 minutes!*

- 3/4 cup reduced-fat creamy peanut butter
- 3 Tbsp. water
- 3 Tbsp. lime juice
- 3 Tbsp. molasses
- 4-1/2 tsp. reduced-sodium soy sauce
- 3 garlic cloves, minced
- 1-1/2 tsp. rice vinegar
- 1-1/2 tsp. sesame oil
- 1/4 tsp. crushed red pepper flakes

SALAD:
- 12 oz. uncooked whole wheat spaghetti
- 2 large carrots, julienned
- 8 cups finely shredded Chinese or napa cabbage
- 2 cups shredded cooked chicken breast
- 2/3 cup minced fresh cilantro
- 3 Tbsp. unsalted dry roasted peanuts, chopped

**1.** For dressing, in a small bowl, whisk the first nine ingredients until smooth; set aside.

**2.** In a large saucepan, cook spaghetti according to package directions, adding the carrots during the last 2 minutes of cooking; drain. Transfer to a large bowl; stir in cabbage and chicken.

**3.** Whisk dressing and pour over spaghetti mixture; toss to coat. Sprinkle with cilantro and peanuts. Serve immediately or chill before serving.

**Nutrition Facts:** 1-1/2 cups equals 400 calories, 12 g fat (2 g saturated fat), 27 mg cholesterol, 298 mg sodium, 51 g carbohydrate, 9 g fiber, 25 g protein.

THAI CHICKEN PASTA SALAD

# Italian Baked Chicken

PREP: 15 min. + marinating BAKE: 20 min.
YIELD: 2 servings

LADONNA REED • PONCA CITY, OKLAHOMA

*This scrumptious chicken entree is low in fat but bursting with flavor from the marinade and bread crumb coating. The meat is tender and moist—and so easy to prepare.*

- 3/4 cup fat-free ranch salad dressing
- 4 garlic cloves, minced
- 2 boneless skinless chicken breast halves (5 oz. *each*)
- 1/2 cup seasoned bread crumbs
- 3 Tbsp. grated Parmesan cheese
- 1/4 tsp. pepper

**1.** In a large resealable plastic bag, combine salad dressing and garlic; add the chicken. Seal bag and turn to coat; refrigerate for at least 30 minutes.

**2.** Meanwhile, in a small shallow bowl, combine the bread crumbs, Parmesan cheese and pepper. Drain and discard marinade. Roll chicken in crumb mixture. Place in an 8-in. square baking dish coated with cooking spray. Bake, uncovered, at 325° for 20-25 minutes or until chicken juices run clear.

**Nutrition Facts:** 1 chicken breast half equals 297 calories, 6 g fat (2 g saturated fat), 82 mg cholesterol, 813 mg sodium, 26 g carbohydrate, 1 g fiber, 33 g protein. **Diabetic Exchanges:** 4 lean meat, 1-1/2 starch.

# Chicken with Cherry Pineapple Sauce

PREP/TOTAL TIME: 25 min. YIELD: 4 servings

SALLY MALONEY • DALLAS, GEORGIA

*Sweet and colorful, this tender, lower-fat chicken dish is simply fantastic! The quick prep time, fresh flavors and cherries will make it a family favorite in no time.*

- 4 boneless skinless chicken breast halves (4 oz. *each*)
- 1/2 tsp. garlic salt
- 1/4 tsp. ground ginger
- 2 tsp. canola oil
- 1 can (8 oz.) unsweetened pineapple chunks
- 1/2 cup sweet-and-sour sauce
- 1/4 cup dried cherries
- 2 green onions, sliced

**1.** Sprinkle chicken with garlic salt and ginger. In a large nonstick skillet coated with cooking spray, brown chicken in oil.

**2.** Drain pineapple, reserving 1/4 cup juice. In a small bowl, combine the sauce, cherries and reserved juice; pour over chicken. Bring to a boil. Reduce heat; cover and simmer for 8-10 minutes or until a thermometer reads 170°, turning chicken once. Stir in pineapple and onions; heat through.

**Nutrition Facts:** 1 chicken breast half with about 1/4 cup sauce equals 238 calories, 5 g fat (1 g saturated fat), 63 mg cholesterol, 473 mg sodium, 24 g carbohydrate, 1 g fiber, 24 g protein. **Diabetic Exchanges:** 3 lean meat, 1/2 starch, 1/2 fruit, 1/2 fat.

CHICKEN WITH CHERRY PINEAPPLE SAUCE

BARBECUED TURKEY SANDWICHES

OPEN-FACED FENNEL TURKEY BURGERS

ITALIAN SAUSAGE MARINARA WITH PENNE

# Turkey Specialties

Trying to eat right but getting tired of chicken? The dishes in this chapter are your supper-time solutions! Turkey breast, turkey sausage, ground turkey and more star in these family-friendly entrees.

## Italian Sausage Marinara with Penne

**PREP:** 30 min. **COOK:** 1 hour **YIELD:** 8 servings

TERESA KRIESE • EAU CLAIRE, WISCONSIN

*Fill your house with the warm, wonderful aroma of this rich, bold-flavored sauce. It's my first original recipe and a family favorite from the start. We love its zesty blend of veggies and Italian turkey links.*

- 1 pkg. (19-1/2 oz.) Italian turkey sausage links, cut into 1/2-in. slices
- 3 small zucchini, cut into 1/2-in. slices
- 1 medium sweet yellow pepper, julienned
- 1 cup sliced fresh mushrooms
- 2 Tbsp. olive oil
- 2 garlic cloves, minced
- 1/2 cup dry red wine *or* reduced-sodium chicken broth
- 1 can (28 oz.) Italian crushed tomatoes
- 1 can (14-1/2 oz.) fire-roasted diced tomatoes, undrained
- 1/3 cup grated Parmesan cheese
- 4-1/2 tsp. Louisiana-style hot sauce
- 3 tsp. Italian seasoning
- 1 tsp. sugar
- 1/4 tsp. salt
- 4 cups uncooked whole wheat penne pasta

**1.** In a Dutch oven, saute sausage until no longer pink; drain. Remove and set aside. In the same pan, saute the zucchini, pepper and mushrooms in oil until tender. Add garlic; cook 1 minute longer. Add wine, stirring to loosen browned bits from pan.

**2.** Add the crushed tomatoes, diced tomatoes, cheese, hot sauce, Italian seasoning, sugar and salt. Stir in sausage. Bring to a boil. Reduce heat; simmer, uncovered, for 1 hour or until slightly thickened.

**3.** Meanwhile, cook pasta according to package directions; drain. Serve with sauce.

**Nutrition Facts:** 1 cup sauce with 1 cup pasta equals 441 calories, 12 g fat (2 g saturated fat), 44 mg cholesterol, 991 mg sodium, 56 g carbohydrate, 8 g fiber, 24 g protein.

## Open-Faced Fennel Turkey Burgers

**PREP:** 20 min. + chilling **COOK:** 15 min.
**YIELD:** 5 servings

HEALTHY COOKING TEST KITCHEN

*Fresh fennel and crunchy vegetables pump up the flavor and nutrition of these mouthwatering burgers. They're topped with chopped tomatoes and served on toasted Italian bread.*

- 1/2 cup chopped fennel bulb
- 1/2 cup chopped sweet onion
- 1/2 cup chopped green pepper
- 2 tsp. butter
- 1/4 cup seasoned bread crumbs
- 1/4 tsp. plus 1/8 tsp. salt, *divided*
- 1/4 tsp. pepper
- 1 pkg. (20 oz.) lean ground turkey
- 1 cup chopped tomato
- 2 Tbsp. minced fresh parsley
- 2 tsp. olive oil
- 5 slices Italian bread (3/4 in. thick), toasted

Chopped fennel fronds, optional

**1.** In a large nonstick skillet, saute fennel, onion and green pepper in butter until crisp-tender. Transfer to a large bowl; cool slightly. Add the bread crumbs, 1/4 tsp. salt and pepper. Crumble turkey over mixture and mix well. Shape into five patties. Cover and refrigerate for at least 1 hour.

**2.** In a small bowl, combine the tomato, parsley, oil and remaining salt; set aside.

**3.** Using long handled tongs, moisten a paper towel with cooking oil and lightly coat the grill rack. Grill burgers, covered, over medium heat or broil 4 in. from the heat for 6-8 minutes or until a thermometer reads 165° and the juices run clear. Serve on toast with the tomato mixture. Sprinkle with fennel fronds if desired.

**Nutrition Facts:** 1 burger with 1 toast slice and 3 Tbsp. tomato mixture equals 321 calories, 14 g fat (4 g saturated fat), 94 mg cholesterol, 571 mg sodium, 24 g carbohydrate, 2 g fiber, 24 g protein. **Diabetic Exchanges:** 3 lean meat, 1 starch, 1 vegetable, 1/2 fat.

# Terrific Turkey Chili

**PREP:** 10 min. **COOK:** 35 min.
**YIELD:** 6 servings (about 2 qt.)

**KIM SEEGER • BROOKLYN PARK, MINNESOTA**

*This satisfying medley is full of tomato flavor and also provides a good dose of fiber. To keep it light, top with reduced-fat cheese, cilantro and green onions.*

> 1 lb. lean ground turkey
> 1 cup chopped onion
> 1 cup chopped green pepper
> 2 tsp. minced garlic
> 1 can (28 oz.) crushed tomatoes
> 1 can (16 oz.) kidney beans, rinsed and drained
> 1 can (11-1/2 oz.) tomato juice
> 1 can (6 oz.) tomato paste
> 1 can (4 oz.) chopped green chilies
> 2 Tbsp. brown sugar
> 1 Tbsp. dried parsley flakes
> 1 Tbsp. ground cumin
> 3 tsp. chili powder
> 2 tsp. dried oregano
> 1-1/2 tsp. pepper

**1.** In a large saucepan, cook the turkey, onion, green pepper over medium heat until meat is no longer pink. Add garlic; cook 1 minute longer. Drain.

**2.** Stir in the remaining ingredients. Bring to a boil. Reduce heat; cover and simmer for 25 minutes or until heated through.

**3.** Serve desired amount. Cool the remaining chili; transfer to freezer containers. May be frozen for up to 3 months.

**To use frozen chili:** Thaw in the refrigerator. Place in a saucepan; heat through.

**Nutrition Facts:** 1-1/3 cups equals 315 calories, 8 g fat (2 g saturated fat), 60 mg cholesterol, 706 mg sodium, 43 g carbohydrate, 11 g fiber, 23 g protein. **Diabetic Exchanges:** 3 starch, 2 lean meat.

# Slow Cooker Turkey Breast F C

**PREP:** 10 min. **COOK:** 5 hours **YIELD:** 14 servings

**MARIA JUCO • MILWAUKEE, WISCONSIN**

*Try this wonderfully flavored, easy-fixing, tender, slow cooker entree when you're craving turkey.*

> 1 bone-in turkey breast (6 to 7 lbs.), skin removed
> 1 Tbsp. olive oil
> 1 tsp. dried minced garlic
> 1 tsp. seasoned salt
> 1 tsp. paprika
> 1 tsp. Italian seasoning
> 1 tsp. pepper

**1.** Brush turkey with oil. Combine the remaining ingredients; rub over turkey. Transfer to a 6-qt. slow cooker. Cover and cook on low for 5-6 hours or until turkey is tender.

**Nutrition Facts:** 4 oz. cooked turkey equals 174 calories, 2 g fat (trace saturated fat), 101 mg cholesterol, 172 mg sodium, trace carbohydrate, trace fiber, 37 g protein. **Diabetic Exchange:** 4 lean meat.

# Turkey Sausage Jambalaya

**PREP:** 20 min. **COOK:** 20 min. **YIELD:** 4 servings

**JAMES MCNAUGHTON • QUINCY, FLORIDA**

*Creole cooking is delicious but frequently calls for lots of high-fat meats and oils. This is a spicy adaptation of an old favorite that is tasty, healthy and fast.*

> 3/4 lb. reduced-fat smoked turkey sausage, cut into 1/4-in. slices
> 1 small onion, chopped
> 1 small green pepper, chopped
> 1 Tbsp. canola oil
> 1 garlic clove, minced
> 1-1/2 cups water
> 1/2 cup uncooked long grain rice
> 1/4 tsp. salt
> 1/4 tsp. cayenne pepper
> 1/4 tsp. hot pepper sauce
> 1 can (14-1/2 oz.) diced tomatoes with green chilies, undrained
> 1/4 lb. uncooked medium shrimp, peeled and deveined

TERRIFIC TURKEY CHILI

BARBECUED TURKEY SANDWICHES

**1.** In a large saucepan, saute the sausage, onion and green pepper in oil until vegetables are tender. Add garlic; cook 1 minute longer. Stir in the water, rice, salt, cayenne and hot pepper sauce. Bring to a boil.

**2.** Reduce heat; cover and simmer for 15 minutes or until rice is tender. Add tomatoes and shrimp; cook and stir until shrimp turn pink.

**Spicy Sausage Jambalaya:** Substitute fully cooked andouille sausage for the turkey sausage. Increase garlic to 2 cloves. Add 1 bay leaf, 1/2 tsp. paprika and 1/4 tsp. dried thyme to the saucepan along with the rice. Proceed with recipe as directed. Discard bay leaf before serving.

**Nutrition Facts:** 1 cup equals 288 calories, 6 g fat (1 g saturated fat), 72 mg cholesterol, 1,311 mg sodium, 38 g carbohydrate, 3 g fiber, 18 g protein.

# Barbecued Turkey Sandwiches

**PREP/TOTAL TIME:** 25 min.  **YIELD:** 6 servings

### JAMARR JAMES • ELKINS PARK, PENNSYLVANIA

*Try these sweet, tangy turkey sandwiches for a fun change from sloppy joes. You could also make them with pork or chicken. One of my best recipes ever!*

- 1 medium onion, finely chopped
- 2 tsp. canola oil

- 3/4 cup chili sauce
- 1/2 cup water
- 2 Tbsp. Worcestershire sauce
- 1 Tbsp. brown sugar
- 3 cups shredded cooked turkey breast
- 6 whole wheat hamburger buns, split

**1.** In a large saucepan, saute onion in oil until tender. Stir in the chili sauce, water, Worcestershire sauce and brown sugar. Bring to a boil. Reduce heat; simmer, uncovered, for 5 minutes. Stir in turkey; heat through. Serve on buns.

**Nutrition Facts:** 1 sandwich equals 279 calories, 4 g fat (1 g saturated fat), 60 mg cholesterol, 762 mg sodium, 36 g carbohydrate, 4 g fiber, 25 g protein. **Diabetic Exchanges:** 3 lean meat, 2 starch.

To remove **onion odors,** when you've finished chopping onions, sprinkle your hands with table salt, rub them together for a few moments, then wash them. Presto! No more smelly hands.

# Turkey Meatballs and Sauce

**PREP:** 30 min.  **COOK:** 6 hours  **YIELD:** 8 servings

**JANE MCMILLAN • DANIA BEACH, FLORIDA**

*My sweetie and I have fought the battle of the bulge forever. This is my less-fattening take on meatballs. They're slow-cooker easy and so flavorful!*

- 1/4  cup egg substitute
- 1/2  cup seasoned bread crumbs
- 1/3  cup chopped onion
- 1/2  tsp. pepper
- 1/4  tsp. salt-free seasoning blend
- 1-1/2 lb. lean ground turkey

**SAUCE:**
- 1  can (15 oz.) tomato sauce
- 1  can (14-1/2 oz.) diced tomatoes, undrained
- 1  small zucchini, chopped
- 1  medium green pepper, chopped
- 1  medium onion, chopped
- 1  can (6 oz.) tomato paste
- 2  bay leaves
- 2  garlic cloves, minced
- 1  tsp. dried oregano
- 1  tsp. dried basil
- 1  tsp. dried parsley flakes
- 1/4 tsp. crushed red pepper flakes
- 1/4 tsp. pepper
- 1  pkg. (16 oz.) whole wheat spaghetti

**1.** In a large bowl, combine the egg substitute, bread crumbs, onion, pepper and seasoning blend. Crumble turkey over mixture and mix well. Shape into 1-in. balls; place on a rack coated with cooking spray in a shallow baking pan. Bake, uncovered, at 400° for 15 minutes or until no longer pink.

**2.** Meanwhile, in a 4- or 5-qt. slow cooker, combine the tomato sauce, tomatoes, zucchini, green pepper, onion, tomato paste, bay leaves, garlic and seasonings. Stir in meatballs. Cover and cook on low for 6 hours. Meanwhile, cook spaghetti according to package directions; serve with sauce.

**Nutrition Facts:** 4 meatballs with 3/4 cup sauce and 1 cup spaghetti equals 416 calories, 8 g fat (2 g saturated fat), 67 mg cholesterol, 533 mg sodium, 61 g carbohydrate, 10 g fiber, 28 g protein.

## Mexican Turkey Hash Brown Bake

**PREP:** 20 min. **BAKE:** 35 min. **YIELD:** 6 servings

**TIM ASH • SALEM, INDIANA**

*Here's an easy, stick-to-your-ribs casserole that really delivers on nutrition and flavor!*

- 1 lb. lean ground turkey
- 1/4 cup chopped onion
- 3 garlic cloves, minced
- 1 pkg. (32 oz.) frozen cubed hash brown potatoes, thawed
- 1 can (10 oz.) enchilada sauce
- 1 can (8 oz.) tomato sauce
- 1 can (4 oz.) chopped green chilies
- 1 Tbsp. reduced-sodium taco seasoning
- 1 cup (4 oz.) shredded cheddar cheese

Reduced-fat sour cream, optional

**1.** In a large skillet, cook the turkey, onion and garlic over medium heat until meat is no longer pink. Add the hash browns, enchilada sauce, tomato sauce, chilies and taco seasoning; heat through. Transfer to a 13-in. x 9-in. baking dish coated with cooking spray.

**2.** Cover and bake at 375° for 30 minutes. Sprinkle with cheese; bake, uncovered, 5-10 minutes longer or until cheese is melted. Serve with sour cream if desired.

**Nutrition Facts:** 1-1/3 cups (calculated without sour cream) equals 330 calories, 12 g fat (6 g saturated fat), 80 mg cholesterol, 799 mg sodium, 35 g carbohydrate, 4 g fiber, 23 g protein. **Diabetic Exchanges:** 3 lean meat, 2 starch, 1 fat.

## Makeover Sausage & Potato Bake

**PREP:** 30 min. **BAKE:** 65 min. **YIELD:** 8 servings

**SHANNON JONES • ASHLAND, VIRGINIA**

*This hearty dish makes an awesome breakfast bake, so we enjoy it on Christmas morning!*

- 1 lb. lean ground turkey
- 1 small onion, chopped
- 1 tsp. fennel seed
- 1/4 tsp. salt
- 1/4 tsp. pepper
- 1/4 tsp. cayenne pepper
- 1/8 tsp. ground nutmeg
- 1 garlic clove, minced
- 1 can (10-3/4 oz.) condensed cream of potato soup, undiluted

- 3/4 cup 2% milk
- 2 lb. potatoes, peeled and thinly sliced
- 1 cup (4 oz.) shredded sharp cheddar cheese
- 1 cup (4 oz.) shredded part-skim mozzarella cheese

**1.** In a large nonstick skillet, cook the turkey, onion, fennel seed, salt, pepper, cayenne and nutmeg over medium heat until turkey is no longer pink. Add garlic; cook 1 minute longer. Drain. In a small bowl, combine soup and milk.

**2.** In a 2-qt. baking dish coated with cooking spray, layer half of the potatoes, soup mixture, sausage mixture and cheeses. Top with remaining potatoes, soup mixture and sausage mixture.

**3.** Cover and bake at 350° for 60-70 minutes or until bubbly and potatoes are tender. Sprinkle with remaining cheeses. Bake, uncovered, 5-10 minutes longer or until cheese is melted.

**Nutrition Facts:** 1 cup equals 281 calories, 12 g fat (6 g saturated fat), 71 mg cholesterol, 483 mg sodium, 23 g carbohydrate, 2 g fiber, 19 g protein.

Flavor your Italian sausage with **fennel seed.** Crush the seed, then heat it in a small amount of water and mix it into the sausage. It permeates the meat quicker this way and gives it a rich, sweet taste.

MAKEOVER SAUSAGE & POTATO BAKE

# Turkey Stir-Fry with Cabbage

**PREP/TOTAL TIME:** 30 min. **YIELD:** 4 servings

**DIDI DESJARDINS • DARTMOUTH, MASSACHUSETTS**

*Crunchy cabbage is a nice change of pace from rice in this sweet and savory stir-fry. You'll especially love the mango chutney and the nutty flavor from sesame oil.*

|  |  |
|---|---|
| 1 | Tbsp. cornstarch |
| 1-1/4 | cups reduced-sodium chicken broth |
| 1/3 | cup plus 2 Tbsp. mango chutney |
| 4-1/4 | tsp. reduced-sodium soy sauce |
| 1 | tsp. Chinese five-spice powder |
| 1 | garlic clove, minced |
| 1 | pkg. (20 oz.) turkey breast tenderloins, cut into thin strips |
| 7 | tsp. sesame oil, *divided* |
| 1 | large sweet red pepper, julienned |
| 1-1/2 | cups fresh snow peas |
| 6 | cups shredded cabbage |

**1.** In a small bowl, combine cornstarch and broth until smooth; stir in the chutney, soy sauce, five-spice powder and garlic.

**2.** In a large skillet, saute turkey in 3 tsp. oil for 6-8 minutes or until no longer pink; set aside. In the same skillet, saute red pepper and snow peas in 2 tsp. oil for 2-3 minutes or until crisp-tender. Stir soy sauce mixture and add to skillet. Bring to a boil; cook and stir for 2 minutes or until thickened. Add the turkey; heat through.

**3.** Meanwhile, in a large nonstick skillet coated with cooking spray, saute cabbage in remaining oil for 5 minutes or until crisp-tender. Serve with turkey stir-fry mixture.

**Nutrition Facts:** 1-1/4 cups stir-fry with 1 cup cabbage equals 410 calories, 10 g fat (2 g saturated fat), 69 mg cholesterol, 803 mg sodium, 42 g carbohydrate, 5 g fiber, 38 g protein.

# Turkey Sloppy Joes

**PREP:** 15 min. **COOK:** 4 hours **YIELD:** 8 servings

**MARYLOU LARUE • FREELAND, MICHIGAN**

*This tangy sandwich filling is so easy to prepare in the slow cooker, and it goes over well at gatherings large and small. I frequently take it to potlucks, and I'm always asked for my secret ingredient.*

|  |  |
|---|---|
| 1 | lb. lean ground turkey |
| 1 | small onion, chopped |
| 1/2 | cup chopped celery |
| 1/4 | cup chopped green pepper |
| 1 | can (10-3/4 oz.) reduced-sodium condensed tomato soup, undiluted |
| 1/2 | cup ketchup |
| 2 | Tbsp. prepared mustard |
| 1 | Tbsp. brown sugar |
| 1/4 | tsp. pepper |
| 8 | hamburger buns, split |

**1.** In a large skillet coated with cooking spray, cook the turkey, onion, celery and green pepper over medium heat until meat is no longer pink; drain. Stir in the tomato soup, ketchup, mustard, brown sugar and pepper.

**2.** Transfer to a 3-qt. slow cooker. Cover and cook on low for 4 hours. Serve on buns.

**Nutrition Facts:** 1 sandwich equals 247 calories, 7 g fat (2 g saturated fat), 45 mg cholesterol, 553 mg sodium, 32 g carbohydrate, 2 g fiber, 14 g protein. **Diabetic Exchanges:** 2 starch, 1-1/2 lean meat.

# Roasted Turkey a l'Orange  Ⓢ Ⓒ

**PREP:** 40 min. **BAKE:** 3-1/2 hours + standing **YIELD:** 28 servings

**ROBIN HAAS • CRANSTON, RHODE ISLAND**

*My niece says this is the best turkey she's ever had—she even requests it in the middle of summer!*

|  |  |
|---|---|
| 1 | whole garlic bulb, cloves separated and peeled |
| 1 | large navel orange |
| 1/4 | cup orange marmalade |
| 2 | Tbsp. lemon juice |
| 1 | Tbsp. honey |
| 2 | tsp. dried parsley flakes |
| 1 | tsp. paprika |
| 1 | tsp. dried oregano |
| 1/2 | tsp. salt |
| 1/2 | tsp. dried thyme |
| 1/2 | tsp. pepper |
| 1 | turkey (14 lb.) |
| 4 | celery ribs, quartered |
| 4 | large carrots, quartered |
| 1 | large onion, quartered |

TURKEY STIR-FRY WITH CABBAGE

ROASTED TURKEY A L'ORANGE

1 large potato, peeled and cut into 2-in. cubes

1 large sweet potato, peeled and cut into 2-in. cubes

**1.** Mince four garlic cloves; transfer to a small bowl. Juice half of the orange; add to bowl. Stir in the marmalade, lemon juice, honey, parsley, paprika, oregano, salt, thyme and pepper. With fingers, carefully loosen skin from the turkey; rub 1/2 cup marmalade mixture under the skin.

**2.** Thinly slice remaining orange half; place under the skin. Brush turkey with remaining marmalade mixture. Place remaining garlic cloves inside the cavity. Tuck the wings under turkey; tie the drumsticks together.

**3.** Combine the celery, carrots, onion and potatoes in a roasting pan. Place the turkey, breast side up, over the vegetables.

**4.** Bake at 325° for 3-1/2 to 4 hours or until a thermometer reads 180°, basting occasionally with

pan drippings. Cover loosely with foil if turkey browns too quickly. Cover and let stand for 20 minutes before carving.

**Nutrition Facts:** 4 oz. cooked turkey (calculated without skin and vegetables) equals 207 calories, 6 g fat (2 g saturated fat), 86 mg cholesterol, 123 mg sodium, 4 g carbohydrate, trace fiber, 33 g protein. **Diabetic Exchange:** 4 lean meat.

You can store whole or partial **garlic bulbs** in a cool dry dark place in a well-ventilated container, like a mesh bag, for up to 2 months. Leaving the cloves on the bulb with the papery skin attached will help prevent them from drying out.

# Quinoa Turkey Chili

**PREP:** 40 min. **COOK:** 35 min.
**YIELD:** 9 servings (2-1/4 qt.)

**SHARON GILJUM • SAN DIEGO, CALIFORNIA**

*This heart-healthy chili is not only tasty, it's a vitamin and protein powerhouse!*

| | |
|---|---|
| 1 | cup quinoa, rinsed |
| 3-1/2 | cups water, *divided* |
| 1/2 | lb. lean ground turkey |
| 1 | large sweet onion, chopped |
| 1 | medium sweet red pepper, chopped |
| 4 | garlic cloves, minced |
| 1 | Tbsp. chili powder |
| 1 | Tbsp. ground cumin |
| 1/2 | tsp. ground cinnamon |

| | |
|---|---|
| 2 | cans (15 oz. *each*) black beans, rinsed and drained |
| 1 | can (28 oz.) crushed tomatoes |
| 1 | medium zucchini, chopped |
| 1 | chipotle pepper in adobo sauce, chopped |
| 1 | Tbsp. adobo sauce |
| 1 | bay leaf |
| 1 | tsp. dried oregano |
| 1/2 | tsp. salt |
| 1/4 | tsp. pepper |
| 1 | cup frozen corn, thawed |
| 1/4 | cup minced fresh cilantro |

**1.** In a large saucepan, bring quinoa and 2 cups water to a boil. Reduce heat; cover and simmer for 12-15 minutes or until water is absorbed. Remove from the heat; fluff with a fork and set aside.

**2.** Meanwhile, in a large saucepan coated with cooking spray, cook the turkey, onion, red pepper and garlic over medium heat until meat is no longer pink and vegetables are tender; drain. Stir in the chili powder, cumin and cinnamon; cook 2 minutes longer.

**3.** Add the black beans, tomatoes, zucchini, chipotle pepper, adobo sauce, bay leaf, oregano, salt, pepper and remaining water. Bring to a boil. Reduce heat; cover and simmer for 30 minutes. Stir in corn and quinoa; heat through. Discard the bay leaf; stir in the cilantro.

**Editor's Note:** Look for quinoa in the cereal, rice or organic food aisle.

**Nutrition Facts:** 1 cup equals 264 calories, 5 g fat (1 g saturated fat), 20 mg cholesterol, 514 mg sodium, 43 g carbohydrate, 9 g fiber, 15 g protein. **Diabetic Exchanges:** 2 starch, 2 lean meat, 2 vegetable.

# Enchilada Stuffed Shells

**PREP:** 20 min. **BAKE:** 30 min. **YIELD:** 5 servings

**REBECCA STOUT • CONROE, TEXAS**

*I served this entree to my husband, my sister and my brother-in-law, who is a hard-to-please eater. He said he liked it and even took leftovers for his lunch the next day; I was just thrilled!*

| | |
|---|---|
| 15 | uncooked jumbo pasta shells |
| 1 | lb. lean ground turkey |
| 1 | can (10 oz.) enchilada sauce |
| 1/2 | tsp. dried minced onion |
| 1/4 | tsp. dried basil |
| 1/4 | tsp. dried oregano |
| 1/4 | tsp. ground cumin |
| 1/2 | cup fat-free refried beans |
| 1 | cup (4 oz.) shredded reduced-fat cheddar cheese |

**1.** Cook pasta according to package directions; drain and rinse in cold water. In a nonstick skillet, cook turkey over medium heat until no longer pink; drain. Stir in enchilada sauce and seasonings; set aside.

**2.** Place a rounded teaspoonful of refried beans in each pasta shell, then fill with the turkey mixture. Place in an 11-in. x 7-in. baking dish coated with cooking spray.

**3.** Cover and bake at 350° for 25 minutes. Uncover; sprinkle with cheese. Bake 5 minutes longer or until cheese is melted.

**Nutrition Facts:** 3 stuffed shells equals 379 calories, 15 g fat (6 g saturated fat), 89 mg cholesterol, 591 mg sodium, 33 g carbohydrate, 2 g fiber, 28 g protein. **Diabetic Exchanges:** 3 lean meat, 2 starch, 1 fat.

# Italian Turkey Tenders

**PREP:** 25 min. **BAKE:** 20 min. **YIELD:** 6 servings

**MARY SHIVERS • ADA, OKLAHOMA**

*Flavorful and crispy, this healthier version of a kids' favorite should delight the whole family. Seasoned bread crumbs or ranch dressing would make tasty variations.*

| | |
|---|---|
| 1 | egg, beaten |
| 1/2 | cup fat-free creamy Italian salad dressing |
| 1/2 | cup all-purpose flour |
| 1-1/4 | cups dry bread crumbs |
| 1 | tsp. dried parsley flakes |
| 1 | tsp. Italian seasoning |
| 3/4 | tsp. salt |
| 1/2 | tsp. onion powder |
| 1/2 | tsp. garlic powder |
| 1/2 | tsp. dried oregano |
| 1/2 | tsp. pepper |
| 2 | lb. boneless skinless turkey breast halves, cut into 1-in. strips |
| | Cooking spray |

**1.** In a shallow bowl, whisk egg and salad dressing. Place flour in another shallow bowl. In a third shallow bowl, combine bread crumbs and seasonings. Coat turkey with flour, then dip in egg mixture and coat with bread crumb mixture.

**2.** Place on baking sheets coated with cooking spray. Spritz turkey with cooking spray. Bake at 375° for 20-25 minutes or until juices run clear, turning once.

**Nutrition Facts:** 1 serving equals 329 calories, 4 g fat (1 g saturated fat), 129 mg cholesterol, 766 mg sodium, 29 g carbohydrate, 2 g fiber, 42 g protein.

Dry bread crumbs may be purchased or made from very dry bread or crackers. Simply place **dry bread slices** in a plastic bag and crush with a rolling pin.

ITALIAN TURKEY TENDERSS

## Lightened-Up Gumbo

**PREP:** 30 min. **COOK:** 20 min. **YIELD:** 6 servings

**HEALTHY COOKING TEST KITCHEN**

*Full of flavor and color, this gumbo tastes like the real deal, except for being lower in calories and fat.*

| | |
|---|---|
| 1/2 | cup all-purpose flour |
| 3 | cups reduced-sodium chicken broth |
| 1 | small onion, chopped |
| 1 | celery rib, chopped |
| 1 | small green pepper, chopped |
| 1 | Tbsp. canola oil |
| 2 | garlic cloves, minced |
| 8 | oz. smoked turkey sausage, sliced |
| 1 | cup frozen sliced okra |
| 2 | bay leaves |
| 1 | tsp. Creole seasoning |
| 1/4 | tsp. salt |
| 1/4 | tsp. pepper |
| 1 | lb. uncooked medium shrimp, peeled and deveined |
| 1 | cup cubed cooked chicken breast |
| 3 | cups cooked brown rice |

**1.** In a large skillet over medium-high heat, cook and stir flour for 6-7 minutes or until light brown in color. Immediately transfer to a small bowl; whisk in broth until smooth.

**2.** In the same skillet, saute the onion, celery and green pepper in oil until tender. Add garlic; cook 1 minute longer. Stir flour mixture; add to the pan. Bring to a boil; cook and stir for 2 minutes or until mixture is thickened.

**3.** Add the sausage, okra, bay leaves, Creole seasoning, salt and pepper. Simmer, uncovered, for 4-5 minutes or until okra is tender. Stir in shrimp and chicken. Cook and stir 5-6 minutes longer or until shrimp turn pink. Discard bay leaves. Serve with rice.

**Nutrition Facts:** 1-1/3 cups gumbo with 1/2 cup rice equals 336 calories, 7 g fat (1 g saturated fat), 134 mg cholesterol, 981 mg sodium, 35 g carbohydrate, 3 g fiber, 31 g protein. **Diabetic Exchanges:** 4 lean meat, 2 starch, 1/2 fat.

## Sausage Penne Bake

**PREP:** 35 min. **BAKE:** 20 min. **YIELD:** 8 servings

**BARBARA KEMPEN • CAMBRIDGE, MINNESOTA**

*No one will guess a dish this cheesy and filling could be healthy, but this one's chock-full of eggplant, whole wheat pasta, tomatoes and fabulous flavor.*

| | |
|---|---|
| 2 | cups uncooked whole wheat penne pasta |
| 3/4 | lb. Italian turkey sausage links, casings removed |
| 1 | small eggplant, peeled and cut into 1/2-in. cubes |
| 1 | medium onion, chopped |
| 1/2 | cup dry red wine or chicken broth |
| 3 | garlic cloves, minced |
| 1 | can (28 oz.) crushed tomatoes |
| 2 | cups (8 oz.) shredded part-skim mozzarella cheese, *divided* |
| 3 | Tbsp. chopped ripe olives |
| 2 | tsp. dried basil |
| 1/4 | tsp. pepper |
| 1/2 | cup grated Parmesan cheese |

**1.** Cook pasta according to package directions. Meanwhile, in a large skillet, cook the sausage, eggplant and onion over medium heat until meat is no longer pink; drain.

**2.** Stir in wine and garlic, stirring to loosen browned bits from pan. Add tomatoes. Bring to a boil. Reduce heat; simmer, uncovered, for 10 minutes or until slightly thickened. Drain pasta. Add the pasta, 1-1/2 cups mozzarella cheese, olives, basil and pepper to the skillet.

**3.** Transfer to a 3-qt. baking dish coated with cooking spray. Sprinkle with Parmesan cheese and remaining mozzarella cheese. Bake, uncovered, at 350° for 20-25 minutes or until heated through.

**Nutrition Facts:** 1 cup equals 325 calories, 11 g fat (5 g saturated fat), 46 mg cholesterol, 623 mg sodium, 35 g carbohydrate, 7 g fiber, 23 g protein. **Diabetic Exchanges:** 3 lean meat, 1-1/2 starch, 1 vegetable, 1 fat.

## Italian Turkey Burgers

**PREP:** 15 min. **BAKE:** 20 min. **YIELD:** 6 servings

**BRENDA DIMARCO • WHITEFORD, MARYLAND**

*We eat burgers a lot in warm weather. I cut down on fat and calories by using ground turkey, then spicing it up. My husband is picky about his burgers, but he loves these!*

| | |
|---|---|
| 1/2 | cup sun-dried tomatoes (not packed in oil) |
| 3/4 | cup boiling water |

LIGHTENED-UP GUMBO

ITALIAN TURKEY BURGERS

1 egg white, beaten
1/2 cup dry bread crumbs
1 small onion, finely chopped
1/4 cup ketchup
1 Tbsp. minced fresh basil *or* 1 tsp. dried basil
1 Tbsp. minced fresh parsley
1 Tbsp. spicy brown mustard
2 garlic cloves, minced
1 tsp. dried oregano
1/4 tsp. Italian seasoning
1 lb. lean ground turkey
1/2 lb. extra-lean ground turkey
3 slices reduced-fat provolone cheese, halved
6 whole wheat hamburger buns, split
Ketchup and mustard, optional

**1.** Place tomatoes in a small bowl; add boiling water. Cover and let stand for 5 minutes.

**2.** In a large bowl, combine the egg white, bread crumbs, onion, ketchup, basil, parsley, mustard, garlic, oregano and Italian seasoning. Drain and chop tomatoes; add to egg white mixture. Crumble turkey over mixture and mix well. Shape into six burgers.

**3.** Place in a 15-in. x. 10-in. x 1-in. baking pan coated with cooking spray. Bake at 350° for 16-20 minutes or until a thermometer reads 165° and juices run clear. Top with cheese; bake 1-2 minutes longer or until melted. Serve on buns with ketchup and mustard if desired.

**Nutrition Facts:** 1 burger (calculated without optional condiments) equals 362 calories, 11 g fat (3 g saturated fat), 80 mg cholesterol, 698 mg sodium, 35 g carbohydrate, 5 g fiber, 31 g protein. **Diabetic Exchanges:** 4 lean meat, 2 starch.

Packed in oil or dry packed, **sun-dried tomatoes** are available in most grocery stores today. The dry-packed variety are usually soaked in a liquid to soften them before they're used in recipes.

PORK ROAST WITH GRAVY

PORK CHOPS CHARCUTIERE

SPICY PORK
TENDERLOIN

# Pork, Ham & More

Health-minded family cooks know the value of a meal featuring lean cuts of pork and ham. That's why this chapter is so popular. Loaded with flavor and weeknight ease, these recipes are sure to become new favorites!

## Spicy Pork Tenderloin

**PREP:** 20 min. + chilling  **GRILL:** 25 min.
**YIELD:** 4 servings (2 cups salsa)

**CAROLYN CARTELLI • PARSIPPANY, NEW JERSEY**

*Cool, sweet mango salsa melds with the spicy rub on this pork tenderloin for a delicious, bold-flavored main dish. The colors and presentation are elegant.*

- 1  pork tenderloin (1 lb.)
- 1  Tbsp. olive oil
- 2  tsp. coarsely ground pepper
- 1-1/2  tsp. paprika
- 1/2  tsp. salt
- 1/2  tsp. garlic powder
- 1/2  tsp. chili powder
- 1/2  tsp. ground cinnamon
- 1/4  tsp. cayenne pepper

MANGO SALSA:
- 1  medium mango, peeled and cubed
- 2  Tbsp. minced fresh cilantro
- 2  Tbsp. lime juice
- 1  Tbsp. honey

**1.** Rub pork with oil. Combine the pepper, paprika, salt, garlic powder, chili powder, cinnamon and cayenne; rub over pork. Refrigerate for 30 minutes.

**2.** Using long-handled tongs, moisten a paper towel with cooking oil and lightly coat the grill rack. Prepare grill for indirect heat using a drip pan. Place pork over drip pan and grill, covered, over indirect medium-hot heat for 25-30 minutes or until a thermometer reads 160°. Let stand for 5 minutes before slicing.

**3.** In a small bowl, combine the mango, cilantro, lime juice and honey; serve with pork.

**Nutrition Facts:** 3 oz. cooked pork with 1/2 cup salsa equals 222 calories, 8 g fat (2 g saturated fat), 63 mg cholesterol, 345 mg sodium, 16 g carbohydrate, 2 g fiber, 23 g protein. **Diabetic Exchanges:** 3 lean meat, 1/2 starch, 1/2 fruit, 1/2 fat.

## Pork Chops Charcutiere  C

**PREP:** 25 min.  **COOK:** 25 min.  **YIELD:** 4 servings

**MONIQUE HOOKER • DESOTO, WISCONSIN**

*The peppery Dijon-mustard sauce spooned over these tender chops makes for a recipe special enough to serve guests.*

- 4  boneless pork loin chops (5 oz. *each*)
- 1  to 3 tsp. pepper
- 4-1/2  tsp. olive oil
- 1  small onion, finely chopped
- 4  shallots, finely chopped
- 1  cup reduced-sodium beef broth
- 1/2  cup white wine *or* additional reduced-sodium beef broth
- 2  Tbsp. Dijon mustard
- 2  Tbsp. chopped celery leaves *or* minced fresh parsley

**1.** Sprinkle pork chops with pepper. In a large nonstick skillet coated with cooking spray, brown chops in oil. Remove and keep warm. In the same skillet, saute onion and shallots until tender. Add broth and wine, stirring to loosen browned bits from skillet. Bring to a boil. Reduce heat; simmer, uncovered, for 3 minutes.

**2.** Return chops to skillet. Cover and cook 8-10 minutes longer or until meat is tender. Place chops on a serving platter and keep warm. Stir mustard into skillet. Return to a boil. Reduce heat; simmer, uncovered, for 12-15 minutes or until sauce is thickened. Spoon sauce over chops; sprinkle with celery leaves.

**Nutrition Facts:** 1 pork chop with 1/4 cup sauce equals 292 calories, 13 g fat (4 g saturated fat), 70 mg cholesterol, 339 mg sodium, 11 g carbohydrate, 1 g fiber, 29 g protein. **Diabetic Exchanges:** 4 lean meat, 1 starch, 1 fat.

> Cuts of pork vary little in tenderness. Use dry-heat cooking methods (broiling, grilling, roasting and stir-frying) when a **firm texture** is desired.

# Pork Tenderloin with Raspberry Dijon Sauce

PREP/TOTAL TIME: 25 min.  YIELD: 4 servings

LISA VARNER • CHARLESTON, SOUTH CAROLINA

*Try this tempting pork tenderloin with its peppery, slightly sweet raspberry tang for a fast, full-flavored entree your whole family will enjoy.*

    1  pork tenderloin (1 lb.), cut into 1/2-in. slices
    1  tsp. garlic pepper blend
    2  tsp. canola oil
  1/2  cup seedless raspberry jam
    2  Tbsp. red wine vinegar
    2  tsp. Dijon mustard

**1.** Flatten pork slices to 1/4-in. thickness; sprinkle with pepper blend. In a large nonstick skillet coated with cooking spray over medium heat, cook pork in oil in batches for 2-3 minutes on each side or until juices run clear. Remove and keep warm.

**2.** In the same skillet, add the jam, vinegar and mustard, stirring to loosen browned bits. Bring to a boil. Reduce heat; simmer, uncovered, for 1 minute or until thickened. Serve with pork.

**Nutrition Facts:** 3 oz. cooked pork with 2 Tbsp. sauce equals 256 calories, 6 g fat (1 g saturated fat), 63 mg cholesterol, 175 mg sodium, 27 g carbohydrate, 0 fiber, 22 g protein. **Diabetic Exchanges:** 3 lean meat, 1-1/2 starch, 1/2 fat.

PORK TENDERLOIN WITH RASPBERRY DIJON SAUCE

# Onion-Dijon Pork Chops

PREP/TOTAL TIME: 25 min.  YIELD: 4 servings

HEALTHY COOKING TEST KITCHEN

*Coated in a flavorful sauce, these chops are cooked to tender perfection. Serve with rice and carrots for a full meal.*

    4  boneless pork loin chops (5 oz.each)
  1/4  tsp. salt
  1/4  tsp. pepper
  3/4  cup thinly sliced red onion
  1/4  cup water
  1/4  cup cider vinegar
    3  Tbsp. brown sugar
    2  Tbsp. honey Dijon mustard

**1.** Sprinkle pork chops with salt and pepper. In a large nonstick skillet coated with cooking spray, cook pork over medium heat for 4-6 minutes on each side or until lightly browned. Remove and keep warm.

**2.** Add the remaining ingredients to the skillet, stirring to loosen browned bits from pan. Bring to a boil; cook and stir for 2 minutes or until thickened. Return chops to the pan. Reduce heat; cover and simmer for 4-5 minutes or until a thermometer reads 160°.

**Nutrition Facts:** 1 pork chop with 2 Tbsp. onion mixture equals 261 calories, 9 g fat (3 g saturated fat), 69 mg cholesterol, 257 mg sodium, 17 g carbohydrate, 1 g fiber, 28 g protein. **Diabetic Exchanges:** 4 lean meat, 1 starch.

# Pork Roast with Gravy

PREP: 10 min.  COOK: 50 min.  YIELD: 8 servings

JEAN VIRZI LOWREY • DUBACH, LOUISIANA

*I've been making this juicy roast for 40 years. Lower in calories, it's a favorite of mine.*

ONION-DIJON PORK CHOPS

1 boneless pork sirloin roast (2-1/2 lbs.)
1-1/2 tsp. canola oil
3/4 cup white wine or chicken broth
2 Tbsp. brown sugar
2 Tbsp. reduced-sodium soy sauce
1 tsp. minced fresh gingerroot
1 garlic clove, minced
1/2 tsp. chicken bouillon granules
4-1/2 tsp. cornstarch
4-1/2 tsp. cold water

**1.** In a Dutch oven, brown roast in oil on all sides. In a small bowl, combine the wine, brown sugar, soy sauce, ginger, garlic and bouillon; pour over roast.

**2.** Bring to a boil. Reduce heat to low; cover and cook for 45-60 minutes or until a thermometer reads 160°, basting occasionally with pan juices.

**3.** Remove roast to a serving platter; keep warm. Pour drippings and loosened browned bits into a 2-cup measuring cup; skim fat. Add enough water to measure 1-1/2 cups. Return to the pan.

**4.** Combine cornstarch and water until smooth; gradually stir into the pan. Bring to a boil; cook and stir for 1-2 minutes or until thickened. Serve with the roast.

**Nutrition Facts:** 4 oz. cooked pork with 3 Tbsp. gravy equals 241 calories, 9 g fat (3 g saturated fat), 85 mg cholesterol, 262 mg sodium, 5 g carbohydrate, trace fiber, 29 g protein. **Diabetic Exchange:** 4 lean meat.

GLAZED PORK MEDALLIONS

# Glazed Pork Medallions [C]

**PREP/TOTAL TIME:** 30 min.  **YIELD:** 4 servings

**MICHELE FLAGEL • SHELLSBURG, IOWA**

*After my husband was told to lower his cholesterol, he was sure he'd never taste good food again. He was so surprised by this entree, which proves you don't have to eat fish every night to keep fat down.*

- 1   pork tenderloin (1-1/4 lbs.)
- 1/4   tsp. salt
- 1/3   cup reduced-sugar orange marmalade
- 2   tsp. cider vinegar
- 2   tsp. Worcestershire sauce
- 1/2   tsp. minced fresh gingerroot
- 1/8   tsp. crushed red pepper flakes

**1.** Cut pork into 1-in. slices and flatten to 1/4-in. thickness; sprinkle with salt. In a large nonstick skillet coated with cooking spray, cook pork in batches over medium-high heat until juices run clear. Reduce heat to low; return all meat to the pan. Combine the remaining ingredients; pour over pork and turn to coat. Heat through.

**Nutrition Facts:** 4 oz. cooked pork equals 200 calories, 5 g fat (2 g saturated fat), 79 mg cholesterol, 231 mg sodium, 9 g carbohydrate, trace fiber, 28 g protein. **Diabetic Exchanges:** 4 lean meat, 1/2 fruit, 1/2 fat.

# Spiced Orange Glaze for Ham [F] [S] [C]

**PREP/TOTAL TIME:** 5 min.  **YIELD:** 2/3 cup

**SUE GRONHOLZ • BEAVER DAM, WISCONSIN**

*Add something new to your traditional ham with this easy glaze. It covers an 8- to 10-lb. ham and provides about 20 servings. The blend of citrus and spice makes it especially lovely for the holidays.*

- 1/4   cup packed brown sugar
- 1/4   cup orange juice
- 2   Tbsp. honey
- 1   Tbsp. stone-ground mustard
- 2   tsp. dried basil
- 1   tsp. grated orange peel
- 1/8   tsp. ground cloves

**1.** In a small bowl, combine all ingredients. Brush over ham during the last 30 minutes of cooking.

**Nutrition Facts:** 1-1/2 tsp. equals 20 calories, trace fat (trace saturated fat), 0 cholesterol, 17 mg sodium, 5 g carbohydrate, trace fiber, trace protein. **Diabetic Exchange:** Free food.

# Pork Chops with Cranberry Dijon Sauce [C]

**PREP/TOTAL TIME:** 30 min.  **YIELD:** 4 servings

**LISA HERRING BRIDGES • ATLANTA, GEORGIA**

*Here's a rich-tasting dish with bold flavors that blend so well together. Quick yet special, it's a terrific choice for both family and unexpected guests.*

- 1   medium apple, peeled and thinly sliced
- 2   Tbsp. dried cranberries
- 2   Tbsp. Dijon mustard
- 1   Tbsp. cider vinegar
- 1   Tbsp. honey
- 1   tsp. Worcestershire sauce
- 1/8   tsp. dried thyme
- 1/8   tsp. rubbed sage
- 1/8   tsp. dried rosemary, crushed
- 1/8   tsp. pepper

Dash salt

Dash ground nutmeg

- 4   boneless pork loin chops (4 oz. *each*)
- 1   Tbsp. butter

**1.** In a small bowl, combine the first 12 ingredients. In a large skillet coated with cooking spray, brown pork chops in butter. Stir in fruit mixture. Bring to a boil. Reduce heat; cover and simmer for 3-4 minutes on each side or until a thermometer reads 160°.

**Nutrition Facts:** 1 serving equals 229 calories, 9 g fat (4 g saturated fat), 62 mg cholesterol, 283 mg sodium, 13 g carbohydrate, 1 g fiber, 22 g protein. **Diabetic Exchanges:** 3 lean meat, 1 starch, 1/2 fat.

Dried herbs don't spoil, but they lose flavor and potency over time. For maximum flavor in your cooking, replace herbs that are more than a year old. Store dried herbs in airtight containers and keep them away from heat and light.

PORK CHOPS WITH CRANBERRY DIJON SAUCE

## Tangy Pineapple Glaze F S C

**PREP/TOTAL TIME:** 5 min. **YIELD:** 1 cup

### JOAN HALLFORD • NORTH RICHLAND HILLS, TEXAS

*A few basic ingredients can easily dress up a ham. This glaze will cover an 8- to 10-lb. ham and provides about 20 servings.*

| | |
|---|---|
| 1 | can (8 oz.) unsweetened crushed pineapple, drained |
| 1/2 | cup apricot jam |
| 1 | Tbsp. spicy brown mustard |
| 2 | tsp. prepared horseradish |

**1.** In a small bowl, combine all ingredients. Brush over ham during the last 30 minutes of cooking.

**Nutrition Facts:** 2-1/2 tsp. equals 27 calories, trace fat (trace saturated fat), 0 cholesterol, 15 mg sodium, 7 g carbohydrate, trace fiber, trace protein. **Diabetic Exchange:** 1/2 starch.

## Peachy Pork with Rice

**PREP/TOTAL TIME:** 30 min. **YIELD:** 4 servings

### MELISSA MOLAISON • HAWKINSVILLE, GEORGIA

*Peach preserves sweeten the spicy salsa in this delicious dish that's nice enough for company. Adjust the heat level to taste by using mild or spicy salsa and seasoning.*

| | |
|---|---|
| 1-1/2 | cups instant brown rice |
| 1 | pork tenderloin (1 lb.), cut into 1-in. cubes |
| 2 | Tbsp. olive oil |
| 2 | Tbsp. reduced-sodium taco seasoning |
| 1 | cup salsa |
| 3 | Tbsp. peach preserves |

**1.** Cook rice according to package directions. Meanwhile, place pork in a large bowl; drizzle with oil. Sprinkle with taco seasoning; toss to coat.

**2.** In a large nonstick skillet coated with cooking spray, cook pork for 8-10 minutes or until no longer pink. Stir in salsa and preserves; heat through. Serve with rice.

**Nutrition Facts:** 1 cup pork mixture with 1/2 cup rice equals 387 calories, 12 g fat (2 g saturated fat), 63 mg cholesterol, 540 mg sodium, 42 g carbohydrate, 2 g fiber, 25 g protein. **Diabetic Exchanges:** 3 lean meat, 2-1/2 starch, 1-1/2 fat.

## Pork with Blueberry Herb Sauce

**PREP:** 25 min. **COOK:** 10 min. **YIELD:** 4 servings

### LIBBY WALP • CHICAGO, ILLINOIS

*A different and delicious way to use blueberries, this tangy, sweet-savory sauce would also be great over chicken. The blend of berries and balsamic vinegar is wonderful!*

| | |
|---|---|
| 1 | garlic clove, minced |
| 1 | tsp. pepper |
| 1/2 | tsp. salt |
| 1/8 | tsp. cayenne pepper |
| 4 | boneless pork loin chops (6 oz.each) |
| 2 | cups fresh blueberries |
| 1/4 | cup packed brown sugar |
| 2 | Tbsp. minced fresh parsley |
| 1 | Tbsp. balsamic vinegar |
| 2 | tsp. butter |
| 1 | tsp. minced fresh thyme *or* 1/4 tsp. dried thyme |
| 1 | tsp. fresh sage *or* 1/4 tsp. dried sage leaves |

**1.** In a small bowl, combine the garlic, pepper, salt and cayenne; sprinkle over pork.

**2.** In a large ovenproof skillet coated with cooking spray, brown pork chops. Bake uncovered, at 350° for 10-15 minutes or until a thermometer reads 160°. Remove pork and keep warm.

**3.** In the same skillet, add the remaining ingredients. Cook and stir over medium heat until thickened, about 8 minutes. Serve with pork.

**Nutrition Facts:** 1 pork chop with 1/4 cup sauce equals 343 calories, 12 g fat (5 g saturated fat), 87 mg cholesterol, 364 mg sodium, 25 g carbohydrate, 2 g fiber, 33 g protein. **Diabetic Exchanges:** 5 lean meat, 1 starch, 1/2 fruit.

PEACHY PORK WITH RICE

PORK WITH BLUEBERRY HERB SAUCE

# Spice-Rubbed Ham  C

**PREP:** 15 min.  **BAKE:** 3-1/4 hours + standing
**YIELD:** 24 servings

**SHARON TIPTON • WINTER GARDEN, FLORIDA**

*Now this is a ham—sweet and smoky, with just enough clove
and ginger flavor to let you know you're in for a holiday treat.*

1 fully cooked semi-boneless ham (8 to 10 lbs.)
1/2 cup spicy brown mustard
1/4 cup packed brown sugar
1/4 tsp. ground ginger
1/4 tsp. ground cinnamon
Whole cloves

**1.** Place ham on a rack in a shallow roasting pan.
Score the surface of the ham, making diamond shapes
1/2 in. deep. Combine the mustard, brown sugar,
ginger and cinnamon; rub over surface of ham. Insert
a clove in each diamond.

**2.** Bake, uncovered, at 325° for 1-1/2 hours. Cover
and bake 1-3/4 to 2 hours longer or until a
thermometer reads 140°. Cover loosely with foil if
ham browns too quickly. Discard cloves. Let stand for
10 minutes before slicing.

**Nutrition Facts:** 3 oz. cooked ham equals 139 calories, 4 g fat
(1 g saturated fat), 66 mg cholesterol, 858 mg sodium, 3 g
carbohydrate, trace fiber, 22 g protein. **Diabetic Exchange:**
3 lean meat.

> When a label reads that a ham is "fully cooked" it means
> that the meat is cooked and smoked and/or cured. The
> ham can be eaten without being warmed, but it is
> generally heated to an internal temperature of 140° for
> optimal flavor.

PORK CHOPS
WITH APRICOT GLAZE

# Pork Chops
# With Apricot Glaze

**PREP/TOTAL TIME:** 30 min.  **YIELD:** 6 servings

**KATHY HARDING • RICHMOND, MISSOURI**

*Wow! What an impressive-looking main course. No one will guess it came together in about a half hour!*

1-1/2  tsp. ground ginger
   1  tsp. salt
 1/2  tsp. garlic powder
 1/2  tsp. pepper
   6  boneless pork loin chops (6 oz. *each*)
   1  cup apricot preserves
   2  Tbsp. hoisin sauce
 1/2  tsp. crushed red pepper flakes
   2  green onions, chopped
   3  Tbsp. chopped unsalted peanuts

**1.** Combine the ginger, salt, garlic powder and pepper; rub over chops. In a small saucepan, combine the preserves, hoisin sauce and pepper flakes. Cook and stir over medium heat until preserves are melted. Set aside 1/2 cup sauce for brushing.

**2.** Moisten a paper towel with cooking oil; using long-handled tongs, lightly coat the grill rack. Grill pork, covered, over medium heat or broil 4-5 in. from the heat for 4-5 minutes on each side or until a thermometer reads 145°, basting frequently with sauce. Let stand 5 minutes before serving. Brush with reserved sauce before serving; sprinkle with green onions and peanuts.

**Nutrition Facts:** 1 pork chop equals 399 calories, 12 g fat (4 g saturated fat), 82 mg cholesterol, 549 mg sodium, 39 g carbohydrate, 1 g fiber, 34 g protein.

# Raspberry Chipotle Glaze for Ham F S C

**PREP/TOTAL TIME:** 15 min.
**YIELD:** 1-2/3 cups (enough for an 8- to 10-lb. ham)

**MARY LOU WAYMAN • SALT LAKE CITY, UTAH**

*A wonderfully different combination of flavors creates my terrific glaze. It easily covers an 8- to 10-lb. ham and provides about 20 servings.*

- 1 jar (12 oz.) seedless raspberry jam
- 2 Tbsp. white vinegar
- 2 chipotle peppers in adobo sauce, drained, seeded and minced
- 2 to 3 garlic cloves, minced
- 2 tsp. coarsely ground pepper

**1.** In a small saucepan, combine the jam, vinegar, peppers and garlic. Bring to a boil. Reduce heat; simmer, uncovered, for 5 minutes. Brush over ham during the last 30 minutes of cooking. Sprinkle with pepper before serving.

**Nutrition Facts:** 4 tsp. equals 45 calories, trace fat (0 saturated fat), 0 cholesterol, 10 mg sodium, 11 g carbohydrate, trace fiber, trace protein. **Diabetic Exchange:** 1 starch.

# Ham Noodle Casserole

**PREP:** 15 min. **BAKE:** 20 min. **YIELD:** 6 servings

**SHERI SWITZER • CRAWFORDVILLE, INDIANA**

*My mom used to make the original version of this mild curry casserole, which I loved. It didn't fit my healthier eating habits until I made a few changes. Now our entire family can enjoy it without the guilt.*

- 6 cups uncooked no-yolk medium noodles
- 1 can (10-3/4 oz.) reduced-fat reduced-sodium condensed cream of celery soup, undiluted
- 1 cup cubed fully cooked lean ham
- 2/3 cup cubed reduced-fat process American cheese
- 1/2 cup fat-free milk
- 1/4 cup thinly sliced green onions
- 1/2 tsp. curry powder

**1.** Cook noodles according to package directions; drain and place in a large bowl. Stir in the remaining ingredients.

**2.** Transfer to a 2-1/2-qt. baking dish coated with cooking spray. Cover and bake at 375° for 20-30 minutes or until heated through.

**Nutrition Facts:** 1 cup equals 241 calories, 4 g fat (2 g saturated fat), 20 mg cholesterol, 725 mg sodium, 35 g carbohydrate, 3 g fiber, 15 g protein. **Diabetic Exchanges:** 2-1/2 starch, 1 lean meat.

# Pineapple Pork Tenderloin

**PREP:** 10 min. + marinating **GRILL:** 30 min.
**YIELD:** 4 servings

**DONNA NOEL • GRAY, MAINE**

*Just a handful of ingredients creates this easy, elegant entree that pairs juicy, grilled pineapple slices and ginger-flavored pork tenderloin. It's sure to be popular with all ages. It's simply delicious!*

- 1 cup unsweetened pineapple juice
- 1/4 cup minced fresh gingerroot
- 1/4 cup reduced-sodium soy sauce
- 4 garlic cloves, minced
- 1 tsp. ground mustard
- 2 pork tenderloins (3/4 lb. *each*)
- 1 fresh pineapple, cut into 12 slices

**1.** In a small bowl, combine the first five ingredients. Pour 2/3 cup marinade into a large resealable plastic bag. Add the pork; seal bag and turn to coat. Refrigerate for 8 hours or overnight. Cover and refrigerate remaining marinade.

**2.** Drain and discard marinade. Moisten a paper towel with cooking oil; using long-handled tongs, lightly coat the grill rack.

**3.** Prepare grill for indirect heat, using a drip pan. Place pork over drip pan and grill, covered, over indirect medium-hot heat for 25-30 minutes or until a thermometer reads 160°, basting occasionally with the reserved marinade. Let stand for 5 minutes before slicing.

**4.** Meanwhile, grill pineapple slices for 2-3 minutes on each side or until heated through; serve with pork.

**Nutrition Facts:** 5 oz. cooked pork with 3 pineapple slices equals 295 calories, 6 g fat (2 g saturated fat), 95 mg cholesterol, 523 mg sodium, 23 g carbohydrate, 2 g fiber, 36 g protein. **Diabetic Exchanges:** 5 lean meat, 1 fruit.

> Keep tenderloin in the freezer for last-minute meals since it thaws and cooks quickly. Thaw the **pork tenderloin** using the "defrost" cycle of your microwave according to the manufacturer's directions.

PINEAPPLE PORK TENDERLOIN

## Makeover Linguine With Ham & Swiss Cheese

**PREP:** 15 min. **BAKE:** 45 min. **YIELD:** 8 servings

**MIKE TCHOU • PEPPER PIKE, OHIO**

*This rich linguine casserole recipe eliminates nearly half the saturated fat from the original, but keeps the creamy texture and distinctive Swiss cheese flavor.*

8 oz. uncooked multigrain linguine, broken in half
2 cups cubed fully cooked lean ham
1-3/4 cups (7 oz.) shredded Swiss cheese, *divided*
1 can (10-3/4 oz.) reduced-fat reduced-sodium condensed cream of mushroom soup, undiluted
1 cup (8 oz.) reduced-fat sour cream
1 medium onion, chopped
1 small green pepper, finely chopped

**1.** Cook linguine according to package directions. Meanwhile, in a large bowl, combine the ham, 1-1/2 cups cheese, soup, sour cream, onion and green pepper. Drain the pasta; add to the ham mixture and stir to coat.

**2.** Transfer to a 13-in. x 9-in. baking dish coated with cooking spray. Cover and bake at 350° for 35 minutes. Uncover; sprinkle with remaining cheese. Bake 10-15 minutes longer or until cheese is melted.

**Nutrition Facts:** 1 cup equals 293 calories, 12 g fat (7 g saturated fat), 47 mg cholesterol, 665 mg sodium, 29 g carbohydrate, 4 g fiber, 19 g protein. **Diabetic Exchanges:** 2 starch, 2 lean meat, 1 fat.

Feel free to get creative with this **casserole.** Use cream of onion soup or toss in a handful of frozen peas or fresh sliced mushrooms.

MAKEOVER LINGUINE WITH HAM & SWISS CHEESE

## Pork Chops with Cherry Sauce

**PREP/TOTAL TIME:** 25 min. **YIELD:** 2 servings

**KENDRA DOSS • KANSAS CITY, MISSOURI**

*Enjoy the rich flavor of this dish, which is just right for two. The spice rub also works well on lamb or beef.*

1 Tbsp. finely chopped shallot
1 tsp. olive oil
1 cup fresh *or* frozen pitted dark sweet cherries, halved
1/3 cup ruby port wine
1 tsp. balsamic vinegar
1/8 tsp. salt
PORK CHOPS:
1 tsp. coriander seeds, crushed
3/4 tsp. ground mustard
1/4 tsp. salt
1/4 tsp. pepper
2 bone-in pork loin chops (7 oz. *each*)
2 tsp. olive oil

**1.** In a small saucepan, saute the shallot in oil until tender. Stir in the cherries, wine, vinegar and salt. Bring to a boil; cook until liquid is reduced by half, about 10 minutes.

**2.** Meanwhile, in a small bowl, combine the coriander, mustard, salt and pepper; rub over chops. In a large skillet, cook chops in oil over medium heat for 4-6 minutes on each side or until a thermometer reads 160°. Serve with sauce.

**Nutrition Facts:** 1 pork chop with 1/3 cup sauce equals 356 calories, 16 g fat (4 g saturated fat), 86 mg cholesterol, 509 mg sodium, 16 g carbohydrate, 2 g fiber, 32 g protein. **Diabetic Exchanges:** 4 lean meat, 1-1/2 fat, 1 fruit.

## Oven-Barbecued Pork Tenderloins C

**PREP:** 5 min. **BAKE:** 35 min. **YIELD:** 6 servings

**RUBY WILLIAMS • BOGALUSA, LOUISIANA**

*Pork tenderloin is one of the leanest cuts of meat. This luscious heirloom recipe is a wonderful way to serve it with very little preparation time.*

3 Tbsp. ketchup
2 Tbsp. cider vinegar
1 Tbsp. maple syrup
2 tsp. Dijon mustard
1 tsp. Worcestershire sauce
1/8 tsp. cayenne pepper
2 pork tenderloins (3/4 lb. *each*)

**1.** In a small bowl, combine the first six ingredients. Place tenderloins on a rack in a shallow roasting pan; spoon some of the sauce over pork.

**2.** Bake, uncovered, at 425° for 35-40 minutes or until a thermometer reads 160°, basting occasionally with remaining sauce.

**3.** Let stand for 5 minutes before slicing.

CRUMB-CRUSTED PORK ROAST
WITH ROOT VEGETABLES

**Nutrition Facts:** 3 oz. cooked pork equals 151 calories, 4 g fat (1 g saturated fat), 63 mg cholesterol, 185 mg sodium, 5 g carbohydrate, trace fiber, 23 g protein. **Diabetic Exchange:** 3 lean meat.

# Crumb-Crusted Pork Roast With Root Vegetables

**PREP:** 25 min.  **BAKE:** 1-1/2 hours + standing
**YIELD:** 8 servings

**HEALTHY COOKING TEST KITCHEN**

*Perfect for fall, this hearty meal combines sweet roasted veggies with a savory crumb coating.*

- 1 boneless pork loin roast (2 to 3 lbs.)
- 4-1/2 tsp. honey
- 1 Tbsp. molasses
- 1-1/2 tsp. spicy brown mustard
- 2 tsp. rubbed sage
- 1 tsp. dried thyme
- 1 tsp. dried rosemary, crushed
- 1/2 cup soft whole wheat bread crumbs
- 2 Tbsp. grated Parmesan cheese
- 1 large celery root, peeled and cut into 1/2-in. cubes
- 1 large rutabaga, peeled and cut into 1/2-in. cubes
- 1 large sweet potato, peeled and cut into 1/2-in. cubes
- 1 large onion, cut into wedges
- 2 Tbsp. canola oil
- 1/2 tsp. salt
- 1/4 tsp. pepper

**1.** Place roast on a rack in a shallow roasting pan coated with cooking spray. In a small bowl, combine the honey, molasses and mustard; brush over roast. In another small bowl, combine the sage, thyme and rosemary; set aside. Combine the bread crumbs, Parmesan cheese and 2 tsp. of the herb mixture; press onto roast.

**2.** In a resealable plastic bag, combine the celery root, rutabaga, sweet potato, onion, oil, salt, pepper and remaining herb mixture; toss to coat. Arrange vegetables around roast.

**3.** Bake, uncovered, at 350° for 1-1/2 to 1-3/4 hours or until a thermometer reads 160°. Transfer to a warm serving platter. Let stand for 10-15 minutes before slicing.

**Nutrition Facts:** 3 oz. cooked pork with 3/4 cup vegetables equals 302 calories, 10 g fat (2 g saturated fat), 57 mg cholesterol, 313 mg sodium, 29 g carbohydrate, 5 g fiber, 25 g protein. **Diabetic Exchanges:** 3 lean meat, 2 starch, 1/2 fat.

THAI SHRIMP SOUP

GLAZED SALMON SALAD

PINEAPPLE PICO TUNA STEAKS

# Fish & Seafood

Light and refreshing, seafood is a natural choice for those looking to cut calories and eat healthy. Turn here for change-of-pace menu options you'll adore...most of which pare down carbs and come together in no time!

## Pineapple Pico Tuna Steaks

**PREP:** 10 min. + marinating **GRILL:** 10 min.
**YIELD:** 4 servings

**SALLY SIBTHORPE • SHELBY TOWNSHIP, MICHIGAN**

*Bursting with flavor from a quick and easy marinade, these tuna steaks are topped with pico de gallo made of pineapple, tomatoes, lime juice and a nice kick of jalapeno.*

- 1/2 cup tequila
- 3 Tbsp. brown sugar
- 2 Tbsp. lime juice
- 1 Tbsp. chili powder
- 1 Tbsp. olive oil
- 1 tsp. salt
- 4 tuna steaks (6 oz. *each*)

PICO DE GALLO:
- 1 cup chopped fresh pineapple
- 1 plum tomato, finely chopped
- 1/3 cup finely chopped onion
- 1/4 cup minced fresh cilantro
- 2 Tbsp. minced seeded jalapeno pepper
- 2 Tbsp. lime juice
- 1 Tbsp. olive oil
- 2 tsp. grated lime peel
- 1/2 tsp. salt

**1.** In a large resealable plastic bag, combine the first six ingredients. Add the tuna; seal bag and turn to coat. Refrigerate for 30 minutes. Meanwhile, in a small bowl, combine pico de gallo ingredients. Cover and refrigerate until serving.

**2.** Drain and discard marinade. Using long-handled tongs, moisten a paper towel with cooking oil and lightly coat the grill rack. For medium-rare, grill tuna, covered, over high heat or broil 3-4 in. from the heat for 3-4 minutes on each side or until slightly pink in the center. Serve with pico de gallo.

**Editor's Note:** Wear disposable gloves when cutting hot peppers; the oils can burn skin. Avoid touching your face.

**Nutrition Facts:** 1 tuna steak with 1/2 cup salsa equals 385 calories, 9 g fat (1 g saturated fat), 77 mg cholesterol, 974 mg sodium, 20 g carbohydrate, 2 g fiber, 41 g protein. **Diabetic Exchanges:** 5 lean meat, 1/2 starch, 1/2 fat.

## Thai Shrimp Soup  **C**

**PREP:** 20 min.  **COOK:** 20 min.  **YIELD:** 8 servings (2 qt.)

**JESSIE GREARSON-SAPAT • FALMOUTH, MAINE**

*This tasty, crowd-pleasing soup comes together in minutes, and I like the fact that the ingredients are available in my little local grocery store.*

- 1 medium onion, chopped
- 1 Tbsp. olive oil
- 3 cups reduced-sodium chicken broth
- 1 cup water
- 1 Tbsp. brown sugar
- 1 Tbsp. minced fresh gingerroot
- 1 Tbsp. fish *or* soy sauce
- 1 Tbsp. red curry paste
- 1 lemon grass stalk
- 1 lb. uncooked large shrimp, peeled and deveined
- 1-1/2 cups frozen shelled edamame
- 1 can (14 oz.) light coconut milk
- 1 can (8-3/4 oz.) whole baby corn, drained and cut in half
- 1/2 cup bamboo shoots
- 1/4 cup fresh basil leaves, torn
- 1/4 cup minced fresh cilantro
- 2 Tbsp. lime juice
- 1-1/2 tsp. grated lime peel
- 1 tsp. curry powder

**1.** In a Dutch oven, saute onion in oil until tender. Add the broth, water, brown sugar, ginger, fish sauce, curry paste and lemon grass. Bring to a boil. Reduce heat; carefully stir in shrimp and edamame. Cook, uncovered, for 5-6 minutes or until shrimp turn pink.

**2.** Add the coconut milk, corn, bamboo shoots, basil, cilantro, lime juice, lime peel and curry powder; heat through. Discard lemon grass.

**Nutrition Facts:** 1 cup equals 163 calories, 7 g fat (3 g saturated fat), 69 mg cholesterol, 505 mg sodium, 9 g carbohydrate, 2 g fiber, 14 g protein. **Diabetic Exchanges:** 2 lean meat, 1 vegetable, 1 fat.

## Creole Baked Tilapia F C

**PREP/TOTAL TIME:** 25 min. **YIELD:** 4 servings

**CAROLYN COLLINS • FREEPORT, TEXAS**

*Since I'm originally from Louisiana, I love Creole cooking. This is quick and easy as well as healthy. It's great served with your favorite rice dish. Enjoy!*

|     |                                      |
| --- | ------------------------------------ |
| 4   | tilapia fillets (6 oz. *each*)       |
| 1   | can (8 oz.) tomato sauce             |
| 1   | small green pepper, thinly sliced    |
| 1/2 | cup chopped red onion                |
| 1   | tsp. Creole seasoning                |

**1.** Place tilapia in an ungreased 13-in. x 9-in. baking dish. In a small bowl, combine the tomato sauce, green pepper, onion and Creole seasoning; pour over the fillets.

**2.** Bake, uncovered, at 350° for 20-25 minutes or until fish flakes easily with a fork.

**Editor's Note:** The following spices may be substituted for 1 tsp. Creole seasoning: 1/4 tsp. each salt, garlic powder and paprika; and a pinch each of dried thyme, ground cumin and cayenne pepper.

**Nutrition Facts:** 1 fish fillet with 1/3 cup topping equals 166 calories, 2 g fat (1 g saturated fat), 83 mg cholesterol, 488 mg sodium, 6 g carbohydrate, 1 g fiber, 33 g protein. **Diabetic Exchanges:** 5 lean meat, 1 vegetable.

## Glazed Salmon Salad C

**PREP:** 20 min. **BAKE:** 20 min. **YIELD:** 4 servings

**ELIZABETH DEHART • WEST JORDAN, UTAH**

*Honey and smoked paprika lend delightful flavors and a bright color to this beautiful dish. It has a special feeling but is quick enough for weeknights, too.*

|       |                                   |
| ----- | --------------------------------- |
| 4     | salmon fillets (4 oz. *each*)     |
| 1     | Tbsp. olive oil                   |
| 2     | tsp. smoked paprika               |
| 2     | tsp. honey                        |
| 1     | garlic clove, minced              |
| 1/2   | tsp. salt                         |
| 1/2   | tsp. pepper                       |
| 1/4   | tsp. crushed red pepper flakes    |

SALAD:

|       |                                   |
| ----- | --------------------------------- |
| 4     | cups fresh baby spinach           |
| 1/2   | cup shredded carrot               |
| 1/4   | cup chopped red onion             |
| 1/4   | cup olive oil                     |
| 2     | Tbsp. cider vinegar               |
| 1-1/2 | tsp. finely chopped shallot       |
| 1     | tsp. Dijon mustard                |

**1.** Place salmon in an 11-in. x 7-in. baking dish coated with cooking spray.

**2.** In a small bowl, combine the oil, paprika, honey, garlic, salt, pepper and pepper flakes; brush over salmon. Bake, uncovered, at 350° for 20-25 minutes or until fish flakes easily with a fork. Cut salmon into 1-in. pieces.

**3.** In a large bowl, combine the spinach, carrot and onion. Divide among four serving plates; top with salmon. In a small bowl, combine the oil, vinegar, shallot and mustard; drizzle over the salads. Serve the salads immediately.

**Nutrition Facts:** 1 serving equals 362 calories, 28 g fat (4 g saturated fat), 57 mg cholesterol, 417 mg sodium, 8 g carbohydrate, 2 g fiber, 21 g protein.

CREOLE BAKED TILAPIA

GLAZED SALMON SALAD

# Broiled Parmesan Tilapia C

**PREP/TOTAL TIME:** 20 min.  **YIELD:** 6 servings

**TRISHA KRUSE • EAGLE, IDAHO**

*Even picky families will change their minds about eating fish with this toasty, cheesy Parmesan-coated dish. I serve it with mashed cauliflower and a green salad for a low-carb meal everyone loves.*

| | |
|---|---|
| 6 | tilapia fillets (6 oz. *each*) |
| 1/4 | cup grated Parmesan cheese |
| 1/4 | cup reduced-fat mayonnaise |
| 2 | Tbsp. lemon juice |
| 1 | Tbsp. butter, softened |
| 1 | garlic clove, minced |
| 1 | tsp. minced fresh basil *or* 1/4 tsp. dried basil |
| 1/2 | tsp. seafood seasoning |

**1.** Place fillets on a broiler pan coated with cooking spray. In a small bowl, combine the remaining ingredients; spread over fillets.

**2.** Broil 3-4 in. from the heat for 10-12 minutes or until fish flakes easily with a fork.

**Nutrition Facts:** 1 fillet equals 207 calories, 8 g fat (3 g saturated fat), 94 mg cholesterol, 260 mg sodium, 2 g carbohydrate, trace fiber, 33 g protein. **Diabetic Exchanges:** 5 lean meat, 1 fat.

# Scallops with Citrus Glaze C

**PREP/TOTAL TIME:** 20 min.  **YIELD:** 4 servings

**PATRICIA NIEH • PORTOLA VALLEY, CALIFORNIA**

*These scallops are especially scrumptious when served on steamed rice with a green veggie on the side.*

| | |
|---|---|
| 12 | sea scallops (about 1-1/2 lbs.) |
| 1/2 | tsp. pepper |
| 1/4 | tsp. salt |
| 2 | Tbsp. olive oil, *divided* |
| 4 | garlic cloves, minced |
| 1/2 | cup orange juice |
| 1/4 | cup lemon juice |
| 1 | Tbsp. reduced-sodium soy sauce |
| 1/2 | tsp. grated orange peel |

**1.** Sprinkle scallops with pepper and salt. In a large skillet, saute scallops in 1 Tbsp. oil until firm and opaque. Remove and keep warm.

**2.** In the same skillet, cook garlic in remaining oil for 1 minute. Add the juices, soy sauce and orange peel. Bring to a boil; cook and stir for 5 minutes or until thickened. Serve with scallops.

**Nutrition Facts:** 3 scallops with 2 tsp. glaze equals 235 calories, 8 g fat (1 g saturated fat), 56 mg cholesterol, 574 mg sodium, 10 g carbohydrate, trace fiber, 29 g protein. **Diabetic Exchanges:** 4 lean meat, 1-1/2 fat.

FIRECRACKER GRILLED SALMON

## Firecracker Grilled Salmon c

**PREP:** 20 min. + marinating **GRILL:** 5 min.
**YIELD:** 4 servings

**MELISSA ROGERS • TUSCALOOSA, ALABAMA**

*Let this sensational salmon perk up dinner tonight. With a super flavorful glaze that kicks you right in the taste buds, this dish is anything but boring!*

|     |                              |
| --- | ---------------------------- |
| 2   | Tbsp. balsamic vinegar       |
| 2   | Tbsp. reduced-sodium soy sauce |
| 1   | green onion, thinly sliced   |
| 1   | Tbsp. olive oil              |
| 1   | Tbsp. maple syrup            |
| 2   | garlic cloves, minced        |
| 1   | tsp. ground ginger           |
| 1   | tsp. crushed red pepper flakes |
| 1/2 | tsp. sesame oil              |
| 1/4 | tsp. salt                    |
| 4   | salmon fillets (6 oz. *each*) |

**1.** In a small bowl, combine the first ten ingredients. Pour 1/4 cup marinade into a large resealable plastic bag. Add the salmon; seal bag and turn to coat. Refrigerate for up to 30 minutes. Cover and refrigerate remaining marinade. Drain and discard the marinade.

**2.** Using long-handled tongs, moisten a paper towel with cooking oil and lightly coat the grill rack. Place salmon skin side down on grill rack. Grill, covered, over high heat or broil 3-4 in. from the heat for 5-10 minutes or until fish flakes easily with a fork, basting occasionally with remaining marinade.

**Nutrition Facts:** 1 fillet equals 306 calories, 18 g fat (4 g saturated fat), 85 mg cholesterol, 367 mg sodium, 4 g carbohydrate, trace fiber, 29 g protein. **Diabetic Exchanges:** 5 lean meat, 1 fat.

## Spicy Mango Scallops

**PREP/TOTAL TIME:** 30 min. **YIELD:** 4 servings

**NICOLE FILIZETTI • JACKSONVILLE, FLORIDA**

*This sweet and spicy seafood combo gives off enough heat to make the whole family warm up to its great flavors! Be sure to buy the larger sea scallops for this recipe; cooking times would be off for the smaller bay scallops.*

|     |                                   |
| --- | --------------------------------- |
| 12  | sea scallops (1-1/2 lbs.)         |
| 1   | Tbsp. peanut oil                  |
| 1   | medium red onion, chopped         |
| 1   | garlic clove, minced              |
| 1/4 | to 1/2 tsp. crushed red pepper flakes |
| 1/2 | cup unsweetened pineapple juice   |
| 1/4 | cup mango chutney                 |
| 2   | cups hot cooked basmati rice      |

Minced fresh cilantro

**1.** In a large skillet, saute scallops in oil for 1-1/2 to 2 minutes on each side or until firm and opaque. Remove and keep warm.

**2.** In the same skillet, saute onion until tender. Add garlic and pepper flakes; cook 1 minute longer. Stir in pineapple juice. Bring to a boil; cook until liquid is reduced by half. Remove from the heat. Add chutney and scallops; stir to coat. Serve with rice; drizzle with sauce. Sprinkle with cilantro.

**Nutrition Facts:** 3 scallops with 1/2 cup cooked rice and 2 Tbsp. sauce equals 371 calories, 5 g fat (1 g saturated fat), 56 mg cholesterol, 447 mg sodium, 47 g carbohydrate, 1 g fiber, 31 g protein. **Diabetic Exchanges:** 4 lean meat, 3 starch, 1/2 fat.

# Curried Halibut Skillet

**PREP/TOTAL TIME:** 25 min.  **YIELD:** 4 servings

**KAREN KUEBLER • DALLAS, TEXAS**

*My friend in England told me coconut is all the rage there, so I've been experimenting with it in main dishes here at home. This is one of my most successful recipes.*

| | |
|---|---|
| 4 | halibut fillets (4 oz. *each*) |
| 1/2 | tsp. salt |
| 4 | tsp. curry powder |
| 2 | Tbsp. olive oil, *divided* |
| 1 | large sweet onion, chopped |
| 1 | can (14-1/2 oz.) diced tomatoes, undrained |
| 2 | Tbsp. lime juice |
| 1-1/2 | tsp. grated lime peel |
| 1 | tsp. minced fresh gingerroot |
| 1/4 | cup flaked coconut, toasted |
| 1/4 | cup minced fresh cilantro |

**1.** Sprinkle fillets with salt; coat with curry. In a large nonstick skillet coated with cooking spray, brown fillets in 1 Tbsp. oil; remove and set aside.

**2.** In the same pan, saute onion in remaining oil for 1 minute. Stir in the tomatoes, lime juice, lime peel and ginger. Bring to a boil. Return fillets to the pan; cover and simmer for 10-12 minutes or until fish flakes easily with a fork. Serve with tomato mixture; sprinkle with coconut and cilantro.

**Nutrition Facts:** 1 serving equals 270 calories, 12 g fat (3 g saturated fat), 36 mg cholesterol, 510 mg sodium, 16 g carbohydrate, 3 g fiber, 26 g protein. **Diabetic Exchanges:** 3 lean meat, 2 vegetable, 1-1/2 fat.

# Spicy Shrimp Kabobs ▣F

**PREP:** 15 min. + marinating  **GRILL:** 5 min.
**YIELD:** 4 servings

**MICHELE TUNGETT • ROCHESTER, ILLINOIS**

*Shrimp lovers will adore these spicy, juicy kabobs. Adjust the cayenne to suit your preference for more or less heat. They are so quick and easy!*

| | |
|---|---|
| 1/4 | cup tomato sauce |
| 2 | Tbsp. minced fresh basil or 2 tsp. dried basil |
| 2 | Tbsp. red wine vinegar |
| 3 | garlic cloves, minced |
| 1 | Tbsp. olive oil |
| 1/4 | tsp. salt |
| 1/4 | tsp. cayenne pepper |
| 1 | lb. uncooked medium shrimp, peeled and deveined |
| 1-1/2 | cups pineapple chunks |
| 1 | medium onion, cut into wedges |

**1.** In a large resealable plastic bag, combine the first seven ingredients. Add the shrimp; seal bag and turn to coat. Refrigerate for up to 2 hours.

**2.** Drain and discard marinade. On eight metal or soaked wooden skewers, alternately thread the shrimp, pineapple and onion. Using long-handled tongs, moisten a paper towel with cooking oil and lightly coat the grill rack. Grill kabobs, covered, over medium heat or broil 4 in. from the heat for 2-3 minutes on each side or until shrimp turn pink.

**Nutrition Facts:** 2 kabobs equals 187 calories, 3 g fat (1 g saturated fat), 138 mg cholesterol, 245 mg sodium, 20 g carbohydrate, 2 g fiber, 20 g protein. **Diabetic Exchanges:** 3 lean meat, 1 fruit.

CURRIED HALIBUT SKILLET

SPICY SHRIMP KABOBS

# Crusty Red Snapper

**PREP:** 25 min. **BAKE:** 20 min. **YIELD:** 6 servings

KELLY REMINGTON • ARCATA, CALIFORNIA

*This is an amazing dish. It's so easy, yet so elegant. The veggies steam the fish from the bottom, and covering the fillets with a crunchy topping keeps them moist.*

- 2 medium tomatoes, chopped
- 1 each medium green, sweet yellow and red pepper, chopped
- 1 cup chopped leeks (white portion only)
- 1/2 cup chopped celery leaves
- 2 garlic cloves, minced
- 6 red snapper fillets (4 oz. each)

TOPPING:
- 1/2 cup panko (Japanese) bread crumbs
- 1/2 cup coarsely crushed baked Parmesan and Tuscan herb potato chips
- 1/4 cup grated Parmesan cheese
- 1/2 tsp. salt
- 1/2 tsp. paprika
- 1/4 tsp. cayenne pepper
- 1/4 tsp. pepper
- 2 Tbsp. butter, melted

**1.** In a 15-in. x 10-in. x 1-in. baking pan coated with cooking spray, combine the tomatoes, peppers, leeks, celery leaves and garlic; arrange fillets over vegetable mixture.

**2.** In a small bowl, combine the bread crumbs, chips, cheese, salt, paprika, cayenne and pepper; stir in butter. Sprinkle over the fillets. Bake, uncovered, at 425° for 18-22 minutes or until the fish flakes easily with a fork.

**Nutrition Facts:** 1 fillet with 2/3 cup vegetable mixture equals 237 calories, 7 g fat (3 g saturated fat), 53 mg cholesterol, 396 mg sodium, 16 g carbohydrate, 3 g fiber, 26 g protein. **Diabetic Exchanges:** 3 lean meat, 1 vegetable, 1 fat, 1/2 starch.

# Grilled Salmon with Marmalade Dijon Glaze

**PREP/TOTAL TIME:** 20 min. **YIELD:** 4 servings

JUDY GREBETZ • RACINE, WISCONSIN

*This tender salmon takes just a handful of ingredients and is pretty enough to serve guests.*

- 1/2 cup orange marmalade
- 1 Tbsp. Dijon mustard
- 1/2 tsp. salt
- 1/2 tsp. garlic powder
- 1/4 tsp. pepper
- 1/8 tsp. ground ginger
- 4 salmon fillets (6 oz. each)

**1.** In a small bowl, combine the first six ingredients; set aside 1/4 cup. Brush remaining glaze over salmon.

**2.** Moisten a paper towel with cooking oil; using long-handled tongs, lightly coat the grill rack. Place salmon skin side down on grill rack.

**3.** Grill, covered, over medium heat or broil 4 in. from the heat for 10-12 minutes or until fish flakes easily with a fork, basting occasionally with the remaining glaze.

**Nutrition Facts:** 1 fillet equals 368 calories, 16 g fat (3 g saturated fat), 85 mg cholesterol, 493 mg sodium, 28 g carbohydrate, trace fiber, 29 g protein. **Diabetic Exchanges:** 4 lean meat, 1-1/2 starch, 1-1/2 fat.

CRUSTY RED SNAPPER

GRILLED SALMON WITH MARMALADE DIJON GLAZE

# Feta Shrimp with Linguine

**PREP/TOTAL TIME:** 30 min.  **YIELD:** 4 servings

**CHARLENE CHAMBERS • ORMOND BEACH, FLORIDA**

*Great Mediterranean flavors, full-fat feta cheese and a little heat make this one recipe to die for! I serve it with crusty bread, a green salad and red wine.*

|   |   |
|---|---|
| 8 | oz. uncooked multigrain linguine |
| 4 | garlic cloves, minced |
| 1 | tsp. olive oil |
| 1 | can (28 oz.) diced tomatoes, undrained |
| 1/4 | cup sun-dried tomatoes (not packed in oil), chopped |
| 1/4 | cup Greek olives, coarsely chopped |
| 1/4 | tsp. salt |
| 1/4 | tsp. pepper |
| 1 | lb. uncooked medium shrimp, peeled and deveined |
| 1/4 | cup minced fresh parsley |
| 2 | Tbsp. lemon juice |
| 1/4 | tsp. crushed red pepper flakes |
| 1/2 | cup crumbled feta cheese |

**1.** Cook linguine according to package directions. Meanwhile, in a large skillet, saute garlic in oil for 1 minute. Add the diced tomatoes, sun-dried tomatoes, olives, salt and pepper. Bring to a boil. Reduce heat; simmer, uncovered, for 8-10 minutes or until thickened, stirring occasionally.

**2.** Add the shrimp to the tomato mixture; cook, uncovered, for 5-6 minutes or until shrimp turn pink. Stir in the parsley, lemon juice and pepper flakes. Drain pasta; serve with shrimp mixture. Sprinkle with feta cheese.

**Nutrition Facts:** 1-1/4 cups shrimp mixture with 1 cup cooked linguine and 2 Tbsp. feta cheese equals 404 calories, 8 g fat (2 g saturated fat), 145 mg cholesterol, 881 mg sodium, 58 g carbohydrate, 10 g fiber, 30 g protein.

# Soy-Glazed Scallops C

**PREP:** 25 min. + marinating  **BROIL:** 5 min.
**YIELD:** 4 servings

**APRIL KORANDO • AVA, ILLINOIS**

*These yummy broiled scallops are a great source of vitamin B12 and heart-healthy minerals such as magnesium.*

|   |   |
|---|---|
| 1/4 | cup lemon juice |
| 2 | Tbsp. canola oil |
| 2 | Tbsp. reduced-sodium soy sauce |
| 2 | Tbsp. honey |
| 2 | garlic cloves, minced |
| 1/2 | tsp. ground ginger |
| 12 | sea scallops (about 1-1/2 lbs.) |

**1.** In a small bowl, combine the first six ingredients. Pour 1/3 cup marinade into a large resealable plastic bag. Add the scallops; seal bag and turn to coat. Refrigerate for 20 minutes.

**2.** Place remaining marinade in a small saucepan. Bring to a boil. Reduce heat; simmer, uncovered, for 8-10 minutes or until slightly thickened.

**3.** Drain and discard marinade. Thread scallops onto four metal or soaked wooden skewers. Broil 4 in. from the heat for 2-4 minutes on each side or until scallops are firm and opaque, basting occasionally with remaining marinade.

**Nutrition Facts:** 3 scallops equals 250 calories, 8 g fat (1 g saturated fat), 54 mg cholesterol, 567 mg sodium, 15 g carbohydrate, trace fiber, 28 g protein. **Diabetic Exchanges:** 4 lean meat, 1 fat, 1/2 starch.

# Chipotle Salmon with Strawberry Mango Salsa

**PREP/TOTAL TIME:** 25 min. **YIELD:** 4 servings

**NAYLET LAROCHELLE • MIAMI, FLORIDA**

*I've made this recipe several times for family dinners and have always received compliments. Even the kids like this sweet berry salsa with the spicy, savory salmon.*

- 2  Tbsp. brown sugar
- 3  garlic cloves, minced
- 2  tsp. finely chopped chipotle peppers in adobo sauce
- 1/4  tsp. salt
- 4  salmon fillets (6 oz. *each*)

SALSA:
- 2  cups chopped fresh strawberries
- 2/3  cup chopped peeled mango
- 1/3  cup chopped red onion
- 2  Tbsp. lime juice
- 1  Tbsp. minced fresh cilantro
- 1  Tbsp. minced fresh mint
- 2  tsp. olive oil

**1.** In a small bowl, combine the brown sugar, garlic, chipotle peppers and salt; rub over salmon.

**2.** Moisten a paper towel with cooking oil; using long-handled tongs, lightly coat the grill rack. Place salmon skin side down on grill rack. Grill salmon, covered, over high heat or broil 3-4 in. from heat for 5-10 minutes or until the fish flakes easily with a fork.

**3.** In a small bowl, combine the salsa ingredients; serve with salmon.

**Nutrition Facts:** 1 salmon fillet with 1/2 cup salsa equals 368 calories, 18 g fat (4 g saturated fat), 85 mg cholesterol, 255 mg sodium, 21 g carbohydrate, 3 g fiber, 30 g protein. **Diabetic Exchanges:** 5 lean meat, 1-1/2 fat, 1/2 starch, 1/2 fruit.

# Grapefruit Shrimp Salad c

**PREP/TOTAL TIME:** 15 min. **YIELD:** 4 servings

**JOANNE BEAUPRE • MANCHESTER, CONNECTICUT**

*A simple combination of shrimp, avocado and grapefruit add up to one simply fabulous salad.*

- 1  head Bibb *or* Boston lettuce
- 1  large grapefruit, peeled and sectioned
- 1  medium ripe avocado, peeled and thinly sliced
- 1  lb. cooked medium shrimp, peeled and deveined

CITRUS VINAIGRETTE:
- 2  Tbsp. orange juice
- 2  Tbsp. red wine vinegar
- 1  Tbsp. olive oil
- 2  tsp. Dijon mustard
- 1/4  tsp. salt

**1.** Place lettuce on four serving plates. Arrange the grapefruit, avocado and shrimp over lettuce. In a small bowl, whisk the vinaigrette ingredients. Drizzle over each salad.

**Nutrition Facts:** 1 serving equals 266 calories, 12 g fat (2 g saturated fat), 221 mg cholesterol, 445 mg sodium, 14 g carbohydrate, 4 g fiber, 26 g protein. **Diabetic Exchanges:** 3 lean meat, 2 fat, 1 vegetable, 1/2 fruit.

# Grilled Tilapia with Raspberry Chipotle Chutney

**PREP:** 40 min. **GRILL:** 5 min. **YIELD:** 4 servings

**MEGAN DICOU • BENTONVILLE, ARKANSAS**

*I eat a lot of fish and am always looking for healthy, tasty ways to prepare it. This recipe has become a family favorite because of the great flavors—and it's so easy to prepare, especially if you make the chutney ahead. I serve it with herbed couscous.*

- 1 medium red onion, chopped
- 1 medium sweet red pepper, chopped
- 2 tsp. olive oil
- 3 garlic cloves, minced
- 2 tsp. minced fresh gingerroot
- 1-1/2 cups fresh raspberries
- 3/4 cup reduced-sodium chicken broth
- 1/4 cup honey
- 2 Tbsp. cider vinegar
- 1 Tbsp. minced chipotle peppers in adobo sauce
- 1/2 tsp. salt, *divided*
- 1/2 tsp. pepper, *divided*
- 4 tilapia fillets (6 oz. *each*)

**1.** In a large saucepan, saute onion and pepper in oil until tender. Add garlic and ginger; cook 1 minute longer. Stir in the raspberries, broth, honey, vinegar, chipotle peppers, 1/4 tsp. salt and 1/4 tsp. pepper. Bring to a boil. Reduce heat; simmer, uncovered, for 25-30 minutes or until thickened.

**2.** Meanwhile, sprinkle fillets with remaining salt and pepper. Using long-handled tongs, moisten a paper towel with cooking oil and lightly coat the grill rack. Grill fish, covered, over high heat or broil 3-4 in. from the heat for 3-5 minutes or until fish flakes easily with a fork. Serve with chutney.

**Nutrition Facts:** 1 fillet with 1/4 cup chutney equals 277 calories, 4 g fat (1 g saturated fat), 83 mg cholesterol, 491 mg sodium, 29 g carbohydrate, 5 g fiber, 33 g protein. **Diabetic Exchanges:** 5 lean meat, 2 starch, 1/2 fat.

# Grilled Salmon Packets [c]

**PREP/TOTAL TIME:** 25 min. **YIELD:** 4 servings

**MIKE MILLER • CRESTON, IOWA**

*I don't like plain salmon, but this has a nice stir-fried flavor! It's a healthy meal-in-one favorite.*

- 4 salmon fillets (6 oz. *each*)
- 3 cups fresh sugar snap peas
- 1 small sweet red pepper, cut into strips
- 1 small sweet yellow pepper, cut into strips
- 1/4 cup reduced-fat Asian toasted sesame salad dressing

**1.** Place each salmon fillet on a double thickness of heavy-duty foil (about 12 in. square). Combine sugar snap peas and peppers; spoon over salmon. Drizzle with dressing. Fold foil around mixture and seal tightly.

**2.** Grill, covered, over medium heat for 15-20 minutes or until fish flakes easily with a fork. Open foil carefully to allow steam to escape.

**Nutrition Facts:** 1 salmon fillet with 1 cup vegetables equals 350 calories, 17 g fat (3 g saturated fat), 85 mg cholesterol, 237 mg sodium, 14 g carbohydrate, 4 g fiber, 34 g protein. **Diabetic Exchanges:** 4 lean meat, 2 vegetable, 2 fat.

GRILLED TILAPIA WITH RASPBERRY CHIPOTLE CHUTNEY

GRILLED SALMON PACKETS

## Halibut Steaks With Papaya Mint Salsa [S] [C]

**PREP/TOTAL TIME:** 20 min. **YIELD:** 4 servings

**SONYA LABBE • LOS ANGELES, CALIFORNIA**

*An amazing mix of fresh, zesty salsa and good, smoky flavor—plus 161 mg of magnesium—makes this dish the catch of the day!*

- 1 medium papaya, peeled, seeded and chopped
- 1/4 cup chopped red onion
- 1/4 cup fresh mint leaves
- 1 tsp. finely chopped chipotle pepper in adobo sauce
- 1 Tbsp. olive oil
- 1 Tbsp. honey
- 4 halibut steaks (6 oz. *each*)
- 1 Tbsp. olive oil

**1.** In a small bowl, combine the papaya, onion, mint, chipotle pepper, oil and honey. Cover and refrigerate until serving.

**2.** In a large skillet, cook halibut in oil for 4-6 minutes on each side or until fish flakes easily with a fork. Serve with salsa.

**Nutrition Facts:** 1 halibut steak with 1/2 cup salsa equals 300 calories, 11 g fat (2 g saturated fat), 54 mg cholesterol, 105 mg sodium, 13 g carbohydrate, 2 g fiber, 36 g protein. **Diabetic Exchanges:** 5 lean meat, 1 starch, 1 fat.

HALIBUT STEAKS WITH PAPAYA MINT SALSA

## Colorful Crab Stir-Fry

**PREP/TOTAL TIME:** 30 min. **YIELD:** 4 servings

**LEE DENEAU • LANSING, MICHIGAN**

*My love for seafood has carried over from childhood, when we used to fish together as a family. So I was happy to find this change-of-pace recipe that combines stir-fry with seafood. It tastes like a special treat but is a breeze to prepare.*

- 2 tsp. cornstarch
- 1 tsp. chicken bouillon granules
- 3/4 cup water
- 1/2 tsp. reduced-sodium soy sauce
- 1 cup sliced fresh carrots
- 1 Tbsp. canola oil
- 1 cup fresh *or* frozen snow peas
- 1/2 cup julienned sweet red pepper
- 1 tsp. minced fresh gingerroot
- 1 tsp. minced garlic
- 1 pkg. (8 oz.) imitation crabmeat

Hot cooked rice, optional

**1.** In a small bowl, combine the cornstarch, bouillon, water and soy sauce until smooth; set aside. In a large skillet or wok, stir-fry carrots in oil. Add the peas, red pepper, ginger and garlic; stir-fry 1-2 minutes longer or until vegetables are crisp-tender.

**2.** Stir cornstarch mixture and gradually add to the pan. Bring to a boil; cook and stir for 2 minutes or until thickened. Add crab; heat through. Serve with rice if desired.

**Nutrition Facts:** 3/4 cup (calculated without rice) equals 126 calories, 4 g fat (trace saturated fat), 7 mg cholesterol, 562 mg sodium, 16 g carbohydrate, 2 g fiber, 7 g protein. **Diabetic Exchanges:** 3 vegetable, 1 lean meat.

COLORFUL CRAB STIR-FRY

# Baked Italian Tilapia [C]

**PREP:** 10 min. **BAKE:** 40 min. **YIELD:** 4 servings

**KIMBERLY MCGEE • MOSHEIM, TENNESSEE**

*It's easy to include healthful fish in your weekly menus with recipes as tasty and simple as this one!*

| | |
|---|---|
| 4 | tilapia fillets (6 oz. *each*) |
| 1/4 | tsp. pepper |
| 1 | can (14-1/2 oz.) diced tomatoes with basil, oregano and garlic, drained |
| 1 | large onion, halved and julienned |
| 1 | medium green pepper, halved and julienned |
| 1/4 | cup shredded Parmesan cheese |

**1.** Place tilapia in a 13-in. x 9-in. baking dish coated with cooking spray; sprinkle with the pepper. Spoon the tomatoes over tilapia; top with the onion and the green pepper.

**2.** Cover and bake at 350° for 30 minutes. Uncover; sprinkle with cheese.

**3.** Bake 10-15 minutes longer or until fish flakes easily with a fork.

**Nutrition Facts:** 1 serving equals 215 calories, 4 g fat (2 g saturated fat), 86 mg cholesterol, 645 mg sodium, 12 g carbohydrate, 2 g fiber, 36 g protein. **Diabetic Exchanges:** 4 lean meat, 2 vegetable.

If you're looking for fish that doesn't taste "fishy," try widely available tilapia. It offers a delightfully mild flavor that works well with many herbs and seasonings. It's a great way to get your family accustomed to main courses featuring fish and seafood.

# Egg Foo Yong C

**PREP:** 15 min.  **COOK:** 5 min./batch  **YIELD:** 4 servings

**SHERRI MELOTIK • OAK CREEK, WISCONSIN**

*Forget the Chinese takeout! You'll have fun making this colorful, crunchy and delicious version of an Asian classic at home in just about 20 minutes.*

> 1 can (14 oz.) chop suey vegetables, drained
> 1/2 lb. peeled and deveined cooked small shrimp, coarsely chopped
> 4 green onions, thinly sliced
> 4 eggs, beaten
> 2 Tbsp. canola oil

GREEN PEA SAUCE:
> 2 Tbsp. cornstarch
> 1 tsp. chicken bouillon granules
> 2 cups water
> 1-1/2 tsp. reduced-sodium soy sauce
> 1/2 cup frozen peas, thawed

**1.** In a large bowl, combine the chop suey vegetables, shrimp and green onions. Stir in eggs.

**2.** In a large nonstick skillet, heat 1 tsp. oil. Drop vegetable mixture by 1/4 cupfuls into skillet. Cook in batches until browned on both sides, using remaining oil as needed.

**3.** In a small saucepan, combine cornstarch and bouillon. Gradually stir in the water and soy sauce. Bring to a boil; cook and stir for 2 minutes or until sauce is thickened.

**4.** Stir peas into the sauce; heat through. Serve with egg foo yong.

**Nutrition Facts:** 3 patties with 1/2 cup sauce equals 242 calories, 13 g fat (2 g saturated fat), 298 mg cholesterol, 497 mg sodium, 10 g carbohydrate, 2 g fiber, 20 g protein. **Diabetic Exchanges:** 3 lean meat, 1-1/2 fat, 1/2 starch.

# Walnut-Crusted Salmon [c]

PREP/TOTAL TIME: 25 min.  YIELD: 4 servings

**EDIE DESPAIN • LOGAN, UTAH**

*Whenever I can get salmon for a good price, I always turn to this simple and delicious recipe. It's wonderful served with mashed potatoes and fresh green beans.*

- 4 salmon fillets (4 oz. *each*)
- 4 tsp. Dijon mustard
- 4 tsp. honey
- 2 slices whole wheat bread
- 3 Tbsp. finely chopped walnuts
- 2 tsp. canola oil
- 1/2 tsp. dried thyme

**1.** Place salmon on a baking sheet coated with cooking spray. Combine mustard and honey; brush over salmon. Place bread in a food processor; cover and process until crumbly. Transfer to a small bowl. Add the walnuts, oil and thyme; press onto salmon.

**2.** Bake at 400° for 12-15 minutes or until fish flakes easily with a fork and topping is lightly browned.

**Nutrition Facts:** 1 fillet equals 326 calories, 19 g fat (3 g saturated fat), 67 mg cholesterol, 253 mg sodium, 13 g carbohydrate, 1 g fiber, 25 g protein. **Diabetic Exchanges:** 3 lean meat, 1 starch, 1/2 fat.

# Poached Salmon with Grapefruit Salsa [c]

PREP/TOTAL TIME: 30 min.  YIELD: 4 servings

**PATRICIA NIEH • PORTOLA VALLEY, CALIFORNIA**

*Family and friends often request this recipe ahead of time when they know they'll be dining with me. I gladly fill their requests because this is so easy, the dish is delicious—and it especially pleases those who are counting calories.*

- 5 cups strong brewed green tea
- 4 fresh basil sprigs
- 4 fresh thyme sprigs
- 4 fresh cilantro sprigs
- 3 Tbsp. lemon juice
- 3 Tbsp. minced fresh gingerroot
- 4 salmon fillets (4 oz. *each*)

SALSA:
- 1 large pink grapefruit, sectioned and chopped
- 4 green onions, thinly sliced
- 1 Tbsp. minced fresh cilantro
- 1 Tbsp. finely chopped crystallized ginger
- 1/4 tsp. salt

**1.** In a large skillet, combine the first six ingredients. Bring to a boil. Reduce heat; add salmon and poach, uncovered, for 8-10 minutes or until fish flakes easily with a fork.

**2.** Meanwhile, in a small bowl, combine the salsa ingredients. Remove salmon with a slotted spoon. Serve with salsa.

**Nutrition Facts:** 1 salmon fillet with 1/4 cup salsa equals 220 calories, 11 g fat (2 g saturated fat), 57 mg cholesterol, 209 mg sodium, 11 g carbohydrate, 1 g fiber, 20 g protein. **Diabetic Exchanges:** 3 lean meat, 1 starch.

When sectioning grapefruit, it can be hard to remove the white pith. Place the whole fruit in boiling water. Remove from heat; let stand 5 minutes before draining. Peel and section when it's cool enough to handle.

WALNUT-CRUSTED SALMON

POACHED SALMON WITH GRAPEFRUIT SALSA

CORN BREAD-TOPPED FRIJOLES

CURRIED QUINOA AND CHICKPEAS

PESTO VEGGIE PIZZA

# Meatless Mains

For some, meat-free dinners are a way of life. For others, they're a way to mix up dinnertime lineups. Consider these entrees when you want to try something new yet keep your commitment to eating right.

## Pesto Veggie Pizza M

PREP: 30 min. + standing BAKE: 10 min.
YIELD: 6 servings

DANA DIRKS • SAN DIEGO, CALIFORNIA

*When I started thinking of recipes I could submit to Healthy Cooking magazine, I thought about what my family really likes to eat and what I like to cook, and the answer was...pizza!*

> 1 pkg. (1/4 oz.) active dry yeast
> 1 cup warm water (110° to 115°)
> 1/3 cup grated Parmesan cheese
> 2 Tbsp. canola oil
> 1 Tbsp. sugar
> 1 Tbsp. dried basil
> 1/2 tsp. salt
> 3/4 cup all-purpose flour
> 1 to 1-1/2 cups whole wheat flour
> 3-1/2 cups fresh baby spinach
> 1/4 cup prepared pesto
> 1-3/4 cups coarsely chopped fresh broccoli
> 3/4 cup chopped green pepper
> 2 green onions, chopped
> 4 garlic cloves, minced
> 2 cups (8 oz.) shredded part-skim mozzarella cheese

**1.** In a small bowl, dissolve yeast in warm water. Add Parmesan cheese, oil, sugar, basil, salt, all-purpose flour and 3/4 cup whole wheat flour. Beat until smooth. Stir in enough remaining whole wheat flour to form a soft dough (dough will be sticky).

**2.** Turn onto a lightly floured surface; knead until smooth and elastic, about 6-8 minutes. Cover and let rest for 10 minutes.

**3.** Roll dough into a 16-in. x 12-in. rectangle. Transfer to a baking sheet coated with cooking spray; build up edges slightly. Prick dough with a fork. Bake at 375° for 8-10 minutes or until lightly browned.

**4.** Meanwhile, in a large saucepan, bring 1/2 in. of water to a boil. Add spinach; cover and boil for 3-5 minutes or until wilted. Drain and place in a food processor. Add pesto; cover and process until mixture is blended.

**5.** Spread over pizza crust. Top with broccoli, green pepper, green onions, garlic and mozzarella cheese. Bake 10-12 minutes longer or until cheese is melted.

**Nutrition Facts:** 1 piece equals 364 calories, 17 g fat (6 g saturated fat), 29 mg cholesterol, 543 mg sodium, 35 g carbohydrate, 5 g fiber, 19 g protein **Diabetic Exchanges:** 2 starch, 2 medium-fat meat, 2 fat, 1 vegetable.

## Curried Quinoa And Chickpeas M

PREP: 15 min. COOK: 25 min. YIELD: 4 servings

SUZANNE BANFIELD • BASKING RIDGE, NEW JERSEY

*Quinoa contains more protein than other grains, and that protein is of unusually high quality for a plant food. That makes this a great, filling main dish. The blend of flavors and colors will bring everyone at the table back for more.*

> 1-1/2 cups water
> 1/2 cup orange juice
> 1 can (15 oz.) chickpeas or garbanzo beans, rinsed and drained
> 2 medium tomatoes, seeded and chopped
> 1 medium sweet red pepper, julienned
> 1 cup quinoa, rinsed
> 1 small red onion, finely chopped
> 1/2 cup raisins
> 1 tsp. curry powder
> 1/2 cup minced fresh cilantro

**1.** In a large saucepan, bring water and orange juice to a boil. Stir in chickpeas, tomatoes, red pepper, quinoa, onion, raisins and curry. Return to a boil. Reduce heat; cover and simmer for 15-20 minutes or until liquid is absorbed.

**2.** Remove from the heat; fluff with a fork. Sprinkle with cilantro.

**Editor's Note:** Look for quinoa in the cereal, rice or organic food aisle.

**Nutrition Facts:** 1-1/2 cups equals 355 calories, 5 g fat (trace saturated fat), 0 cholesterol, 155 mg sodium, 70 g carbohydrate, 9 g fiber, 12 g protein.

# Zucchini Enchiladas

**PREP:** 1-1/2 hours **BAKE:** 30 min. **YIELD:** 12 servings

**ANGELA LEINENBACH • MECHANICSVLLE, VIRGINIA**

*I love this recipe because it helps me serve a healthy but tasty meal to my family. Plus, zucchini is so plentiful in my garden, and this dish makes a great way to use it up.*

- 1 medium sweet yellow pepper, chopped
- 1 medium green pepper, chopped
- 1 large sweet onion, chopped
- 2 Tbsp. olive oil
- 2 garlic cloves, minced
- 2 cans (15 oz. *each*) tomato sauce
- 2 cans (14-1/2 oz. *each*) no-salt-added diced tomatoes, undrained
- 2 Tbsp. chili powder
- 2 tsp. sugar
- 2 tsp. dried marjoram
- 1 tsp. dried basil
- 1 tsp. ground cumin
- 1/4 tsp. salt
- 1/4 tsp. cayenne pepper
- 1 bay leaf
- 3 lb. zucchini, shredded (about 8 cups)
- 24 corn tortillas (6 in.), warmed
- 4 cups (16 oz.) shredded reduced-fat cheddar cheese
- 2 cans (2-1/4 oz. *each*) sliced ripe olives, drained
- 1/2 cup minced fresh cilantro

Reduced-fat sour cream, optional

**1.** In a large saucepan, saute peppers and onion in oil until tender. Add garlic; cook 1 minute longer. Stir in the tomato sauce, tomatoes, chili powder, sugar, marjoram, basil, cumin, salt, cayenne and bay leaf. Bring to a boil. Reduce heat; simmer, uncovered, for 30-35 minutes or until slightly thickened. Discard bay leaf.

**2.** Place 1/3 cup zucchini down the center of each tortilla; top with 2 Tbsp. cheese and 1 Tbsp. olives. Roll up and place seam side down in two 13-in. x 9-in. baking dishes coated with cooking spray. Pour sauce over the top; sprinkle with remaining cheese.

**3.** Bake, uncovered, at 350° for 30-35 minutes or until heated through. Sprinkle with cilantro. Serve with sour cream if desired.

**Nutrition Facts:** 2 enchiladas (calculated without sour cream) equals 326 calories, 13 g fat (6 g saturated fat), 27 mg cholesterol, 846 mg sodium, 42 g carbohydrate, 7 g fiber, 16 g protein. **Diabetic Exchanges:** 2 starch, 2 medium-fat meat, 2 vegetable, 1/2 fat.

ZUCCHINI ENCHILADAS

# Southwestern Frittata

**PREP/TOTAL TIME:** 25 min. **YIELD:** 4 servings

**MARY RELYEA • CANASTOTA, NEW YORK**

*This tasty egg dish makes a great breakfast entree but could easily be served for lunch or dinner, too. Fresh eggs are jazzed up with red tomatoes, onion and green bell pepper, then treated to a topping of savory mozzarella cheese. What a fantastic way to spice up your meals.*

- 4 eggs
- 1 Tbsp. fat-free milk
- 1/4 tsp. salt
- 1/4 tsp. ground mustard
- 1/4 tsp. pepper

Dash to 1/8 tsp. cayenne pepper

- 1/2 cup chopped onion
- 1/2 cup chopped green pepper
- 1/2 tsp. minced garlic
- 1 tsp. olive oil
- 1 large tomato, chopped
- 2 Tbsp. sliced ripe olives, drained
- 1/2 cup shredded part-skim mozzarella cheese

**1.** In a small bowl, whisk the eggs, milk, salt, mustard, pepper and cayenne; set aside.

**2.** In a large skillet over medium heat, cook the onion, green pepper and garlic in oil until tender. Add tomato and olives; heat through.

**3.** Pour egg mixture over vegetables. As eggs set, lift edges, letting uncooked portion flow underneath. When eggs are set, sprinkle with cheese. Remove from the heat. Cover and let stand for 1-2 minutes or until cheese is melted. Cut into four wedges.

**Nutrition Facts:** 1 slice equals 152 calories, 9 g fat (3 g saturated fat), 221 mg cholesterol, 320 mg sodium, 7 g carbohydrate, 1 g fiber, 11 g protein.

FIERY STUFFED POBLANOS

# Fiery Stuffed Poblanos  M

PREP: 50 min. + standing BAKE: 20 min.
YIELD: 8 servings

**AMBER MASSEY • FORT WORTH, TEXAS**

*I love Southwest-inspired cuisine, but since it's often laden with fatty meat and cheese, I tend to steer clear. As a future dietitian, I try to come up with healthy twists on recipes. That's how my stuffed chili dish was born.*

- 8 poblano peppers
- 1 can (15 oz.) black beans, rinsed and drained
- 1 medium zucchini, chopped
- 1 small red onion, chopped
- 4 garlic cloves, minced
- 1 can (15-1/4 oz.) whole kernel corn, drained
- 1 can (14-1/2 oz.) fire-roasted diced tomatoes, undrained
- 1 cup cooked brown rice
- 1 Tbsp. ground cumin
- 1 to 1-1/2 tsp. ground ancho chili pepper
- 1/4 tsp. salt
- 1/4 tsp. pepper
- 1 cup (4 oz.) shredded reduced-fat Mexican cheese blend, *divided*
- 3 green onions, chopped
- 1/2 cup reduced-fat sour cream

**1.** Broil peppers 3 in. from the heat until skins blister, about 5 minutes. With tongs, rotate peppers a quarter turn. Broil and rotate until all sides are blistered and blackened. Immediately place peppers in a large bowl; cover and let stand for 20 minutes.

**2.** Meanwhile, in a small bowl, coarsely mash beans; set aside. In a large nonstick skillet coated with cooking spray, cook and stir zucchini and onion until tender. Add garlic; cook 1 minute longer. Add the corn, tomatoes, rice, seasonings and beans. Remove from the heat; stir in 1/2 cup cheese. Set aside.

**3.** Peel off and discard charred skins from poblanos. Cut a lengthwise slit down each pepper, leaving the stem intact; remove membranes and seeds. Fill each pepper with 2/3 cup filling.

**4.** Place peppers in a 13-in. x 9-in. baking dish coated with cooking spray. Bake, uncovered, at 375° for 18-22 minutes or until heated through, sprinkling with green onions and remaining cheese during last 5 minutes of baking. Garnish with sour cream.

**Nutrition Facts:** 1 stuffed pepper with 1 Tbsp. sour cream equals 223 calories, 5 g fat (2 g saturated fat), 15 mg cholesterol, 579 mg sodium, 32 g carbohydrate, 7 g fiber, 11 g protein.
**Diabetic Exchanges:** 2 vegetable, 1 starch, 1 lean meat, 1 fat.

RAVIOLI WITH SNAP PEAS & MUSHROOMS

## Ravioli with Snap Peas & Mushrooms **M**

PREP/TOTAL TIME: 30 min. YIELD: 8 servings

**CHARLENE CHAMBERS • ORMOND BEACH, FLORIDA**

*Topped with the toasty texture and flavor of hazelnuts, this pasta makes an easy, earthy weeknight dinner. I like to serve it with an herbed lettuce salad and white wine.*

- 1 pkg. (20 oz.) refrigerated cheese ravioli
- 1 lb. fresh sugar snap peas, trimmed
- 1/2 lb. sliced fresh mushrooms
- 3 shallots, chopped
- 2 garlic cloves, minced
- 1 Tbsp. butter
- 2 cups fat-free evaporated milk
- 8 fresh sage leaves, thinly sliced *or* 2 tsp. rubbed sage
- 1 tsp. lemon-pepper seasoning
- 1 tsp. grated lemon peel
- 1/4 tsp. white pepper
- 1/4 cup shredded Parmesan cheese
- 1/4 cup hazelnuts, coarsely chopped and toasted

**1.** In a large saucepan, cook ravioli according to the package directions, adding the peas during the last 3 minutes of cooking; drain.

**2.** Meanwhile, in a large skillet, saute the mushrooms, shallots and garlic in butter until tender. Stir in the milk, sage, lemon-pepper, lemon peel and white pepper. Bring to a boil. Reduce heat; simmer, uncovered, for 2 minutes or until slightly thickened.

**3.** Add ravioli and peas to skillet; heat through. Sprinkle with cheese and hazelnuts.

**Nutrition Facts:** 1 cup equals 347 calories, 11 g fat (5 g saturated fat), 36 mg cholesterol, 470 mg sodium, 44 g carbohydrate, 4 g fiber, 20 g protein. **Diabetic Exchanges:** 2-1/2 starch, 1 medium-fat meat, 1 vegetable, 1 fat.

## Curried Tofu with Rice **M**

PREP: 15 min. COOK: 20 min. YIELD: 4 servings

**CRYSTAL BRUNS • ILIFF, COLORADO**

*Tofu takes the place of meat in this bold dish with lots of curry and cilantro flavor.*

- 1 pkg. (12.3 oz.) extra-firm tofu, drained and cubed
- 1 tsp. seasoned salt

1 Tbsp. canola oil
1 small onion, chopped
3 garlic cloves, minced
1/2 cup light coconut milk
1/4 cup minced fresh cilantro
1 tsp. curry powder
1/4 tsp. salt
1/4 tsp. pepper
2 cups cooked brown rice

**1.** Sprinkle tofu with seasoned salt. In a large nonstick skillet coated with cooking spray, saute tofu in oil until lightly browned. Remove and keep warm.

**2.** In the same skillet, saute onion and garlic for 1-2 minutes or until crisp-tender. Stir in the coconut milk, cilantro, curry, salt and pepper. Bring to a boil. Reduce heat; simmer, uncovered, for 4-5 minutes or until sauce is slightly thickened. Stir in tofu; heat through. Serve with rice.

**Nutrition Facts:** 1/2 cup tofu mixture with 1/2 cup rice equals 240 calories, 11 g fat (3 g saturated fat), 0 cholesterol, 540 mg sodium, 27 g carbohydrate, 3 g fiber, 10 g protein. **Diabetic Exchanges:** 1-1/2 starch, 1 medium-fat meat, 1 fat.

# Corn Bread-Topped Frijoles ⓜ

**PREP:** 20 min. **COOK:** 3 hours **YIELD:** 8 servings

SUZANNE CALDWELL • ARTESIA, NEW MEXICO

*My family often requests this economical, slow-cooker favorite. It's loaded with fresh Southwestern flavors. One batch makes several servings, but it never lasts long at our house!*

1 medium onion, chopped
1 medium green pepper, chopped
1 Tbsp. canola oil
2 garlic cloves, minced
1 can (16 oz.) kidney beans, rinsed and drained
1 can (15 oz.) pinto beans, rinsed and drained
1 can (14-1/2 oz.) diced tomatoes, undrained

1 can (8 oz.) tomato sauce
1 tsp. chili powder
1/2 tsp. pepper
1/8 tsp. hot pepper sauce

CORN BREAD TOPPING:
1 cup all-purpose flour
1 cup yellow cornmeal
1 Tbsp. sugar
1-1/2 tsp. baking powder
1/2 tsp. salt
2 eggs, lightly beaten
1-1/4 cups fat-free milk
1 can (8-1/4 oz.) cream-style corn
3 Tbsp. canola oil

**1.** In a large skillet, saute onion and green pepper in oil until tender. Add garlic; cook 1 minute longer. Transfer to a greased 5-qt. slow cooker.

**2.** Stir in the beans, tomatoes, tomato sauce, chili powder, pepper and pepper sauce. Cover and cook on high for 1 hour.

**3.** In a large bowl, combine the flour, cornmeal, sugar, baking powder and salt. Combine the eggs, milk, corn and oil; add to dry ingredients and mix well. Spoon evenly over bean mixture.

**4.** Cover and cook on high 2 hours longer or until a toothpick inserted near the center of corn bread comes out clean.

**Nutrition Facts:** 1 serving equals 367 calories, 9 g fat (1 g saturated fat), 54 mg cholesterol, 708 mg sodium, 59 g carbohydrate, 9 g fiber, 14 g protein.

CURRIED TOFU WITH RICE

CORN BREAD-TOPPED FRIJOLES

## Veggie Bean Tacos **M**

PREP: 20 min. COOK: 20 min. YIELD: 6 servings

**TONYA BURKHARD-JONES • DAVIS, ILLINOIS**

*Here's a delicious way to use up your summer bounty of vegetables. Fresh tomatoes, corn and zucchini star in these sensational tacos. Avocado, salsa verde and black beans round out the flavor.*

- 2 cups fresh corn
- 2 Tbsp. canola oil, *divided*
- 4 medium tomatoes, seeded and chopped
- 3 small zucchini, chopped
- 1 large red onion, chopped
- 3 garlic cloves, minced
- 1 cup black beans, rinsed and drained
- 1 tsp. minced fresh oregano or 1/4 tsp. dried oregano
- 1/2 tsp. salt
- 1/4 tsp. pepper
- 12 corn tortillas (6 in.), warmed
- 3/4 cup shredded Monterey Jack cheese
- 1/4 cup salsa verde
- 1 medium ripe avocado, peeled and thinly sliced

Reduced-fat sour cream, optional

**1.** In a large skillet, saute corn in 1 Tbsp. oil until lightly browned. Remove and keep warm. In the same skillet, saute tomatoes, zucchini and onion in remaining oil until tender. Add garlic; cook 1 minute longer. Stir in the beans, oregano, salt, pepper and corn; heat through.

**2.** Divide filling among tortillas. Top with cheese, salsa, avocado and sour cream if desired.

**Nutrition Facts:** 2 tacos (calculated without sour cream) equals 378 calories, 16 g fat (4 g saturated fat), 13 mg cholesterol, 517 mg sodium, 52 g carbohydrate, 10 g fiber, 13 g protein.

## Bow Ties with Walnut-Herb Pesto **M**

PREP/TOTAL TIME: 20 min. YIELD: 6 servings

**DIANE NEMITZ • LUDINGTON, MICHIGAN**

*A homemade pesto turns whole wheat pasta into a sensational meatless main course. If you've never made pesto before, this is an easy recipe to start with. Skip the red pepper flakes if you don't like that much extra spice.*

- 4 cups uncooked whole wheat bow tie pasta
- 1 cup fresh arugula
- 1/2 cup packed fresh parsley sprigs
- 1/2 cup loosely packed basil leaves
- 1/4 cup grated Parmesan cheese
- 1/2 tsp. salt
- 1/8 tsp. crushed red pepper flakes
- 1/4 cup chopped walnuts
- 1/3 cup olive oil
- 1 plum tomato, seeded and chopped

**1.** Cook pasta according to the package directions. Meanwhile, place the arugula, parsley, basil, cheese, salt and pepper flakes in a food processor; cover and pulse until chopped. Add walnuts; cover and process until blended. While processing, gradually add oil in a steady stream.

**2.** Drain pasta, reserving 3 Tbsp. cooking water. In a large bowl, toss pasta with pesto, tomato and reserved water.

**Nutrition Facts:** 1 cup equals 323 calories, 17 g fat (3 g saturated fat), 3 mg cholesterol, 252 mg sodium, 34 g carbohydrate, 6 g fiber, 10 g protein. **Diabetic Exchanges:** 2-1/2 fat, 2 starch.

VEGGIE BEAN TACOS

BOW TIES WITH WALNUT-HERB PESTO

GREEK PITA PIZZAS

# Greek Pita Pizzas M

**PREP/TOTAL TIME:** 25 min.  **YIELD:** 6 servings

**TRISHA KRUSE • EAGLE, IDAHO**

*Colorful, crunchy and packed with fresh veggies and flavor, these quick pizzas taste just like a Greek salad. Whole wheat pitas were never more delicious!*

  6  whole wheat pita breads (6 in.)
1-1/2  cups meatless spaghetti sauce
  1  can (14 oz.) water-packed artichoke hearts, rinsed, drained and quartered
  2  cups fresh baby spinach, chopped
1-1/2  cups sliced fresh mushrooms
  1/2  cup crumbled feta cheese
  1  small green pepper, thinly sliced
  1/4  cup thinly sliced red onion
  1/4  cup sliced ripe olives
  3  Tbsp. grated Parmesan cheese
  1/4  tsp. pepper

**1.** Place the pita breads on an ungreased baking sheet; spread with the spaghetti sauce. Top with the remaining ingredients.

**2.** Bake at 350° for 8-12 minutes or until cheese is melted. Serve immediately.

**Nutrition Facts:** 1 pizza equals 273 calories, 5 g fat (2 g saturated fat), 7 mg cholesterol, 969 mg sodium, 48 g carbohydrate, 7 g fiber, 13 g protein. **Diabetic Exchanges:** 2 starch, 1 medium-fat meat, 1 vegetable.

If you decide to buy a chunk of Parmesan cheese and grate your own, be sure to use the finest section on your grating tool. You can also use a blender or food processor. Simply cut **Parmesan cheese** into 1-inch cubes and process 1 cup of cubes at a time on high until finely grated.

FOUR-CHEESE BAKED PENNE

## Four-Cheese Baked Penne M

**PREP:** 30 min. + cooling  **BAKE:** 20 min.
**YIELD:** 6 servings

### JANET ELROD • NEWNAN, GEORGIA

*This cheesy pasta dish is comforting, hearty, delicious
and—surprise—meatless. Filling whole grains, low-fat
protein and a touch of heat make this recipe a keeper! Serve
with a salad and crusty bread.*

|       |                                             |
| ----- | ------------------------------------------- |
| 4     | cups uncooked whole wheat penne pasta       |
| 1     | medium onion, chopped                       |
| 2     | tsp. olive oil                              |
| 4     | garlic cloves, minced                       |
| 1     | can (15 oz.) crushed tomatoes               |
| 1     | can (8 oz.) tomato sauce                    |
| 3     | Tbsp. minced fresh parsley *or* 1 Tbsp. dried parsley flakes |
| 1     | tsp. dried oregano                          |
| 1     | tsp. dried rosemary, crushed                |
| 1/2   | tsp. crushed red pepper flakes              |
| 1/4   | tsp. pepper                                 |
| 1-1/2 | cups (12 oz.) 2% cottage cheese             |
| 1-1/4 | cups (5 oz.) shredded part-skim mozzarella cheese, *divided* |
| 1     | cup part-skim ricotta cheese                |
| 1/4   | cup grated Parmesan cheese                  |

**1.** Cook penne according to package directions.

**2.** Meanwhile, in a large skillet, saute onion in oil
until tender. Add garlic; cook 1 minute longer. Stir in
the tomatoes, tomato sauce, parsley, oregano,
rosemary, pepper flakes and pepper. Bring to a boil.
Remove from the heat; cool for 15 minutes.

**3.** Drain penne; add to sauce. Stir in the cottage
cheese, 1/2 cup mozzarella and all of the ricotta.
Transfer to a 13-in. x 9-in. baking dish coated with
cooking spray. Top with Parmesan cheese and
remaining mozzarella.

**4.** Bake, uncovered, at 400° for 20-25 minutes or
until bubbly.

**Nutrition Facts:** 1-1/3 cups equals 523 calories, 12 g fat (6 g
saturated fat), 37 mg cholesterol, 682 mg sodium, 72 g
carbohydrate, 11 g fiber, 32 g protein.

## Spanako-Pasta M

**PREP:** 20 min.  **COOK:** 15 min.  **YIELD:** 4 servings

### LINDSAY WILLIAMS • HASTINGS, MINNESOTA

*I love spanakopita, so I made it into a wonderful creamy pasta
dish. If you don't have fresh dill, try 2 tablespoons of dried.*

|       |                                           |
| ----- | ----------------------------------------- |
| 4-1/2 | cups uncooked whole wheat spiral pasta    |
| 1     | medium onion, chopped                     |
| 2     | tsp. olive oil                            |
| 2     | garlic cloves,  minced                    |

2 Tbsp. all-purpose flour

3/4 cup reduced-sodium chicken broth *or* vegetable broth

3/4 cup fat-free milk

1 pkg. (10 oz.) frozen chopped spinach, thawed and squeezed dry

1/4 cup grated Parmesan cheese

2 oz. reduced-fat cream cheese

2 Tbsp. lemon juice

2 Tbsp. snipped fresh dill

1/4 tsp. ground nutmeg

1/4 tsp. salt

Dash cayenne pepper

3/4 cup crumbled feta cheese

**1.** Cook pasta according to package directions. Meanwhile, in a large skillet, saute onion in oil until tender. Add garlic; cook 1 minute longer. Stir in flour until blended; gradually add broth and milk. Bring to a boil; cook and stir for 2 minutes or until thickened.

**2.** Add the spinach, Parmesan cheese, cream cheese, lemon juice, dill, nutmeg, salt and cayenne; heat through. Drain pasta, reserving 1 cup liquid. Toss pasta with spinach mixture, adding some of the reserved pasta liquid if needed. Sprinkle with the feta cheese.

**Nutrition Facts:** 1-1/2 cups equals 435 calories, 12 g fat (6 g saturated fat), 27 mg cholesterol, 667 mg sodium, 61 g carbohydrate, 11 g fiber, 23 g protein.

# Spinach Cheese Manicotti Ⓜ

**PREP:** 55 min. **BAKE:** 55 min. **YIELD:** 7 servings

**JULIE LOWER • KATY, TEXAS**

*No one will even miss the meat in this hearty, delicious meal. Cream cheese and cottage cheese "beef up" the filling and give this lasagna-like dish a creamy base.*

1 large onion, chopped

2 garlic cloves, minced

1 Tbsp. olive oil

3 cans (8 oz. *each*) no-salt-added tomato sauce

2 cans (6 oz. *each*) tomato paste

1-1/2 cups water

1/2 cup dry red wine *or* vegetable broth

2 Tbsp. Italian seasoning

2 tsp. sugar

2 tsp. dried oregano

FILLING:

1 pkg. (8 oz.) fat-free cream cheese

1-1/4 cups (10 oz.) 2% cottage cheese

1 pkg. (10 oz.) frozen chopped spinach, thawed and squeezed dry

1/4 cup grated Parmesan cheese

2 eggs, lightly beaten

1/2 tsp. salt

1 pkg. (8 oz.) manicotti shells

1 cup (4 oz.) shredded part-skim mozzarella cheese

**1.** In a large saucepan, saute onion and garlic in oil until tender. Stir in the tomato sauce, tomato paste, water, wine, Italian seasoning, sugar and oregano. Bring to a boil. Reduce heat; simmer, uncovered, for 15-20 minutes, stirring occasionally.

**2.** Meanwhile, for filling, in a large bowl, beat cream cheese until smooth. Stir in the cottage cheese, spinach, Parmesan cheese, eggs and salt.

**3.** Stuff cream cheese mixture into uncooked manicotti shells. Spread 1 cup sauce into a 13-in. x 9-in. baking dish coated with cooking spay. Arrange manicotti over sauce. Pour remaining sauce over top.

**4.** Cover and bake at 350° for 50-55 minutes or until pasta is tender. Uncover; sprinkle with mozzarella cheese. Bake 5-10 minutes longer or until the cheese is melted.

**Nutrition Facts:** 2 stuffed manicotti equals 389 calories, 9 g fat (4 g saturated fat), 80 mg cholesterol, 722 mg sodium, 50 g carbohydrate, 5 g fiber, 25 g protein.

SPANAKO-PASTA

SPINACH CHEESE MANICOTTI

# Bean 'n' Rice Burritos

**PREP/TOTAL TIME:** 25 min.  **YIELD:** 8 servings

**KIM HARDISON • MAITLAND, FLORIDA**

*I love that these hearty, zippy burritos can be whipped up in a jiffy. They're ideal for weeknights.*

| | |
|---|---|
| 1-1/2 | cups water |
| 1-1/2 | cups uncooked instant brown rice |
| 1 | medium green pepper, diced |
| 1/2 | cup chopped onion |
| 1 | Tbsp. olive oil |
| 1 | tsp. minced garlic |
| 1 | Tbsp. chili powder |
| 1 | tsp. ground cumin |
| 1/8 | tsp. crushed red pepper flakes |
| 1 | can (15 oz.) black beans, rinsed and drained |
| 8 | flour tortillas (8 in.), warmed |
| 1 | cup salsa |

Reduced-fat shredded cheddar cheese and reduced-fat sour cream, optional

**1.** In a small saucepan, bring water to a boil. Add rice. Return to a boil. Reduce heat; cover and simmer for 5 minutes. Remove from the heat. Let stand for 5 minutes or until water is absorbed.

**2.** Meanwhile, in a large skillet, saute green pepper and onion in oil for 3-4 minutes or until tender. Add garlic; cook 1 minute longer. Stir in the chili powder, cumin and pepper flakes until combined. Add beans and rice; cook and stir for 4-6 minutes or until the mixture is heated through.

**3.** Spoon about 1/2 cup of filling off-center on each tortilla; top with 2 Tbsp. salsa. Fold sides and ends over filling and roll up. Serve with cheese and sour cream if desired.

**Nutrition Facts:** 1 burrito (calculated without cheese and sour cream) equals 290 calories, 6 g fat (1 g saturated fat), 0 cholesterol, 504 mg sodium, 49 g carbohydrate, 4 g fiber, 9 g protein.

# Eggplant Parmesan

**PREP:** 40 min.  **COOK:** 25 min.  **YIELD:** 8 servings

**LACI HOOTEN • MCKINNEY, TEXAS**

*Because my recipe calls for baking the eggplant instead of frying it, it's much healthier. The prep time is a little longer than for some recipes, but the Italian flavors and rustic elegance are well worth it.*

| | |
|---|---|
| 3 | eggs, beaten |
| 2-1/2 | cups panko (Japanese) bread crumbs |
| 3 | medium eggplants, cut into 1/4-in. slices |
| 2 | jars (4-1/2 oz. *each*) sliced mushrooms, drained |
| 1/2 | tsp dried basil |
| 1/8 | tsp. dried oregano |
| 2 | cups (8 oz.) shredded part-skim mozzarella cheese |
| 1/2 | cup grated Parmesan cheese |
| 1 | jar (28 oz.) spaghetti sauce |

**1.** Place eggs and bread crumbs in separate shallow bowls. Dip eggplant in eggs, then coat in crumbs. Place on baking sheets coated with cooking spray. Bake at 350° for 15-20 minutes or until tender and golden brown, turning once.

**2.** In a small bowl, combine the mushrooms, basil and oregano. In another small bowl, combine mozzarella and Parmesan cheeses.

**3.** Spread 1/2 cup sauce into a 13-in. x 9-in. baking dish coated with cooking spray. Layer with a third of the mushroom mixture, eggplant, 3/4 cup sauce and a third of the cheese mixture. Repeat layers twice.

**4.** Bake, uncovered, at 350° for 25-30 minutes or until heated through and cheese is melted.

**Nutrition Facts:** 1 serving equals 305 calories, 12 g fat (5 g saturated fat), 102 mg cholesterol, 912 mg sodium, 32 g carbohydrate, 9 g fiber, 18 g protein. **Diabetic Exchanges:** 2 starch, 2 vegetable, 1 medium-fat meat.

BEAN 'N' RICE BURRITOS

EGGPLANT PARMESAN

CREAMY MAKEOVER
MACARONI AND CHEESE

# Creamy Makeover Macaroni and Cheese  Ⓜ

PREP: 30 min.  BAKE: 25 min.  YIELD: 10 servings

**APRIL TAYLOR • FORT RILEY, KANSAS**

*Your family will love the rich, creamy flavor of this mac and cheese dish—and you'll feel good knowing there is less saturated fat than most recipes.*

- 1   pkg. (16 oz.) elbow macaroni
- 2   Tbsp. butter
- 1/3 cup all-purpose flour
- 2   cups fat-free half-and-half
- 2   cups fat-free milk
- 1/2 tsp. garlic powder
- 1/2 tsp. pepper
- 1/4 tsp. salt
- 3   cups (12 oz.) shredded reduced-fat sharp cheddar cheese

TOPPING:
- 1   medium onion, chopped
- 2   Tbsp. butter
- 5   cups cubed bread
- 1/2 cup shredded reduced-fat cheddar cheese

**1.** Cook macaroni according to package directions. Meanwhile, in a large saucepan, melt butter over medium heat.

**2.** Combine flour and half-and-half; stir into pan. Add milk and seasonings. Bring to a gentle boil; remove from the heat. Stir in cheese until melted. Drain macaroni; add to the cheese sauce and stir to coat.

**3.** Transfer to a 13-in. x 9-in. baking dish coated with cooking spray. In a large skillet, saute onion in butter until tender. Add bread; saute 2-3 minutes longer. Sprinkle bread mixture and cheese over macaroni mixture. Bake, uncovered, at 350° for 25-30 minutes or until heated through.

**Nutrition Facts:** 1 cup equals 432 calories, 15 g fat (9 g saturated fat), 41 mg cholesterol, 526 mg sodium, 55 g carbohydrate, 2 g fiber, 21 g protein.

> Using milk and half-and-half that's fat free, reducing the butter and taking advantage of reduced-fat cheeses, our Test Kitchen **cut the fat** from the original version of this dish by 27 g, including 19 g of saturated fat.

# Hearty Shepherd's Pie Ⓜ

PREP: 50 min. BAKE: 30 min. YIELD: 6 servings

**KIMBERLY HAMMOND • KINGWOOD, TEXAS**

*Mushrooms, carrots, celery, peas and potatoes pack this full-flavored meal-maker. You'll never even miss the meat.*

- 6 garlic cloves
- 1/4 tsp. olive oil
- 1-1/2 lb. medium potatoes, peeled and cubed
- 3 Tbsp. vegetable broth
- 1/4 tsp. salt
- 1/8 tsp. pepper

FILLING:
- 1 medium onion, chopped
- 1 Tbsp. olive oil
- 2 garlic cloves, minced
- 1 lb. sliced baby portobello mushrooms
- 8 oz. frozen vegetarian meat crumbles
- 2 medium carrots, sliced
- 2 celery ribs, chopped
- 3/4 cup vegetable broth, *divided*
- 2 Tbsp. minced fresh rosemary *or* 2 tsp. dried rosemary, crushed
- 1 Tbsp. reduced-sodium soy sauce
- 1/2 tsp. salt
- 1/4 tsp. pepper
- 2 Tbsp. all-purpose flour
- 1 cup frozen peas

**1.** Place garlic on a double thickness of heavy-duty foil. Drizzle with oil. Wrap foil around garlic. Bake at 425° for 15-20 minutes. Cool for 10-15 minutes.

**2.** Place potatoes in a Dutch oven and cover with water. Bring to a boil. Reduce heat; cover and cook for 10-15 minutes or until tender; drain. Mash potatoes with broth, salt and pepper; squeeze softened garlic into potatoes and mix well.

**3.** In a large nonstick skillet coated with cooking spray, saute onion in oil until tender. Add garlic; cook 1 minute longer. Stir in the mushrooms, meat crumbles, carrots and celery; cook and stir for 5 minutes. Add 1/2 cup broth, rosemary, soy sauce, salt and pepper; cover and cook for 10 minutes.

**4.** Combine flour and remaining broth until smooth. Gradually stir into the pan. Bring to a boil; cook and stir for 1 minute or until thickened. Stir in peas.

**5.** Transfer vegetable mixture to an 8-in. square baking dish coated with cooking spray; cover with potato mixture. Bake, uncovered, at 350° for 30-35 minutes or until heated through.

**Editor's Note:** Vegetarian meat crumbles are a nutritious protein source made from soy. Look for them in the natural foods freezer section.

**Nutrition Facts:** 1-1/2 cups equals 223 calories, 5 g fat (1 g saturated fat), trace cholesterol, 753 mg sodium, 34 g carbohydrate, 6 g fiber, 13 g protein. **Diabetic Exchanges:** 2 vegetable, 1 starch, 1 lean meat, 1 fat.

# Provolone Ziti Bake Ⓜ

PREP: 20 min. BAKE: 65 min. YIELD: 8 servings

**VICKY PALMER • ALBUQUERQUE, NEW MEXICO**

*As easy as it is filling and delicious, this Italian meal appeals to everyone—and they won't even miss the meat.*

- 1 medium onion, chopped
- 1 Tbsp. olive oil
- 3 garlic cloves, minced
- 2 cans (28 oz. *each*) Italian crushed tomatoes
- 1-1/2 cups water
- 1/2 cup dry red wine *or* reduced-sodium chicken broth
- 1 Tbsp. sugar
- 1 tsp. dried basil
- 1 pkg. (16 oz.) ziti *or* small tube pasta
- 8 slices provolone cheese

**1.** In a Dutch oven, saute onion in oil until tender. Add garlic; cook 1 minute longer. Stir in the tomatoes, water, wine, sugar and basil. Bring to a boil; remove from the heat. Stir in ziti.

**2.** Transfer to a 13-in. x 9-in. baking dish coated with cooking spray. Cover and bake at 350° for 1 hour. Top with cheese. Bake, uncovered, 4-6 minutes longer or until the ziti is tender and the cheese is melted.

**Nutrition Facts:** 1-1/2 cups equals 381 calories, 8 g fat (4 g saturated fat), 15 mg cholesterol, 763 mg sodium, 60 g carbohydrate, 4 g fiber, 16 g protein.

# Lentil Sweet Potato Curry Ⓜ

PREP: 20 min. COOK: 35 min. YIELD: 6 servings

**TRISHA KRUSE • EAGLE, IDAHO**

*This is one of those suppers you can start when you get home, then relax while it cooks. (Or help the kids with homework or hop on the stair-stepper.) Apple and brown sugar sweeten this delicious meatless meal.*

- 1 cup dried lentils, rinsed
- 3 cups water, *divided*
- 1 large onion, chopped
- 1 Tbsp. olive oil
- 2 medium carrots, chopped
- 3 garlic cloves, minced
- 2 medium sweet potatoes, peeled and chopped
- 4 tsp. curry powder
- 3/4 tsp. salt
- 1/2 tsp. pepper
- 2 medium tomatoes, chopped
- 1 medium apple, peeled and chopped
- 1 Tbsp. brown sugar
- 3 cups hot cooked brown rice

**1.** In a small saucepan, combine lentils and 2 cups water; bring to a boil. Reduce heat; cover and simmer for 20-25 minutes or until tender. Drain.

**2.** Meanwhile, in a large saucepan, saute onion in oil until tender. Add carrots and garlic; cook 2 minutes longer. Stir in the sweet potatoes, curry, salt, pepper and remaining water. Bring to a boil. Reduce heat; cover and simmer for 10 minutes.

**3.** Add the tomatoes, apple and brown sugar; cover and cook 10-15 minutes longer or until apple is tender. Stir in lentils; heat through. Serve with rice.

**Nutrition Facts:** 1 cup lentil mixture with 1/2 cup rice equals 333 calories, 4 g fat (1 g saturated fat), 0 cholesterol, 325 mg sodium, 63 g carbohydrate, 15 g fiber, 13 g protein.

PROVOLONE ZITI BAKE

LENTIL SWEET POTATO CURRY

GLUTEN-FREE CORNMEAL MUFFINS

BANANA NUT BREAD

SAGE FONTINA FOCACCIA

# The Bread Basket

The next time the bread basket comes around, don't be shy! Go ahead and grab a slice. This chapter proves that you can enjoy hearty loaves and rolls, as well as coffee cakes, muffins and more without any guilt.

## Sage Fontina Focaccia S C

**PREP:** 30 min. + rising **BAKE:** 10 min.
**YIELD:** 1 loaf (8 wedges)

**BETH DAUENHAUER • PUEBLO, COLORADO**

*These rustic loaves have plenty of sage flavor—a tasty addition to just about any feast.*

1-1/4 tsp. active dry yeast
1/2 cup warm water (110° to 115°)
1/2 tsp. honey
3/4 to 1 cup all-purpose flour
1/4 cup whole wheat flour
1 Tbsp. olive oil
2 tsp. minced fresh sage
1/4 tsp. salt

TOPPING:
1-1/2 tsp. olive oil, *divided*
8 fresh sage leaves
1/2 cup shredded fontina cheese

**1.** In a large bowl, dissolve yeast in warm water. Stir in honey; let stand for 5 minutes. Add 3/4 cup all-purpose flour, whole wheat flour, oil, minced sage and salt. Beat on medium speed for 3 minutes or until smooth. Stir in enough remaining flour to form a soft dough (dough will be sticky).

**2.** Turn onto a lightly floured surface; knead until smooth and elastic, about 6-8 minutes. Place in a large bowl coated with cooking spray, turning once to coat the top. Cover and let rise in a warm place until doubled, about 1 hour.

**3.** Punch dough down. Cover and let rest for 5 minutes. Shape into an 8-in. circle; place on a baking sheet coated with cooking spray. Cover and let rise until doubled, about 30 minutes. Using the end of a wooden spoon handle, make several 1/4-in. indentations in the loaf.

**4.** For topping, brush dough with 1 tsp. oil. Top with sage leaves; brush leaves with remaining oil. Sprinkle with cheese. Bake at 400° for 8-10 minutes or until golden brown. Remove to a wire rack.

**Nutrition Facts:** 1 wedge equals 112 calories, 5 g fat (2 g saturated fat), 8 mg cholesterol, 131 mg sodium, 12 g carbohydrate, 1 g fiber, 4 g protein. **Diabetic Exchanges:** 1 starch, 1 fat.

## Banana Nut Bread

**PREP:** 20 min. **BAKE:** 50 min. + cooling
**YIELD:** 1 loaf (12 slices)

**BRITTANY CARRINGTON • TEHACHAPI, CALIFORNIA**

*I made up this recipe when I was a vegetarian and didn't eat eggs. It's packed with fiber, omega-3s and soy protein yet tastes delicious! Silken tofu is a wonderful egg substitute.*

1 cup all-purpose flour
1 cup whole wheat flour
1 tsp. baking powder
1/2 tsp. baking soda
1/4 tsp. salt
1 cup sugar
1 cup mashed ripe bananas (2 medium)
3/4 cup silken soft tofu
1/4 cup canola oil
1 tsp. vanilla extract
1/2 cup chopped walnuts

**1.** In a large bowl, combine the first five ingredients. In a small bowl, beat the sugar, bananas, tofu, oil and and vanilla. Beat into dry ingredients just until moistened. Fold in walnuts.

**2.** Transfer to an 8-in. x 4-in. loaf pan coated with cooking spray. Bake at 350° for 50-55 minutes or until a toothpick inserted near the center comes out clean. Cool for 10 minutes before removing from pan to a wire rack.

**Nutrition Facts:** 1 slice equals 234 calories, 9 g fat (1 g saturated fat), 0 cholesterol, 140 mg sodium, 37 g carbohydrate, 2 g fiber, 4 g protein.

To test baking powder for freshness, place 1 teaspoon **baking powder** in a cup and add 1/3 cup hot tap water. If active bubbling occurs, the product is fine. If not, you should discard the powder and replace it.

# Cinnamon Pull-Apart Loaf

**PREP:** 30 min. + rising **BAKE:** 25 min.
**YIELD:** 1 loaf (12 slices)

JUDY EDDY • BALDWIN CITY, KANSAS

*If you like the fun of monkey bread, you'll adore this unique take on cinnamon bread. The flaky layers are heavenly topped with a creamy drizzle.*

  1   pkg. (1/4 oz.) active dry yeast
3/4   cup warm water (110° to 115°)
1/2   cup quick-cooking oats
1/2   cup whole wheat flour
1/4   cup packed brown sugar
  2   Tbsp. butter, melted
  1   egg
  1   tsp. salt
1-3/4 to 2-1/4 cups all-purpose flour

FILLING:
  3   Tbsp. butter, softened
1/3   cup sugar
  2   tsp. ground cinnamon

GLAZE:
  1   cup confectioners' sugar
6-1/2 tsp. half-and-half cream
4-1/2 tsp. butter, softened

**1.** In a large bowl, dissolve yeast in warm water. Add the oats, whole wheat flour, brown sugar, butter, egg, salt and 1 cup all-purpose flour. Beat on medium speed until smooth. Stir in enough remaining flour to form a soft dough (dough will be sticky).

**2.** Turn onto a lightly floured surface; knead until smooth and elastic, about 6-8 minutes. Place in a bowl coated with cooking spray, turning once to coat the top. Cover and let rise in a warm place until doubled, about 1 hour.

**3.** Punch dough down. Roll into an 18-in. x 12-in. rectangle; spread with butter. Combine the sugar and the cinnamon; sprinkle mixture over dough to within 1/2 in. of edges.

**4.** Cut into thirty-six 3-in. x 2-in. rectangles. Make two stacks of 18 rectangles. Place, cut sides up, in a 9-in. x 5-in. loaf pan coated with cooking spray. Cover and let rise until doubled, about 45 minutes.

**5.** Bake at 375° for 25-30 minutes or until golden brown. Cool for 10 minutes before removing from pan to a wire rack. For glaze, in a small bowl, beat the confectioners' sugar, cream and butter until smooth. Drizzle over warm loaf.

**Nutrition Facts:** 1 slice equals 240 calories, 7 g fat (4 g saturated fat), 35 mg cholesterol, 251 mg sodium, 40 g carbohydrate, 2 g fiber, 4 g protein.

# Lime Coconut Biscotti ⬛F⬛S⬛C

**PREP:** 25 min. **BAKE:** 30 min. **YIELD:** 32 cookies

DIANA BURRINK • CRETE, ILLINOIS

*My family loves this recipe! It's great with a morning cup of coffee, delicious as an afternoon snack or after-dinner dessert. Citrusy, crunchy and not too sweet, it always hits the spot.*

3/4   cup sugar
1/4   cup canola oil
  2   eggs
1/4   cup lime juice
  1   tsp. vanilla extract
1/4   tsp. coconut extract
1-3/4 cups all-purpose flour
2/3   cup cornmeal
1-1/2 tsp. baking powder
1/4   tsp. salt
  1   cup flaked coconut
  1   tsp. grated lime peel

**1.** In a small bowl, beat sugar and oil until blended. Beat in the eggs, lime juice, and vanilla and coconut extracts. Combine the flour, cornmeal, baking powder and salt; gradually add to sugar mixture and mix well (dough will be sticky). Stir in coconut and lime peel.

**2.** Divide dough in half. With lightly floured hands, shape each half into a 12-in. x 2-in. rectangle on a parchment paper-lined baking sheet. Bake at 350° for 20-25 minutes or until set.

**3.** Place pan on a wire rack. When cool enough to handle, transfer to a cutting board; cut diagonally with a serrated knife into 3/4-in. slices. Place cut side down on ungreased baking sheets. Bake for 5-6 minutes on each side or until golden brown. Remove to wire racks to cool. Store in an airtight container.

**Nutrition Facts:** 1 cookie equals 89 calories, 3 g fat (1 g saturated fat), 13 mg cholesterol, 49 mg sodium, 14 g carbohydrate, 1 g fiber, 1 g protein. **Diabetic Exchanges:** 1 starch, 1/2 fat.

CINNAMON PULL-APART LOAF

GLUTEN-FREE
SANDWICH BREAD

# Gluten-Free Sandwich Bread ⑤

**PREP:** 20 min. + rising **BAKE:** 30 min. + cooling
**YIELD:** 1 loaf (16 slices)

**DORIS KINNEY • MERRIMACK, NEW HAMPSHIRE**

*In my quest to find an enjoyable gluten-free bread, this recipe emerged. It's moist and has no cardboard texture!*

|       |                                         |
|-------|-----------------------------------------|
| 1     | Tbsp. active dry yeast                  |
| 2     | Tbsp. sugar                             |
| 1     | cup warm fat-free milk (110° to 115°)   |
| 2     | eggs                                    |
| 3     | Tbsp. canola oil                        |
| 1     | tsp. cider vinegar                      |
| 2-1/2 | cups gluten-free all-purpose baking flour |
| 2-1/2 | tsp. xanthan gum                        |
| 1     | tsp. unflavored gelatin                 |
| 1/2   | tsp. salt                               |

**1.** Grease a 9-in. x 5-in. loaf pan and sprinkle with gluten-free flour; set aside.

**2.** In a small bowl, dissolve yeast and sugar in warm milk. In a stand mixer with a paddle attachment, combine the eggs, oil, vinegar and yeast mixture. Gradually beat in the flour, xanthan gum, gelatin and salt. Beat on low speed for 1 minute. Beat on medium for 2 minutes. (Dough will be softer than yeast bread dough with gluten.)

**3.** Transfer to prepared pan. Smooth the top with a wet spatula. Cover and let rise in a warm place until dough reaches the top of pan, about 25 minutes.

**4.** Bake at 375° for 20 minutes; cover loosely with foil. Bake 10-15 minutes longer or until golden brown. Remove from pan to a wire rack to cool.

**Editor's Note:** Read all ingredient labels for possible gluten content prior to use. Ingredient formulas can change, and production facilities vary among brands. If you're concerned that your brand may contain gluten, contact the company.

**Nutrition Facts:** 1 slice equals 110 calories, 4 g fat (trace saturated fat), 27 mg cholesterol, 95 mg sodium, 17 g carbohydrate, 2 g fiber, 4 g protein. **Diabetic Exchanges:** 1 starch, 1/2 fat.

MULTI-GRAIN CINNAMON ROLLS

# Multi-Grain Cinnamon Rolls

**PREP:** 30 min. + rising **BAKE:** 15 min. **YIELD:** 1 dozen

**JUDY EDDY • BALDWIN CITY, KANSAS**

*This simple and easy-to-work-with recipe is sure to become a family favorite. The wholesome cinnamon rolls will fill your kitchen with a wonderful, warm aroma.*

| | |
|---|---|
| 1 | pkg. (1/4 oz.) active dry yeast |
| 3/4 | cup warm water (110° to 115°) |
| 1/2 | cup quick-cooking oats |
| 1/2 | cup whole wheat flour |
| 1/4 | cup packed brown sugar |
| 2 | Tbsp. butter, melted |
| 1 | egg |
| 1 | tsp. salt |
| 1-3/4 to 2-1/4 | cups all-purpose flour |

FILLING:
| | |
|---|---|
| 3 | Tbsp. butter, softened |
| 1/3 | cup sugar |
| 2 | tsp. ground cinnamon |

GLAZE:
| | |
|---|---|
| 1 | cup confectioners' sugar |
| 6-1/2 | tsp. half-and-half cream |
| 4-1/2 | tsp. butter, softened |

**1.** In a large bowl, dissolve yeast in warm water. Add the oats, whole wheat flour, brown sugar, butter, egg, salt and 1 cup all-purpose flour. Beat on medium speed until smooth. Stir in enough remaining flour to form a soft dough (dough will be sticky).

**2.** Turn onto a lightly floured surface; knead until smooth and elastic, about 6-8 minutes. Place in a bowl coated with cooking spray, turning once to coat the top. Cover and let rise in a warm place until doubled, about 1 hour.

**3.** Punch dough down. Roll into an 18-in. x 12-in. rectangle; spread with butter. Combine the sugar and cinnamon; sprinkle over dough to within 1/2 in. of edges.

**4.** Roll up jelly-roll style, starting with a short side; pinch seams to seal. Cut into 12 slices. Place cut sides down in a 13-in. x 9-in. baking pan coated with cooking spray. Cover and let rise until doubled, about 45 minutes.

**5.** Bake at 375° for 15-20 minutes or until golden brown. For icing, in a small bowl, beat the confectioners' sugar, cream and butter until smooth. Drizzle over warm rolls.

**Nutrition Facts:** 1 cinnamon roll equals 240 calories, 7 g fat (4 g saturated fat), 35 mg cholesterol, 251 mg sodium, 40 g carbohydrate, 2 g fiber, 4 g protein.

# Gluten-Free Banana Walnut Muffins

**PREP:** 20 min. **BAKE:** 20 min. **YIELD:** 16 muffins

**TRISH PANNELL • COLLEGE STATION, TEXAS**

*I've been cooking gluten-free since 2003, when my husband was diagnosed with celiac disease. Over the years, I've managed to perfect some recipes so when family and friends join us, they can't tell that what they're eating is gluten-free. This is one of those recipes.*

| | |
|---|---|
| 1 | cup mashed ripe bananas (2 medium) |
| 3/4 | cup sugar |
| 2 | eggs |
| 1/2 | cup unsweetened applesauce |
| 1/4 | cup canola oil |
| 1/4 | cup orange juice |
| 1 | tsp. vanilla extract |
| 1-1/2 | cups gluten-free all-purpose baking flour |
| 3/4 | tsp. baking soda |
| 3/4 | tsp. xanthan gum |
| 1/2 | tsp. salt |
| 1/2 | tsp. ground cinnamon |
| 1/3 | cup finely chopped walnuts |

**1.** In a large bowl, beat the first seven ingredients until well blended. In a large bowl, combine the flour, baking soda, xanthan gum, salt and cinnamon; gradually beat into banana mixture until blended.

**2.** Coat muffin cups with cooking spray or use paper liners; fill three-fourths full with batter. Sprinkle with the walnuts. Bake at 350° for 20-25 minutes or until a toothpick inserted near the center comes out clean. Cool for 5 minutes before removing from pans to wire racks.

**Editor's Note:** Read all ingredient labels for possible gluten content prior to use. Ingredient formulas can change, and production facilities vary among brands. If you're concerned that your brand may contain gluten, contact the company.

**Nutrition Facts:** 1 muffin equals 148 calories, 6 g fat (1 g saturated fat), 26 mg cholesterol, 143 mg sodium, 23 g carbohydrate, 2 g fiber, 2 g protein. **Diabetic Exchanges:** 1-1/2 starch, 1 fat.

# Makeover Maple Coffee Cake

**PREP:** 20 min. **BAKE:** 30 min. + cooling
**YIELD:** 12 servings

SHARON BOYNAK • LA PORTE, INDIANA

*Downsizing the sugar and margarine, and switching to fat-free milk made all the difference in this coffee cake recipe—without sacrificing one tasty crumb of flavor!*

| | |
|---|---|
| 1/3 | cup butter, softened |
| 3/4 | cup sugar |

| | |
|---|---|
| 2 | eggs |
| 1 | cup fat-free milk |
| 1/2 | cup unsweetened applesauce |
| 3 | cups all-purpose flour |
| 2-1/2 | tsp. baking powder |
| 1/2 | tsp. salt |
| 1/4 | tsp. baking soda |

FILLING:
| | |
|---|---|
| 1/2 | cup finely chopped pecans |
| 1/3 | cup packed brown sugar |
| 2 | Tbsp. all-purpose flour |
| 2 | Tbsp. butter, melted |
| 2 | tsp. ground cinnamon |

ICING:
| | |
|---|---|
| 1/4 | cup confectioners' sugar |
| 1-1/2 | tsp. fat-free milk |
| 1/4 | tsp. maple flavoring |

**1.** In a large bowl, beat butter and sugar until crumbly, about 2 minutes. Add eggs; mix well. Beat in milk and applesauce (mixture may appear curdled). Combine the flour, baking powder, salt and baking soda; add to butter mixture just until moistened. Spread half of the batter into a 13-in. x 9-in. baking pan coated with cooking spray.

**2.** Combine filling ingredients; sprinkle half of filling over the batter. Gently top with remaining batter and filling. Bake at 350° for 30-35 minutes or until a toothpick inserted near the center comes out clean. Cool on a wire rack.

**3.** Combine icing ingredients until smooth; drizzle over coffee cake.

**Nutrition Facts:** 1 piece equals 318 calories, 11 g fat (5 g saturated fat), 54 mg cholesterol, 281 mg sodium, 49 g carbohydrate, 1 g fiber, 6 g protein.

GLUTEN-FREE BANANA WALNUT MUFFINS

MAKEOVER MAPLE COFFEE CAKE

# Maple-Walnut Coffee Cake

**PREP:** 25 min. **BAKE:** 35 min. + cooling
**YIELD:** 24 servings

**ANGELA SPENGLER • CLOVIS, NEW MEXICO**

*Wake up the sleepy heads in your household with this moist, tender coffee cake that's both sweet and savory. Bacon and nuts in the crumbly topping blend with flavors of maple, nutmeg and cinnamon. Yum!*

| | |
|---|---|
| 2-1/2 | cups all-purpose flour |
| 1 | cup packed brown sugar |
| 1/2 | tsp. salt |
| 1/3 | cup cold butter |
| 2 | tsp. baking powder |
| 1/2 | tsp. baking soda |
| 1/2 | tsp. ground cinnamon |
| 1/4 | tsp. ground nutmeg |
| 2 | eggs |
| 1-1/2 | cups buttermilk |
| 1/2 | cup maple syrup |
| 1/3 | cup unsweetened applesauce |
| 5 | bacon strips, cooked and crumbled |
| 1/2 | cup chopped walnuts |

**1.** In a large bowl, combine the flour, brown sugar and salt. Cut in butter until crumbly. Set aside 1/2 cup for topping. Combine the baking powder, baking soda, cinnamon and nutmeg; stir into the remaining flour mixture.

**2.** In a small bowl, whisk the eggs, buttermilk, syrup and applesauce until well blended. Gradually stir into flour mixture until combined.

**3.** Spread into a 13-in. x 9-in. baking pan coated with cooking spray. Sprinkle with reserved topping, then bacon and walnuts. Bake at 350° for 35-40 minutes or until a toothpick inserted near the center comes out clean. Cool on a wire rack.

**Nutrition Facts:** 1 piece equals 160 calories, 5 g fat (2 g saturated fat), 27 mg cholesterol, 183 mg sodium, 25 g carbohydrate, 1 g fiber, 3 g protein. **Diabetic Exchanges:** 1-1/2 starch, 1 fat.

MAPLE-WALNUT COFFEE CAKE

# Multigrain Nutrition Loaves  **F**

**PREP:** 30 min. + rising **BAKE:** 35 min. + cooling
**YIELD:** 3 loaves (16 slices each)

**BARB TROY • NEW BERLIN, WISCONSIN**

*As a dietitian, I'm always hunting for healthful, homemade additions to my family's meals, and this is a delicious one.*

| | |
|---|---|
| 6-1/2 to 7 | cups all-purpose flour |
| 1-1/2 | cups whole wheat flour |
| 1 | cup bran flakes |
| 1 | cup quick-cooking oats |
| 2 | pkg. (1/4 oz. *each*) active dry yeast |
| 2 | tsp. salt |
| 2-1/2 | cups water |
| 1-1/2 | cups (12 oz.) 1% cottage cheese |
| 1 | cup raisins |
| 1/2 | cup molasses |
| 2 | Tbsp. butter |
| 2 | eggs |

**1.** In a large mixing bowl, combine 2 cups all-purpose flour, whole wheat flour, bran flakes, oats, yeast and salt. In a small saucepan, heat the water, cottage cheese, raisins, molasses and butter to 120°-130°. Add to dry ingredients; beat until blended. Beat in eggs. Stir in enough remaining all-purpose flour to form a soft dough.

**2.** Turn onto a lightly floured surface; knead until smooth and elastic, about 6-8 minutes. Place in a bowl coated with cooking spray, turning once to coat the top. Cover and let rise in a warm place until doubled, about 1 hour.

**3.** Punch dough down. Turn onto a lightly floured surface; divide into thirds. Shape into loaves. Place in three 9-in. x 5-in. loaf pans coated with cooking spray. Cover and let rise until doubled, about 40 minutes.

**4.** Bake at 375° for 35-40 minutes or until golden brown. Remove from pans to wire racks.

**Nutrition Facts:** 1 slice equals 110 calories, 1 g fat (trace saturated fat), 10 mg cholesterol, 143 mg sodium, 21 g carbohydrate, 1 g fiber, 4 g protein. **Diabetic Exchange:** 1-1/2 starch.

# Bananas Foster Bread

**PREP:** 20 min. + cooling **BAKE:** 50 min. + cooling
**YIELD:** 1 loaf (16 slices)

**CHRISTEN CHALMERS • HOUSTON, TEXAS**

*This moist, tender bread has all the flavors of New Orleans' famous dessert. And the rum-flavored glaze is amazing!*

| | |
|---|---|
| 5 | Tbsp. butter, cubed |
| 1 | cup packed brown sugar, *divided* |
| 1-1/2 | cups mashed ripe bananas |
| 3 | Tbsp. dark rum |
| 1-1/2 | cups all-purpose flour |
| 1/4 | cup ground flaxseed |
| 3/4 | tsp. baking soda |
| 1/2 | tsp. salt |
| 1/2 | tsp. ground cinnamon |

2 eggs
1/3 cup fat-free plain yogurt
GLAZE:
1/3 cup confectioners' sugar
1 Tbsp. butter, melted
1 Tbsp. dark rum

**1.** In a small saucepan, melt butter. Stir in 1/2 cup brown sugar and bananas. Bring to a boil. Reduce heat; simmer, uncovered, for 3-4 minutes or until slightly thickened. Remove from the heat. Stir in rum; set aside to cool.

**2.** In a large bowl, combine the flour, flax, baking soda, salt and cinnamon. In another large bowl, whisk the eggs, yogurt, banana mixture and remaining brown sugar. Stir into dry ingredients just until moistened.

**3.** Transfer to a 9-in. x 5-in. loaf pan coated with cooking spray. Bake at 350° for 50-55 minutes or until a toothpick inserted near the center comes out clean. Cool for 10 minutes before removing from pan to a wire rack to cool completely.

**4.** Combine the glaze ingredients; drizzle over bread.

**Nutrition Facts:** 1 slice equals 189 calories, 6 g fat (3 g saturated fat), 38 mg cholesterol, 181 mg sodium, 31 g carbohydrate, 1 g fiber, 3 g protein. **Diabetic Exchanges:** 2 starch, 1 fat.

# Gluten-Free Cornmeal Muffins

**PREP:** 20 min. **BAKE:** 15 min. **YIELD:** 1 dozen

**LAURA FALL-SUTTON • BUHL, IDAHO**

*I serve these muffins warm with butter, honey or even salsa. Reheat leftovers in foil in the oven...if there are any!*

3/4 cup fat-free milk
1/4 cup honey
2 Tbsp. canola oil
1 egg
1 egg white
1-1/2 cups cornmeal
1/2 cup amaranth flour
2-1/2 tsp. baking powder
1/2 tsp. xanthan gum
1/2 tsp. salt
1 cup frozen corn, thawed
3/4 cup shredded reduced-fat Monterey Jack cheese *or* Mexican cheese blend

**1.** In a large bowl, beat the first five ingredients until well blended.

**2.** Combine the cornmeal, amaranth flour, baking powder, xanthan gum and salt; gradually beat into milk mixture until blended. Stir in corn and cheese.

**3.** Coat muffin cups with cooking spray or use foil liners; fill three-fourths full with batter. Bake at 375° for 15-18 minutes or until a toothpick inserted near the center comes out clean.

**4.** Cool for 5 minutes before removing from pan to a wire rack.

**Editor's Note:** Read all ingredient labels for possible gluten content prior to use. Ingredient formulas can change, and production facilities vary among brands. If you're concerned that your brand may contain gluten, contact the company.

**Nutrition Facts:** 1 muffin equals 169 calories, 5 g fat (1 g saturated fat), 23 mg cholesterol, 263 mg sodium, 27 g carbohydrate, 2 g fiber, 6 g protein. **Diabetic Exchanges:** 1-1/2 starch, 1 fat.

# Cafe Mocha Mini Muffins S C

PREP/TOTAL TIME: 30 min. YIELD: 1-1/2 dozen

TINA SAWCHUK • ARDMORE, ALBERTA

*These mini muffins freeze well, so it's always easy to keep some on hand. They're just the right size for a low-carb snack!*

|       |                                                      |
|-------|------------------------------------------------------|
| 2     | tsp. instant coffee granules                         |
| 1/3   | cup boiling water                                    |
| 1/4   | cup quick-cooking oats                               |
| 3     | Tbsp. butter, softened                               |
| 1/4   | cup sugar                                            |
| 3     | Tbsp. brown sugar                                    |
| 1     | egg yolk                                             |
| 1/2   | tsp. vanilla extract                                 |
| 1/2   | cup all-purpose flour                                |
| 1     | Tbsp. baking cocoa                                   |
| 1/2   | tsp. baking powder                                   |
| 1/8   | tsp. baking soda                                     |
| 1/8   | tsp. salt                                            |
| 1/2   | cup miniature semisweet chocolate chips, *divided*   |

**1.** In a small bowl, dissolve coffee granules in water. Stir in the oats; set aside. In a small bowl, cream butter and sugars. Beat in egg yolk, vanilla and oat mixture. Combine the flour, cocoa, baking powder, baking soda and salt; add to oat mixture just until moistened. Stir in 1/3 cup chocolate chips.

**2.** Coat miniature muffin cups with cooking spray or use paper liners; fill three-fourths full with batter. Sprinkle with remaining chips. Bake at 350° for 12-15 minutes or until a toothpick inserted near the center comes out clean. Cool for 5 minutes before removing from pans to wire racks.

**Editor's Note:** Muffins may be frozen for up to 2 months.

**Nutrition Facts:** 1 muffin equals 81 calories, 4 g fat (2 g saturated fat), 17 mg cholesterol, 53 mg sodium, 12 g carbohydrate, 1 g fiber, 1 g protein. **Diabetic Exchanges:** 1 starch, 1/2 fat.

CAFE MOCHA MINI MUFFINS

# Moist Mexican Corn Bread

PREP: 20 min. BAKE: 25 min. YIELD: 9 servings

KATHERINE THOMPSON • TYBEE ISLAND, GEORGIA

*The name of this recipe says it all. The bread is perfect for scooping up that last drop of soup or stew.*

|         |                                                                           |
|---------|---------------------------------------------------------------------------|
| 1       | cup all-purpose flour                                                     |
| 1       | cup cornmeal                                                              |
| 1/4     | cup ground flaxseed                                                       |
| 1       | Tbsp. sugar                                                               |
| 2-1/2   | tsp. baking powder                                                        |
| 1       | tsp. salt                                                                 |
| 2       | eggs                                                                      |
| 1-1/2   | cups fat-free milk                                                        |
| 1       | Tbsp. olive oil                                                           |
| 1-1/2   | cups frozen corn, thawed                                                  |
| 1-1/2   | cups (6 oz.) shredded reduced-fat Colby-Monterey Jack cheese, *divided*   |
| 1/2     | cup finely chopped sweet red pepper                                       |

**1.** In a large bowl, combine the flour, cornmeal, flax, sugar, baking powder and salt. In a small bowl, whisk the eggs, milk and oil. Stir into dry ingredients just until moistened. Fold in the corn, 1 cup cheese and pepper.

**2.** Transfer to an 11-in. x 7-in. baking pan coated with cooking spray. Sprinkle with remaining cheese. Bake at 350° for 25-30 minutes or until a toothpick inserted near the center comes out clean. Serve warm.

**Nutrition Facts:** 1 piece equals 251 calories, 8 g fat (3 g saturated fat), 58 mg cholesterol, 563 mg sodium, 34 g carbohydrate, 3 g fiber, 12 g protein.

# Parmesan Herb Loaf F M

PREP: 10 min. + rising BAKE: 20 min. YIELD: 1 loaf (12 slices)

SHIRLEY SIBIT RUDDER • BURKEVILLE, TEXAS

*A frozen loaf of whole wheat bread makes this recipe a snap to toss together. Flavored with garlic, butter and Parmesan cheese, it's a wonderful addition to an Italian menu.*

|         |                                          |
|---------|------------------------------------------|
| 1       | loaf (1 lb.) frozen whole wheat bread dough |
| 1/4     | cup shredded Parmesan cheese             |
| 1-1/2   | tsp. dried parsley flakes                |
| 1-1/2   | tsp. dried minced garlic                 |
| 1/4     | tsp. dill weed                           |
| 1/4     | tsp. salt                                |
| 1       | Tbsp. butter, melted                     |

**1.** Place dough in an 8-in. x 4-in. loaf pan coated with cooking spray. Thaw according to package directions. In a small bowl, combine the cheese, parsley, garlic, dill and salt. Brush dough with butter; sprinkle with cheese mixture. Cover and let rise in a warm place until nearly doubled, about 2-1/2 hours.

**2.** Bake at 350° for 20-25 minutes or until golden brown. Remove from pan to a wire rack to cool.

**Nutrition Facts:** 1 slice equals 111 calories, 3 g fat (1 g saturated fat), 4 mg cholesterol, 250 mg sodium, 18 g carbohydrate, 2 g fiber, 6 g protein. **Diabetic Exchange:** 1 starch.

# Swirl Cinnamon Bread  ⓢ

**PREP:** 25 min. **BAKE:** 45 min. + cooling
**YIELD:** 1 loaf (12 slices)

**MERYL SHEPPARD • GREENSBORO, NORTH CAROLINA**

*If you like cinnamon, you'll love this quick bread. It's crusty on top, soft and moist inside—and one of my most-requested recipes. I always make extra loaves for the holidays and give them to family and friends.*

|   |   |
|---|---|
| 2 | cups all-purpose flour |
| 3/4 | cup sugar |
| 1/2 | tsp. baking soda |
| 1/2 | tsp. plus 1-1/2 tsp. ground cinnamon, *divided* |
| 1/4 | tsp. salt |
| 1 | egg |
| 1 | cup (8 oz.) reduced-fat plain yogurt |
| 1/4 | cup canola oil |
| 1 | tsp. vanilla extract |
| 1/4 | cup packed brown sugar |

**1.** In a large bowl, combine the flour, sugar, baking soda, 1/2 tsp. cinnamon and salt. In a small bowl, whisk the egg, yogurt, oil and vanilla. Stir into dry ingredients just until moistened. In a small bowl, combine brown sugar and remaining cinnamon.

**2.** Spoon a third of the batter into an 8-in. x 4-in. loaf pan coated with cooking spray. Top with a third of the brown sugar mixture. Repeat layers twice. Cut through batter with a knife to swirl the brown sugar mixture.

**3.** Bake at 350° for 45-55 minutes or until a toothpick inserted near the center comes out clean. Cool for 10 minutes before removing from pan to a wire rack.

**Nutrition Facts:** 1 slice equals 203 calories, 6 g fat (1 g saturated fat), 19 mg cholesterol, 124 mg sodium, 35 g carbohydrate, 1 g fiber, 4 g protein.

For quick breads, bake in a **light aluminum pan**, rather than a darker nonstick pan, and bake so the top of the loaf is in the center of the oven. Bake as directed. Cool for 10 minutes, then remove to a wire rack.

HOLIDAY HERB-CHEESE ROLLS

## Holiday Herb-Cheese Rolls F

PREP: 45 min. + rising  BAKE: 20 min.  YIELD: 2 dozen

NANCY BOYD • MIDLOTHIAN, VIRGINIA

*These low-fat hot rolls are flavored with garlic, dill and cheese—they're yummy even without butter! Or stuff with your favorite fixings for mini sandwiches.*

|  |  |
|---|---|
| 4 | to 4-1/2 cups all-purpose flour |
| 1/4 | cup sugar |
| 2 | Tbsp. mashed potato flakes |
| 1 | pkg. (1/4 oz.) active dry yeast |
| 2 | tsp. salt |
| 1/2 | tsp. dill weed |
| 1/4 | tsp. garlic powder |
| 2 | cups water |
| 4-1/2 | tsp. butter |
| 1 | cup old-fashioned oats |
| 1 | egg |
| 3/4 | cup shredded part-skim mozzarella cheese |

TOPPING:

|  |  |
|---|---|
| 2 | Tbsp. fat-free milk |
| 4-1/2 | tsp. grated Parmesan cheese |
| 1/2 | tsp. garlic powder |
| 1/2 | tsp. dill weed |
| 1/2 | tsp. dried basil |

**1.** In a large bowl, combine 1-1/2 cups flour, sugar, potato flakes, yeast, salt, dill and garlic powder. In a small saucepan, bring water and butter just to a boil.

**2.** In a small bowl, pour boiling liquid over oats. Let stand until mixture cools to 120°-130°, stirring occasionally. Add to dry ingredients; beat just until moistened. Add egg;

beat until smooth. Stir in enough remaining flour to form a firm dough (dough will be sticky).

**3.** Turn onto a floured surface; knead until smooth and elastic, about 6-8 minutes. Knead in mozzarella cheese. Place in a large bowl coated with cooking spray, turning once to coat the top. Cover and let rise in a warm place until doubled, about 1-1/4 hours.

**4.** Punch dough down. Turn onto a lightly floured surface; divide into 24 pieces. Shape each into a ball. Place in a 13-in. x 9-in. baking pan coated with cooking spray; brush milk over rolls.

**5.** In a small bowl, combine the remaining ingredients; sprinkle over tops. Cover and let rise until nearly doubled, about 45 minutes. Bake at 375° for 20-25 minutes or until golden brown. Remove from pan to a wire rack.

**Nutrition Facts:** 1 roll equals 119 calories, 2 g fat (1 g saturated fat), 13 mg cholesterol, 228 mg sodium, 21 g carbohydrate, 1 g fiber, 4 g protein. **Diabetic Exchange:** 1-1/2 starch.

## Honey Whole Wheat Bread F

PREP: 20 min. + rising  BAKE: 35 min. + cooling
YIELD: 2 loaves (16 slices each)

ROBYN LINDBERG • KECHI, KANSAS

*Here's a recipe that turns out two beautiful golden loaves.*

|  |  |
|---|---|
| 2 | pkg. (1/4 oz. *each*) active dry yeast |
| 3 | cups warm water (110° to 115°) |
| 1/2 | cup nonfat dry milk powder |
| 1/2 | cup honey |
| 1/3 | cup wheat bran |
| 1/3 | cup toasted wheat germ |
| 1/4 | cup ground flaxseed |

2 Tbsp. canola oil

2 tsp. salt

4 cups whole wheat flour

3-1/2 to 4 cups all-purpose flour

**1.** In a large bowl, dissolve yeast in warm water. Add the milk powder, honey, wheat bran, wheat germ, flax, oil, salt, whole wheat flour and 3 cups all-purpose flour. Beat until smooth. Stir in enough of the remaining flour to form a soft dough (dough will be sticky).

**2.** Turn onto a lightly floured surface; knead until smooth and elastic, about 6-8 minutes. Place in a bowl coated with cooking spray, turning once to coat the top. Cover and let rise in a warm place until doubled, about 1 hour.

**3.** Punch dough down and turn onto a floured surface; shape into two loaves. Place in two 9-in. x 5-in. loaf pans coated with cooking spay. Cover and let rise until doubled, about 30 minutes.

**4.** Bake at 350° for 35-40 minutes or until golden brown. Remove from pans to a wire rack to cool.

**Nutrition Facts:** 1 slice equals 139 calories, 2 g fat (trace saturated fat), trace cholesterol, 155 mg sodium, 28 g carbohydrate, 3 g fiber, 5 g protein. **Diabetic Exchange:** 2 starch.

# Ginger Pear Bread

**PREP:** 25 min. **BAKE:** 45 min. + cooling
**YIELD:** 2 loaves (12 slices each)

**CARLY CURTIN • ELLICOTT CITY, MARYLAND**

*A great way to use up extra pears, this bread is packed with juicy chunks of them, along with ginger, cinnamon, brown sugar and whole wheat flour. It's a healthier choice than many other baked items—and it freezes well, too.*

4 medium pears, peeled and chopped

1 tsp. lemon juice

1-1/2 cups all-purpose flour

1 cup whole wheat flour

1 cup sugar

1/4 cup plus 2 tsp. packed brown sugar, *divided*

2 tsp. baking powder

1 tsp. baking soda

1 tsp. salt

1 tsp. ground ginger

1 tsp. ground cinnamon

3 eggs

3/4 cup canola oil

1 tsp. vanilla extract

**1.** In a large bowl, drizzle the pears with lemon juice; set aside.

**2.** In another large bowl, combine the flours, sugar, 1/4 cup brown sugar, baking powder, baking soda, salt, ginger and cinnamon. In a small bowl, whisk the eggs, oil and vanilla. Stir into dry ingredients just until moistened. Fold in pear mixture.

**3.** Transfer to two 8-in. x 4-in. loaf pans coated with cooking spray. Sprinkle with remaining brown sugar. Bake at 350° for 45-55 minutes or until a toothpick

inserted near the center comes out clean. Cool for 10 minutes before removing from pans to wire racks.

**Nutrition Facts:** 1 slice equals 175 calories, 8 g fat (1 g saturated fat), 26 mg cholesterol, 195 mg sodium, 25 g carbohydrate, 2 g fiber, 2 g protein. **Diabetic Exchanges:** 1-1/2 starch, 1-1/2 fat.

# Cranberry Pistachio Biscotti  **F** **S** **C**

**PREP:** 25 min. **BAKE:** 30 min. **YIELD:** about 2-1/2 dozen

**DIANE GRUBER • SIOUX CITY, IOWA**

*This tasty biscotti is studded with dried cranberries and crunchy pistachios. It's delicious with tea or coffee.*

3/4 cup sugar

1/4 cup canola oil

2 eggs

2 tsp. vanilla extract

1 tsp. almond extract

1-3/4 cups all-purpose flour

1 tsp. baking powder

1/4 tsp. salt

2/3 cup chopped pistachios

1/2 cup dried cranberries

**1.** In a small bowl, beat sugar and oil until blended. Beat in eggs, then extracts. Combine the flour, baking powder and salt; gradually add to sugar mixture and mix well (dough will be stiff). Stir in the pistachios and cranberries.

**2.** Divide dough in half. With floured hands, shape each half into a 12-in. x 2-in. rectangle on a parchment paper-lined baking sheet. Bake at 350° for 18-22 minutes or until set.

**3.** Place pan on wire rack. When cool enough to handle, transfer to a cutting board; cut diagonally with a serrated knife into 3/4-in. slices. Place cut side down on ungreased baking sheets. Bake for 12-14 minutes or until firm. Remove to wire racks to cool. Store in an airtight container.

**Nutrition Facts:** 1 cookie equals 85 calories, 3 g fat (trace saturated fat), 13 mg cholesterol, 46 mg sodium, 12 g carbohydrate, 1 g fiber, 2 g protein. **Diabetic Exchange:** 1 starch.

CRANBERRY PISTACHIO BISCOTTI

# Twisted Cinnamon Ring

**PREP:** 30 min. + rising **BAKE:** 20 min.
**YIELD:** 1 ring (12 slices)

**JUDY EDDY • BALDWIN CITY, KANSAS**

*Here's a fun take on a no-fuss dough I created! The presentation is lovely, and it's really quite simple!*

|       |                                          |
| ----- | ---------------------------------------- |
| 1     | pkg. (1/4 oz.) active dry yeast          |
| 3/4   | cup warm water (110° to 115°)            |
| 1/2   | cup quick-cooking oats                   |
| 1/2   | cup whole wheat flour                    |
| 1/4   | cup packed brown sugar                   |
| 2     | Tbsp. butter, melted                     |
| 1     | egg                                      |
| 1     | tsp. salt                                |
| 1-3/4 to 2-1/4 | cups all-purpose flour          |

FILLING:

|     |                      |
| --- | -------------------- |
| 3   | Tbsp. butter, softened |
| 1/3 | cup sugar            |
| 2   | tsp. ground cinnamon |

GLAZE:

|       |                        |
| ----- | ---------------------- |
| 1     | cup confectioners' sugar |
| 6-1/2 | tsp. half-and-half cream |
| 4-1/2 | tsp. butter, softened  |

**1.** In a large bowl, dissolve yeast in warm water. Add the oats, whole wheat flour, brown sugar, butter, egg, salt and 1 cup all-purpose flour. Beat on medium speed until smooth. Stir in enough remaining flour to form a soft dough (dough will be sticky).

**2.** Turn onto a lightly floured surface; knead until smooth and elastic, about 6-8 minutes. Place in a bowl coated with cooking spray, turning once to coat the top. Cover and let rise in a warm place until doubled, about 1 hour.

**3.** Punch dough down. Roll into an 18-in. x 12-in. rectangle; spread with butter. Combine sugar and cinnamon; sprinkle over dough to within 1/2 in. of the edges.

**4.** Roll up jelly-roll style, starting with a long side; pinch seams to seal. Cut roll in half lengthwise. Place doughs side by side on a baking sheet coated with cooking spray. Twist together, cut side up, and shape into a ring. Pinch ends together. Cover and let rise until doubled, about 45 minutes.

**5.** Bake at 375° for 20-25 minutes or until golden brown. Remove from pan to a wire rack. For glaze, in a small bowl, beat the confectioners' sugar, cream and butter until smooth. Drizzle over ring.

**Nutrition Facts:** 1 slice equals 240 calories, 7 g fat (4 g saturated fat), 35 mg cholesterol, 251 mg sodium, 40 g carbohydrate, 2 g fiber, 4 g protein.

# Walnut Apple Bread  `F` `S`

**PREP:** 40 min. + rising **BAKE:** 30 min. + cooling
**YIELD:** 2 loaves (16 slices each)

**NANCY DAUGHERTY • CORTLAND, OHIO**

*Whenever I make this bread, it's like being in my Grandma's kitchen. Swirled with apples, walnuts and cinnamon, it's one of the best breads I've ever tasted.*

|       |                                   |
| ----- | --------------------------------- |
| 2     | pkg. (1/4 oz.) active dry yeast   |
| 1/2   | cup warm water (110° to 115°)     |
| 3/4   | cup sugar                         |
| 1/2   | cup warm 2% milk (110° to 115°)   |
| 1/4   | cup reduced-fat butter, softened  |
| 2     | eggs                              |
| 1     | tsp. salt                         |
| 4 to 4-1/2 | cups all-purpose flour       |

FILLING:

|     |                             |
| --- | --------------------------- |
| 2   | cups chopped peeled apples  |
| 1/2 | cup chopped walnuts         |
| 2/3 | cup sugar                   |
| 1   | Tbsp. all-purpose flour     |
| 2   | tsp. ground cinnamon        |
| 2   | Tbsp. reduced-fat butter, softened |

GLAZE:

|   |                             |
| - | --------------------------- |
| 1 | cup confectioners' sugar    |
| 2 | Tbsp. apple cider *or* juice |

**1.** In a large bowl, dissolve yeast in warm water. Add the sugar, milk, butter, eggs, salt and 2 cups flour. Beat until smooth. Stir in enough remaining flour to form a soft dough (dough will be sticky).

**2.** Turn onto a lightly floured surface; knead until smooth and elastic, about 6-8 minutes. Place in a bowl coated with cooking spray, turning once to coat the top. Cover and let rise in a warm place until doubled, about 1 hour.

**3.** For filling, in a small bowl, combine apples and walnuts. Combine the sugar, flour and cinnamon; stir into apple mixture. Punch dough down. Roll into a 14-in. x 12-in. rectangle. Spread butter to within 1/2 in. of edges; sprinkle with apple mixture. Roll up jelly-roll style, starting with a long side. Cut in half. Pinch seams to seal and tuck ends under.

**4.** Place loaves seam side down in two 9-in. x 5-in. loaf pans coated with cooking spray. Cover and let rise until doubled, about 30 minutes. With a sharp knife, make eight shallow slashes across top of each loaf.

TWISTED CINNAMON RING

**5.** Bake at 350° for 30-35 minutes or until golden brown. Remove from pans to wire racks to cool. In a small bowl, combine the glaze ingredients; drizzle over the bread.

**Editor's Note:** This recipe was tested with Land O'Lakes light stick butter.

**Nutrition Facts:** 1 slice equals 140 calories, 3 g fat (1 g saturated fat), 16 mg cholesterol, 99 mg sodium, 27 g carbohydrate, 1 g fiber, 3 g protein. **Diabetic Exchanges:** 1-1/2 starch, 1/2 fat.

# Rhubarb-Lemon Coffee Cake

**PREP:** 25 min.  **BAKE:** 35 min. + cooling
**YIELD:** 12 servings

**STEPHANIE OTTEN • BYRON CENTER, MICHIGAN**

*And you thought rhubarb was just for pie—not so in the case of this tart and tasty coffee cake.*

2-1/4 cups all-purpose flour
  3/4 cup sugar
  1/2 tsp. baking powder
  1/2 tsp. baking soda
  1/4 tsp. salt
  1/3 cup butter, melted
  2/3 cup vanilla yogurt
    2 eggs
    1 Tbsp. lemon juice
    2 tsp. grated lemon peel
    1 cup chopped fresh or frozen rhubarb
    1 tsp. ground cinnamon
  1/2 tsp. ground nutmeg

**STREUSEL:**
  1/2 cup all-purpose flour
  1/3 cup sugar
    1 tsp. ground cinnamon
    2 Tbsp. cold butter

**GLAZE:**
  1/3 cup confectioners' sugar
    2 tsp. lemon juice

**1.** In a large bowl, combine the flour, sugar, baking powder, baking soda and salt. In a small bowl, whisk the butter, yogurt, eggs, lemon juice and lemon peel. Stir into dry ingredients just until moistened.

**2.** Coat a 9-in. springform pan with cooking spray and sprinkle with flour. Spread half the batter into prepared pan. Add rhubarb to within 1/2 in. of the edges. Sprinkle with cinnamon and nutmeg. Top with remaining batter.

**3.** For streusel, combine the flour, sugar and cinnamon in a small bowl; cut in butter until crumbly. Sprinkle over batter. Bake at 350° for 35-45 minutes or until a toothpick inserted near the center comes out clean. Cool for 10 minutes.

**4.** For glaze, in a small bowl combine confectioners' sugar and lemon juice. Drizzle over warm cake. Cool for 1 hour.

**Editor's Note:** If using frozen rhubarb, measure rhubarb while still frozen, then thaw completely.  Drain in a colander, but do not press liquid out.

**Nutrition Facts:** 1 slice equals 273 calories, 8 g fat (5 g saturated fat), 54 mg cholesterol, 187 mg sodium, 46 g carbohydrate, 1 g fiber, 5 g protein.

PINEAPPLE-APPLE CHICKEN SALAD

AVOCADO TURKEY WRAPS

TURKEY & SWISS QUESADIILLAS

# Table for Two

Now it's easier than ever for empty nesters, newlyweds and single cooks to prepare healthy fare without having to deal with lots of leftovers. Simply consider these sensational dishes, sized right for small households.

## Turkey & Swiss Quesadillas

PREP/TOTAL TIME: 20 min.  YIELD: 2 servings

**KAREN O'SHEA • SPARKS, NEVADA**

*Light, lean and nutritious, this quick supper idea goes together in just minutes.*

- 2　Tbsp. reduced-fat Parmesan peppercorn ranch salad dressing
- 1　Tbsp. Dijon mustard
- 2　whole wheat tortillas (8 in.)
- 2　slices reduced-fat Swiss cheese, halved
- 1/2　medium ripe avocado, peeled and thinly sliced
- 6　oz. sliced cooked turkey breast

Diced sweet red pepper, optional

**1.** In a small bowl, combine salad dressing and mustard; spread over one side of each tortilla. Place tortillas, spread side up, on a griddle coated with cooking spray.

**2.** Layer cheese, avocado and turkey over half of each tortilla. Fold over and cook over low heat for 1-2 minutes on each side or until cheese is melted. Garnish with red pepper if desired.

**Nutrition Facts:** 1 quesadilla equals 421 calories, 16 g fat (3 g saturated fat), 86 mg cholesterol, 566 mg sodium, 32 g carbohydrate, 5 g fiber, 38 g protein. **Diabetic Exchanges:** 4 lean meat, 2 starch, 2 fat.

## Avocado Turkey Wraps

PREP/TOTAL TIME: 15 min.  YIELD: 2 servings

**HEALTHY COOKING TEST KITCHEN**

*These delicious sandwiches are perfect for brown-bag lunches. With sliced turkey, avocado and cheese, they'll add extra flavor to noontime meals. If you like, substitute tomato slices with a well-drained chunky salsa.*

- 2　whole wheat tortillas (8 in.), room temperature
- 2　Tbsp. fat-free mayonnaise
- 1/4　lb. thinly sliced deli turkey
- 8　thin slices tomato
- 2　tsp. finely chopped jalapeno pepper
- 1/4　cup shredded reduced-fat cheddar cheese
- 2　tsp. minced fresh cilantro
- 1/2　medium ripe avocado, peeled and thinly sliced

**1.** Spread tortillas with mayonnaise. Top each with turkey, tomato, jalapeno, cheese, cilantro and avocado. Roll up and cut in half.

**Editor's Note:** Wear disposable gloves when cutting hot peppers; the oils can burn skin. Avoid touching your face.

**Nutrition Facts:** 1 wrap equals 342 calories, 15 g fat (4 g saturated fat), 37 mg cholesterol, 1,079 mg sodium, 34 g carbohydrate, 6 g fiber, 18 g protein.

## Pineapple-Apple Chicken Salad

PREP/TOTAL TIME: 10 min.  YIELD: 2 servings

**PRISCILLA COTE • NEW HARTFORD, NEW YORK**

*This just might be the fastest chicken salad recipe ever! The fruit gives it a sweet touch, the almonds lend crunch, and the curry adds depth of flavor and color. Using a snack-size cup of pineapple means you won't have leftovers after you make this. You can replace the apple with a chopped pear if you like.*

- 1　cup cubed cooked chicken breast
- 1/2　medium apple, chopped
- 1　snack-size cup (4 oz.) pineapple tidbits, drained
- 1/4　cup reduced-fat mayonnaise
- 2　Tbsp. slivered almonds
- 1/4　to 1/2 tsp. curry powder
- 2　cups torn mixed salad greens

**1.** In a large bowl, combine the first six ingredients. Serve with greens.

**Nutrition Facts:** 1 cup chicken salad with 1 cup salad greens equals 301 calories, 16 g fat (2 g saturated fat), 64 mg cholesterol, 302 mg sodium, 17 g carbohydrate, 4 g fiber, 23 g protein. **Diabetic Exchanges:** 3 lean meat, 2-1/2 fat, 1 vegetable, 1/2 fruit.

Any cooked chicken can be used when making chicken salad, regardless of cooking method or seasonings. Just remove all chicken skin to keep fat at bay. When mixing your own **chicken salad,** get creative with healthy additions such as diced cucumber, peas and red onion.

# Skillet Tacos

**PREP/TOTAL TIME:** 30 min. **YIELD:** 2 servings

**MARIA GOBEL • GREENFIELD, WISCONSIN**

*If you like Mexican food, you'll be whipping up this fast and healthy version of tacos often. It's a great meal-in-one dish!*

- 1/4 lb. lean ground turkey
- 2 Tbsp. chopped onion
- 2 Tbsp. chopped green pepper
- 1 can (8 oz.) tomato sauce
- 1/2 cup uncooked elbow macaroni
- 1/2 cup water
- 1/4 cup picante sauce
- 2 Tbsp. shredded fat-free cheddar cheese
- 1/4 cup crushed baked tortilla chip scoops
- 1/4 cup chopped avocado

Iceberg lettuce wedges and fat-free sour cream, optional

**1.** In a large nonstick skillet coated with cooking spray, cook the turkey, onion and green pepper over medium heat until turkey is no longer pink.

**2.** Stir in the tomato sauce, macaroni, water and picante sauce. Bring to a boil. Reduce heat; cover and simmer for 10-15 minutes or until macaroni is tender.

**3.** Divide between two plates; top with cheese, tortilla chips and avocado. Serve with lettuce and sour cream if desired.

**Nutrition Facts:** 1 serving (calculated without lettuce and sour cream) equals 267 calories, 9 g fat (2 g saturated fat), 46 mg cholesterol, 795 mg sodium, 30 g carbohydrate, 3 g fiber, 18 g protein. **Diabetic Exchanges:** 2 lean meat, 1-1/2 starch, 1 vegetable, 1/2 fat.

# Baked Apple Surprise **F**

**PREP:** 10 min. **BAKE:** 35 min. **YIELD:** 2 servings

**JESSICA LEVINSON • NYACK, NEW YORK**

*This sweet-savory recipe is a favorite. Use Brie instead of blue cheese if you like things creamier. My tip? Bake the apples in a muffin tin so they won't roll around.*

- 2 medium apples
- 2 Tbsp. crumbled blue cheese, *divided*
- 2 Tbsp. quick-cooking oats
- 2 Tbsp. bran flakes
- 1 Tbsp. golden raisins
- 1 Tbsp. raisins
- 1 Tbsp. brown sugar

**1.** Cut apples in half lengthwise; remove cores. Place in an ungreased 8-in. square baking dish. Fill each half with 1 tsp. blue cheese.

**2.** In a small bowl, combine the oats, bran flakes, golden raisins, raisins and brown sugar; spoon into apples. Top with remaining cheese. Bake, uncovered, at 350° for 35-40 minutes or until tender.

**Nutrition Facts:** 2 filled apple halves equals 181 calories, 3 g fat (2 g saturated fat), 6 mg cholesterol, 141 mg sodium, 39 g carbohydrate, 5 g fiber, 3 g protein.

# Fruity Crab Pasta Salad **F**

**PREP/TOTAL TIME:** 30 min. **YIELD:** 2 servings

**DARLENE JUREK • FOLEY, MINNESOTA**

*A sweet ginger dressing spices up this tasty medley of oranges, grapes, crabmeat and pasta. It's an ideal warm-weather entree.*

- 3/4 cup uncooked spiral pasta
- 1 pkg. (8 oz.) imitation crabmeat
- 1 snack-size cup (4 oz.) mandarin oranges, drained
- 1/4 cup halved seedless red grapes
- 1/4 cup halved seedless green grapes
- 1/4 cup reduced-fat plain yogurt
- 2 Tbsp. fat-free mayonnaise
- 1-1/2 tsp. honey
- 1/4 tsp. ground ginger

SKILLET TACOS

BAKED APPLE SURPRISE

CRISPY ASIAN CHICKEN SALAD

**1.** Cook pasta according to package directions; drain and rinse in cold water. In a small bowl, combine the pasta, crab, oranges and grapes.

**2.** Combine the yogurt, mayonnaise, honey and ginger; pour over salad and toss to coat. Refrigerate until serving.

**Nutrition Facts:** 1-1/2 cups (prepared with reduced-fat yogurt and fat-free mayonnaise) equals 322 calories, 2 g fat (1 g saturated fat), 59 mg cholesterol, 215 mg sodium, 55 g carbohydrate, 2 g fiber, 21 g protein.

## Crispy Asian Chicken Salad

**PREP/TOTAL TIME:** 30 min.  **YIELD:** 2 servings

BETH DAUENHAUER • PUEBLO, COLORADO

*Asian flavor, crunchy almonds and crispy breaded chicken make this hearty salad something special.*

|   |   |
|---|---|
| 2 | boneless skinless chicken breast halves (4 oz. *each*) |
| 2 | tsp. hoisin sauce |
| 1 | tsp. sesame oil |
| 1/2 | cup panko (Japanese) bread crumbs |
| 4 | tsp. sesame seeds |
| 2 | tsp. canola oil |
| 4 | cups spring mix salad greens |
| 1 | small green pepper, julienned |
| 1 | small sweet red pepper, julienned |
| 1 | medium carrot, julienned |
| 1/2 | cup sliced fresh mushrooms |
| 2 | Tbsp. thinly sliced onion |
| 2 | Tbsp. sliced almonds, toasted |
| 1/4 | cup reduced-fat sesame ginger salad dressing |

**1.** Flatten chicken breasts to 1/2-in. thickness. Combine hoisin sauce and sesame oil; brush over chicken. In a shallow bowl, combine panko and sesame seeds; dip chicken in mixture.

**2.** In a large nonstick skillet coated with cooking spray, cook chicken in oil for 4-5 minutes on each side or until a thermometer reads 170°.

**3.** Meanwhile, divide salad greens between two plates. Top with the peppers, carrot, mushrooms and onion.

**4.** Slice chicken; place over vegetables. Sprinkle with almonds and drizzle with dressing.

**Nutrition Facts:** 1 salad equals 386 calories, 17 g fat (2 g saturated fat), 63 mg cholesterol, 620 mg sodium, 29 g carbohydrate, 6 g fiber, 30 g protein. **Diabetic Exchanges:** 3 lean meat, 2 vegetable, 2 fat, 1 starch.

CHICKEN CAESAR SALAD

## Chicken Caesar Salad

PREP/TOTAL TIME: 25 min.  YIELD: 2 servings

KAY ANDERSEN • BEAR, DELAWARE

*Topping a delicious Caesar salad with a tender grilled chicken breast ensures a healthy, filling meal that always satisfies.*

- 2 boneless skinless chicken breast halves (4 oz. *each*)
- 2 tsp. olive oil
- 1/4 tsp. garlic salt
- 1/4 tsp. paprika
- 1/4 tsp. pepper
- 1/8 tsp. dried basil
- 1/8 tsp. dried oregano
- 4 cups torn romaine
- 1 small tomato, thinly sliced
- 1/4 cup fat-free creamy Caesar salad dressing
- Caesar salad croutons, optional

**1.** Brush chicken with oil. Combine the garlic salt, paprika, pepper, basil and oregano; sprinkle over chicken. Grill, uncovered, over medium heat or broil 4 in. from the heat for 4-7 minutes on each side or until a thermometer reads 170°.

**2.** Arrange romaine and tomato on plates. Cut chicken into strips; place over salads. Drizzle with dressing. Sprinkle with croutons if desired.

**Nutrition Facts:** 1 serving (calculated without croutons) equals 236 calories, 8 g fat (1 g saturated fat), 63 mg cholesterol, 653 mg sodium, 17 g carbohydrate, 4 g fiber, 26 g protein. **Diabetic Exchanges:** 3 lean meat, 2 vegetable, 1 starch, 1 fat.

## Italian Chicken Skillet Supper C

PREP/TOTAL TIME: 30 min.  YIELD: 2 servings

BARBARA LENTO • HOUSTON, PENNSYLVANIA

*Romano cheese, sliced vegetables and pine nuts jazz up this saucy chicken dinner. It's easy, and we love it!*

- 2 boneless skinless chicken breast halves (4 oz. *each*)
- 1/4 tsp. garlic salt
- 1/4 tsp. pepper
- 2 tsp. reduced-fat butter
- 1 tsp. olive oil
- 1/4 lb. small fresh mushrooms
- 1/2 medium onion, chopped
- 1/4 cup chopped sweet red pepper

1 Tbsp. pine nuts
2 cups fresh baby spinach
1 Tbsp. all-purpose flour
1/2 cup reduced-sodium chicken broth
1-1/2 tsp. spicy brown mustard
2 tsp. shredded Romano cheese

**1.** Flatten chicken slightly; sprinkle with garlic salt and pepper. In a large nonstick skillet, cook chicken in butter and oil over medium heat for 3-4 minutes on each side or until no longer pink. Remove chicken and keep warm.

**2.** In the same skillet, saute the mushrooms, onion, red pepper and pine nuts until vegetables are tender. Add spinach; cook and stir for 2-3 minutes or until wilted. Stir in flour. Gradually stir in broth and mustard. Bring to a boil. Reduce heat; cook and stir for 2 minutes or until thickened.

**3.** Return chicken to the pan; heat through. Sprinkle with the cheese.

**Editor's Note:** This recipe was tested with Land O'Lakes light stick butter.

**Nutrition Facts:** 1 chicken breast half with 1/2 cup vegetable mixture equals 248 calories, 10 g fat (3 g saturated fat), 70 mg cholesterol, 548 mg sodium, 12 g carbohydrate, 3 g fiber, 29 g protein. **Diabetic Exchanges:** 3 lean meat, 2 vegetable, 1-1/2 fat.

# Puffy Apple Omelet  S

**PREP/TOTAL TIME:** 30 min.  **YIELD:** 2 servings

**MELISSA DAVENPORT • CAMPBELL, MINNESOTA**

*This is one omelet you won't forget because of its unique and delicious flavors!*

3 Tbsp. all-purpose flour
1/4 tsp. baking powder
2 eggs, *separated*
3 Tbsp. fat-free milk

1 Tbsp. lemon juice
3 Tbsp. sugar
TOPPING:
1 large tart apple, peeled and thinly sliced
1 tsp. sugar
1/4 tsp. ground cinnamon

**1.** In a small bowl, combine flour and baking powder. In a small bowl, whisk the egg yolks, milk and lemon juice. Stir into dry ingredients and mix well; set aside.

**2.** In another small bowl, beat egg whites on medium speed until soft peaks form. Gradually beat in sugar, 1 Tbsp. at a time, on high until stiff peaks form. Fold into yolk mixture.

**3.** Pour into a shallow 1-1/2-qt. baking dish coated with cooking spray. Arrange apple slices on top. Combine sugar and cinnamon; sprinkle over apples.

**4.** Bake, uncovered, at 375° for 18-20 minutes or until a knife inserted near the center comes out clean. Cut in half.

**Nutrition Facts:** 1 serving equals 249 calories, 5 g fat (2 g saturated fat), 212 mg cholesterol, 130 mg sodium, 44 g carbohydrate, 2 g fiber, 9 g protein. **Diabetic Exchanges:** 2 starch, 1 lean meat, 1 fruit.

For quick preparation, use an **apple corer.** Simply push apple corer down into center of a washed apple. Twist and remove the center seeds and membranes.

ITALIAN CHICKEN SKILLET SUPPER

PUFFY APPLE OMELET

# Salmon Bean Wraps

**PREP:** 20 min. + chilling **YIELD:** 2 servings

**JESS APF • BERKELEY, CALIFORNIA**

*Here's a healthy wrap low in saturated fat and full of the wonderful nutrients found in avocado, black beans and smoked salmon. It's super easy and great for a quick meal.*

| | |
|---|---|
| 1/4 | cup cubed avocado |
| 3/4 | cup canned black beans, rinsed and drained |
| 1/4 | cup finely chopped tomato |
| 3 | Tbsp. minced fresh cilantro |
| 3 | Tbsp. fat-free sour cream |
| 2 | Tbsp. finely chopped red onion |
| 1-1/2 | tsp. lemon juice |
| 1/4 | tsp. pepper |
| 2 | whole wheat tortillas (8 in.), room temperature |
| 2 | oz. flaked smoked salmon fillets |
| 1 | cup shredded lettuce |

**1.** In a large bowl, mash avocado. Stir in the beans, tomato, cilantro, sour cream, red onion, lemon juice and pepper. Cover and refrigerate for at least 30 minutes.

**2.** Spread 3/4 cup over each tortilla. Top with salmon and lettuce; roll up and secure with toothpicks.

**Nutrition Facts:** 1 wrap equals 315 calories, 7 g fat (1 g saturated fat), 10 mg cholesterol, 603 mg sodium, 44 g carbohydrate, 8 g fiber, 16 g protein. **Diabetic Exchanges:** 2 starch, 2 lean meat, 1 vegetable, 1/2 fat.

# Persian Poached Pears  S

**PREP:** 15 min.  **COOK:** 50 min. + chilling
**YIELD:** 2 servings

**TRISHA KRUSE • EAGLE, IDAHO**

*These fragrant pears are a dramatic way to finish off a Middle Eastern feast. They're delicious, aromatic and a unique twist on basic poached pears.*

| | |
|---|---|
| 2 | medium firm pears |
| 1 | vanilla bean |
| 2-1/4 | cups water |
| 1/2 | cup white grape juice |
| 2 | dried apricots, chopped |
| 1 | Tbsp. sugar |
| 1 | Tbsp. honey |
| 1 | lemon peel strip |
| 1 | whole clove |
| 2 | Tbsp. chopped almonds, toasted |

**1.** Core pears from the bottom, leaving stems intact. Peel pears; cut 1/4 in. from the bottom of each to level if necessary. Split vanilla bean and scrape seeds; set aside.

**2.** In a small saucepan, combine the water, grape juice, apricots, sugar, honey, lemon strip, clove, vanilla bean and seeds. Bring to a boil. Reduce heat; place the pears on their sides in the saucepan and poach, uncovered, for 18-22 minutes or until the pears are almost tender, basting occasionally with poaching liquid.

**3.** Remove pears and apricots with a slotted spoon; cool slightly. Cover and refrigerate. Bring poaching liquid to a boil; cook until liquid is reduced to 1/4 cup. Discard the vanilla bean, lemon strip and clove. Cover and refrigerate for at least 1 hour.

**4.** Place pears on dessert plates. Drizzle with poaching liquid. Sprinkle with apricots and almonds.

**Nutrition Facts:** 1 pear with 2 Tbsp. sauce and 1 Tbsp. almonds equals 258 calories, 4 g fat (trace saturated fat), 0 cholesterol, 6 mg sodium, 56 g carbohydrate, 7 g fiber, 3 g protein.

SALMON BEAN WRAPS

PERSIAN POACHED PEARS

# Grilled Beef Tenderloins C

**PREP:** 10 min. + marinating  **GRILL:** 10 min.
**YIELD:** 2 servings

**PATRICIA SWART • GALLOWAY, NEW JERSEY**

*Who says that healthy foods have to be bland? Bold flavors bring out the best in these super tender steaks.*

| | |
|---|---|
| 1/4 | cup dry red wine |
| 1/4 | cup reduced-sodium soy sauce |
| 1/2 | tsp. garlic powder |
| 1/2 | tsp. dried oregano |
| 1/4 | tsp. ground cumin |
| 1/4 | tsp. ground ancho chili pepper |
| 1/4 | tsp. pepper |
| 2 | beef tenderloin steaks (6 oz. *each*) |

**1.** In a large resealable plastic bag, combine the first seven ingredients. Add the steaks; seal bag and turn to coat. Refrigerate for up to 4 hours.

**2.** Drain and discard marinade. Using long-handled tongs, moisten a paper towel with cooking oil and lightly coat the grill rack. Grill steaks, covered, over medium heat or broil 4 in. from the heat for 4-6 minutes on each side or until meat reaches desired doneness (for medium-rare, a thermometer should read 145°; medium, 160°; well-done, 170°).

**Nutrition Facts:** 1 steak equals 263 calories, 10 g fat (4 g saturated fat), 75 mg cholesterol, 402 mg sodium, 1 g carbohydrate, trace fiber, 37 g protein. **Diabetic Exchange:** 5 lean meat.

# Garlic-Dill
# Smashed Potatoes F M

**PREP:** 25 min.  **COOK:** 20 min.  **YIELD:** 2 servings

**AMBER HUFF • ATHENS, GEORGIA**

*These delicious potatoes are so creamy you simply won't believe they are light.*

| | |
|---|---|
| 3 | garlic cloves |
| 1/4 | tsp. olive oil |
| 3/4 | lb. red potatoes, cubed |
| 2 | Tbsp. fat-free milk |
| 2 | Tbsp. reduced-fat sour cream |
| 1-1/2 | tsp. grated Parmesan cheese |
| 1 | tsp. snipped fresh dill |
| 1/4 | tsp. salt |
| 1/8 | tsp. pepper |

Dash cayenne pepper

**1.** Place garlic on a double thickness of heavy-duty foil. Drizzle with oil. Wrap foil around garlic. Bake at 425° for 15-20 minutes. Cool for 10-15 minutes.

**2.** Meanwhile, place potatoes in a small saucepan and cover with water. Bring to a boil. Reduce heat; cover and cook for 10-15 minutes or until tender. Drain. Transfer potatoes to a small bowl; squeeze softened garlic into bowl. Add the remaining ingredients; mash potatoes.

**Nutrition Facts:** 3/4 cup equals 165 calories, 2 g fat (1 g saturated fat), 6 mg cholesterol, 342 mg sodium, 30 g carbohydrate, 3 g fiber, 6 g protein. **Diabetic Exchange:** 2 starch.

VERY VEGGIE OMELET

## Very Veggie Omelet C M

**PREP/TOTAL TIME:** 20 min. **YIELD:** 2 servings

**JAN HOUBERG • REDDICK, ILLINOIS**

*This tasty omelet packed with veggies is a great wake-up call any morning. Because it's loaded with cheese, vegetables, and herbs and seasonings, however, it's great any time of the day. It's a delicious way to use up summer's bounty!*

|       |                                               |
|-------|-----------------------------------------------|
| 1     | small onion, chopped                          |
| 1/4   | cup chopped green pepper                       |
| 1     | Tbsp. butter                                  |
| 1     | small zucchini, chopped                       |
| 3/4   | cup chopped tomato                            |
| 1/4   | tsp. dried oregano                            |
| 1/8   | tsp. pepper                                   |
| 4     | egg whites                                    |
| 1/4   | cup water                                      |
| 1/4   | tsp. cream of tartar                          |
| 1/4   | tsp. salt                                      |
| 1/4   | cup egg substitute                            |
| 1/2   | cup shredded reduced-fat cheddar cheese, *divided* |

**1.** In a large nonstick skillet, saute onion and green pepper in butter until tender. Add the zucchini, tomato, oregano and pepper. Cook and stir for 5-8 minutes or until vegetables are tender and liquid is nearly evaporated. Set aside and keep warm.

**2.** In a small bowl, beat egg whites, water, cream of tartar and salt until stiff peaks form. Place egg substitute in another bowl; fold in egg white mixture. Pour into a 10-in. ovenproof skillet coated with cooking spray. Cook for 5 minutes over medium heat or until lightly browned on bottom.

**3.** Bake, uncovered, at 350° for 9-10 minutes or until a knife inserted near the center comes out clean. Carefully run a knife around edge of pan to loosen.

**4.** With a knife, score center of omelet. Place vegetable mixture and half of cheese on one side; fold other side over filling. Sprinkle with remaining cheese. Cut in half to serve.

**Nutrition Facts:** 1/2 omelet equals 197 calories, 9 g fat (5 g saturated fat), 21 mg cholesterol, 639 mg sodium, 10 g carbohydrate, 2 g fiber, 19 g protein. **Diabetic Exchanges:** 3 lean meat, 2 vegetable, 1-1/2 fat.

## Breakfast Mushroom Cups C M

**PREP/TOTAL TIME:** 25 min. **YIELD:** 2 servings

**SARA MORRIS • LAGUNA BEACH, CALIFORNIA**

*Here's a fun and surprisingly hearty breakfast dish packed with flavor and richness.*

|       |                                         |
|-------|-----------------------------------------|
| 2     | large portobello mushrooms, stems removed |
| 1/8   | tsp. garlic salt                        |
| 1/8   | tsp. pepper, *divided*                  |

1 small onion, chopped
1/2 tsp. olive oil
1 cup fresh baby spinach
1/2 cup egg substitute
1/8 tsp. salt
1/4 cup crumbled goat or feta cheese
2 Tbsp. minced fresh basil

**1.** Place mushrooms on a 15-in. x 10-in. x 1-in. baking pan. Spray with cooking spray; sprinkle with garlic salt and dash pepper. Bake at 425° for 10 minutes or until tender.

**2.** In a large saucepan, saute onion in oil until tender. Stir in spinach and cook until wilted. In a small bowl, whisk the egg substitute, salt and remaining pepper; add to pan. Cook and stir until set.

**3.** Spoon egg mixture into mushrooms; sprinkle with cheese and basil.

**Nutrition Facts:** 1 stuffed mushroom equals 126 calories, 5 g fat (2 g saturated fat), 18 mg cholesterol, 472 mg sodium, 10 g carbohydrate, 3 g fiber, 11 g protein. **Diabetic Exchanges:** 2 vegetable, 1 lean meat, 1/2 fat.

# Pork Tenderloin with Horseradish Sauce [C]

**PREP:** 15 min. **BAKE:** 30 min. + standing
**YIELD:** 2 servings

ANN BERGER OSOWSKI • ORANGE CITY, FLORIDA

*This delicious combo of tenderloin and savory sauce receives rave reviews each time I make it, and I've shared the recipe with numerous friends. The entree is very versatile; the pork can be served hot or cold, and the creamy sauce can also be used as a zesty dip for fresh veggies.*

1/2 tsp. steak seasoning
1/2 tsp. dried rosemary, crushed
1/2 tsp. dried thyme
1 pork tenderloin (3/4 lb.)
2 garlic cloves, peeled and quartered

1 tsp. balsamic vinegar
1 tsp. olive oil
HORSERADISH SAUCE:
2 Tbsp. fat-free mayonnaise
2 Tbsp. reduced-fat sour cream
1 tsp. prepared horseradish
1/8 tsp. grated lemon peel
Dash salt and pepper

**1.** In a small bowl, combine the steak seasoning, rosemary and thyme; rub over meat. Using the point of a sharp knife, make eight slits in the tenderloin. Insert garlic into slits. Place meat on a rack in a foil-lined shallow roasting pan. Drizzle with vinegar and oil.

**2.** Bake, uncovered, at 350° for 30-40 minutes or until a thermometer reads 160°. Let stand for 10 minutes before slicing. Meanwhile, combine the sauce ingredients; chill until serving. Serve with pork.

**Nutrition Facts:** 4 oz. cooked pork with 2 Tbsp. sauce equals 258 calories, 10 g fat (3 g saturated fat), 101 mg cholesterol, 450 mg sodium, 5 g carbohydrate, 1 g fiber, 35 g protein. **Diabetic Exchanges:** 5 lean meat, 1 fat.

A pinch is thought to be the amount of a dry ingredient that can be held between your thumb and forefinger. However, **a dash** is a very small amount of seasoning added with a quick downward stroke of the hand.

BREAKFAST MUSHROOM CUPS

PORK TENDERLOIN WITH HORSERADISH SAUCE

PEPPERMINT-KISSED FUDGE MALLOW COOKIES

CHOCOLATE ANGEL CUPCAKES WITH COCONUT CREAM FRO

PUMPKIN OATMEAL BARS

# Cookies, Bars & More

Searching for a sweet snack to enjoy with morning coffee or to tuck into a bag lunch? Look no further! These sugar bites are sure to keep your family smiling and asking for more!

## Pumpkin Oatmeal Bars

PREP: 30 min. BAKE: 30 min. + cooling YIELD: 2 dozen

**ERIN ANDREWS • EDGEWATER, FLORIDA**

*It took me a long time to develop this effortless recipe, but I'm so happy with how it turned out. These bars have it all—sugar and spice and a creamy-rich pumpkin layer that's especially nice!*

   1  pkg. (18-1/4 oz.) yellow cake mix
2-1/2  cups quick-cooking oats
   5  Tbsp. butter, melted
   3  Tbsp. honey
   1  Tbsp. water

FILLING:
   1  can (15 oz.) solid-pack pumpkin
1/4  cup reduced-fat cream cheese
1/4  cup fat-free milk
   3  Tbsp. brown sugar
   2  Tbsp. maple syrup
   1  tsp. ground cinnamon
   1  tsp. vanilla extract
1/4  tsp. ground allspice
1/4  tsp. ground cloves
   1  egg
   1  egg white
1/4  cup chopped walnuts
   1  Tbsp. butter, melted

**1.** In a large bowl, combine cake mix and oats; set aside 1/2 cup for topping. Add the butter, honey and water to the remaining cake mixture. Press onto the bottom of a 13-in. x 9-in. baking pan coated with cooking spray.

**2.** For filling, in a large bowl, beat the pumpkin, cream cheese, milk, brown sugar, maple syrup, cinnamon, vanilla, allspice and cloves until blended. Add egg and egg white; beat on low speed just until combined. Pour over crust. In a small bowl, combine the walnuts, butter and reserved cake mixture; sprinkle over filling.

**3.** Bake at 350° for 30-35 minutes or until set and edges are lightly browned. Cool on a wire rack. Cut into bars.

**Nutrition Facts:** 1 bar equals 186 calories, 7 g fat (3 g saturated fat), 18 mg cholesterol, 180 mg sodium, 30 g carbohydrate, 2 g fiber, 3 g protein. **Diabetic Exchanges:** 2 starch, 1 fat.

## Chocolate Angel Cupcakes with Coconut Cream Frosting  F

PREP: 15 min. BAKE: 15 min. + cooling YIELD: 2 dozen

**MANDY RIVERS • LEXINGTON, SOUTH CAROLINA**

*Sweeten any meal with these fun, frosted chocolate cupcakes that take just minutes to make. The finger-licking flavor packs far fewer calories and fat than traditional desserts!*

   1  pkg. (16 oz.) angel food cake mix
3/4  cup baking cocoa
   1  cup (8 oz.) reduced-fat sour cream
   1  cup confectioners' sugar
1/8  tsp. coconut extract
2-1/2  cups reduced-fat whipped topping
3/4  cup flaked coconut, toasted

**1.** Prepare cake mix according to package directions for cupcakes, adding cocoa when mixing.

**2.** Fill foil- or paper-lined muffin cups two-thirds full. Bake at 375° for 11-15 minutes or until cake springs back when lightly touched and cracks feel dry. Cool for 10 minutes before removing from pans to wire racks to cool completely.

**3.** For frosting, in a large bowl, combine the sour cream, confectioners' sugar and extract until smooth. Fold in whipped topping. Frost cupcakes. Sprinkle with coconut. Refrigerate leftovers.

**Nutrition Facts:** 1 cupcake equals 142 calories, 3 g fat (2 g saturated fat), 3 mg cholesterol, 154 mg sodium, 27 g carbohydrate, 1 g fiber, 3 g protein. **Diabetic Exchanges:** 1-1/2 starch, 1/2 fat.

> To quickly **frost cupcakes,** place frosting in a bowl. The frosting should be a soft, spreadable consistency. Dip top of cupcake into the frosting, twist slightly and lift up.

# Cherry-Chocolate Coconut Meringues F S C

**PREP:** 15 min.  **BAKE:** 25 min./batch + cooling
**YIELD:** 3 dozen

**MARY SHIVERS • ADA, OKLAHOMA**

*Dried cherries lend sweetness and texture to these easy meringue cookies fit for any occasion. They're simply delicious and very low in fat. They also provide a great guiltless dessert for those family members on a gluten-free diet.*

| | |
|---|---|
| 3 | egg whites |
| 1/2 | tsp. almond extract |
| Dash salt | |
| 1/3 | cup sugar |
| 2/3 | cup confectioners' sugar |
| 1/4 | cup baking cocoa |
| 1-1/4 | cups finely shredded unsweetened coconut |
| 1/2 | cup dried cherries, finely chopped |

**1.** Place egg whites in a large bowl; let stand at room temperature for 30 minutes.

**2.** Add extract and salt; beat on medium speed until soft peaks form. Gradually add sugar, 1 Tbsp. at a time, beating on high until stiff glossy peaks form and sugar is dissolved. Combine confectioners' sugar and cocoa; beat into egg white mixture. Fold in coconut and cherries.

**3.** Drop by rounded tablespoonfuls 2 in. apart onto baking sheets coated with cooking spray. Bake at 325° for 25-28 minutes or until firm to the touch. Cool completely on pans on wire racks. Store meringues in an airtight container.

**Editor's Note:** Look for unsweetened coconut in the baking or health food section.

**Nutrition Facts:** 1 cookie equals 42 calories, 2 g fat (1 g saturated fat), 0 cholesterol, 10 mg sodium, 6 g carbohydrate, 1 g fiber, 1 g protein. **Diabetic Exchange:** 1/2 starch.

# Striped Cutouts F S C

**PREP:** 30 min. + chilling  **BAKE:** 5 min. per batch
**YIELD:** 2 dozen

**HEALTHY COOKING TEST KITCHEN**

*Here's a fun take on the classic sugar cookie. The unique look means no additional decorating for you!*

| | |
|---|---|
| 1/4 | cup butter, softened |
| 1/2 | cup sugar |
| 1/2 | cup packed brown sugar |
| 1 | egg |
| 2 | Tbsp. canola oil |
| 1/4 | tsp. vanilla extract |
| 1-1/2 | cups all-purpose flour |
| 1/4 | tsp. salt |
| 1/8 | tsp. baking soda |
| 5 | drops yellow food coloring |
| 2 | drops red food coloring |
| 1 | egg white, beaten |

**1.** In a large bowl, beat butter and sugars until crumbly, about 2 minutes. Add egg, oil and vanilla. Combine the flour, salt and baking soda; gradually add to creamed mixture and mix well.

**2.** Divide dough into four portions; mix both yellow and red food coloring into two portions to create two orange rolls. Roll each portion of dough between waxed paper into a 12-in. x 6-in. rectangle. Refrigerate for 30 minutes.

**3.** Remove waxed paper; brush tops with egg white. Stack rectangles, alternating colors. Cut into eight 3-in. x 3-in. squares. Stack squares; wrap in plastic wrap. Chill for 2 hours or until firm. Cut into 1/8-in. slices. Cut each slice with a cookie cutter. Place 1 in. apart on greased baking sheets coated with cooking spray. Bake at 350° for 5-7 minutes or until set. Cool for 1 minute before removing from pans to wire racks.

**Nutrition Facts:** 1 cookie equals 92 calories, 3 g fat (1 g saturated fat), 14 mg cholesterol, 49 mg sodium, 15 g carbohydrate, trace fiber, 1 g protein. **Diabetic Exchanges:** 1 starch, 1/2 fat.

CHERRY-CHOCOLATE COCONUT MERINGUES

STRIPED CUTOUTS

# Peppermint-Kissed Fudge Mallow Cookies F S

**PREP:** 30 min. **BAKE:** 10 min./batch + cooling
**YIELD:** 2 dozen

**PRISCILLA YEE • CONCORD, CALIFORNIA**

*At my house, Christmas just wouldn't be the same without these cute-as-can-be treats. Fudgy-rich chocolate cookies with refreshing mint flavor, soft marshmallow, crunchy candy... it's a must-try recipe for any event!*

- 1/3 cup reduced-fat plain yogurt
- 5 Tbsp. butter, melted
- 3/4 tsp. peppermint extract
- 1 cup all-purpose flour
- 3/4 cup sugar
- 1/2 cup baking cocoa
- 1/4 tsp. salt
- 1/4 tsp. baking soda
- 12 large marshmallows, cut in half lengthwise

CHOCOLATE GLAZE:
- 2 Tbsp. semisweet chocolate chips
- 3/4 cup confectioners' sugar
- 3 Tbsp. baking cocoa
- 3 Tbsp. fat-free milk
- 1/4 tsp. peppermint extract
- 1/4 cup crushed peppermint candies

**1.** In a large bowl, beat the yogurt, butter and extract until well blended. Combine the flour, sugar, cocoa, salt and baking soda; gradually add to yogurt mixture and mix well.

**2.** Drop by tablespoonfuls onto baking sheets coated with cooking spray. Bake at 350° for 8 minutes. Place a marshmallow half on each cookie; bake 1-2 minutes longer or until marshmallow is puffed. Cool for 2 minutes before removing from pans to wire racks to cool completely.

**3.** For glaze, in a microwave, melt chocolate chips; stir until smooth. Stir in the confectioners' sugar, cocoa, milk and extract until smooth. Drizzle over marshmallows; sprinkle with candies.

**Nutrition Facts:** 1 cookie equals 109 calories, 3 g fat (2 g saturated fat), 7 mg cholesterol, 60 mg sodium, 20 g carbohydrate, 1 g fiber, 1 g protein.

To easily separate **sticky marshmallows,** place a spoonful of powdered sugar in the bag and shake it well. A few stubborn marshmallows might still need to be separated by hand, but overall, this works seamlessly!

## Toffee Cheesecake Bars s

**PREP:** 25 min. **BAKE:** 20 min. + chilling
**YIELD:** 2-1/2 dozen

**EDIE DESPAIN • LOGAN, UTAH**

*These melt-in-your-mouth treats are absolutely delicious, and everyone will want seconds. A must for homemade gift giving, no one would ever guess they're on the lighter side.*

| | |
|---|---|
| 1 | cup all-purpose flour |
| 3/4 | cup confectioners' sugar |
| 1/3 | cup baking cocoa |
| 1/8 | tsp. baking soda |
| 1/2 | cup cold butter |
| 1 | pkg. (8 oz.) reduced-fat cream cheese |
| 1 | can (14 oz.) sweetened condensed milk |
| 2 | eggs, lightly beaten |
| 1 | tsp. vanilla extract |
| 1-1/4 | cups milk chocolate English toffee bits, *divided* |

**1.** In a small bowl, combine the flour, confectioners' sugar, cocoa and baking soda. Cut in butter until mixture resembles coarse crumbs. Press onto the bottom of an ungreased 13-in. x 9-in. baking dish. Bake at 350° for 12-15 minutes or until set.

**2.** In a large bowl, beat cream cheese until fluffy. Add the milk, eggs and vanilla; beat until smooth. Stir in 3/4 cup toffee bits. Pour over crust. Bake 18-22 minutes longer or until center is almost set.

**3.** Cool on a wire rack for 15 minutes. Sprinkle with remaining toffee bits; cool completely. Cover and refrigerate for 8 hours or overnight.

**Nutrition Facts:** 1 bar equals 169 calories, 9 g fat (5 g saturated fat), 39 mg cholesterol, 120 mg sodium, 19 g carbohydrate, trace fiber, 3 g protein. **Diabetic Exchanges:** 2 fat, 1 starch.

# Gluten-Free Almond Cookies F S C

**PREP:** 15 min. **BAKE:** 15 min./batch **YIELD:** 2 dozen

SHERRI COX • LUCASVILLE, OHIO

*My friend on a gluten-free diet loved these fantastic cookies so much, she had to ask for the recipe! Quick and easy, they taste as good as the decadent treats I make using puff pastry and almond paste. Everyone loves these!*

|     |                        |
| --- | ---------------------- |
| 1   | can (8 oz.) almond paste |
| 1/2 | cup sugar              |
| 2   | egg whites            |
| 1/8 | tsp. salt             |

**1.** In a large bowl, beat almond paste and sugar until crumbly. Beat in egg whites and salt until smooth. Shape dough into 1-in. balls.

**2.** Place 1 in. apart on parchment paper-lined baking sheets. Bake at 350° for 15-18 minutes or until lightly browned. Cool for 1 minute before removing from pans to wire racks. Store in an airtight container.

**Editor's Note:** Read all ingredient labels for possible gluten content prior to use. Ingredient formulas can change, and production facilities vary among brands. If you're concerned that your brand may contain gluten, contact the company.

**Nutrition Facts:** 1 cookie equals 61 calories, 3 g fat (trace saturated fat), 0 cholesterol, 18 mg sodium, 9 g carbohydrate, trace fiber, 1 g protein. **Diabetic Exchanges:** 1/2 starch, 1/2 fat.

# Lighter Cookie Cutouts F S C

**PREP:** 20 min. **BAKE:** 5 min./batch **YIELD:** 2 dozen

HEALTHY COOKING TEST KITCHEN

*These cookie cutouts are so light and fuss-free, you'll want to bake up several batches to decorate in different ways.*

|       |                        |
| ----- | ---------------------- |
| 1/4   | cup butter, softened   |
| 1/2   | cup sugar              |
| 1/2   | cup packed brown sugar |
| 1     | egg                    |
| 2     | Tbsp. canola oil       |
| 1/4   | tsp. vanilla extract   |
| 1-1/2 | cups all-purpose flour |
| 1/4   | tsp. salt              |
| 1/8   | tsp. baking soda       |

FOR VARIATIONS:
Yellow and red food coloring

Beaten egg white

Popsicle *or* lollipop sticks

**1.** In a large bowl, beat butter and sugars until crumbly, about 2 minutes. Add egg, oil and vanilla. Combine the flour, salt and baking soda; gradually add to creamed mixture and mix well.

**2.** Divide the dough in half. On a lightly floured surface, roll one portion of dough to 1/4-in. thickness. Cut with a floured 3-in. cookie cutter. Place 1 in. apart on baking sheets coated with cooking spray. Repeat.

**3.** Bake at 350° for 5-7 minutes or until set. Cool for 1 minute before removing from pans to wire racks. Decorate as desired.

**Nutrition Facts:** 1 cookie equals 92 calories, 3 g fat (1 g saturated fat), 14 mg cholesterol, 49 mg sodium, 15 g carbohydrate, trace fiber, 1 g protein. **Diabetic Exchanges:** 1 starch, 1/2 fat.

# Gluten-Free Oatmeal Chip Bars S

**PREP:** 20 min. **BAKE:** 20 min. + cooling **YIELD:** 3 dozen

SUSAN JAMES • COKATO, MINNESOTA

*With two busy boys who would rather move around than sit and eat, I needed a gluten-free, hearty, hand-held treat that could double as a quick breakfast, brunch, lunch or snack. This is a favorite of theirs, and I can change it up to accommodate ingredients I have on hand.*

|       |                                    |
| ----- | ---------------------------------- |
| 1/2   | cup packed brown sugar             |
| 4     | eggs                               |
| 1-1/2 | cups mashed ripe bananas (3-4 medium) |
| 1     | cup peanut butter                  |
| 1/2   | tsp. salt                          |
| 6     | cups gluten-free old-fashioned oats |
| 1     | cup gluten-free butterscotch chips |
| 1     | cup (6 oz.) semisweet chocolate chips |

**1.** In a large bowl, beat brown sugar and eggs until well blended. Add bananas, peanut butter and salt until blended. Stir in the oats, butterscotch and chocolate chips.

**2.** Spread the batter into a 15-in. x 10-in. x 1-in. baking pan coated with cooking spray. Bake at 350° for 20-25 minutes or until edges begin to brown. Cool completely on a wire rack. Cut into bars.

**Editor's Note:** Read all ingredient labels for possible gluten content prior to use. Ingredient formulas can change, and production facilities vary among brands. If you're concerned that your brand may contain gluten, contact the company.

**Nutrition Facts:** 1 bar equals 179 calories, 8 g fat (4 g saturated fat), 24 mg cholesterol, 80 mg sodium, 23 g carbohydrate, 2 g fiber, 5 g protein. **Diabetic Exchanges:** 1-1/2 starch, 1 fat.

GLUTEN-FREE OATMEAL CHIP BARS

# Cutout Cookie Pops  F S C

**PREP:** 30 min. + chilling **BAKE:** 5 min. per batch
**YIELD:** 2 dozen

**HEALTHY COOKING TEST KITCHEN**

*Perfect for Halloween classroom snacks, these fun cookie pops don't pile on fat and calories!*

| | |
|---|---|
| 1/4 | cup butter, softened |
| 1/2 | cup sugar |
| 1/2 | cup packed brown sugar |
| 1 | egg |
| 2 | Tbsp. canola oil |
| 1/4 | tsp. vanilla extract |
| 1-1/2 | cups all-purpose flour |
| 1/4 | tsp. salt |
| 1/8 | tsp. baking soda |
| 10 | drops yellow food coloring |
| 4 | drops red food coloring |
| 1 | egg white, beaten |

Popsicle *or* lollipop sticks

**1.** In a large bowl, beat butter and sugars until crumbly, about 2 minutes. Add egg, oil and vanilla. Combine the flour, salt and baking soda; gradually add to creamed mixture and mix well.

**2.** Divide dough in half. Mix yellow and red food coloring into one portion of dough. Cover and refrigerate both portions for 30 minutes.

**3.** On a lightly floured surface, roll doughs to 1/4-in. thickness. Cut with a floured 3-in. pumpkin-shaped cookie cutter. Cut out a face to resemble a jack-o'-lantern. Place the Popsicle sticks on baking sheets coated with cooking spray. Top each with cutout dough; press down gently. Replace face cutouts with opposite colored dough. Bake at 350° for 5-7 minutes or until set. Cool for 1 minute before removing from pans to wire racks.

**Nutrition Facts:** 1 cookie pop equals 92 calories, 3 g fat (1 g saturated fat), 14 mg cholesterol, 49 mg sodium, 15 g carbohydrate, trace fiber, 1 g protein. **Diabetic Exchanges:** 1 starch, 1/2 fat.

# Makeover Pick-Me-Up Cream Cheese Brownies  S

**PREP:** 30 min. **BAKE:** 35 min. + cooling **YIELD:** 2-1/2 dozen

**SONYA LABBE • LOS ANGELES, CALIFORNIA**

*The lightened-up version of these indulgent brownies tastes absolutely divine but weighs in at a modest 159 calories and 8 g fat per serving.*

| | |
|---|---|
| 1/4 | cup reduced-fat butter |
| 1 | cup sugar |
| 2 | eggs |
| 2 | egg whites |
| 4 | oz. bittersweet chocolate, melted |
| 4 | oz. semisweet chocolate, melted |
| 1 | tsp. rum extract |
| 1 | cup all-purpose flour |
| 1 | tsp. baking powder |
| 1/2 | tsp. salt |
| 1 | cup 60% cacao bittersweet chocolate baking chips |

**CHEESECAKE LAYER:**

| | |
|---|---|
| 2 | Tbsp. instant espresso powder |
| 2 | Tbsp. hot water |
| 6 | oz. reduced-fat cream cheese |
| 1/4 | cup sugar |
| 2 | Tbsp. all-purpose flour |
| 1/2 | tsp. rum extract |
| 1 | egg |
| 1/2 | cup 60% cacao bittersweet chocolate baking chips |

**1.** In a large bowl, cream butter and sugar until light and fluffy. Add eggs and egg whites, one at a time, beating well after each addition. Beat in melted chocolate and extract. Combine the flour, baking powder and salt; add to the creamed mixture. Fold in baking chips; set aside.

**2.** In a small bowl, dissolve espresso powder in water; cool to room temperature. In a large bowl, beat cream cheese and sugar until smooth. Beat in the flour, extract and espresso mixture. Add egg; beat on low speed just until combined. Fold in baking chips.

**3.** Spread half of chocolate mixture into a 13-in. x 9-in. baking pan coated with cooking spray; top with cream cheese mixture. Spoon remaining chocolate batter over top; cut through batter with a knife to swirl.

**4.** Bake at 325° for 35-40 minutes or until a toothpick inserted near the center comes out with moist crumbs. Cool completely on a wire rack. Cut into bars.

**Editor's Note:** This recipe was tested with Land O'Lakes light stick butter.

**Nutrition Facts:** 1 brownie equals 159 calories, 8 g fat (4 g saturated fat), 27 mg cholesterol, 101 mg sodium, 22 g carbohydrate, 1 g fiber, 3 g protein. **Diabetic Exchanges:** 1-1/2 fat, 1 starch.

CUTOUT COOKIE POPS

# Blondies with Chips ⑤

**PREP:** 5 min. **BAKE:** 20 min. + cooling **YIELD:** 1 dozen

**KAI SKUPINSKI • CANTON, MICHIGAN**

*My friends and family love my pared-down version of the classic blond brownie and never suspect that I use whole wheat flour. They even encouraged me to enter my recipe in a contest.*

| | |
|---|---|
| 1/3 | cup all-purpose flour |
| 1/3 | cup whole wheat flour |
| 1/4 | cup packed brown sugar |
| 1/2 | tsp. baking powder |
| 1/4 | tsp. salt |
| 1 | egg |
| 1/4 | cup canola oil |
| 2 | Tbsp. honey |
| 1 | tsp. vanilla extract |
| 1/2 | cup semisweet chocolate chips |

**1.** In a small bowl, combine the first five ingredients. In another bowl, whisk the egg, oil, honey and vanilla. Stir into dry ingredients just until combined. Stir in chocolate chips (batter will be thick).

**2.** Spread into an 8-in. square baking dish coated with cooking spray. Bake at 350° for 20-22 minutes or until a toothpick inserted near the center comes out clean. Cool on a wire rack. Cut into bars.

**Nutrition Facts:** 1 bar equals 133 calories, 7 g fat (2 g saturated fat), 18 mg cholesterol, 67 mg sodium, 17 g carbohydrate, 1 g fiber, 2 g protein. **Diabetic Exchanges:** 1 starch, 1 fat.

# Vegan Chocolate Chip Cookies ⑤

**PREP:** 15 min. + chilling **BAKE:** 10 min./batch
**YIELD:** 3-1/2 dozen

**CASSANDRA BRZYCKI • WAUWATOSA, WISCONSIN**

*A busy competitive figure skater came up with this high-energy recipe. The cookies are loaded with nuts, chips and fabulous flavor. Coaches at her skating rink are always snitching two or three when she brings them in!*

| | |
|---|---|
| 1-1/4 | cups packed dark brown sugar |
| 1/2 | cup canola oil |
| 6 | Tbsp. vanilla soy milk |
| 1/4 | cup sugar |
| 1/4 | cup unsweetened applesauce |
| 2 | tsp. vanilla extract |
| 2-1/4 | cups all-purpose flour |
| 1 | tsp. baking soda |
| 3/4 | tsp. salt |
| 1 | cup dairy-free semisweet chocolate chips |
| 1/2 | cup finely chopped walnuts |

**1.** In a large bowl, beat the first six ingredients until well blended. Combine the flour, baking soda and salt; gradually add to sugar mixture and mix well. Stir in the chocolate chips and nuts. Cover and refrigerate for 1 hour.

**2.** Drop by rounded tablespoonfuls 2 in. apart onto parchment paper-lined baking sheets. Bake at 375° for 10-12 minutes or until edges are lightly browned. Cool for 1 minute before removing from pans to wire racks.

**Nutrition Facts:** 1 cookie equals 111 calories, 5 g fat (1 g saturated fat), 0 cholesterol, 76 mg sodium, 16 g carbohydrate, 1 g fiber, 1 g protein.

# Makeover Frosty Lemon Squares

**PREP:** 30 min. **BAKE:** 15 min. + freezing **YIELD:** 20 servings

**HEALTHY COOKING TEST KITCHEN**

*This make-ahead dessert has a lemony filling sandwiched between two creamy layers and a crunchy crust. What's not to love? Simple changes to the original recipe reduced a good portion of the calories and saturated fat, but left a ton of great lemon flavor and a rich cream cheese layer.*

| | |
|---|---|
| 1/4 | cup butter, softened |
| 2 | Tbsp. confectioners' sugar |
| 1/2 | cup all-purpose flour |
| 1/2 | cup cornstarch |
| 1/2 | cup ground pecans |

**CREAM CHEESE LAYER:**

| | |
|---|---|
| 1 | pkg. (8 oz.) reduced-fat cream cheese |
| 1 | pkg. (8 oz.) fat-free cream cheese |
| 3/4 | cup confectioners' sugar |
| 1 | carton (8 oz.) frozen reduced-fat whipped topping, thawed |

**LEMON LAYER:**

| | |
|---|---|
| 1-1/4 | cups sugar |
| 6 | Tbsp. cornstarch |
| 1/4 | tsp. salt |
| 1-1/4 | cups water |
| 3/4 | cup lemon juice |
| 2 | Tbsp. butter |

| | |
|---|---|
| 1 | Tbsp. grated lemon peel |
| 3 | to 4 drops yellow food coloring, optional |

**TOPPING:**

| | |
|---|---|
| 1 | Tbsp. grated lemon peel |
| 1 | carton (8 oz.) frozen reduced-fat whipped topping, thawed |

**1.** In a small bowl, cream butter and confectioners' sugar until light and fluffy. Gradually add flour and cornstarch (mixture will be crumbly). Stir in pecans. Press into a 13-in. x 9-in. baking dish coated with cooking spray. Bake at 350° for 14-16 minutes or until lightly browned. Cool on a wire rack.

**2.** In a large bowl, beat cream cheeses and confectioners' sugar until fluffy. Fold in whipped topping. Spread over crust. Cover and freeze for 1 hour.

**3.** Meanwhile, in a small saucepan, combine the sugar, cornstarch, salt and water until smooth. Bring to a boil; cook and stir for 2 minutes or until thickened. Remove from the heat; stir in the lemon juice, butter, lemon peel and food coloring if desired. Transfer to a bowl; refrigerate for 1 hour.

**4.** Spread lemon mixture over cream cheese layer. Cover and freeze for 1 hour. Fold lemon peel into whipped topping; spread over lemon layer. Cover and freeze for up to 1 month. Remove from the freezer 15 minutes before serving.

**Nutrition Facts:** 1 piece equals 240 calories, 10 g fat (7 g saturated fat), 18 mg cholesterol, 164 mg sodium, 35 g carbohydrate, trace fiber, 3 g protein.

# Chewy Oatmeal Raisin Cookies S

PREP: 15 min. BAKE: 10 min./batch YIELD: 15 cookies

**TRINA BOITNOTT • BOONES MILL, VIRGINIA**

*A glass of milk and one of these warm, chewy cookies make for a perfect before-bed treat.*

| | |
|---|---|
| 1/3 | cup canola oil |
| 1/3 | cup packed brown sugar |
| 2 | Tbsp. sugar |
| 3 | Tbsp. water |
| 1 | egg white |
| 3/4 | tsp. vanilla extract |
| 1/3 | cup all-purpose flour |
| 1/3 | cup whole wheat flour |
| 2 | tsp. ground cinnamon |
| 1/2 | tsp. baking soda |
| 1/4 | tsp. salt |
| 2 | cups old-fashioned oats |
| 1/2 | cup raisins |

**1.** In a large bowl, combine the oil, sugars, water, egg white and vanilla. Combine the flours, cinnamon, baking soda and salt; gradually add to sugar mixture and mix well. Stir in oats and raisins.

**2.** Drop by scant 1/4 cupfuls onto baking sheets coated with cooking spray; flatten slightly with the back of a spoon. Bake at 350° for 10-12 minutes or until golden brown. Cool for 1 minute before removing from pans to wire racks.

**Nutrition Facts:** 1 cookie equals 144 calories, 6 g fat (1 g saturated fat), 0 cholesterol, 88 mg sodium, 22 g carbohydrate, 2 g fiber, 3 g protein. **Diabetic Exchanges:** 1-1/2 starch, 1 fat.

# Mini Sweet Potato Muffins F S C

PREP: 35 min. BAKE: 10 min./batch YIELD: 4-1/2 dozen

**MEREDITH HEDEEN • NEW KENSINGTON, PENNSYLVANIA**

*I'm always looking for ways to "healthify" recipes. My husband loves the airy texture and zesty streusel of these muffins.*

| | |
|---|---|
| 1 | cup all-purpose flour |
| 3/4 | cup whole wheat flour |
| 1/2 | cup sugar |
| 1/2 | cup packed brown sugar |
| 1 | tsp. baking powder |
| 1 | tsp. ground cinnamon |
| 1 | tsp. ground allspice |
| 1/2 | tsp. salt |
| 1/4 | tsp. baking soda |
| 2 | eggs, beaten |
| 1 | cup mashed sweet potatoes |
| 1/2 | cup water |
| 1/4 | cup canola oil |
| 3 | Tbsp. unsweetened applesauce |

STREUSEL:

| | |
|---|---|
| 2 | Tbsp. biscuit/baking mix |
| 2 | Tbsp. quick-cooking oats |
| 1 | Tbsp. sugar |
| 1 | Tbsp. brown sugar |
| 1-1/2 | tsp. cold butter |
| 1 | Tbsp. finely chopped crystallized ginger |

**1.** In a large bowl, combine the first nine ingredients. In another bowl, combine the eggs, potatoes, water, oil and applesauce. Stir into the dry ingredients just until moistened.

**2.** Coat miniature muffin cups with cooking spray or use paper liners; fill two-thirds full. For streusel, combine baking mix, oats and sugars; cut in butter until crumbly. Stir in ginger. Sprinkle over batter.

**3.** Bake at 350° for 10-12 minutes or until a toothpick inserted near the center comes out clean. Cool for 5 minutes before removing from pans to wire racks.

**Nutrition Facts:** 1 muffin equals 51 calories, 1 g fat (trace saturated fat), 8 mg cholesterol, 45 mg sodium, 9 g carbohydrate, trace fiber, 1 g protein. **Diabetic Exchange:** 1/2 starch.

CHEWY OATMEAL RAISIN COOKIES

MINI SWEET POTATO MUFFINS

BEST-EVER SWEET POTATO PIE

PINEAPPLE APPLE PIE

COCONUT-STREUSEL PEAR PIE

# Cakes & Pies

These sensational sweets prove you can enjoy dessert without guilt. From Creamy Lemon Cheesecake and Raspberry Baked Alaska Pie to Chocolate Swirl Cake and Caramel Custard Pie, these specialties are sure to please!

## Pineapple Apple Pie [S]

**PREP:** 20 min. **BAKE:** 40 min. + cooling
**YIELD:** 10 servings

**KAREN BRINK • ATWATER, OHIO**

*This special pie is destined to become a family tradition. The apple and pineapple are mouthwatering together, and the crunchy topping is fabulous! This one's best served warm, perhaps with a scoop of low-fat frozen yogurt on top!*

Pastry for single-crust pie (9 in.)

- 1 can (20 oz.) crushed pineapple in heavy syrup, undrained
- 3 medium tart apples, peeled and chopped
- 1/4 cup all-purpose flour
- 1/2 tsp. ground cinnamon
- 1/2 tsp. ground nutmeg

TOPPING:
- 1/2 cup quick-cooking oats
- 1/3 cup packed brown sugar
- 1/4 cup all-purpose flour
- 2 Tbsp. plus 2 tsp. butter, melted

**1.** Line a 9-in. pie plate with the pastry; trim and flute the edges.

**2.** In a large bowl, combine the pineapple and the chopped apples.

**3.** Combine the flour, cinnamon and nutmeg; add to apple mixture and toss to coat. Transfer to pastry.

**4.** In a small bowl, combine the oats, brown sugar, flour and butter; sprinkle over filling.

**5.** Bake at 375° for 40-45 minutes or until topping is browned. Cover edges with foil during the last 15 minutes to prevent overbrowning if necessary. Cool on a wire rack.

**Nutrition Facts:** 1 piece equals 259 calories, 9 g fat (4 g saturated fat), 12 mg cholesterol, 105 mg sodium, 43 g carbohydrate, 2 g fiber, 3 g protein.

## Coconut-Streusel Pear Pie

**PREP:** 20 min. **BAKE:** 20 min. + cooling
**YIELD:** 8 servings

**PAULA HOFFMAN • PLAINVIEW, NEBRASKA**

*I remember my mom making this pie when I was growing up. I make several while I have fresh pears from the family tree, then freeze them for later. One of my taste testers declared it "the best pear pie ever!"*

Pastry for single-crust pie (9 in.)

- 1/3 cup sugar
- 1/4 cup all-purpose flour
- 1/4 tsp. salt
- 6 cups sliced peeled fresh pears
- 1 Tbsp. lemon juice

TOPPING:
- 3 Tbsp. sugar
- 3 Tbsp. all-purpose flour
- 4-1/2 tsp. cold butter
- 1/3 cup flaked coconut

**1.** Line a 9-in. pie plate with pastry; trim and flute edges. In a large saucepan, combine the sugar, flour and salt. Add pears and lemon juice. Cook and stir over medium heat for 4-5 minutes or until thickened. Pour into pastry.

**2.** For topping, in a small bowl, combine sugar and flour. Cut in butter until crumbly. Stir in coconut; sprinkle over top. Bake at 400° for 20-25 minutes or until filling is bubbly and topping is lightly browned. Cool on a wire rack.

**Nutrition Facts:** 1 piece equals 306 calories, 11 g fat (6 g saturated fat), 11 mg cholesterol, 200 mg sodium, 52 g carbohydrate, 4 g fiber, 2 g protein.

> Brown sugar is a mixture of granulated sugars and molasses, with **dark brown sugar** containing more molasses, giving it a slightly stronger flavor. For the most part, the sugars can be used interchangeably.

# Caramel Custard Pie

PREP: 15 min. BAKE: 55 min. + chilling YIELD: 8 servings

**ROGER CLAPPER • DELAVAN, WISCONSIN**

*Here's a traditional custard pie that's been in our family for over 100 years. A fun layer of caramel jazzes up the creamy old-fashioned flavor. It's great with whipped topping.*

Pastry for single-crust pie (9 in.)
- 2/3  cup packed brown sugar
- 4  tsp. all-purpose flour
- 3  eggs
- 2  cups 2% milk
- 1/4  cup sugar
- 1  tsp. vanilla extract
- 1/8  tsp. salt
- 1/8  tsp. ground nutmeg

**1.** Line a 9-in. pie plate with pastry; trim and flute edges. Combine brown sugar and flour; press into the pastry.

**2.** In a large bowl, combine the eggs, milk, sugar, vanilla and salt; pour over brown sugar mixture.

**3.** Bake at 350° for 55-60 minutes or until a knife inserted near the center comes out clean. Cover edges with foil during the last 15 minutes to prevent overbrowning if necessary. Cool on a wire rack; sprinkle with nutmeg. Refrigerate for at least 2 hours before serving.

**Nutrition Facts:** 1 piece equals 277 calories, 10 g fat (4 g saturated fat), 89 mg cholesterol, 201 mg sodium, 41 g carbohydrate, trace fiber, 6 g protein.

CARAMEL CUSTARD PIE

# Pudding Pumpkin Pie

PREP: 15 min. + chilling YIELD: 8 servings

**SHEILA ROUTION • ANGLETON, TEXAS**

*With this pumpkin pie, you don't have to spend all day in the kitchen whipping up a dessert that keeps calories and fat at bay. The mouthwatering treat has a pleasant level of pumpkin and spice, and it's ready in no time at all.*

- 1  egg white, beaten
- 1  reduced-fat graham cracker crust (8 in.)
- 1  cup cold fat-free milk
- 1  pkg. (1-1/2 oz.) sugar-free instant vanilla pudding mix
- 1  can (15 oz.) solid-pack pumpkin
- 1  tsp. pumpkin pie spice
- 1/2  tsp. ground cinnamon
- 1/2  tsp. ground nutmeg
- 1-1/2  cups reduced-fat whipped topping, *divided*

**1.** Brush egg white over crust. Bake at 375° for 5 minutes or until lightly browned. Cool crust on a wire rack.

**2.** In a large bowl, whisk milk and pudding mix. Stir in the pumpkin, pumpkin pie spice, cinnamon and nutmeg. Fold in 1 cup whipped topping. Pour into crust. Refrigerate for 4 hours or overnight.

**3.** Cut into slices; dollop with remaining whipped topping. Refrigerate leftovers.

**Nutrition Facts:** 1 piece with 1 Tbsp. whipped topping equals 180 calories, 5 g fat (3 g saturated fat), 1 mg cholesterol, 341 mg sodium, 29 g carbohydrate, 2 g fiber, 3 g protein. **Diabetic Exchanges:** 2 starch, 1 fat.

# Creamy Lemon Cheesecake

PREP: 35 min. BAKE: 50 min. + chilling
YIELD: 16 servings

**ANNE HENRY • TORONTO, ONTARIO**

*My friend, Gwen, gave me this creamy, lip-smacking recipe, and it's been a crowd-pleaser at my house ever since. The homemade lemon curd on top adds a tart, special touch. The cake can also be made in three store-bought graham cracker pie shells.*

PUDDING PUMPKIN PIE

CREAMY LEMON CHEESECAKE

1 cup graham cracker crumbs
2 Tbsp. butter, melted

FILLING:
2 pkg. (8 oz. *each*) reduced-fat cream cheese
1 pkg. (8 oz.) fat-free cream cheese
1-1/3 cups sugar
1/3 cup lemon juice
1 Tbsp. grated lemon peel
3 eggs, lightly beaten

TOPPINGS:
1 cup (8 oz.) reduced-fat sour cream
4 tsp. plus 1/2 cup sugar, *divided*
1 tsp. vanilla extract
4-1/2 tsp. cornstarch
1/4 tsp. salt
3/4 cup water
1 egg yolk, beaten
1/3 cup lemon juice
1 Tbsp. butter
2 tsp. grated lemon peel

**1.** Place a 9-in. springform pan coated with cooking spray on a double thickness of heavy-duty foil (about 18 in. square). Securely wrap foil around pan.

**2.** In a small bowl, combine cracker crumbs and butter. Press onto the bottom of prepared pan. Place pan on a baking sheet. Bake at 325° for 6-9 minutes or until set. Cool on a wire rack.

**3.** In a large bowl, beat cream cheeses and sugar until smooth. Beat in lemon juice and peel. Add eggs; beat on low speed just until combined. Pour over crust. Place springform pan in a large baking pan; add 1 in. of hot water to larger pan.

**4.** Bake at 325° for 40-45 minutes or until center is almost set. Let stand for 5 minutes. Combine the sour cream, 4 tsp. sugar and vanilla; spread over top of cheesecake. Bake 10 minutes longer. Remove the springform pan from water bath. Cool on a wire rack for 10 minutes. Carefully run a knife around edge of pan to loosen; cool 1 hour longer.

**5.** In a small heavy saucepan, combine the cornstarch, salt and remaining sugar. Stir in water until smooth. Cook and stir over medium-high heat until thickened and bubbly. Reduce heat; cook and stir 2 minutes longer. Remove from the heat.

**6.** Stir a small amount of hot mixture into egg yolk; return all to the pan, stirring constantly. Bring to a gentle boil; cook and stir 2 minutes longer. Remove from the heat. Gently stir in the lemon juice, butter and lemon peel. Cool to room temperature without stirring.

**7.** Spread over cheesecake. Refrigerate overnight. Remove sides of pan.

**Nutrition Facts:** 1 slice equals 260 calories, 11 g fat (7 g saturated fat), 84 mg cholesterol, 305 mg sodium, 33 g carbohydrate, trace fiber, 8 g protein.

# Raspberry Bavarian Cake  F S

**PREP:** 20 min. + chilling **YIELD:** 16 servings

**LINDA MURRAY • ALLENSTOWN, NEW HAMPSHIRE**

*This recipe is an all-time favorite with my family and everyone else who tastes it. It's so easy but makes an impressive company dessert. Because it doesn't seem light, everyone feels like they're overindulging!*

> 5 pkg. (12 oz. *each*) frozen unsweetened raspberries, thawed
>
> 2 cups confectioners' sugar
>
> 2 envelopes unflavored gelatin
>
> 1/3 cup plus 1/2 cup cold water, *divided*
>
> 38 ladyfingers, split
>
> 2 Tbsp. seedless raspberry jam
>
> 1 tsp. water
>
> 1 carton (12 oz.) frozen reduced-fat whipped topping, thawed, *divided*

**1.** In a large saucepan, combine raspberries and confectioners' sugar. Bring to a boil. Reduce heat; simmer for 5-10 minutes or until bubbly and sugar is dissolved, stirring occasionally. Mash and strain raspberries, reserving syrup. Discard seeds; set aside.

**2.** In a small saucepan, sprinkle gelatin over 1/3 cup cold water; let stand for 1 minute. Heat over low heat stirring until gelatin is completely dissolved. Stir in remaining cold water and raspberry juice. Cover and refrigerate for 1-1/2 to 2 hours or until slightly thickened, stirring occasionally.

**3.** Meanwhile, line the bottom and sides of a 9-in. springform pan with ladyfingers. In a small bowl, combine raspberry jam and water; spread over ladyfingers lining bottom of pan. Fold 3-3/4 cups whipped topping into raspberry mixture. Pour into prepared pan. Cover and refrigerate for at least 3 hours or until firm. Garnish with remaining whipped topping.

**Nutrition Facts:** 1 slice equals 223 calories, 3 g fat (3 g saturated fat), 35 mg cholesterol, 121 mg sodium, 46 g carbohydrate, 3 g fiber, 4 g protein.

# Cran-Orange Pie in a Jar

**PREP:** 20 min. + chilling **YIELD:** 4 servings

### HEALTHY COOKING TEST KITCHEN

*These individual pudding pies in a jar are irresistible to big and little snackers alike! Not only is this an excellent light dessert, but it's a perfect homemade gift, too!*

- 1 cup graham cracker crumbs
- 2 Tbsp. butter, melted
- 2 cups cold fat-free milk
- 1 pkg. (1 oz.) sugar-free instant white chocolate pudding mix
- 1/2 tsp. grated orange peel
- 1/2 cup whole-berry cranberry sauce

**1.** In a small bowl, combine cracker crumbs and butter. Press into the bottom of each of four half-pint canning jars.

**2.** In another bowl, whisk milk and pudding mix for 2 minutes. Stir in orange peel. Let stand for 2 minutes or until soft-set. Spoon over crusts. Top with cranberry sauce. Cover and refrigerate for at least 1 hour.

**Nutrition Facts:** 1 serving equals 253 calories, 8 g fat (4 g saturated fat), 18 mg cholesterol, 439 mg sodium, 40 g carbohydrate, 1 g fiber, 6 g protein.

# Best-Ever Sweet Potato Pie

**PREP:** 25 min. **BAKE:** 1 hour 15 min. **YIELD:** 10 servings

### ERIN GIBBONS • DOWNINGTOWN, PENNSYLVANIA

*My grandmother handed down this recipe and it's amazing! The flavor, with a hint of maple and great spices, totally lives up to its name.*

- 1 extra-servings-size graham cracker crust (9 oz.)
- 1 egg white, beaten
- 1-1/2 cups mashed sweet potatoes
- 1-1/4 cups fat-free milk
- 3 eggs
- 2/3 cup sugar
- 1/2 cup maple syrup
- 1 tsp. ground cinnamon
- 1/2 tsp. salt
- 1/2 tsp. ground ginger
- 1/2 tsp. ground nutmeg
- 1/4 tsp. ground mace

**1.** Brush crust with egg white. Bake at 400° for 6-8 minutes. Cool on a wire rack. Reduce heat to 350°.

**2.** In a large bowl, beat the remaining ingredients until blended. Pour into crust. Bake for 70-80 minutes or until a knife inserted near the center comes out clean. Cool on a wire rack. Refrigerate leftovers.

**Nutrition Facts:** 1 piece equals 292 calories, 8 g fat (2 g saturated fat), 64 mg cholesterol, 318 mg sodium, 51 g carbohydrate, 2 g fiber, 5 g protein.

> Members of the morning glory family and native to Central America, **sweet potatoes** come in two readily available varieties. One has a pale skin with a light yellow flesh and a dry mealy texture. The other has dark skin with a dark orange flesh that cooks to a moist texture.

CRAN-ORANGE PIE IN A JAR

BEST-EVER SWEET POTATO PIE

# Cherry Upside-Down Cake

PREP: 25 min. BAKE: 20 min. + cooling
YIELD: 8 servings

**DOROTHY ERICKSON • BLUE EYE, MISSOURI**

*As a home economics teacher, I used this recipe to demonstrate simple cake- and sauce-making techniques. The kids loved it just as my family always has.*

- 1 can (14-1/2 oz.) pitted tart cherries
- 1/3 cup sugar
- 1 Tbsp. butter

CAKE:
- 1/4 cup shortening
- 1/2 cup sugar
- 1 egg
- 1 cup all-purpose flour
- 1 tsp. baking powder
- 1/4 tsp. salt
- 1/3 cup fat-free milk

SAUCE:
- 3 Tbsp. sugar
- 1 Tbsp. cornstarch
- 5 to 8 drops food coloring, optional

**1.** Drain cherries, reserving liquid in a 1-cup measuring cup. Add enough water to measure 1 cup; set aside for sauce.

**2.** In a small saucepan, combine the cherries, sugar and butter. Cook and stir over medium heat until butter is melted and sugar is dissolved. Pour into a 9-in. round baking pan coated with cooking spray.

**3.** For cake, in a large bowl, cream shortening and sugar until light and fluffy. Add egg; mix well. Combine the flour, baking powder and salt; add to the creamed mixture alternately with milk, beating well after each addition. Spread over cherry mixture.

**4.** Bake at 350° for 20-25 minutes or until a toothpick inserted near the center comes out clean. Cool for 10 minutes before inverting cake onto a serving plate.

**5.** For sauce, in a small saucepan, combine sugar and cornstarch. Gradually add reserved cherry juice mixture. Bring to a boil; cook and stir for 2 minutes or until thickened. Stir in food coloring if desired. Serve with warm cake.

**Nutrition Facts:** 1 slice with 2 Tbsp. sauce equals 258 calories, 8 g fat (3 g saturated fat), 30 mg cholesterol, 151 mg sodium, 43 g carbohydrate, 1 g fiber, 3 g protein.

# Chocolate-Covered Cherry Pudding Cake

PREP: 20 min. COOK: 2 hours + standing
YIELD: 8 servings

**MEREDITH COE • CHARLOTTESVILLE, VIRGINIA**

*Growing up, I remember my grandfather cherishing the chocolate-covered cherries we'd bring him for Christmas. After he passed away, I came up with this rich recipe in his honor. It's delicious served with whipped topping.*

- 1/2 cup reduced-fat sour cream
- 2 Tbsp. canola oil
- 1 Tbsp. butter, melted
- 2 tsp. vanilla extract
- 1 cup all-purpose flour
- 1/4 cup sugar
- 1/4 cup packed brown sugar
- 3 Tbsp. baking cocoa
- 2 tsp. baking powder
- 1/2 tsp. ground cinnamon
- 1/8 tsp. salt
- 1 cup fresh or frozen pitted dark sweet cherries, thawed
- 1 cup fresh or frozen pitted tart cherries, thawed
- 1/3 cup 60% cacao bittersweet chocolate baking chips

PUDDING:
- 1/2 cup packed brown sugar
- 2 Tbsp. baking cocoa
- 1-1/4 cups hot water

CHERRY UPSIDE-DOWN CAKE

CHOCOLATE-COVERED CHERRY PUDDING CAKE

**1.** In a large bowl, beat the sour cream, oil, butter and vanilla until blended. Combine the flour, sugars, cocoa, baking powder, cinnamon and salt. Add to sour cream mixture just until combined. Stir in cherries and chips. Pour into a 3-qt. slow cooker coated with cooking spray.

**2.** In a small bowl, combine brown sugar and cocoa. Stir in hot water until blended. Pour over the batter (do not stir). Cover and cook on high for 2 to 2-1/2 hours or until set. Let stand for 15 minutes. Serve cake warm.

**Nutrition Facts:** 1 serving equals 291 calories, 9 g fat (3 g saturated fat), 9 mg cholesterol, 167 mg sodium, 51 g carbohydrate, 2 g fiber, 4 g protein.

# Raspberry Baked Alaska Pie

**PREP:** 40 min. + freezing **YIELD:** 8 servings (1 cup sauce)

**DAGMAR VENA • NEPEAN, ONTARIO**

*I'm sharing one of my family's very favorite pie recipes. I love making it for special occasions, and assembling it the day before leaves extra time to spend with loved ones.*

- 1  cup graham cracker crumbs
- 3  Tbsp. brown sugar
- 3  Tbsp. butter, melted
- 1  Tbsp. cornstarch
- 1/2  cup cold water
- 3  Tbsp. lemon juice
- 1  pkg. (10 oz.) frozen sweetened raspberries, thawed
- 2  tsp. grated lemon peel

- 4-1/2  cups reduced-fat vanilla ice cream, softened
- 3  egg whites
- 1/2  cup sugar

**1.** In a small bowl, combine the cracker crumbs, brown sugar and butter. Press onto the bottom and up the sides of a 9-in. pie plate; freeze until set.

**2.** Meanwhile, in a large saucepan, combine the cornstarch, water and lemon juice until smooth. Stir in raspberries and lemon peel. Cook, stirring occasionally, over medium heat until mixture just comes to a boil. Remove from the heat; transfer to a small bowl. Cool slightly; refrigerate until chilled.

**3.** Spread 1-1/2 cups ice cream into crust; cover and freeze for 1 hour. Drizzle with 1/2 cup raspberry sauce; freeze until set. Repeat layers, freezing after each layer. Top with remaining ice cream. Cover and freeze for 8 hours or overnight.

**4.** In a large heavy saucepan, combine the egg whites and sugar. With a hand mixer, beat on low speed for 1 minute. Continue beating over low heat until the egg mixture reaches 160°, about 6 minutes. Transfer to a bowl; beat until stiff glossy peaks form and sugar is dissolved.

**5.** Immediately spread meringue over ice cream, sealing to edges of pie. Heat with a creme brulee torch or broil 8 in. from the heat for 3-5 minutes or until meringue is lightly browned. Serve immediately with remaining sauce.

**Nutrition Facts:** 1 piece with 2 Tbsp. sauce equals 321 calories, 9 g fat (5 g saturated fat), 31 mg cholesterol, 172 mg sodium, 56 g carbohydrate, 2 g fiber, 6 g protein.

ZUCCHINI CHOCOLATE CAKE
WITH ORANGE GLAZE

## Zucchini Chocolate Cake with Orange Glaze

**PREP:** 20 min.  **BAKE:** 50 min. + cooling
**YIELD:** 16 servings

**BARBARA WORREL • GRANBURY, TEXAS**

*This moist and mouthwatering cake has a rich chocolate flavor, a hint of orange and is chock-full of zucchini and nuts.*

| | |
|---|---|
| 1/2 | cup butter, softened |
| 1-1/2 | cups sugar |
| 2 | eggs |
| 1/4 | cup unsweetened applesauce |
| 1 | tsp. vanilla extract |
| 2-1/2 | cups all-purpose flour |
| 1/2 | cup baking cocoa |
| 1-1/4 | tsp. baking powder |
| 1 | tsp. salt |
| 1 | tsp. ground cinnamon |
| 1/2 | tsp. baking soda |
| 1/2 | cup fat-free milk |
| 3 | cups shredded zucchini |
| 1/2 | cup chopped walnuts |
| 1 | Tbsp. grated orange peel |

GLAZE:
| | |
|---|---|
| 1-1/4 | cups confectioners' sugar |
| 2 | Tbsp. orange juice |
| 1 | tsp. vanilla extract |

**1.** Coat a 10-in. fluted tube pan with cooking spray and sprinkle with flour.

**2.** In a large bowl, cream butter and sugar until light and fluffy. Add eggs, one at a time, beating well after each addition. Beat in applesauce and vanilla.

**3.** Combine the flour, baking cocoa, baking powder, salt, cinnamon and soda; add to the creamed mixture alternately with milk, beating well after each addition. Fold in the shredded zucchini, walnuts and orange peel.

**4.** Transfer to prepared pan. Bake at 350° for 50-60 minutes or until a toothpick inserted near the center comes out clean.

**5.** Cool for 10 minutes before removing from pan to a wire rack to cool completely.

**6.** In a small bowl, combine glaze ingredients. Drizzle over the cake.

**Nutrition Facts:** 1 slice equals 282 calories, 9 g fat (4 g saturated fat), 42 mg cholesterol, 273 mg sodium, 47 g carbohydrate, 2 g fiber, 4 g protein.

# Caramel-Pecan Cheese Pie

PREP: 20 min. + chilling  YIELD: 8 servings

PATSY MULLINS • TAFT, TENNESSEE

*Family and friends love this tasty no-bake pie, and no one can believe it's not loaded with fat!*

- 1 envelope unflavored gelatin
- 1/3 cup cold water
- 1/4 cup lemon juice
- 3 oz. reduced-fat cream cheese, cubed
- 1 cup nonfat dry milk powder
- Sugar substitute equivalent to 2 Tbsp. sugar
- 1 carton (8 oz.) frozen reduced-fat whipped topping, thawed
- 5 Tbsp. chopped pecans, toasted, *divided*
- 1 reduced-fat graham cracker crust (9 in.)
- 2 Tbsp. fat-free caramel ice cream topping

**1.** In a small saucepan, sprinkle gelatin over cold water; let stand for 1 minute. Heat over low heat, stirring until gelatin is completely dissolved. Cool mixture slightly.

**2.** In a blender, combine the lemon juice, cream cheese and gelatin mixture; cover and process until smooth. Add milk powder and sugar substitute; cover and process for 1 minute or until blended.

**3.** Transfer to a large bowl; fold in the whipped topping. Stir in 3 Tbsp. of pecans. Pour into crust. Sprinkle with remaining pecans. Drizzle with caramel topping. Cover and refrigerate for 2-3 hours or until set.

**Editor's Note:** This recipe was tested with Splenda no-calorie sweetener.

**Nutrition Facts:** 1 piece equals 270 calories, 12 g fat (6 g saturated fat), 6 mg cholesterol, 186 mg sodium, 31 g carbohydrate, 1 g fiber, 7 g protein. **Diabetic Exchanges:** 2 starch, 2 fat.

# Light Strawberry Pie

PREP: 25 min. + chilling  YIELD: 8 servings

LOU WRIGHT • ROCKFORD, ILLINOIS

*This luscious strawberry dessert is a great after-supper sweet. People rave about this pie. And best of all, it's a low-sugar sensation that you won't feel one bit guilty eating.*

- 1 can (8 oz.) unsweetened crushed pineapple
- 1 pkg. (.8 oz.) sugar-free cook-and-serve vanilla pudding mix
- 1 pkg. (.3 oz.) sugar-free strawberry gelatin
- 3 cups sliced fresh strawberries
- 1 reduced-fat graham cracker crust (8 in.)
- 1/2 cup reduced-fat whipped topping

**1.** Drain pineapple, reserving juice in a 2-cup measuring cup. Set pineapple aside. Add enough water to juice to measure 1-1/2 cups; transfer to a saucepan. Whisk in the pudding mix and gelatin until combined. Bring to a boil; cook and stir for 1-2 minutes or until thickened. Stir in pineapple. Remove from the heat; cool for 10 minutes.

**2.** Add the strawberries; toss gently to coat. Pour into crust. Refrigerate until set, about 3 hours. Garnish each piece with 1 Tbsp. whipped topping. Refrigerate leftovers.

**Nutrition Facts:** 1 piece equals 159 calories, 4 g fat (2 g saturated fat), 0 cholesterol, 172 mg sodium, 29 g carbohydrate, 2 g fiber, 2 g protein. **Diabetic Exchanges:** 1 starch, 1 fruit, 1/2 fat.

LIGHT STRAWBERRY PIE

CARAMEL-PECAN CHEESE PIE

## Makeover Pineapple Upside-Down Cake

**PREP:** 15 min. **BAKE:** 35 min. **YIELD:** 9 servings

**MARY LOU MOELLER • WOOSTER, OHIO**

*Both of my boys loved this trimmed-down version of a family favorite. Even my husband, who is a bit picky, takes pieces in his lunch bag!*

| | |
|---|---|
| 3 | Tbsp. butter, melted |
| 1/3 | cup packed brown sugar |
| 9 | canned unsweetened pineapple slices |
| 9 | maraschino cherries halves |
| 2/3 | cup sugar |
| 2/3 | cup fat-free milk |
| 3 | Tbsp. canola oil |
| 1 | egg |
| 1 | tsp. lemon extract |
| 1/2 | tsp. vanilla extract |
| 1-1/3 | cups cake flour |
| 1-1/4 | tsp. baking powder |
| 1/4 | tsp. salt |

**1.** Pour butter into a 9-in. square baking pan; sprinkle with brown sugar. Arrange pineapple slices in a single layer in pan; place cherry halves in center of pineapple slices; set aside.

**2.** In a large bowl, beat the sugar, milk, oil, egg and extracts until well blended. Combine the flour, baking powder and salt; gradually beat into sugar mixture until blended. Pour into prepared pan.

**3.** Bake at 350° for 35-40 minutes or until a toothpick comes out clean. Immediately invert onto a serving plate. Serve warm.

**Nutrition Facts:** 1 piece equals 288 calories, 9 g fat (3 g saturated fat), 34 mg cholesterol, 172 mg sodium, 49 g carbohydrate, 1 g fiber, 3 g protein.

## Chocolate Swirl Cake

**PREP:** 20 min. **BAKE:** 35 min. + cooling
**YIELD:** 15 servings

**GAIL MAKI • MARQUETTE, MICHIGAN**

*This tasty chocolate cake won't ruin your waistline. Pretty swirls of cream cheese dress it up while cherry pie filling provides moistness. Sometimes I add miniature chocolate chips for an extra-special treat.*

| | |
|---|---|
| 1 | pkg. (18-1/4 oz.) chocolate cake mix |
| 1 | can (20 oz.) reduced-sugar cherry pie filling |
| 5 | egg whites |
| 1 | tsp. vanilla extract |

TOPPING:

| | |
|---|---|
| 1 | pkg. (8 oz.) reduced-fat cream cheese |

Sugar substitute equivalent to 1/3 cup sugar

| | |
|---|---|
| 1/2 | tsp. vanilla extract |
| 2 | egg whites |

**1.** In a large bowl, combine the cake mix, pie filling, egg whites and vanilla just until moistened. Spread into a 13-in. x 9-in. baking dish coated with cooking spray; set aside.

**2.** In a small bowl, beat the cream cheese, sugar substitute and vanilla until smooth. Add egg whites; beat on low speed just until combined. Spread over batter; cut through batter with a knife to swirl.

**3.** Bake at 350° for 35-40 minutes or until a toothpick inserted near the center comes out clean and topping is set. Cool on a wire rack. Store cake in the refrigerator.

**Editor's Note:** This recipe was tested with Splenda no-calorie sweetener.

**Nutrition Facts:** 1 piece equals 207 calories, 5 g fat (2 g saturated fat), 5 mg cholesterol, 350 mg sodium, 35 g carbohydrate, 1 g fiber, 5 g protein. **Diabetic Exchanges:** 1-1/2 starch, 1 fat, 1/2 fruit.

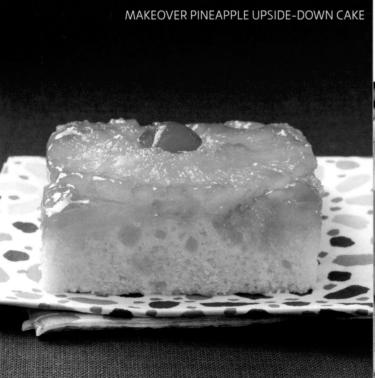

MAKEOVER PINEAPPLE UPSIDE-DOWN CAKE

CHOCOLATE SWIRL CAKE

# Makeover Frozen Chocolate Pie ⓢ

PREP: 40 min. BAKE: 1 hour + freezing YIELD: 8 servings

## HEALTHY COOKING TEST KITCHEN

*The original recipe for this fabulous dessert was absolute heaven—until it came to stepping on the scale! Now the fat's been cut by over half and the calories reduced. Your taste buds will never even know the difference!*

3 egg whites
1/4 tsp. cream of tartar
1-1/2 cups sugar, *divided*
1/4 cup baking cocoa
1 Tbsp. cornstarch
Dash salt
3/4 cup evaporated milk
1 tsp. vanilla extract
2 cups reduced-fat vanilla ice cream, softened
1 carton (8 oz.) frozen whipped topping, thawed

**1.** Place egg whites in a small bowl; let stand at room temperature for 30 minutes. Add cream of tartar; beat until soft peaks form. Gradually add 3/4 cup sugar, 1 Tbsp. at a time, beating until stiff peaks form.

**2.** Spread onto the bottom and up the sides of a greased and floured 9-in. deep-dish pie plate. Bake at 275° for 1 hour. Turn off oven and do not open door; let meringue cool completely inside the oven.

**3.** For chocolate sauce, in a small saucepan, combine the cocoa, cornstarch, salt and remaining sugar. Whisk in milk. Bring to a boil over medium heat, stirring constantly. Reduce heat; simmer, uncovered, for 5-7 minutes or until slightly thickened. Remove from the heat; stir in vanilla. Cool to room temperature. Transfer to a large bowl.

**4.** Spread ice cream into meringue shell. Fold whipped topping into cooled chocolate sauce. Spread over ice cream layer; cover and freeze until firm.

**Nutrition Facts:** 1 piece equals 328 calories, 8 g fat (7 g saturated fat), 16 mg cholesterol, 86 mg sodium, 57 g carbohydrate, 1 g fiber, 5 g protein.

VERY BERRY CRISP

LEMON BLACKBERRY PARFAITS

CHOCOLATE ANISE CANNOLI

Crisps, trifles, ice cream snacks and souffles...you'll find all of these luscious dishes and more in this section. Turn here when you want an extra-special dessert that still keeps your commitment to eating right!

## Chocolate Anise Cannoli

**PREP:** 35 min. **BAKE:** 10 min. + cooling
**YIELD:** 16 servings

**MARIE RIZZIO • INTERLOCHEN, MICHIGAN**

*Here's that something special you've been looking for to add to your holiday cookie tray! We guarantee these wonton-wrapped bites with anise, cherries, chocolate, brandy and pistachios will be gone in a twinkling.*

    16  wonton wrappers
Butter-flavored cooking spray
     1  Tbsp. sugar
  1/4  cup dried cherries
     1  Tbsp. cherry brandy
     2  pkg. (8 oz. *each*) reduced-fat cream cheese
     1  cup confectioners' sugar
  1/2  cup baking cocoa
     3  Tbsp. anise liqueur
  1/4  cup semisweet chocolate chips
  1/4  cup chopped shelled pistachios

**1.** Wrap a wonton wrapper around a metal cannoli tube. Moisten corner with water and seal. Transfer to an ungreased baking sheet. Repeat with remaining wrappers. Spritz with the cooking spray; sprinkle with sugar.

**2.** Bake at 325° for 10-14 minutes or until golden brown. Cool for 5 minutes. Remove shells from tubes; cool on a wire rack.

**3.** Meanwhile, place cherries in a small bowl. Add brandy; let stand for 10 minutes. Drain and coarsely chop cherries. In a large bowl, beat the cream cheese, confectioners' sugar, cocoa, liqueur and chopped cherries until blended.

**4.** In a microwave, melt chocolate chips; stir until smooth. Dip shell ends in chocolate; allow excess to drip off. Press into pistachios. Place on waxed paper; let stand until set.

**5.** Pipe filling into prepared shells. Serve immediately.

**Nutrition Facts:** 1 cannoli equals 175 calories, 9 g fat (5 g saturated fat), 21 mg cholesterol, 174 mg sodium, 19 g carbohydrate, 1 g fiber, 5 g protein.

## Very Berry Crisp  S

**PREP:** 20 min. **BAKE:** 25 min. **YIELD:** 8 servings

**JANET ELROD • NEWNAN, GEORGIA**

*I love this recipe because it's easy, low-fat, versatile and delicious! The crispy topping is flavored with graham cracker crumbs, cinnamon and almonds and doesn't taste light at all. Great with frozen yogurt or whipped topping.*

     2  cups fresh raspberries
     2  cups sliced fresh strawberries
     2  cups fresh blueberries
  1/3  cup sugar
     2  Tbsp. plus 1/4 cup all-purpose flour, *divided*
  1/3  cup graham cracker crumbs
  1/3  cup quick-cooking oats
  1/4  cup packed brown sugar
     2  Tbsp. sliced almonds
  1/2  tsp. ground cinnamon
     1  Tbsp. canola oil
     1  Tbsp. butter, melted
     1  Tbsp. water

**1.** In a large bowl, combine the berries, sugar and 2 Tbsp. flour; transfer to an 11-in. x 7-in. baking dish coated with cooking spray.

**2.** In a small bowl, combine the cracker crumbs, oats, brown sugar, almonds, cinnamon and remaining flour. Stir in the oil, butter and water until moistened. Sprinkle over berries.

**3.** Bake at 375° for 25-30 minutes or until filling is bubbly and topping is golden brown.

**Nutrition Facts:** 1 serving equals 193 calories, 5 g fat (1 g saturated fat), 4 mg cholesterol, 35 mg sodium, 37 g carbohydrate, 5 g fiber, 2 g protein.

Purchase fresh **strawberries** that are shiny, firm and very fragrant. A strawberry should be almost completely red, though a little bit of whiteness near the leafy cap is absolutely acceptable.

# Lemon Blackberry Parfaits

**PREP:** 25 min. + chilling  **YIELD:** 6 servings

**AMBER NEEDHAM • BELLBROOK, OHIO**

*I love the freshness of lemon, and with added seasonal blackberries, this rich, creamy dessert is so wonderful! Serve immediately if you like crisp graham crackers, or within 4 hours for a moister crumb.*

> 3 eggs
> 1/2 cup plus 1/4 cup sugar, *divided*
> 3/4 cup lemon juice
> 1 Tbsp. grated lemon peel
> 2 Tbsp. butter
> 4 oz. fat-free cream cheese
> 1 cup plus 6 Tbsp. reduced-fat whipped topping, *divided*
> 3 cups fresh blackberries
> 3 whole graham crackers, crushed

**1.** In a small heavy saucepan over medium heat, whisk the eggs, 1/2 cup sugar, lemon juice and peel until blended. Add butter; cook, whisking constantly, until mixture is thickened and coats the back of a spoon. Transfer to a small bowl; cool. Cover and refrigerate until chilled.

**2.** In a small bowl, beat cream cheese and remaining sugar until smooth. Fold in lemon mixture and 1 cup whipped topping. Spoon half of the cream cheese mixture into six parfait glasses. Top with half of the berries and half of the cracker crumbs. Repeat layers. Top with remaining whipped topping. Serve immediately.

**Nutrition Facts:** 1 parfait equals 292 calories, 9 g fat (5 g saturated fat), 117 mg cholesterol, 213 mg sodium, 48 g carbohydrate, 4 g fiber, 8 g protein.

# Melon with Serrano-Mint Syrup  F S

**PREP:** 30 min. + chilling  **YIELD:** 12 servings

**JENNIFER FISHER • AUSTIN, TEXAS**

*This is one of the recipes I created to take advantage of the mint I grow. The serrano pepper is a nice contrast to the sweetness of the syrup and salad.*

> 1/3 cup sugar
> 1/3 cup water
> 1/4 cup lemon juice
> 3 Tbsp. honey
> 1/2 tsp. minced serrano pepper
> 1/4 cup minced fresh mint
> 1 Tbsp. grated lemon peel
> 4 cups *each* cubed watermelon, cantaloupe and honeydew

**1.** In a small saucepan, combine the sugar, water, lemon juice, honey and serrano pepper. Bring to a boil; cook for 3-5 minutes or until slightly thickened. Remove from the heat; stir in mint and lemon peel. Cool to room temperature.

**2.** Strain syrup; discard pepper, mint and lemon peel. In a large bowl, combine melon cubes. Add syrup; gently toss to coat. Cover and refrigerate for at least 2 hours, stirring several times. Serve with a slotted spoon.

**Editor's Note:** Wear disposable gloves when cutting hot peppers; the oils can burn skin. Avoid touching your face.

**Nutrition Facts:** 1 cup equals 92 calories, trace fat (trace saturated fat), 0 cholesterol, 13 mg sodium, 25 g carbohydrate, 1 g fiber, 1 g protein. **Diabetic Exchanges:** 1 fruit, 1/2 starch.

# Chocolate Malt Desserts  S

**PREP:** 10 min.  **COOK:** 10 min. + chilling  **YIELD:** 6 servings

**LISA KEYS • MIDDLEBURY, CONNECTICUT**

*I came up with this recipe after my mom gave me a container of malted milk powder. It's so rich you'd never believe it's light.*

LEMON BLACKBERRY PARFAITS

MELON WITH SERRANO-MINT SYRUP

CHOCOLATE MALT DESSERTS

1/2 cup malted milk powder
1/4 cup sugar
  2 Tbsp. baking cocoa
  2 Tbsp. cornstarch
1/2 tsp. instant espresso powder
  2 cups fat-free milk
  2 oz. semisweet chocolate, finely chopped
  1 tsp. vanilla extract
3/4 cup reduced-fat whipped topping
  6 malted milk balls, chopped
  6 maraschino cherries

**1.** In a small saucepan, combine the first five ingredients. Stir in milk until smooth. Cook and stir over medium heat until mixture comes to a boil; cook 1-2 minutes longer or until thickened. Remove from the heat; stir in chocolate and vanilla until smooth.

**2.** Transfer to six dessert dishes, about 1/3 cup in each. Cover and refrigerate for at least 2 hours before serving.

**3.** Garnish each serving with 2 Tbsp. whipped topping, 1/2 tsp. chopped malted milk balls and a cherry.

**Nutrition Facts:** 1 serving equals 239 calories, 5 g fat (3 g saturated fat), 2 mg cholesterol, 87 mg sodium, 45 g carbohydrate, 1 g fiber, 6 g protein.

When you're short on time, you can easily add some frosty fun to dinnertime by serving up a variety of toppings and sauces and letting family members concoct their own scrumptious sundaes.

APPLE TARRAGON GRANITA

## Apple Tarragon Granita  F S

**PREP:** 10 min. + freezing **YIELD:** 6 servings

**DEBBY HARDEN • WILLIAMSTON, MICHIGAN**

*Looking for a something-different twist on a classic Italian treat? Fresh tarragon complements the sweet, bright apple flavor of this icy grown-up dessert.*

- 3 cups unsweetened apple juice
- 1/2 cup sugar
- 2 Tbsp. coarsely chopped fresh tarragon
- 4 tsp. lemon juice

**1.** In an 8-in. square dish, combine all ingredients until sugar is dissolved. Freeze for 1 hour; stir with a fork.

**2.** Freeze 2-3 hours longer or until completely frozen, stirring every 30 minutes. Stir granita with a fork just before serving; spoon into dessert dishes.

**Nutrition Facts:** 1 serving equals 125 calories, trace fat (trace saturated fat), 0 cholesterol, 4 mg sodium, 32 g carbohydrate, trace fiber, trace protein.

## Melon with Ice Cream  F S

**PREP/TOTAL TIME:** 10 min.  **YIELD:** 4 servings

**TINA MEEKINS • PORT ORCHARD, WASHINGTON**

*Three items are all you need for this cool creation. It's particularly yummy on hot days. No granola in the pantry? Top off individual servings with chopped nuts or toasted coconut.*

- 1 medium cantaloupe, cut into 4 wedges
- 1 pint fat-free sugar-free vanilla ice cream
- 4 Tbsp. reduced-fat granola cereal without raisins

**1.** Place cantaloupe wedges in individual bowls. Top each with a scoop of ice cream and 1 Tbsp. granola. Serve immediately.

**Nutrition Facts:** 1 serving equals 156 calories, trace fat (trace saturated fat), 0 cholesterol, 98 mg sodium, 34 g carbohydrate, 1 g fiber, 6 g protein. **Diabetic Exchanges:** 2 fruit, 1/2 fat-free milk.

# Banana Pudding Parfaits F

**PREP:** 15 min. + chilling **YIELD:** 8 servings

**MARGARET ALLEN • ABINGDON, VIRGINIA**

*With bananas, vanilla wafers and a pudding mix, these creamy after-dinner sweets are easy to assemble. If you'd like to mix things up, substitute your favorite fresh berries or other flavors of sugar-free instant pudding.*

- 3-1/3 cups cold fat-free milk
- 2 pkg. (1 oz. *each*) sugar-free instant vanilla pudding mix
- 2/3 cup fat-free sour cream
- 1/4 tsp. vanilla extract
- 1 carton (8 oz.) frozen fat-free whipped topping, thawed, *divided*
- 32 reduced-fat vanilla wafers
- 3 medium ripe bananas, cut into 1/4-in. slices

**1.** In a large bowl, whisk milk and pudding mix for 2 minutes. Let stand for 2 minutes. Whisk in sour cream and vanilla. Fold in three-fourths of the whipped topping.

**2.** Set aside eight vanilla wafers. Place one wafer into each of eight parfait glasses; top with a third of the banana slices and pudding mixture. Repeat layers twice. Top with remaining whipped topping. Refrigerate for at least 1 hour. Garnish with reserved vanilla wafers.

**Nutrition Facts:** 1 parfait equals 231 calories, 1 g fat (trace saturated fat), 5 mg cholesterol, 433 mg sodium, 46 g carbohydrate, 1 g fiber, 6 g protein.

# Banana Souffle S

**PREP:** 30 min. **BAKE:** 25 min. **YIELD:** 6 servings

**CRYSTAL BRUNS • ILIFF, COLORADO**

*This pretty, golden-topped puff is so easy to whip up, but looks like you really fussed. Lightly laced with rum, the moist and tender banana-rich souffle makes that perfect "little something" to wrap up any holiday dinner.*

- 4 eggs, *separated*
- 1 egg white
- 2 Tbsp. butter
- 1 cup mashed ripe bananas
- 1/3 cup sugar
- 1 Tbsp. cornstarch
- 1 Tbsp. lemon juice
- 1 Tbsp. rum
- 1/4 tsp. grated lemon peel

**1.** Let egg whites stand at room temperature for 30 minutes. Coat a 1-1/2-qt. souffle dish with cooking spray; set aside.

**2.** In a small saucepan over medium heat, melt butter. Stir in the bananas, sugar and cornstarch until blended. Bring to a boil, stirring constantly. Cook and stir 1-2 minutes longer or until thickened. Transfer to a large bowl; stir in lemon juice, rum and lemon peel.

**3.** Stir a small amount of hot mixture into egg yolks; return all to the bowl, stirring constantly. Allow to cool slightly.

**4.** In a large bowl with clean beaters, beat egg whites until stiff peaks form. With a spatula, stir a fourth of the egg whites into banana mixture until no white streaks remain. Fold in remaining egg whites until combined. Transfer to prepared dish.

**5.** Bake at 350° for 25-30 minutes or until the top is puffed and center appears set. Serve immediately.

**Nutrition Facts:** 1 serving equals 168 calories, 7 g fat (3 g saturated fat), 151 mg cholesterol, 83 mg sodium, 21 g carbohydrate, 1 g fiber, 5 g protein. **Diabetic Exchanges:** 1 starch, 1 fat, 1/2 fruit.

BANANA SOUFFLE

BANANA PUDDING PARFAITS

# Banana Chocolate Parfaits

**PREP/TOTAL TIME:** 20 min.  **YIELD:** 8 servings

### HEALTHY COOKING TEST KITCHEN

*Chocolate and banana pair in this creamy combination from our Test Kitchen. With chocolate pudding and a crunchy chocolate topping, these pretty parfaits are sure to satisfy all of your sweet-tooth cravings.*

|     |     |
| --- | --- |
| 3 | medium bananas, sliced |
| 1/4 | cup lemon juice |
| 2 | cups cold fat-free milk |
| 1 | pkg. (1.4 oz.) sugar-free instant chocolate pudding mix |
| 1 | cup (8 oz.) reduced-fat sour cream |
| 1-1/2 | cups reduced-fat whipped topping |
| 8 | chocolate wafers, crushed |

**1.** In a small bowl, combine bananas and lemon juice; let stand for 5 minutes. In another bowl, whisk the milk and pudding mix for 2 minutes. Refrigerate for 5 minutes. Stir in sour cream.

**2.** Drain bananas. Place half of the banana slices in eight parfait glasses; layer with pudding mixture, whipped topping, chocolate wafer crumbs and remaining banana slices. Refrigerate until serving.

**Nutrition Facts:** 1 parfait equals 183 calories, 6 g fat (5 g saturated fat), 11 mg cholesterol, 236 mg sodium, 27 g carbohydrate, 2 g fiber, 5 g protein. **Diabetic Exchanges:** 1 starch, 1 fat, 1/2 fruit.

BANANA CHOCOLATE PARFAITS

# Strawberry Shortcake Dessert

**PREP:** 10 min.  **BAKE:** 30 min. + chilling
**YIELD:** 20 servings

### MICHELE TRACHIER • PASADENA, TEXAS

*This recipe was given to me by a coworker. I've used other fruits, including blueberries, cherries and peaches, and it always gets rave reviews.*

|     |     |
| --- | --- |
| 1 | pkg. (18-1/4 oz.) white cake mix |
| 1-1/3 | cups water |
| 1/4 | cup unsweetened applesauce |
| 2 | egg whites |
| 1 | egg |
| 1 | pkg. (.6 oz.) sugar-free strawberry gelatin |
| 2 | cups boiling water |
| 1 | pkg. (16 oz.) frozen unsweetened whole strawberries, thawed, drained and sliced |
| 1 | carton (16 oz.) frozen reduced-fat whipped topping, thawed |
| 10 | fresh strawberries, halved |

**1.** In a large bowl, combine the cake mix, water, applesauce, egg whites and egg; beat on low speed for 30 seconds. Beat on medium for 2 minutes.

**2.** Pour batter into a 13-in. x 9-in. baking dish coated with cooking spray. Bake at 350° for 30-35 minutes or until a toothpick inserted near the center comes out clean.

**3.** In a large bowl, dissolve gelatin in boiling water. Stir in strawberries. Using a sharp knife, make a diamond pattern in the top of the hot cake; immediately pour gelatin mixture over cake. Cool on a wire rack.

**4.** Refrigerate for at least 6 hours. Spread with whipped topping. Garnish with fresh strawberries.

**Nutrition Facts:** 1 piece equals 179 calories, 5 g fat (3 g saturated fat), 11 mg cholesterol, 192 mg sodium, 29 g carbohydrate, 1 g fiber, 2 g protein. **Diabetic Exchanges:** 2 starch, 1/2 fat.

STRAWBERRY SHORTCAKE DESSERT

# Light Chocolate Truffles **F S C**

**PREP:** 25 min. + chilling **YIELD:** about 1-1/2 dozen

**DONNI WORTHEN • BRANSON, MISSOURI**

*I made these for my husband on Valentine's Day and later for Christmas gifts. Everyone loves them!*

1/3 cup semisweet chocolate chips
4 oz. reduced-fat cream cheese
1/3 cup plus 2 tsp. baking cocoa, *divided*
1-1/4 cups plus 2 tsp. confectioners' sugar, *divided*

**1.** In a microwave, melt chocolate chips; stir until smooth. Set aside.

**2.** In a small bowl, beat cream cheese until fluffy. Beat in 1/3 cup cocoa and melted chocolate. Gradually beat in 1-1/4 cups confectioners' sugar. Lightly coat hands with confectioners' sugar; roll chocolate mixture into 1-in. balls. Roll in remaining cocoa or confectioners' sugar. Cover and refrigerate for at least 1 hour.

**Nutrition Facts:** 1 truffle equals 62 calories, 2 g fat (1 g saturated fat), 4 mg cholesterol, 24 mg sodium, 11 g carbohydrate, trace fiber, 1 g protein. **Diabetic Exchanges:** 1/2 starch, 1/2 fat.

You can make the **coconut centers** for these truffles and freeze them in airtight containers for up to 2 months. Then, thaw in the refrigerator, dip in chocolate and decorate as directed.

ENGLISH TRIFLE

# English Trifle F

**PREP:** 45 min. + chilling  **YIELD:** 12 servings

ALDAH BOTHMANN-POWELL • SAN ANTONIO, TEXAS

*You'll impress guests with this lovely dessert layered with angel food cake, fruit, pudding and fat-free whipped topping. It's so creamy and refreshing that no one will know it's light.*

- 1 pkg. (.3 oz.) sugar-free strawberry gelatin
- 1 cup boiling water
- 1 cup cold water
- 1 prepared angel food cake (8 to 10 oz.), cut into 1-in. cubes
- 1 cup mashed strawberries
- 1 tsp. sugar
- 1 can (8 oz.) unsweetened pineapple chunks
- 1 cup sliced firm bananas
- 2 cups sliced fresh strawberries
- 2 cups cold fat-free milk
- 1 pkg. (1 oz.) sugar-free instant vanilla pudding mix
- 1 carton (8 oz.) frozen fat-free whipped topping, thawed
- 1/4 cup slivered almonds, toasted
- 1 fresh strawberry

**1.** In a small bowl, dissolve gelatin powder in boiling water. Stir in cold water. Pour half of gelatin mixture into a small bowl; cover and refrigerate for 1 hour or until slightly thickened. Let remaining gelatin stand at room temperature.

**2.** Place half of cake cubes in a 3-qt. trifle bowl. In a small bowl, combine mashed strawberries and sugar; spoon half over cake.

**3.** Drain pineapple, reserving 1/4 cup juice. Cut pineapple chunks in half; arrange half over mashed strawberries. Toss banana slices with reserved pineapple juice; arrange half of slices over pineapple. Top with 1 cup sliced strawberries. Spoon refrigerated gelatin over fruit. Refrigerate trifle and remaining gelatin mixture for 20 minutes.

**4.** In a small bowl, whisk milk and pudding mix for 2 minutes. Let stand for 2 minutes or until soft-set. Spread half of pudding over trifle. Repeat all layers. Top with whipped topping. Cover and refrigerate. Just before serving, sprinkle with almonds; garnish with the strawberry.

**Nutrition Facts:** 1 cup equals 155 calories, 2 g fat (trace saturated fat), 1 mg cholesterol, 274 mg sodium, 32 g carbohydrate, 2 g fiber, 4 g protein. **Diabetic Exchanges:** 1-1/2 starch, 1/2 fruit.

# Chocolate-Raspberry Bread Pudding

**PREP:** 25 min.  **BAKE:** 30 min. + standing
**YIELD:** 12 servings (3/4 cup sauce)

PHYLLIS DOBSON • LITTLETON, COLORADO

*With lots of chocolate and raspberry flavor, plenty of crunch and less than 300 calories, this no-guilt dessert is to die for!*

- 8 cups cubed day-old French bread
- 1 cup fat-free milk
- 1 cup fat-free half-and-half
- 3/4 cup plus 2 Tbsp. sugar, *divided*
- 1/4 cup baking cocoa
- 2 oz. bittersweet chocolate, coarsely chopped
- 3/4 cup egg substitute
- 2 tsp. vanilla extract
- 1/2 cup semisweet chocolate chips
- 1 pkg. (12 oz.) frozen unsweetened raspberries, thawed, *divided*
- 1 tsp. lemon juice

**1.** Place bread cubes in a large bowl; set aside. In a small saucepan, combine milk, half-and-half, 3/4 cup sugar and cocoa. Bring to a gentle boil. Remove from the heat. Stir in bittersweet chocolate until melted.

**2.** Stir a small amount of hot milk mixture into egg substitute; return all to the pan. Stir in vanilla. Pour mixture over bread cubes. Let stand for 5 minutes. Place half of bread mixture in an 11-in. x 7-in. baking dish coated with cooking spray. Sprinkle with chocolate chips and half of raspberries. Top with remaining bread mixture.

**3.** Bake, uncovered, at 350° for 30-40 minutes or until a knife inserted near the center comes out clean. Let stand for 10 minutes before serving.

**4.** For sauce, place the remaining raspberries in a food processor; add lemon juice and remaining sugar. Cover and process for 2-3 minutes or until blended. Strain and discard seeds and pulp. Serve with pudding. Refrigerate leftovers.

**Nutrition Facts:** 1 serving with 1 Tbsp. sauce equals 297 calories, 7 g fat (3 g saturated fat), 1 mg cholesterol, 289 mg sodium, 54 g carbohydrate, 3 g fiber, 8 g protein.

CHOCOLATE-RASPBERRY BREAD PUDDING

## Sangria Gelatin Dessert F S C

PREP: 15 min. + chilling  YIELD: 6 servings

**HEALTHY COOKING TEST KITCHEN**

*Here's a festive finale that's just ideal for balmy summer nights. White wine gives it a refreshing twist, and the vibrant color dresses up dinners without much effort.*

- 1 pkg. (.3 oz.) sugar-free lemon gelatin
- 1 pkg. (.3 oz.) sugar-free raspberry gelatin
- 1-1/2 cups boiling water
- 1 cup cold water
- 1 cup white wine
- 1 can (11 oz.) mandarin oranges, drained
- 1 cup fresh raspberries
- 1 cup green grapes, halved

**1.** In a large bowl, dissolve gelatins in boiling water. Let stand for 10 minutes. Stir in cold water and the wine; refrigerate for 45 minutes or until partially set.

**2.** Fold in the oranges, raspberries and grapes. Transfer to six large wine glasses, 1 cup in each. Refrigerate for 4 hours or until set.

**Nutrition Facts:** 1 serving equals 95 calories, trace fat (trace saturated fat), 0 cholesterol, 83 mg sodium, 13 g carbohydrate, 2 g fiber, 2 g protein. **Diabetic Exchange:** 1 fruit.

SANGRIA GELATIN DESSERT

## Polynesian Parfaits S

PREP/TOTAL TIME: 15 min.  YIELD: 4 servings

**JANICE MITCHELL • AURORA, COLORADO**

*Pack one of these refreshing, tropical treats in a plastic container to take with you. They're great for lunch boxes!*

- 2 cups (16 oz.) pineapple yogurt
- 1 Tbsp. sugar
- 1/8 tsp. ground nutmeg
- 1 cup granola without raisins
- 1 can (11 oz.) mandarin oranges, drained
- 3/4 cup unsweetened pineapple tidbits
- 1/3 cup fresh raspberries

**1.** Combine the yogurt, sugar and nutmeg; spoon into four dishes. Top with granola and fruit.

**Nutrition Facts:** 1 parfait equals 293 calories, 5 g fat (1 g saturated fat), 6 mg cholesterol, 79 mg sodium, 57 g carbohydrate, 6 g fiber, 11 g protein.

## Cran-Apple Praline Gingerbread

PREP: 25 min.  BAKE: 30 min. + cooling
YIELD: 8 servings

**JEANNE HOLT • MENDOTA HEIGHTS, MINNESOTA**

*Start with a spice-rich batter baked atop apples and cranberries in a creamy caramel sauce, then invert when done for a topsy-turvy dessert that's a real beauty. The old-time holiday taste will delight family and friends!*

- 2/3 cup fat-free caramel ice cream topping
- 2 medium tart apples, peeled and thinly sliced
- 2/3 cup fresh or frozen cranberries
- 1/4 cup butter, softened
- 1/4 cup sugar

POLYNESIAN PARFAITS

1 egg
6 Tbsp. molasses
1/4 cup unsweetened applesauce
1-1/4 cups all-purpose flour
3/4 tsp. baking soda
1/2 tsp. ground ginger
1/2 tsp. apple pie spice
1/4 tsp. salt
1/2 cup hot water

YOGURT CREAM:
3/4 cup reduced-fat whipped topping
1/2 cup fat-free vanilla yogurt

**1.** Coat a 9-in. round baking pan with cooking spray. Pour caramel topping into pan and tilt to coat bottom evenly. Arrange apples and cranberries in a single layer over caramel.

**2.** In a large bowl, beat butter and sugar until crumbly, about 2 minutes. Add egg; mix well. Beat in molasses and applesauce (mixture may appear curdled). Combine the flour, baking soda, ginger, pie spice and salt; add to butter mixture just until moistened. Stir in hot water.

**3.** Pour over fruit; smooth top. Bake at 350° for 30-35 minutes or until a toothpick inserted near the center comes out clean. Cool for 10 minutes before inverting onto a serving plate. Combine whipped topping and yogurt; serve with gingerbread.

**Nutrition Facts:** 1 slice with 2 Tbsp. cream equals 289 calories, 7 g fat (5 g saturated fat), 42 mg cholesterol, 284 mg sodium, 53 g carbohydrate, 2 g fiber, 4 g protein.

Cranberries are only in season from early fall through December. When buying **fresh cranberries**, look for packages with shiny, bright red (light or dark) berries. Avoid berries that are bruised, shriveled or have brown spots.

GRILLED PINEAPPLE DESSERT

# Grilled Pineapple Dessert

PREP/TOTAL TIME: 20 min. YIELD: 6 servings

**KATIE SISSON • VALLEY PARK, MISSOURI**

*This fresh-tasting, fruity dessert is one of my very favorites. Warm, sweet, buttery pineapple topped with cold ice cream. Yum! Granola adds a fun crunch.*

|   |   |
|---|---|
| 1 | can (20 oz.) unsweetened sliced pineapple |
| 1 | Tbsp. butter |
| 1 | tsp. brown sugar |
| 1/2 | tsp. vanilla extract |
| 1/4 | tsp. ground cinnamon |
| 3 | cups reduced-fat vanilla ice cream |
| 6 | Tbsp. hot caramel ice cream topping |
| 6 | Tbsp. granola without raisins |

**1.** Drain pineapple, reserving 1/3 cup juice and six pineapple slices (save remaining juice and pineapple for another use).

**2.** In a small microwave-safe bowl, combine the butter, brown sugar, vanilla, cinnamon and reserved juice. Microwave, uncovered, on high for 1-2 minutes or until butter is melted. Brush half of the mixture on both sides of pineapple slices.

**3.** Grill, uncovered, over medium heat or broil 4 in. from the heat for 3-5 minutes or until lightly browned, turning once and basting with remaining butter mixture.

**4.** Place pineapple in dessert bowls; top with ice cream. Drizzle with caramel topping; sprinkle with granola.

**Editor's Note:** This recipe was tested in a 1,100-watt microwave.

**Nutrition Facts:** 1 serving equals 246 calories, 6 g fat (3 g saturated fat), 23 mg cholesterol, 142 mg sodium, 45 g carbohydrate, 2 g fiber, 5 g protein.

# Cappuccino Pudding  `F` `S`

**PREP/TOTAL TIME:** 20 min.  **YIELD:** 4 servings

CINDY BERTRAND • FLOYDADA, TEXAS

*With its fun combination of chocolate, coffee and cinnamon, this smooth dessert is one of my favorites. A garnish of whipped topping and chocolate wafer crumbs provides additional appeal.*

- 4 tsp. instant coffee granules
- 1 Tbsp. boiling water
- 1-1/2 cups cold fat-free milk
- 1 pkg. (1.4 oz.) sugar-free instant chocolate pudding mix
- 1/2 tsp. ground cinnamon
- 1 cup reduced-fat whipped topping
- Additional whipped topping and chocolate wafer crumbs, optional

**1.** Dissolve coffee in boiling water; set aside. In a large bowl, combine the milk, pudding mix and cinnamon. Beat on low speed for 2 minutes. Let stand for 2 minutes or until set.

**2.** Stir in coffee. Fold in whipped topping. Spoon into serving dishes. Garnish with additional whipped topping and wafer crumbs if desired.

**Nutrition Facts:** 1/2 cup (calculated without additional whipped topping and wafer crumbs) equals 105 calories, 2 g fat (0 saturated fat), 2 mg cholesterol, 48 mg sodium, 17 g carbohydrate, 0 fiber, 3 g protein. **Diabetic Exchanges:** 1/2 starch, 1/2 fat-free milk.

# Gluten-Free Sugarplums  `F` `S` `C`

**PREP/TOTAL TIME:** 25 min.  **YIELD:** 2-1/2 dozen

CORLEEN HEIDGERKEN • MILWAUKEE, WISCONSIN

*Lots of moist, fruity flavor and nutty crunch give these sweet and spicy bites a kind of gumdrop richness. They make a delicious addition to cookie trays. Sneak one early—they'll be gone before you can lick the sugar off your fingers!*

- 1-1/3 cups chopped walnuts
- 1 cup pitted dates
- 1 pkg. (5 oz.) dried cherries
- 1/4 cup honey
- 2 tsp. grated orange peel
- 1 tsp. ground cinnamon
- 1 tsp. ground allspice
- 1/2 tsp. ground nutmeg
- 1/4 tsp. ground ginger
- 1/2 cup coarse sugar

**1.** Place the walnuts, dates and cherries in a food processor; cover and process until finely chopped. Transfer to a small bowl; stir in the honey, orange peel and spices. Roll into 1-in. balls, then roll in sugar. Store in an airtight container in the refrigerator.

**Editor's Note:** Read all ingredient labels for possible gluten content prior to use. Ingredient formulas can change, and production facilities vary among brands. If you're concerned that your brand may contain gluten, contact the company.

**Nutrition Facts:** 1 sugarplum equals 84 calories, 3 g fat (trace saturated fat), 0 cholesterol, 1 mg sodium, 13 g carbohydrate, 1 g fiber, 1 g protein. **Diabetic Exchanges:** 1 starch.

High in fiber and a good source of iron and potassium, dates are one of the sweetest fruits; 70% of their weight can be made up of sugar. To prevent sticking when slicing or chopping dates, spray a knife or kitchen scissors with cooking spray or frequently dip in cold water.

CAPPUCCINO PUDDING

GLUTEN-FREE SUGARPLUMS

## Peach Sorbet  F S

**PREP:** 15 min. **PROCESS:** 20 min. + freezing
**YIELD:** 3 servings

**MARY KAY DIXSON • DECATUR, ALABAMA**

*Since moving to an area where fresh peaches are plentiful, I've made this frosty treat frequently. It's the perfect light dessert. Calorie-conscious guests always say "yes" to this when they might decline a slice of cake or pie.*

- 1/2  cup water
-   3  Tbsp. sugar
-   2  Tbsp. lemon juice
-   4  medium ripe peaches, peeled and sliced

**1.** In a saucepan, combine the water, sugar and lemon juice. Cook and stir over medium heat until sugar is dissolved. Cool slightly; transfer to a blender.

**2.** Add the peaches; cover and process until smooth. Fill cylinder of ice cream freezer; freeze according to manufacturer's directions. Transfer sorbet to a freezer container; cover and freeze for 4 hours or until firm.

**Nutrition Facts:** 1/2 cup equals 104 calories, 0 fat (0 saturated fat), 0 cholesterol, trace sodium, 27 g carbohydrate, 3 g fiber, 1 g protein. **Diabetic Exchanges:** 1-1/2 fruit.

## Sweet Potato Tart  S

**PREP:** 20 min.  **BAKE:** 30 min. + cooling
**YIELD:** 12 servings

**KATE GAUDRY • LA JOLLA, CALIFORNIA**

*I love making desserts. You'd never guess this trimmed-down tart, with its homemade pecan crust and creamy filling, is light.*

- 1-1/2  cups all-purpose flour
-   1/2  cup packed brown sugar
-   1/4  cup cold butter, cubed

PEACH SORBET

-     2  Tbsp. chopped pecans, toasted
-     1  egg

FILLING:
-     1  can (15-3/4 oz.) sweet potatoes
-   1/2  cup packed brown sugar
-   1/2  cup fat-free milk
-     2  egg whites
-   1/3  cup reduced-fat plain yogurt
-     1  Tbsp. all-purpose flour
-   1/2  tsp. ground cinnamon
-   1/4  tsp. ground ginger
-   1/4  tsp. ground nutmeg
-   1/8  tsp. ground cloves

Whipped topping, optional

**1.** In a food processor, combine the flour, brown sugar, butter and pecans. Cover and pulse until blended. Add egg, pulsing until mixture forms a soft dough. Press onto the bottom and up the sides of a 9-in. fluted tart pan with removable bottom.

**2.** Place pan on a baking sheet. Bake at 400° for 8-10 minutes or until lightly browned. Cool on a wire rack. Reduce heat to 350°.

**3.** Drain sweet potatoes, reserving 1/4 cup liquid. Place potatoes in a food processor; cover and process until pureed. Add the brown sugar, milk, egg whites, yogurt, flour, cinnamon, ginger, nutmeg, cloves and reserved liquid; cover and process until blended.

**4.** Pour into crust. Bake for 30-35 minutes or until a knife inserted near the center comes out clean. Cool on a wire rack. Store in the refrigerator. Garnish with whipped topping if desired.

**Nutrition Facts:** 1 slice (calculated without whipped topping) equals 221 calories, 5 g fat (3 g saturated fat), 29 mg cholesterol, 87 mg sodium, 39 g carbohydrate, 2 g fiber, 4 g protein.

## Glazed Spiced Apples  F S

**PREP/TOTAL TIME:** 25 min.  **YIELD:** 10 servings

**MARY JO DUCKWORTH • DENVER, COLORADO**

*My husband and I are watching our fat intake, so I came up with this recipe. It's a lovely dessert or even a great side dish with pork. It was a real success.*

- 1/2  cup packed brown sugar
-   3  Tbsp. cornstarch
-   1  can (12 oz.) diet cream soda
- 1/4  cup honey
- 1/4  tsp. apple pie spice
- 1/4  tsp. ground cinnamon
- 1/8  tsp. ground nutmeg
-   8  large apples, peeled and sliced

**1.** In a microwave-safe bowl, combine the brown sugar and cornstarch. Stir in the soda, honey, apple pie spice, cinnamon and nutmeg until smooth. Microwave, uncovered, on high for 3-4 minutes or until thickened, stirring after each minute.

**2.** Place apples in a 3-qt. microwave-safe dish; pour sauce over apples. Cover and cook on high for 5-1/2 minutes; stir. Cook, uncovered, 5-1/2 to 8 minutes

longer or until apples are tender; stir. Let stand for 5 minutes. Serve warm.

**Editor's Note:** This recipe was tested in a 1,100-watt microwave.

**Nutrition Facts:** 2/3 cup equals 187 calories, 1 g fat (1 g saturated fat), 0 cholesterol, 11 mg sodium, 47 g carbohydrate, 5 g fiber, trace protein.

# Baked Long Johns

**PREP:** 15 min. **BAKE:** 20 min. + cooling **YIELD:** 8 servings

**NICKI LAZORIK • MELLEN, WISCONSIN**

*No one will ever guess how much lighter these scrumptious, chocolate-glazed long johns are than the fried ones you buy at the local doughnut store.*

- 2 cups all-purpose flour
- 1/2 cup sugar
- 2 tsp. baking powder
- 1/2 tsp. salt
- 1/4 tsp. ground cinnamon
- 2 eggs
- 3/4 cup fat-free milk
- 1 Tbsp. butter, melted
- 1 tsp. vanilla extract

GLAZE:
- 3/4 cup semisweet chocolate chips
- 1 Tbsp. butter
- 4-1/2 tsp. fat-free milk

**1.** In a small bowl, combine the flour, sugar, baking powder, salt and cinnamon. In another bowl, whisk the eggs, milk, butter and vanilla. Stir into dry ingredients just until moistened.

**2.** Transfer to eight 4-1/2-in. x 2-1/2-in. x 1-1/2-in. loaf pans coated with cooking spray. Bake at 325° for 18-22 minutes or until golden brown. Immediately remove from pans to a wire rack to cool completely.

**3.** In a microwave, melt chocolate chips and butter. Add milk; stir until smooth. Dip tops of doughnuts in glaze. Return to wire rack; let stand until set.

**Nutrition Facts:** 1 long john equals 291 calories, 9 g fat (5 g saturated fat), 61 mg cholesterol, 298 mg sodium, 48 g carbohydrate, 2 g fiber, 6 g protein.

## Caramel Apple Bread Pudding **F**

PREP: 15 min. BAKE: 35 min. YIELD: 8 servings

**MICHELLE BORLAND • PEORIA, ILLINOIS**

*Tender, sweet pudding with delicious apple pieces, spices and a luscious low-fat caramel topping make a rich-tasting comfort dish without all the fat.*

|     |                               |
| --- | ----------------------------- |
| 1   | cup unsweetened applesauce    |
| 1   | cup fat-free milk             |
| 1/2 | cup packed brown sugar        |
| 1/2 | cup egg substitute            |
| 1   | tsp. vanilla extract          |
| 1/2 | tsp. ground cinnamon          |
| 5   | cups cubed day-old bread      |
| 1/2 | cup chopped peeled apple      |
| 1/2 | cup fat-free whipped topping  |
| 1/2 | cup fat-free caramel ice cream topping |

**1.** In a large bowl, combine the applesauce, milk, brown sugar, egg substitute, vanilla and cinnamon. Fold in bread cubes and apple; let stand for 15 minutes or until bread is softened.

**2.** Pour into an 8-in. square baking dish coated with cooking spray. Bake, uncovered, at 325° for 35-40 minutes or until a knife inserted near the center comes out clean. Serve warm with whipped topping and caramel topping. Refrigerate leftovers.

**Nutrition Facts:** 1 serving equals 187 calories, 1 g fat (trace saturated fat), 1 mg cholesterol, 201 mg sodium, 40 g carbohydrate, 1 g fiber, 4 g protein.

## Cranberry Pear Crisp **S**

PREP: 20 min. BAKE: 35 min. YIELD: 8 servings

**LORI CHOQUETTE • HOLYOKE, MASSACHUSETTS**

*This dessert is perfect for that first autumn day you can feel a nip in the air. It's full of sweet, crunchy fall flavors.*

|     |                                    |
| --- | ---------------------------------- |
| 4   | medium pears, peeled and cut into 1-in. cubes |
| 1/2 | cup dried cranberries              |
| 2   | Tbsp. lemon juice                  |
| 1/4 | cup sugar                          |

1 Tbsp. all-purpose flour
2 tsp. grated lemon peel
1 tsp. ground cinnamon
1/2 tsp. ground nutmeg

TOPPING:
1/3 cup all-purpose flour
1/3 cup old-fashioned oats
1/3 cup packed brown sugar
1/4 cup ground flaxseed
1/4 tsp. salt
2 Tbsp. butter, melted
2 Tbsp. canola oil

**1.** In a large bowl, combine pears and cranberries; drizzle with lemon juice. Combine the sugar, flour, lemon peel, cinnamon and nutmeg; stir into pear mixture. Transfer to an 8-in. square baking dish coated with cooking spray.

**2.** For topping, in a small bowl, combine the flour, oats, brown sugar, flax and salt. Stir in butter and oil until crumbly. Sprinkle over fruit mixture. Bake at 350° for 35-40 minutes or until topping is golden brown and fruit is tender.

**Nutrition Facts:** 1/2 cup equals 241 calories, 8 g fat (2 g saturated fat), 8 mg cholesterol, 101 mg sodium, 43 g carbohydrate, 5 g fiber, 2 g protein.

# Eggnog Mousse **S**

PREP: 15 min. + chilling YIELD: 4 servings

**HEALTHY COOKING TEST KITCHEN**

*Guests will always find room for this light, fluffy and mouthwatering mousse. It makes an elegant, refreshing finish for heavier meals—and it's also a great way to use up any extra eggnog in the fridge.*

2 tsp. unflavored gelatin
2 cups reduced-fat eggnog
2 Tbsp. sugar
1/8 tsp. *each* ground cinnamon and ground nutmeg
1/2 tsp. vanilla extract
1 cup reduced-fat whipped topping, *divided*
Additional ground nutmeg, optional

**1.** In a small saucepan, sprinkle gelatin over eggnog; let stand for 1 minute. Heat over low heat, stirring until gelatin is completely dissolved.

**2.** Stir in the sugar, cinnamon and nutmeg until sugar is dissolved. Transfer to a small bowl; stir in vanilla. Refrigerate until mixture begins to thicken.

**3.** Beat mixture until light and fluffy. Beat in 3/4 cup whipped topping. Divide among four dessert dishes. Refrigerate until firm. Garnish with the remaining whipped topping; sprinkle with additional nutmeg if desired.

**Nutrition Facts:** 3/4 cup equals 165 calories, 6 g fat (4 g saturated fat), 97 mg cholesterol, 80 mg sodium, 21 g carbohydrate, trace fiber, 7 g protein. **Diabetic Exchanges:** 1 starch, 1/2 reduced-fat milk.

# Espresso Banana Breakfast Smoothie **F S**

PREP/TOTAL TIME: 10 min. YIELD: 1 serving

**AIMEE WILSON • CLOVIS, CALIFORNIA**

*Want an early morning pick-me-up that's good for you, too? Fruit and flaxseed give this sweet espresso a nutritious twist. Kids are sure to enjoy the combination of chocolate and banana flavors.*

1/2 cup cold fat-free milk
1 Tbsp. vanilla flavoring syrup
1 cup ice cubes
1/2 medium banana, cut up
1 to 2 tsp. instant espresso powder
1 tsp. ground flaxseed
1 tsp. baking cocoa

**1.** In a blender, combine all the ingredients; cover and process for 1-2 minutes or until blended. Pour into a chilled glass; serve immediately.

**Editor's Note:** This recipe was tested with Torani brand flavoring syrup. Look for it in the coffee section.

**Nutrition Facts:** 1-1/2 cups equals 148 calories, 2 g fat (trace saturated fat), 2 mg cholesterol, 54 mg sodium, 31 g carbohydrate, 3 g fiber, 6 g protein.

Packed with heart-healthy oils and lots of fiber, flaxseed is wonderful sprinkled over your cereal or blended into smoothies. It can even be substituted for some of the fat in breads or muffins.

EGGNOG MOUSSE

## Sensational Tiramisu  S

**PREP:** 25 min. **COOK:** 10 min. + chilling
**YIELD:** 12 servings

### MARY WALTERS • WESTERVILLE, OHIO

*This light version of the popular Italian dessert is moist and creamy, and cuts so well into pretty layered squares. You'll love the blend of coffee, Kahlua and cream cheese flavors.*

|        |                                                   |
|--------|---------------------------------------------------|
| 1      | pkg. (8 oz.) reduced-fat cream cheese             |
| 2/3    | cup confectioners' sugar, *divided*               |
| 1-1/2  | cups reduced-fat whipped topping, *divided*       |
| 1/2    | cup plus 1 Tbsp. sugar                            |
| 3      | egg whites                                        |
| 1/4    | cup water                                         |
| 2      | pkg. (3 oz. *each*) ladyfingers, split            |
| 1/2    | cup boiling water                                 |
| 2      | Tbsp. coffee liqueur                              |
| 1      | Tbsp. instant coffee granules                     |
| 1/2    | tsp. baking cocoa                                 |

**1.** In a small bowl, beat cream cheese and confectioners' sugar until smooth. Fold in 1 cup whipped topping; set aside.

**2.** Combine 1/2 cup sugar, egg whites and water in a small heavy saucepan over low heat. With a hand mixer, beat on low speed for 1 minute. Continue beating on low over low heat until mixture reaches 160°, about 8-10 minutes. Pour into a large bowl. Beat on high until stiff peaks form, about 7 minutes. Fold into cream cheese mixture.

**3.** Arrange half of ladyfingers in an ungreased 11-in. x 7-in. dish. Combine the boiling water, coffee liqueur, coffee granules and remaining sugar; brush half of mixture over ladyfingers. Top with half of cream cheese mixture. Repeat layers. Spread remaining whipped topping over the top; sprinkle with cocoa. Refrigerate for 2 hours before serving.

**Nutrition Facts:** 1 piece equals 223 calories, 7 g fat (4 g saturated fat), 62 mg cholesterol, 127 mg sodium, 34 g carbohydrate, trace fiber, 5 g protein. **Diabetic Exchanges:** 2 starch, 1 fat.

## Pumpkin Pecan Custard

**PREP:** 20 min. **BAKE:** 35 min. + chilling
**YIELD:** 8 servings

### ABBY BOOTH • COWETA, OKLAHOMA

*My family loves pumpkin pie, but this is a delicious, creamy and healthier alternative—and we don't miss the crust at all. It firms up as it cools.*

|        |                                              |
|--------|----------------------------------------------|
| 1      | can (15 oz.) solid-pack pumpkin              |
| 1      | can (12 oz.) reduced-fat evaporated milk     |
| 3/4    | cup egg substitute                           |
| 1/3    | cup packed brown sugar                       |
| 1-1/2  | tsp. vanilla extract                         |
| 1      | tsp. ground cinnamon                         |
| 1/2    | tsp. ground ginger                           |
| 1/4    | tsp. ground cloves                           |
| 1/8    | tsp. salt                                    |

TOPPING:

|      |                              |
|------|------------------------------|
| 3    | Tbsp. all-purpose flour      |
| 3    | Tbsp. brown sugar            |
| 1/2  | tsp. ground cinnamon         |
| 2    | Tbsp. cold butter            |
| 1/2  | cup chopped pecans           |

**1.** In a large bowl, combine the first nine ingredients. Transfer to eight 6-oz. ramekins or custard cups. Place in a baking pan; add 1 in. of boiling water to pan. Bake, uncovered, at 325° for 20 minutes.

**2.** Meanwhile, for topping, in a small bowl, combine the flour, brown sugar and cinnamon. Cut in butter until crumbly. Stir in pecans. Sprinkle over custard. Bake 15-20 minutes longer or until a knife inserted near the center comes out clean.

SENSATIONAL TIRAMISU

PUMPKIN PECAN CUSTARD

**3.** Remove ramekins from water bath; cool for 10 minutes. Cover and refrigerate for at least 4 hours.

**Nutrition Facts:** 1/2 cup equals 213 calories, 9 g fat (3 g saturated fat), 11 mg cholesterol, 160 mg sodium, 27 g carbohydrate, 3 g fiber, 7 g protein. **Diabetic Exchanges:** 2 starch, 1-1/2 fat.

# Makeover Frozen Grasshopper Torte  S

**PREP:** 25 min. + freezing  **YIELD:** 16 servings

### HEALTHY COOKING TEST KITCHEN

*Who doesn't love the frosty, refreshing combo of mint and chocolate? Even better when it comes in the form of an awesome ice cream dessert! This Healthy Cooking Test Kitchen makeover is just as good as the original. The crunch of the chocolate crust and a creamy mint filling make a great pair. Although softer-set than the original, this dessert won't stick around long enough to melt!*

|     |     |
| --- | --- |
| 2   | cups chocolate wafer crumbs |
| 3   | Tbsp. butter, melted |
| 1   | pint reduced-fat vanilla ice cream, softened |
| 1   | jar (7 oz.) marshmallow creme |
| 1/4 | cup fat-free milk |
| 1/2 | tsp. peppermint extract |

3 to 4 drops food coloring, optional
1 carton (8 oz.) frozen whipped topping, thawed

**1.** In a small bowl, combine wafer crumbs and butter. Set aside 2 Tbsp. for garnish; press remaining crumb mixture onto the bottom of a 9-in. springform pan. Chill for 30 minutes. Spread the ice cream over the crust; freeze.

**2.** Meanwhile, in a small bowl, combine marshmallow creme and milk; stir until well blended. Add extract and food coloring if desired. Fold in whipped topping. Spoon over ice cream and sprinkle with reserved crumbs. Freeze until firm.

**Nutrition Facts:** 1 piece equals 189 calories, 7 g fat (5 g saturated fat), 10 mg cholesterol, 120 mg sodium, 28 g carbohydrate, 1 g fiber, 2 g protein. **Diabetic Exchanges:** 2 starch, 1 fat.

> To easily remove **marshmallow creme** from a jar, place the jar in a pan of very hot water. Repeat this once or twice, and then simply spoon out the creme with a wooden spoon.

# Triple Berry Cobbler

**PREP:** 20 min. **BAKE:** 30 min. **YIELD:** 6 servings

### AMANDA MILLARD • COLORADO SPRINGS, COLORADO

*Make any meal extra special by topping it off with this tart, berry-bursting dessert. It's simply wonderful!*

- 2 cups fresh *or* frozen cranberries, thawed
- 1 cup fresh *or* frozen unsweetened raspberries, thawed
- 1 cup fresh *or* frozen unsweetened blueberries, thawed
- 1/2 cup honey
- 1 Tbsp. cornstarch
- 1 tsp. water
- 1 tsp. lemon juice

TOPPING:
- 1 cup all-purpose flour
- 2 Tbsp. sugar
- 1-1/2 tsp. baking powder
- 1/2 tsp. salt
- 1/2 cup fat-free milk
- 3 Tbsp. canola oil

Reduced-fat vanilla ice cream, optional

**1.** In a large saucepan, combine the cranberries, raspberries, blueberries and honey. Combine the cornstarch, water and lemon juice until smooth; stir into fruit mixture. Bring to a boil; cook and stir for 2 minutes or until thickened. Pour into an ungreased 11-in. x 7-in. baking dish.

**2.** For topping, in a small bowl, combine the flour, sugar, baking powder and salt. Gradually add milk and oil, tossing with a fork until dough forms a ball. Drop by tablespoon fulls onto hot berry mixture.

**3.** Bake, uncovered, at 400° for 30-35 minutes or until topping is golden brown. Serve warm with ice cream if desired.

**Nutrition Facts:** 1 serving (calculated without ice cream) equals 290 calories, 7 g fat (1 g saturated fat), trace cholesterol, 308 mg sodium, 55 g carbohydrate, 4 g fiber, 3 g protein.

# Makeover Strawberry Cheesecake Ice Cream

**PREP:** 50 min. + chilling
Process: 20 min./batch + freezing **YIELD:** 3 qt.

### HEALTHY COOKING TEST KITCHEN

*This recipe is rich and velvety, with fantastic strawberry flavor—the perfect treat for the summer's heat, but with just a fraction of the fat and fewer calories than the original recipe.*

- 2 cups *each* half-and-half cream and whole milk
- 2 cups sugar
- 3 eggs, lightly beaten
- 1 cup fat-free sour cream
- 1/4 cup apple jelly
- 2 tsp. vanilla extract
- 3 pkg. (8 oz. *each*) reduced-fat cream cheese
- 1 pkg. (16 oz.) frozen unsweetened strawberries, thawed and sliced

2  Tbsp. lemon juice
1  Tbsp. grated lemon peel

**1.** In a large saucepan, heat half-and-half and milk to 175°; stir in sugar until dissolved. Whisk a small amount of hot mixture into the eggs. Return all to the pan, whisking constantly. Cook and stir over low heat until mixture reaches at least 160° and coats the back of a metal spoon.

**2.** Remove from the heat. Stir in the sour cream, jelly and vanilla. Cool quickly by placing pan in a bowl of ice water; stir for 2 minutes. Press waxed paper onto surface of custard. Refrigerate for several hours or overnight.

**3.** In a large bowl, beat the cream cheese, strawberries, lemon juice and lemon peel until blended. Gradually beat in the custard mixture.

**4.** Fill cylinder of ice cream freezer two-thirds full; freeze according to manufacturer's directions. Refrigerate remaining mixture until ready to freeze. When ice cream is frozen, transfer to a freezer container; freeze for 2-4 hours before serving.

**Nutrition Facts:** 1/2 cup equals 208 calories, 9 g fat (6 g saturated fat), 60 mg cholesterol, 156 mg sodium, 25 g carbohydrate, trace fiber, 6 g protein. **Diabetic Exchanges:** 2 fat, 1-1/2 starch.

# Makeover Old-Fashioned Ice Cream Roll

**PREP:** 30 min. **BAKE:** 15 min. + freezing
**YIELD:** 12 servings (1-3/4 cups sauce)

### HEALTHY COOKING TEST KITCHEN

*This dessert is so convenient to make ahead of time and keep in the freezer for company. The caramel sauce—reduced in fat and calories by our Test Kitchen staff—tastes great and makes a nice topping for ice cream, too!*

4  eggs
3/4  cup sugar
1  tsp. vanilla extract
3/4  cup all-purpose flour
3/4  tsp. baking powder
1/4  tsp. salt
6  cups reduced-fat vanilla ice cream, slightly softened

CARAMEL SAUCE:
1  cup packed brown sugar
3  Tbsp. all-purpose flour
1  cup fat-free milk
2  egg yolks, lightly beaten
2  Tbsp. butter
Chopped pecans, optional

**1.** Line a 15-in. x 10-in. x 1-in. baking pan with waxed paper; coat paper with cooking spray; set aside.

**2.** In a large bowl, beat eggs on high speed for 3 minutes. Gradually add sugar, beating until mixture becomes thick and lemon-colored. Beat in vanilla.

**3.** Combine dry ingredients; fold into egg mixture. Spread batter into prepared pan.

**4.** Bake at 350° for 12-14 minutes or until cake springs back when lightly touched. Cool for 5 minutes. Invert onto a kitchen towel dusted with confectioners' sugar. Gently peel off waxed paper. Roll up cake in the towel jelly-roll style, starting with a short side. Cool completely on a wire rack.

**5.** Unroll cake; spread ice cream over cake to within 1/2 in. of edges. Roll up again. Place seam side down on a serving platter. Cover and freeze until firm.

**6.** Meanwhile, for caramel sauce, in a small saucepan, combine brown sugar and flour. Stir in milk until smooth. Cook and stir over medium-high heat until thickened and bubbly. Reduce heat; cook and stir for 2 minutes.

**7.** Remove from the heat. Stir a small amount of hot mixture into egg yolks; return all to pan, stirring constantly. Bring to a gentle boil; cook and stir for 2 minutes. Remove from the heat; gently stir in butter. Serve with ice cream roll. Sprinkle with pecans if desired.

**Nutrition Facts:** 1 slice with about 2 Tbsp. sauce (calculated without pecans) equals 319 calories, 8 g fat (4 g saturated fat), 128 mg cholesterol, 177 mg sodium, 56 g carbohydrate, trace fiber, 7 g protein.

MAKEOVER STRAWBERRY CHEESECAKE ICE CREAM

MAKEOVER OLD-FASHIONED ICE CREAM ROLL

# General Recipe Index

This handy index lists every recipe by food category, major ingredient and/or cooking method, so you can easily locate recipes to suit your needs.

*•Table-ready in 30 minutes or less.*

# Alphabetical Index

This handy index lists every recipe alphabetically, so you can easily find the dishes you enjoy most.

•*Table-ready in 30 minutes or less.*

# Reference Index

Use this index to find the recipe hints located throughout this cookbook.